If my words had a form

They wouldn't reach you standing in the dark

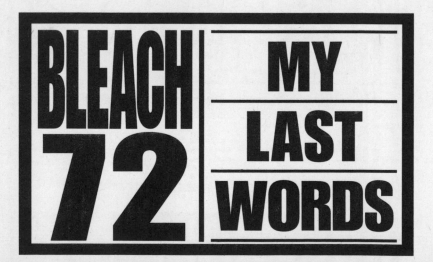

BLEACH 72 | MY LAST WORDS

Shonen Jump Manga

ALL STARS AND

浦原喜助
ウラハラキスケ

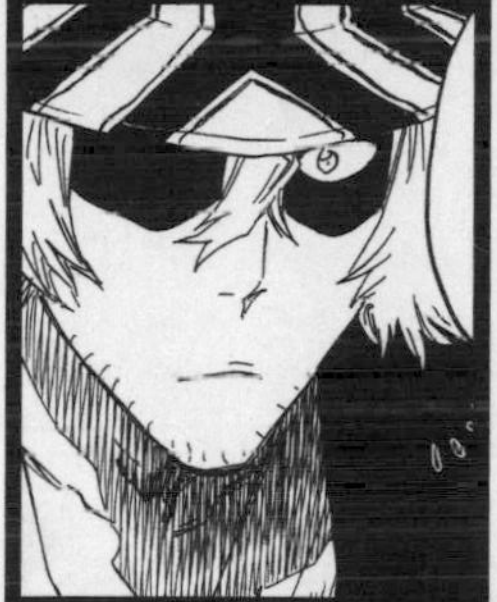

KISUKE URAHARA

YORUICHI SHIHOIN

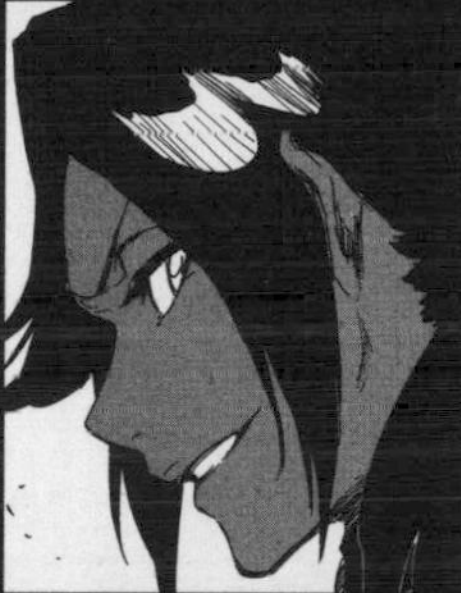

四楓院夜一
シホウインヨルイチ

黒崎一護
クロサキイチゴ

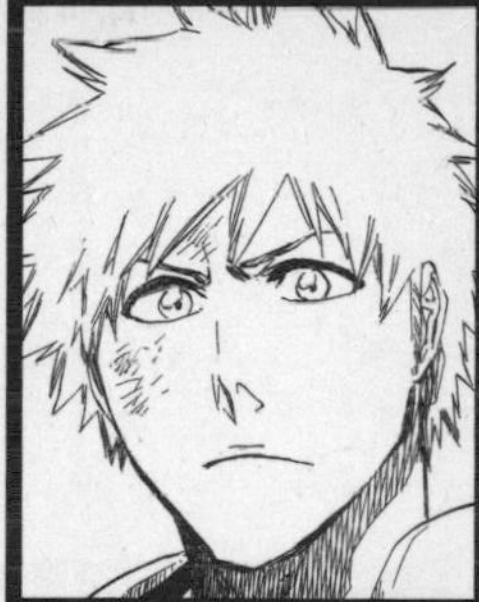

ICHIGO KUROSAKI

plot

Ichigo Kurosaki meets Soul Reaper Rukia Kuchiki and ends up helping her eradicate Hollows. After developing his powers as a Soul Reaper, Ichigo befriends many humans and Soul Reapers and grows as a person...

While making their way into enemy territory, the Soul Reaper captains are attacked by the Quincy forces. Kyoraku stays behind to fight, but is quickly wounded by Lille Barro's powers. Kyoraku releases his bankai and slices off Barro's head, but even that isn't enough. Nanao Ise then appears and saves Kyoraku. She is given the special sword Kyoraku has kept hidden from her, but…

BLEACH

URYU
ISHIDA

石田雨竜
イシダウリュウ

アスキン・
ナックルヴァール

ASKIN
NAKK LE VAAR

GERARD
VALKYRIE

ジェラルド・
ヴァルキリー

STORIES

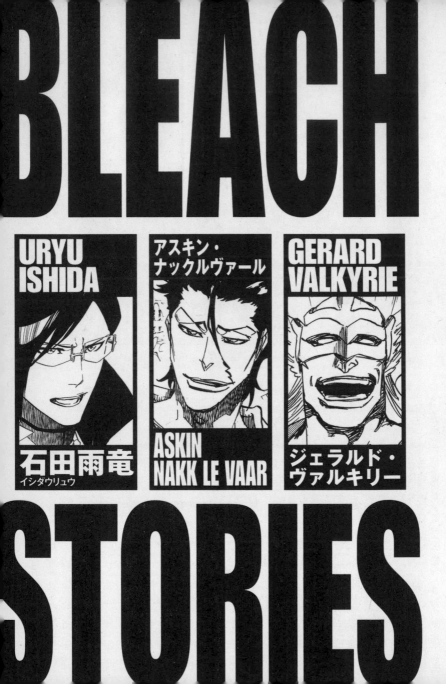

BLEACH 72

MY LAST WORDS

CONTENTS

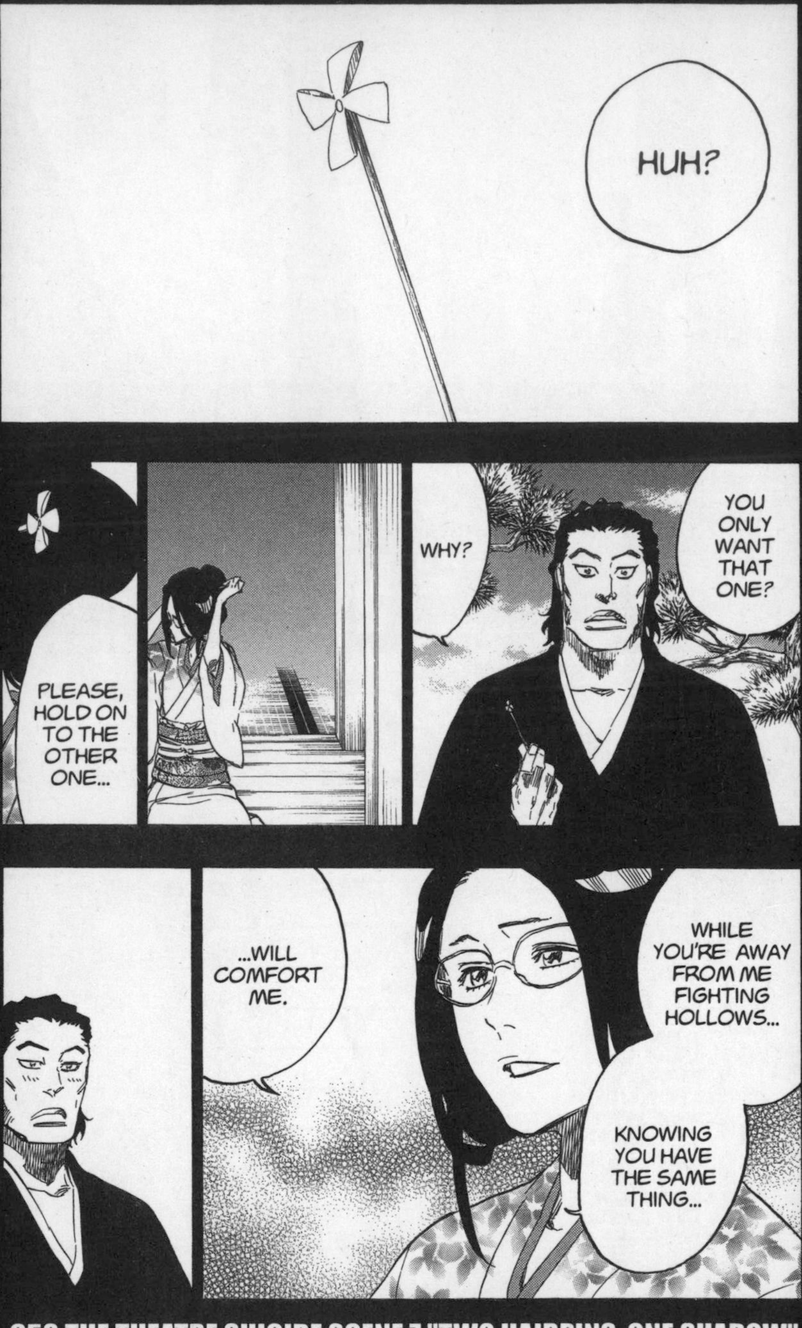
HUH?
YOU ONLY WANT THAT ONE?
WHY?
PLEASE, HOLD ON TO THE OTHER ONE...
WHILE YOU'RE AWAY FROM ME FIGHTING HOLLOWS...
KNOWING YOU HAVE THE SAME THING...
...WILL COMFORT ME.

653.THE THEATRE SUICIDE SCENE 7 "TWO HAIRPINS, ONE SHADOW"

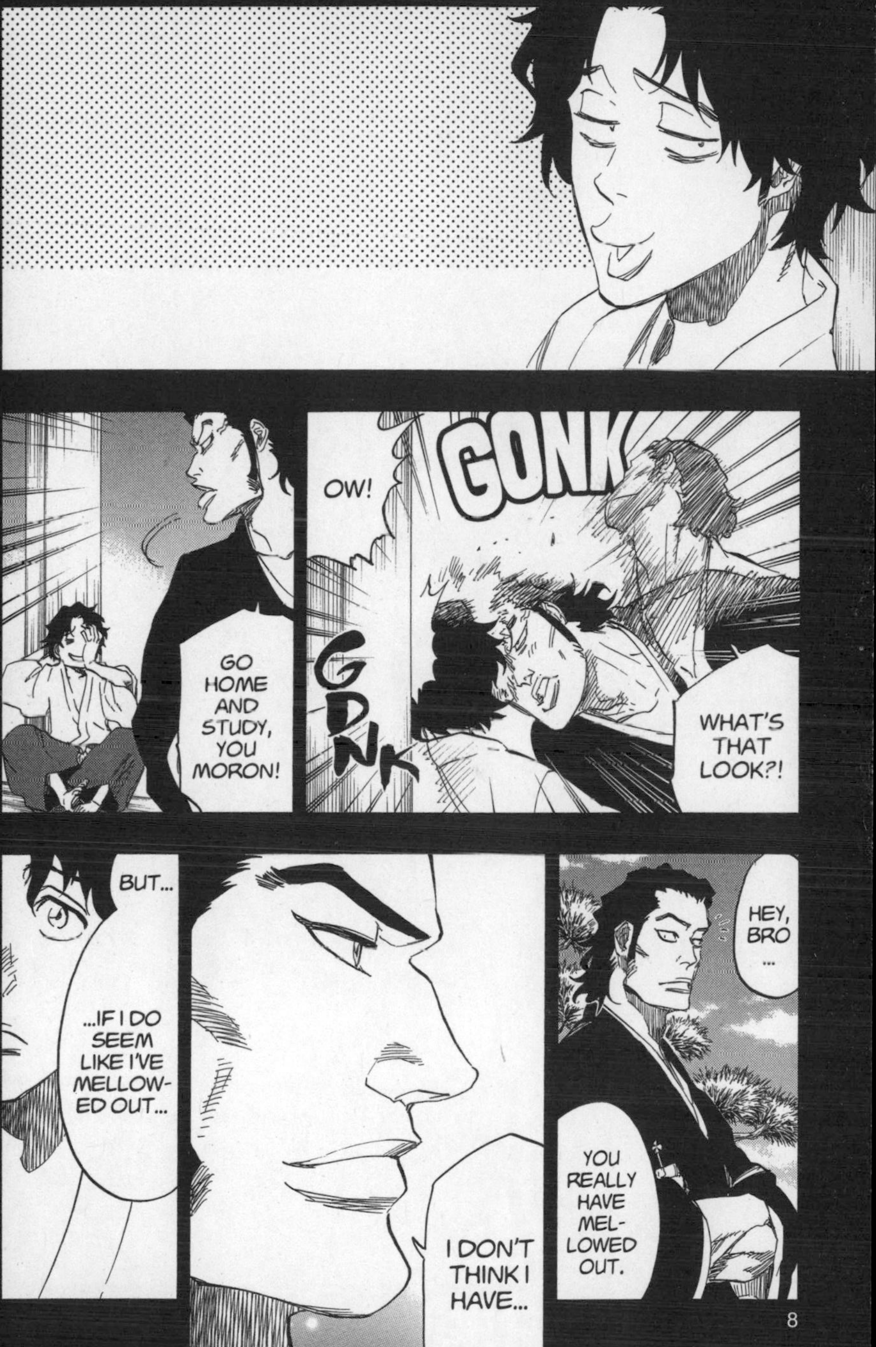
GONK
OW!
WHAT'S THAT LOOK?!
GDNK
GO HOME AND STUDY, YOU MORON!
HEY, BRO...
YOU REALLY HAVE MEL-LOWED OUT.
I DON'T THINK I HAVE...
BUT...
...IF I DO SEEM LIKE I'VE MELLOW-ED OUT...

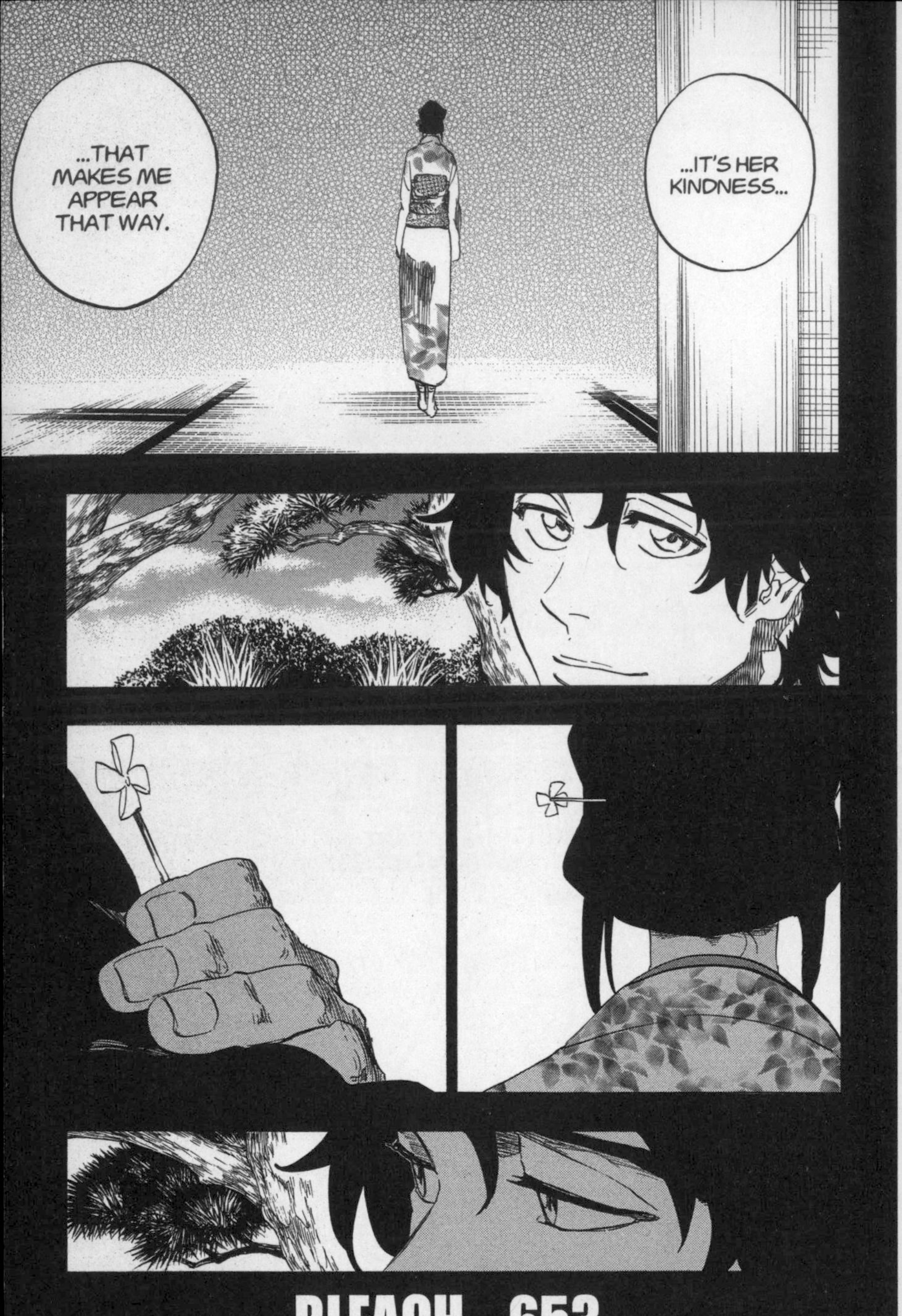
...IT'S HER KINDNESS...
...THAT MAKES ME APPEAR THAT WAY.

BLEACH 653.

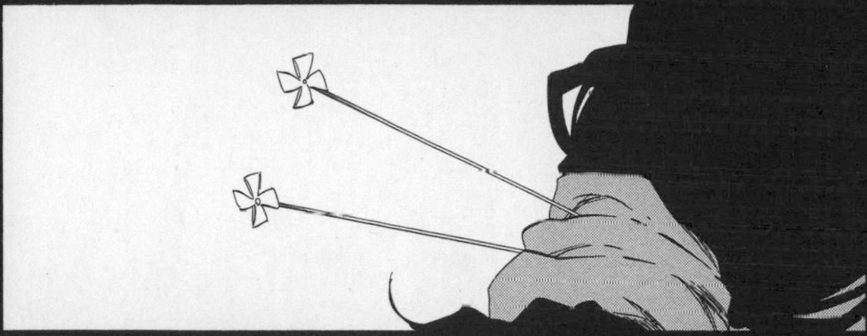

The Theatre Suicide

SCENE 7

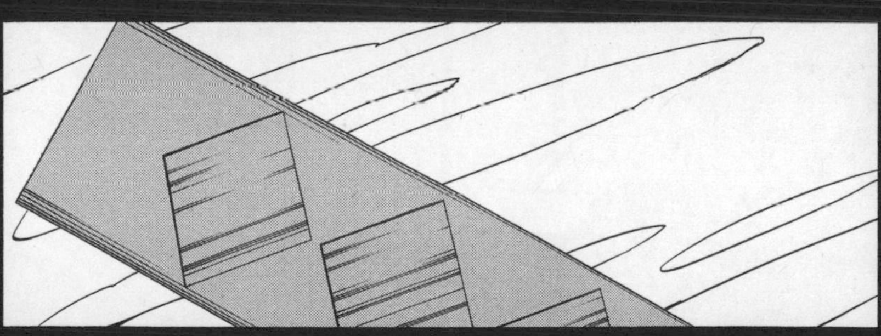

"TWO HAIRPINS, ONE SHADOW"

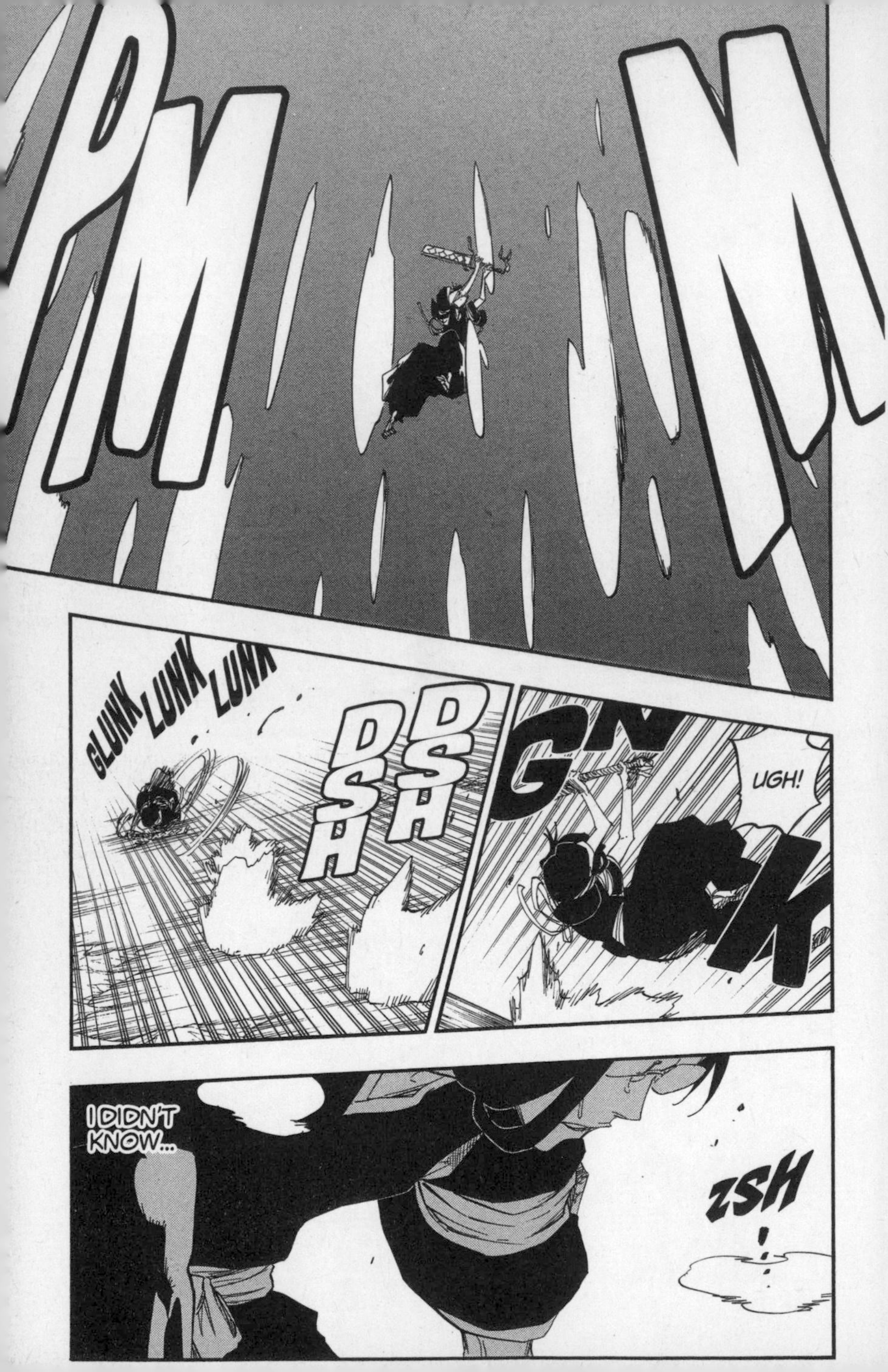
UGH!
DSH
DSH
GLUNK
LUNK
LUNK
I DIDN'T KNOW...
ZSH

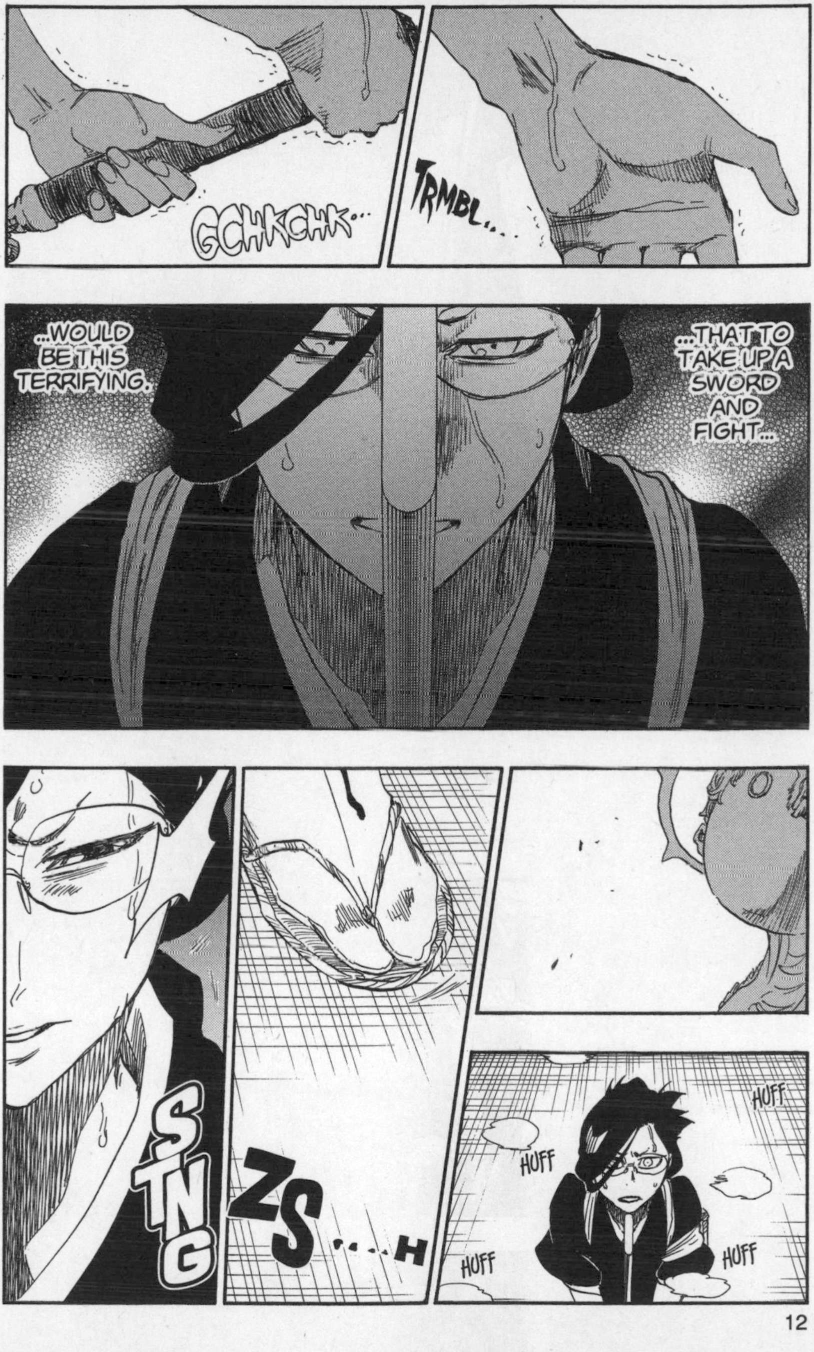
TRMBL...
GCHKCHK...
...THAT TO TAKE UP A SWORD AND FIGHT...
...WOULD BE THIS TERRIFYING.
HUFF
HUFF
HUFF
HUFF
ZS...H
STNG

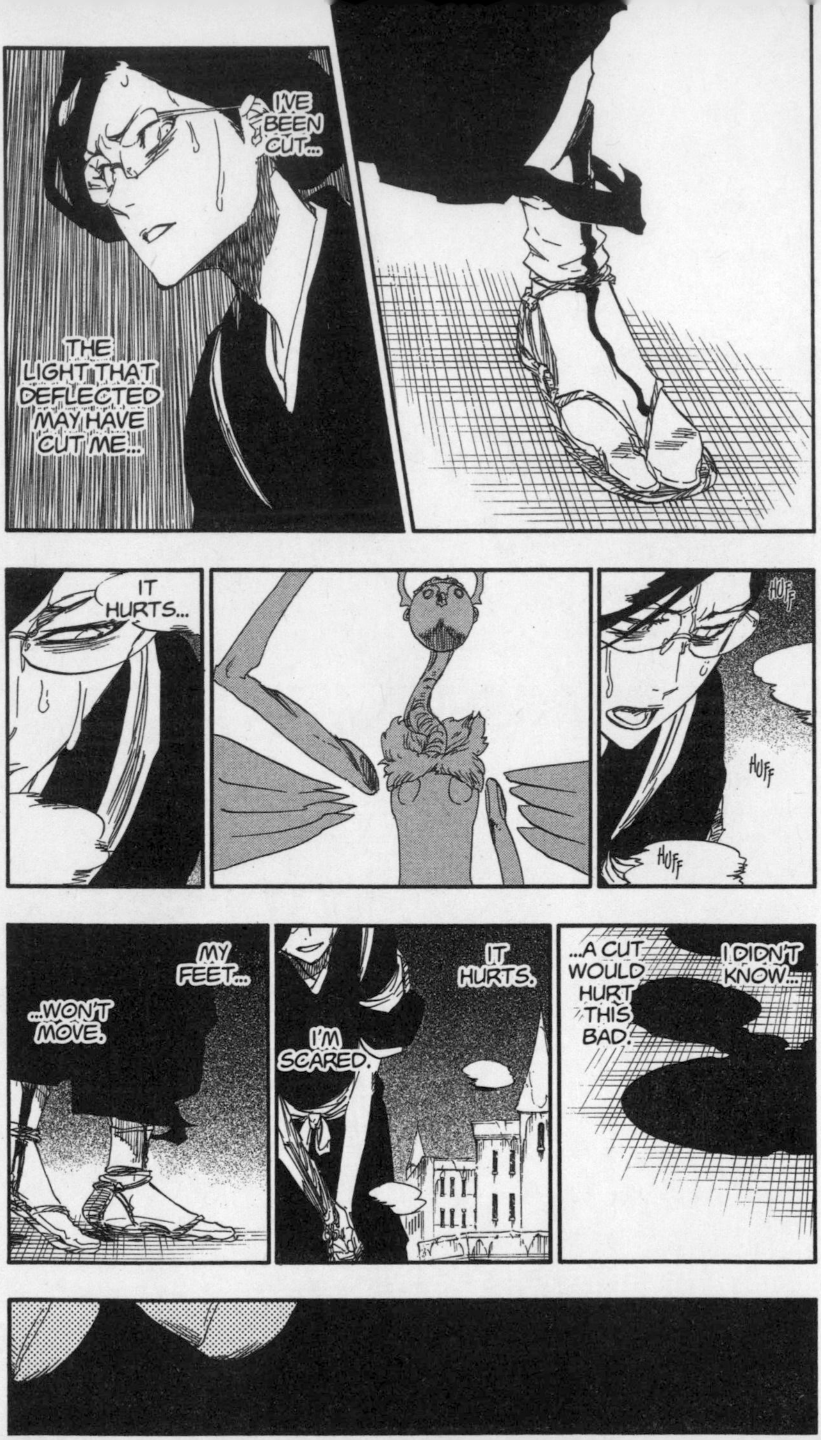
I'VE BEEN CUT...
THE LIGHT THAT DEFLECTED MAY HAVE CUT ME...
HUFF
HUFF
HUFF
IT HURTS...
I DIDN'T KNOW...
...A CUT WOULD HURT THIS BAD.
IT HURTS.
I'M SCARED.
MY FEET...
...WON'T MOVE.

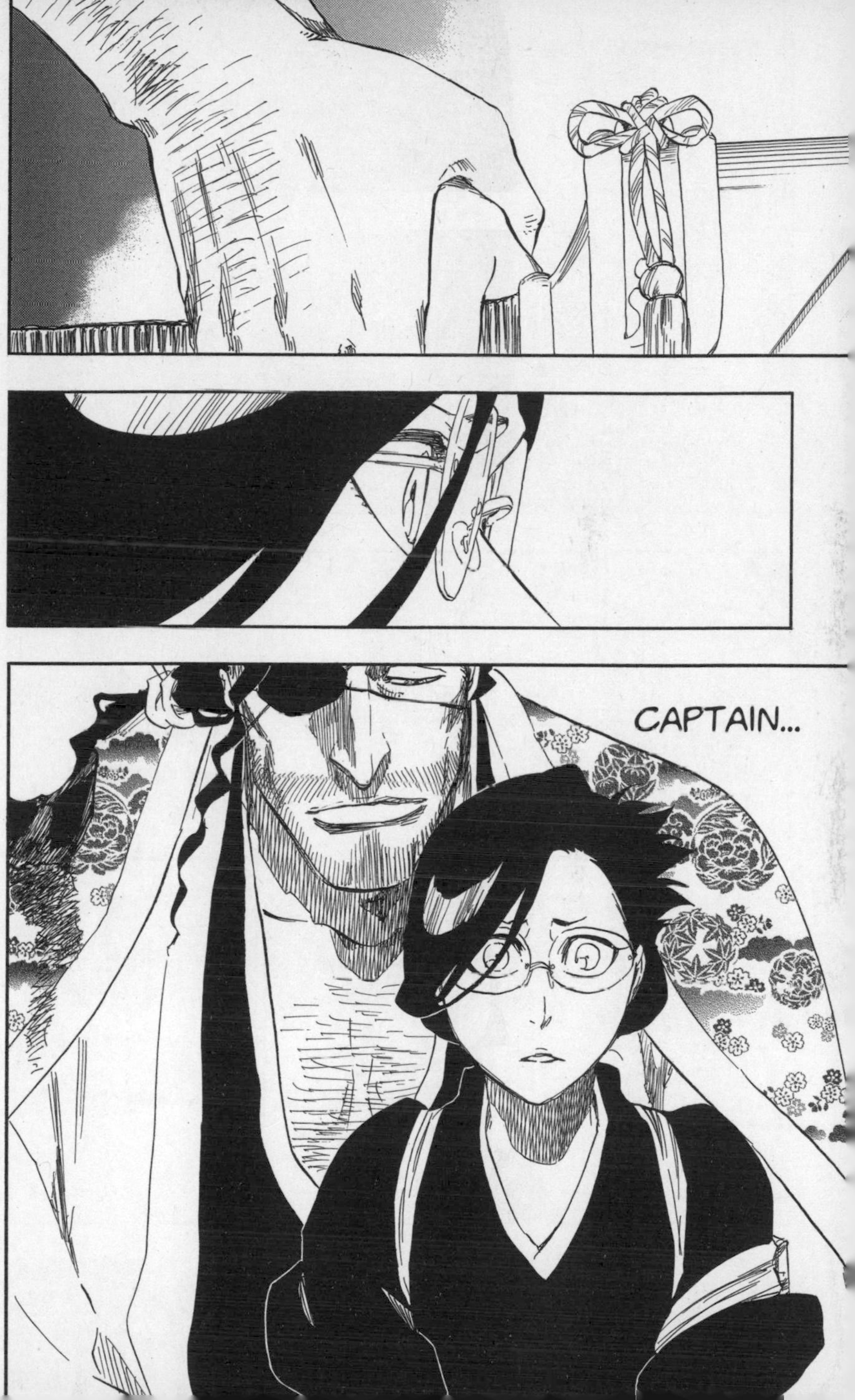
CAPTAIN...

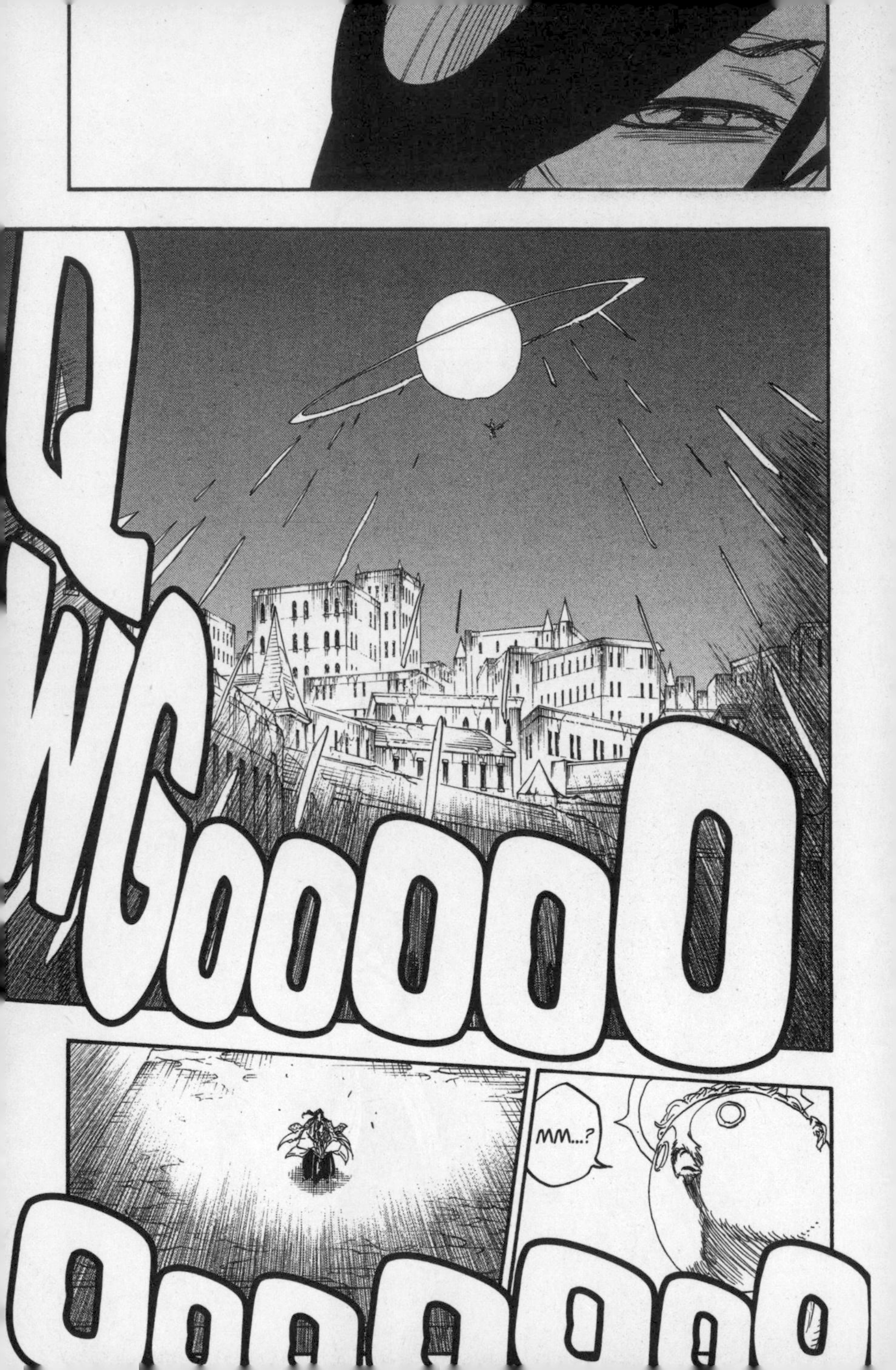
MM...?

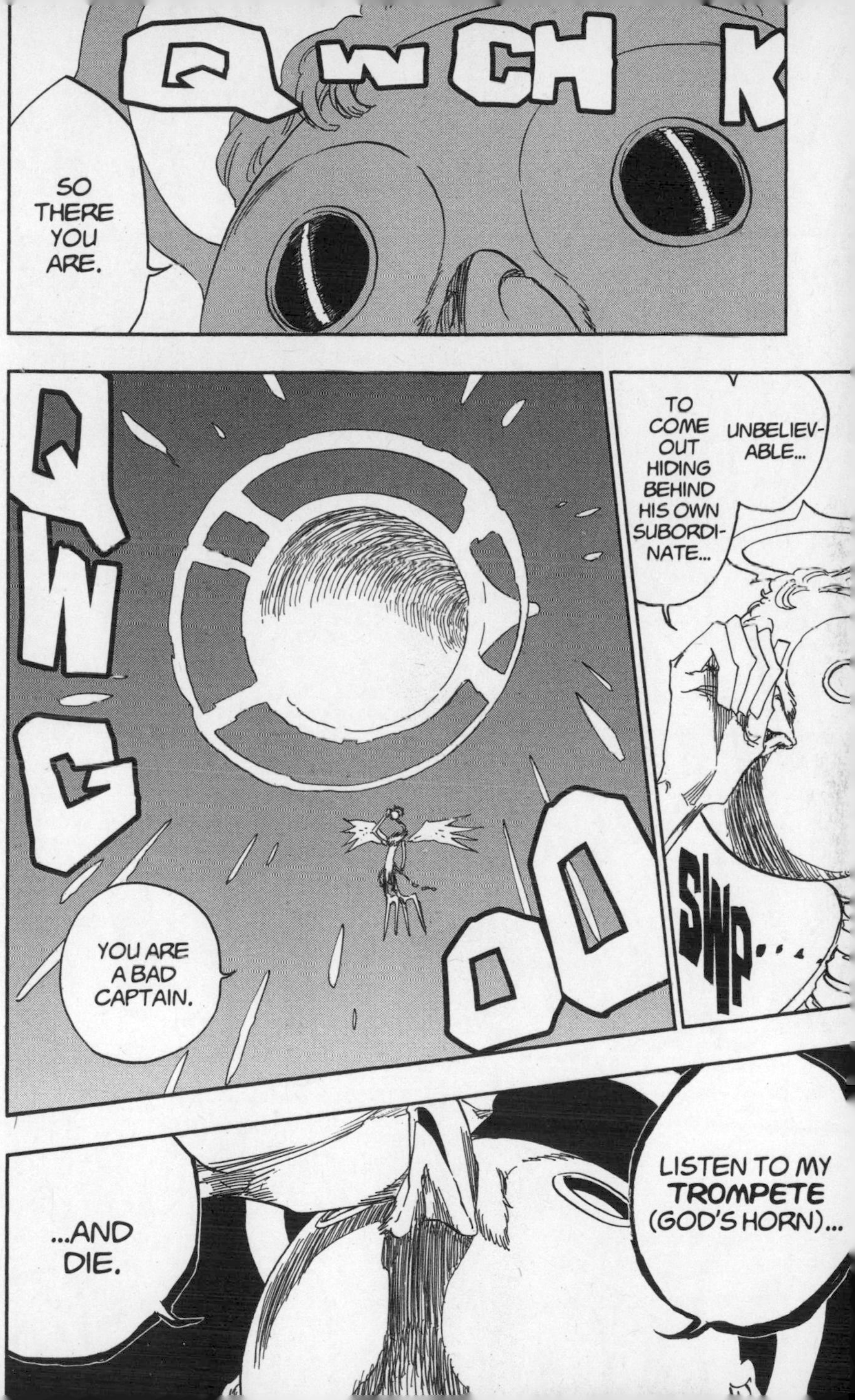
QWCH K
SO THERE YOU ARE.
UNBELIEV-ABLE...
TO COME OUT HIDING BEHIND HIS OWN SUBORDI-NATE...
SWP...
QWGOOO
YOU ARE A BAD CAPTAIN.
LISTEN TO MY TROMPETE (GOD'S HORN)...
...AND DIE.

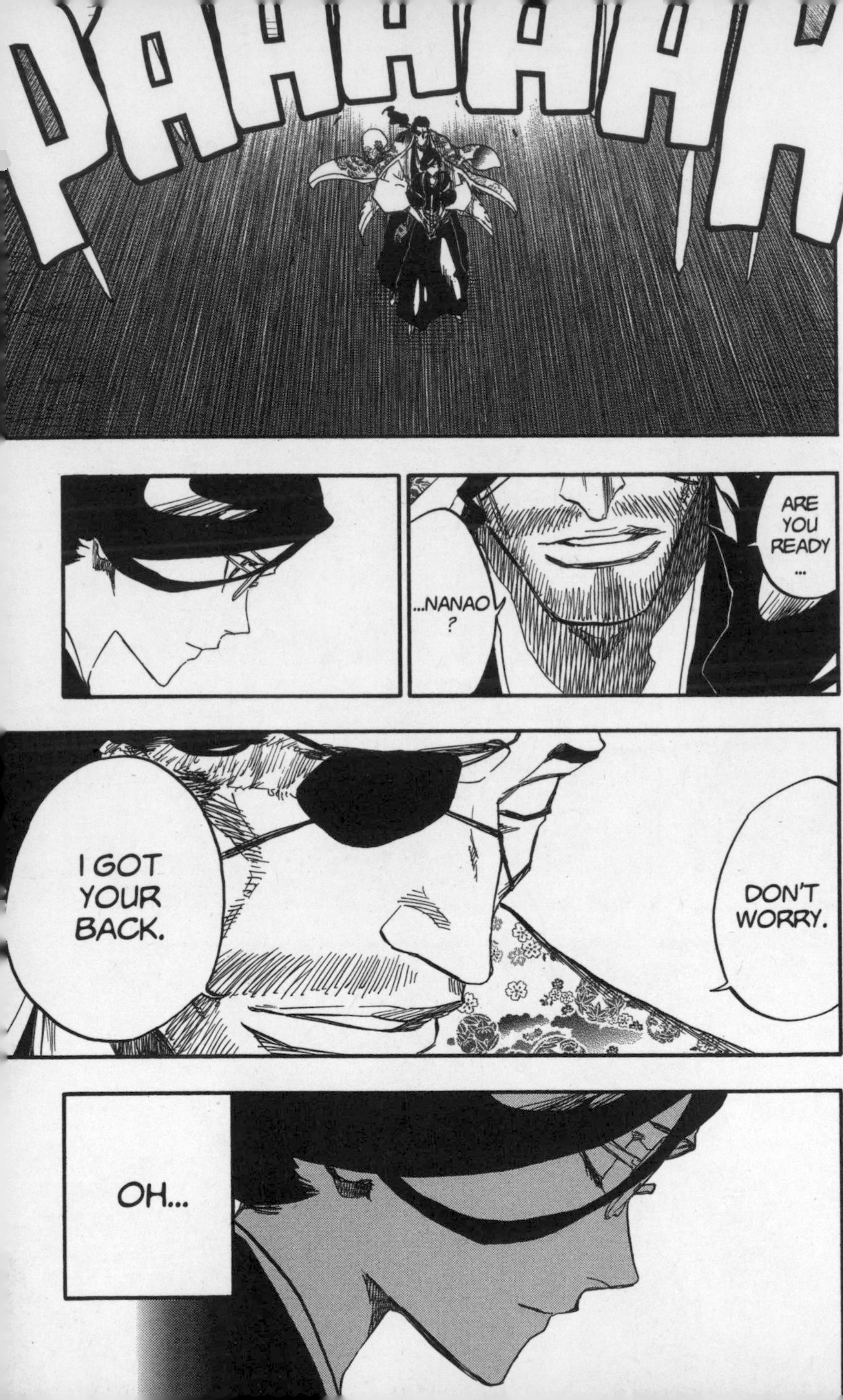
PAAAAAA
ARE YOU READY ...
...NANAO ?
DON'T WORRY.
I GOT YOUR BACK.
OH...

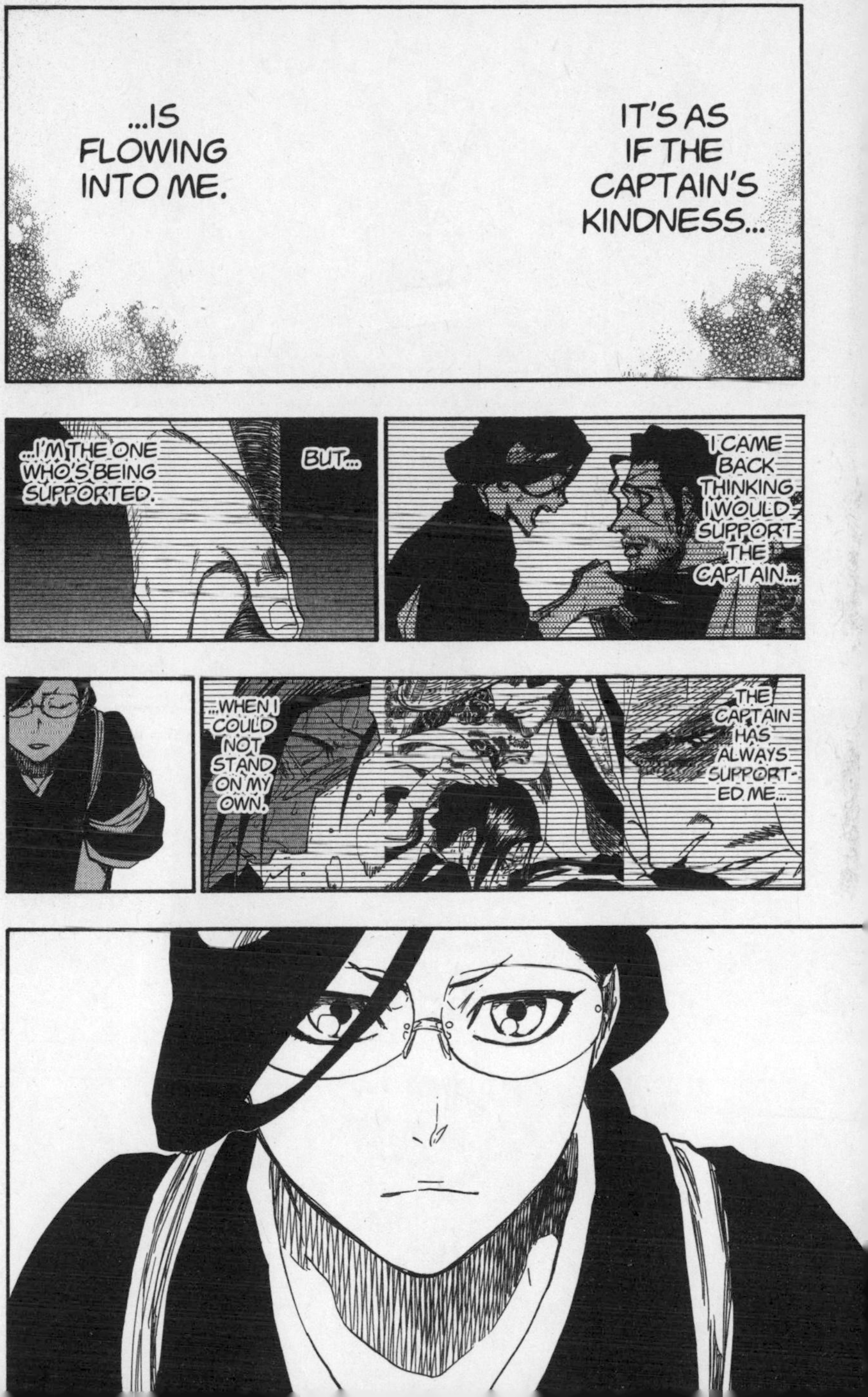
IT'S AS IF THE CAPTAIN'S KINDNESS...
...IS FLOWING INTO ME.
I CAME BACK THINKING I WOULD SUPPORT THE CAPTAIN...
BUT...
...I'M THE ONE WHO'S BEING SUPPORTED.
THE CAPTAIN HAS ALWAYS SUPPORT-ED ME...
...WHEN I COULD NOT STAND ON MY OWN.

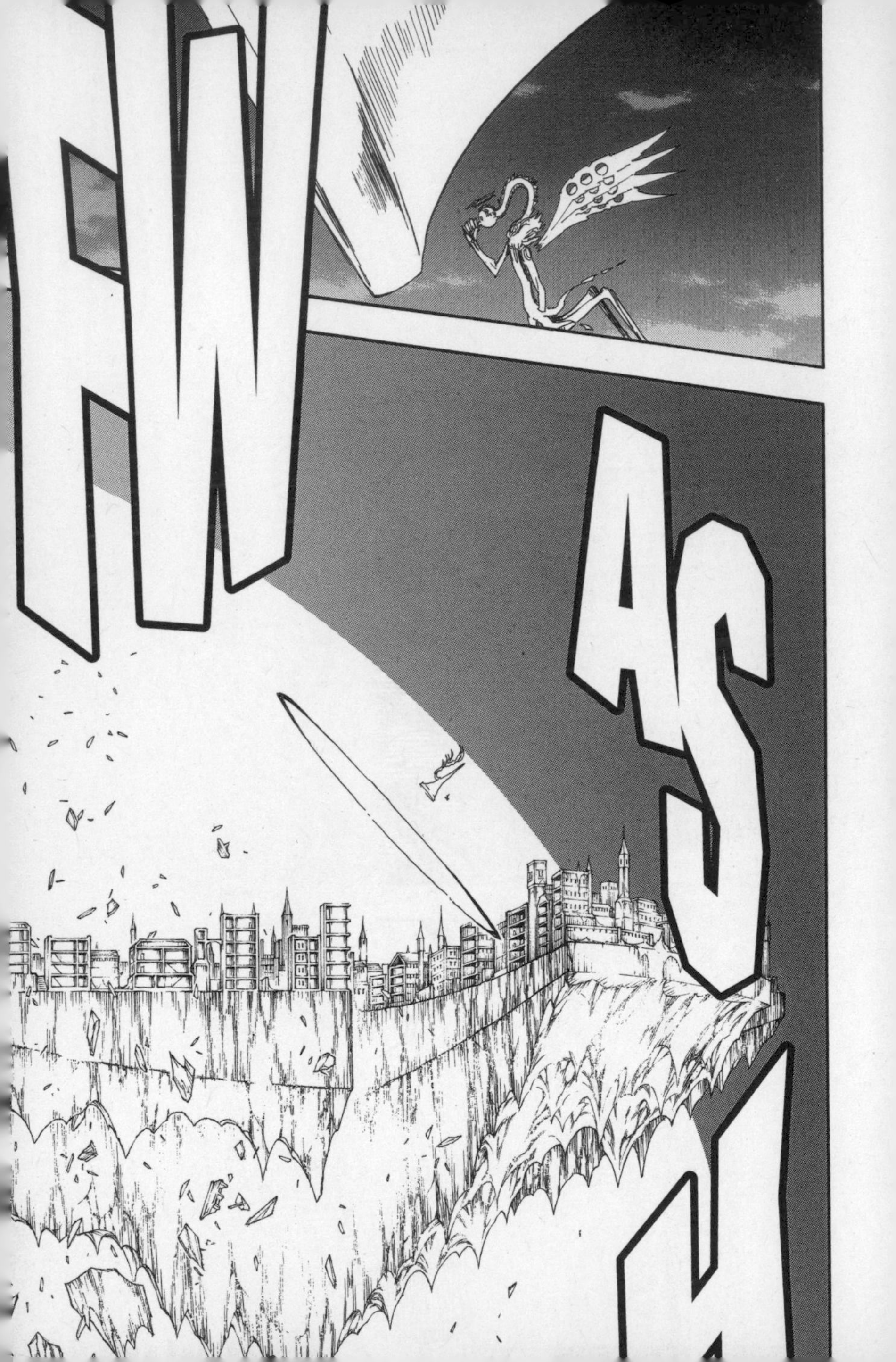
FWASH

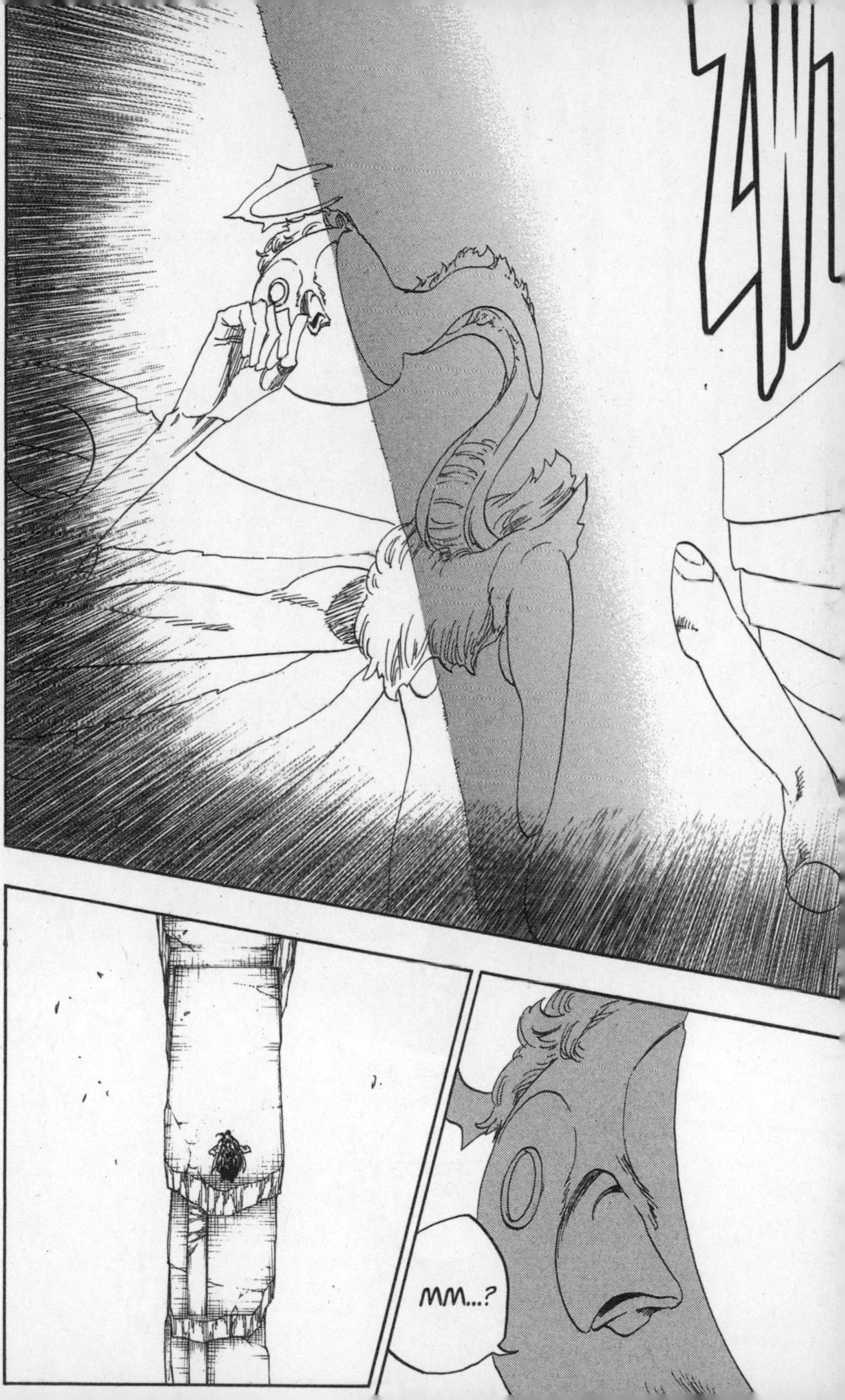
MM...?

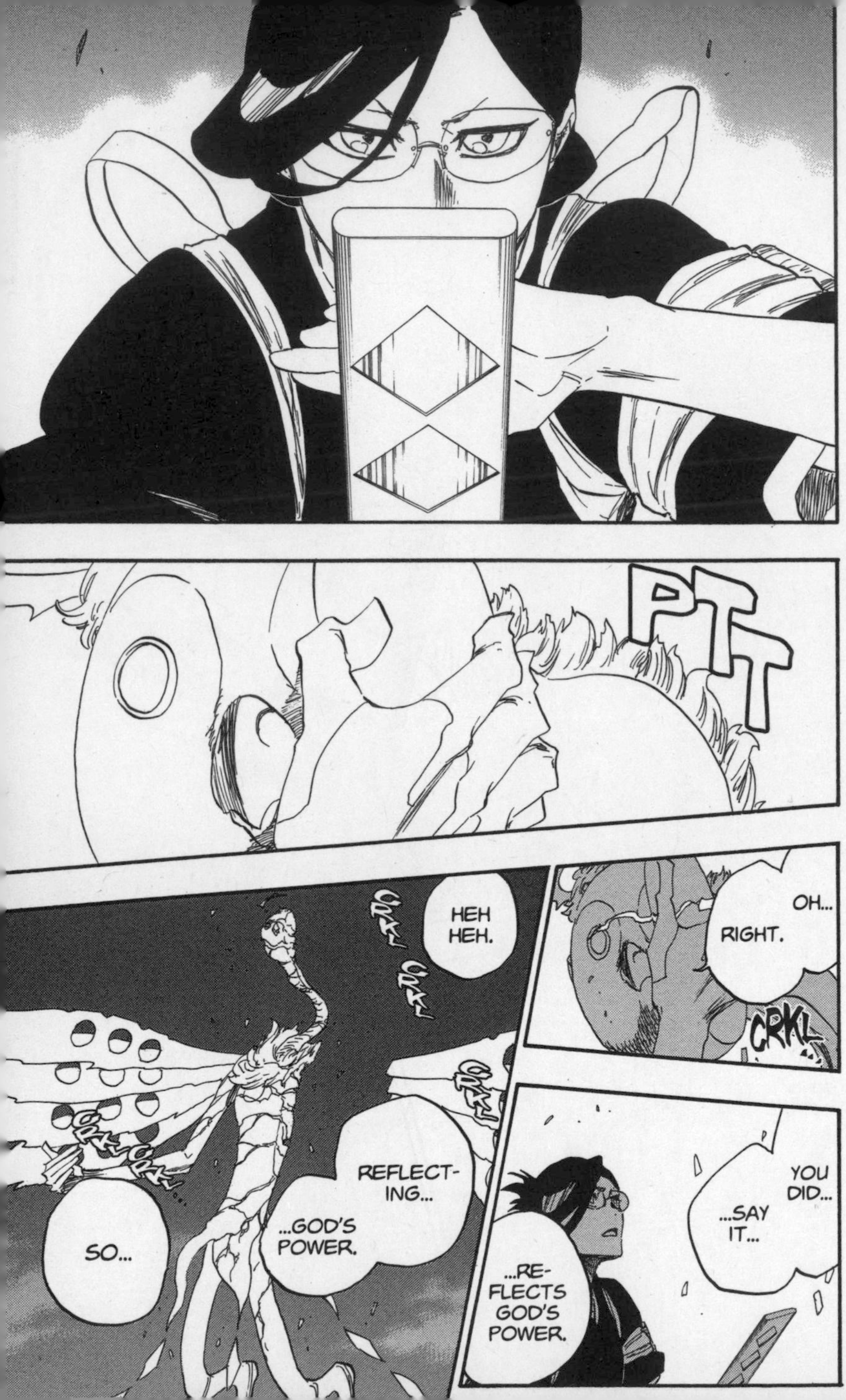
PTT
OH... RIGHT.
CRKL
YOU DID... ...SAY IT...
...RE-FLECTS GOD'S POWER.
HEH HEH.
CRKL CRKL
CRKL
REFLECT-ING...
...GOD'S POWER.
CRKL CRKL...
SO...

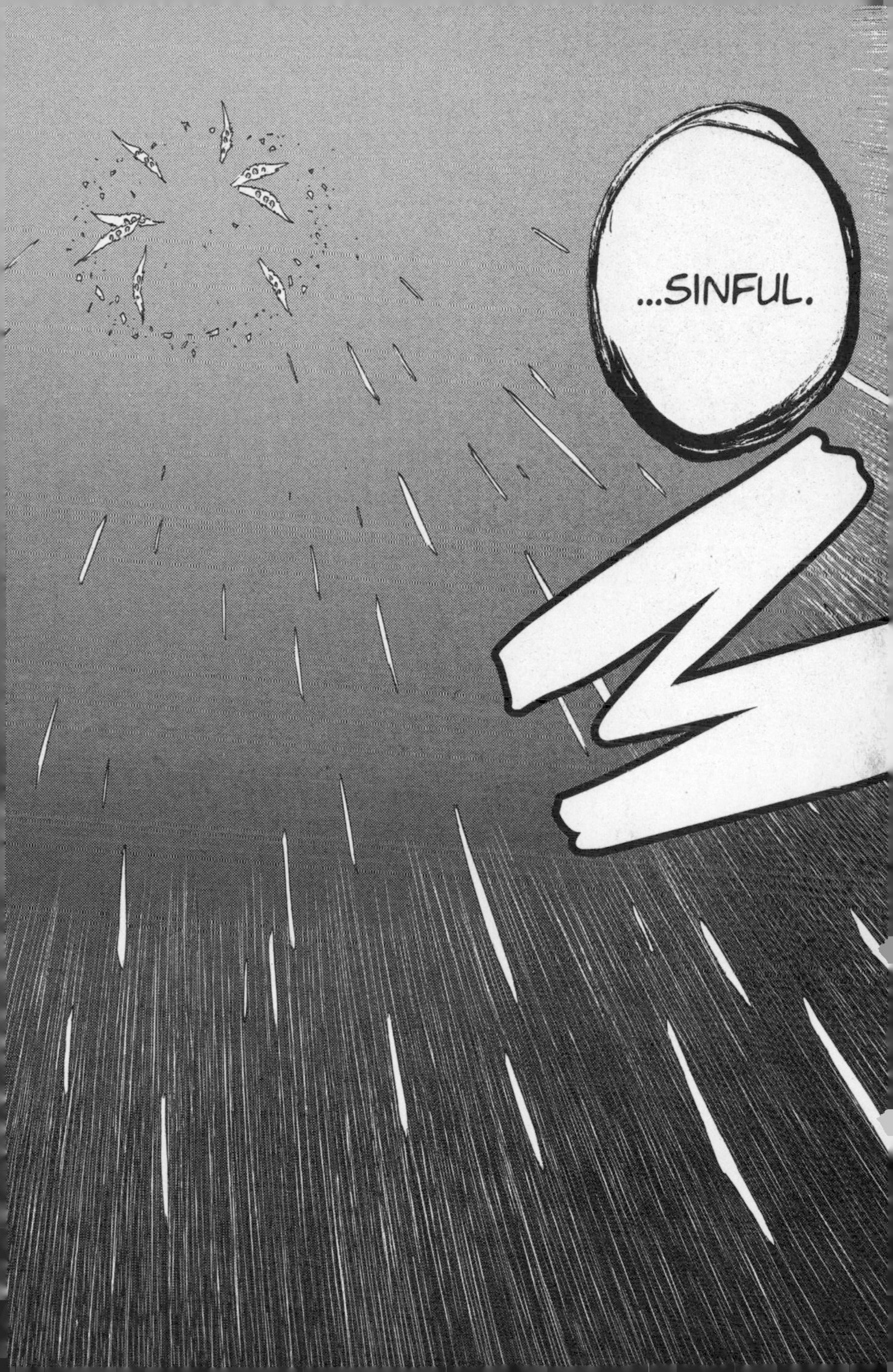
...SINFUL.

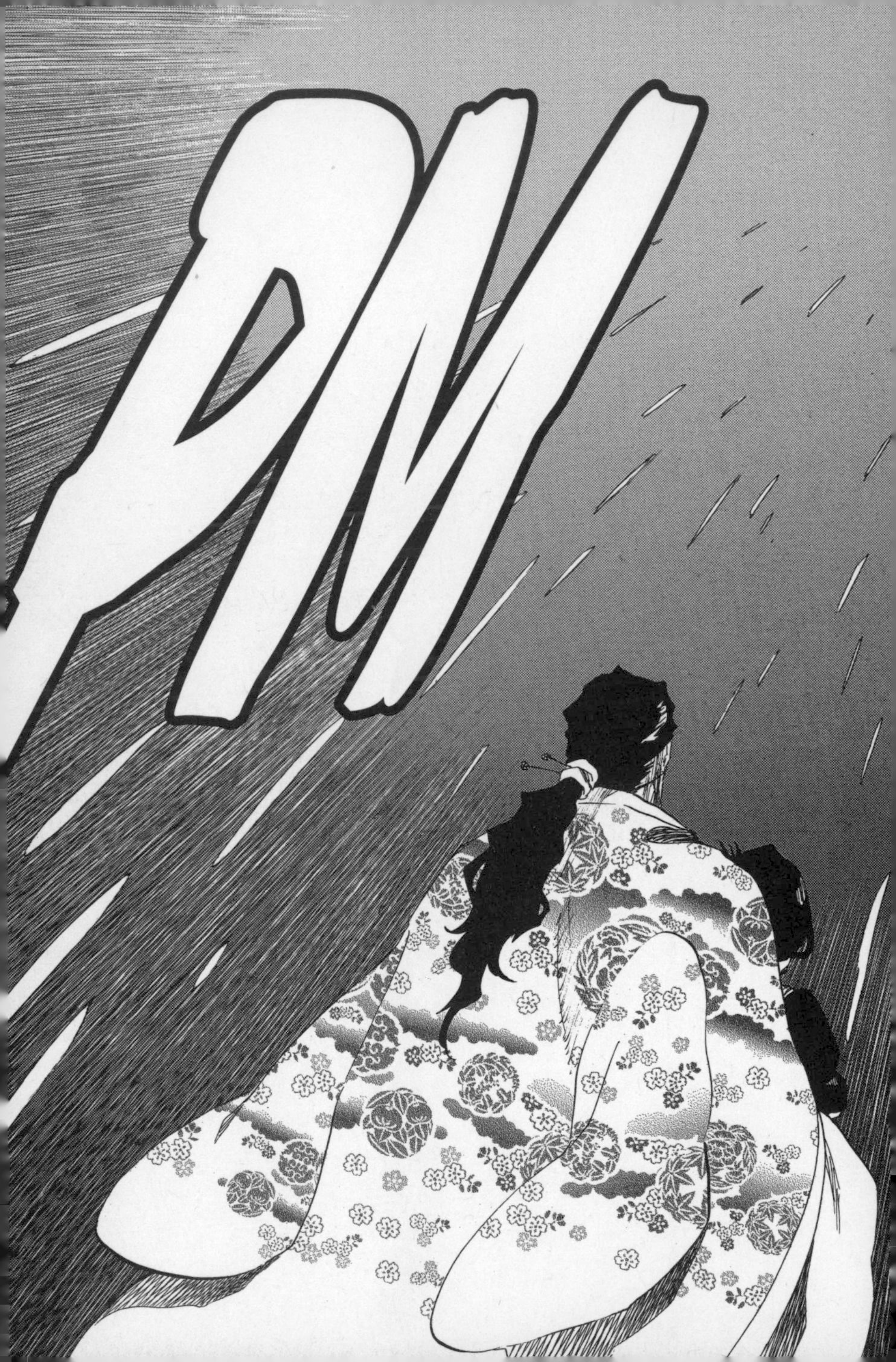

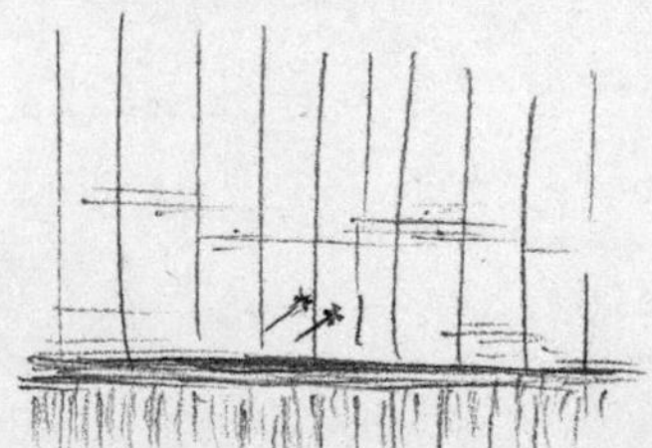

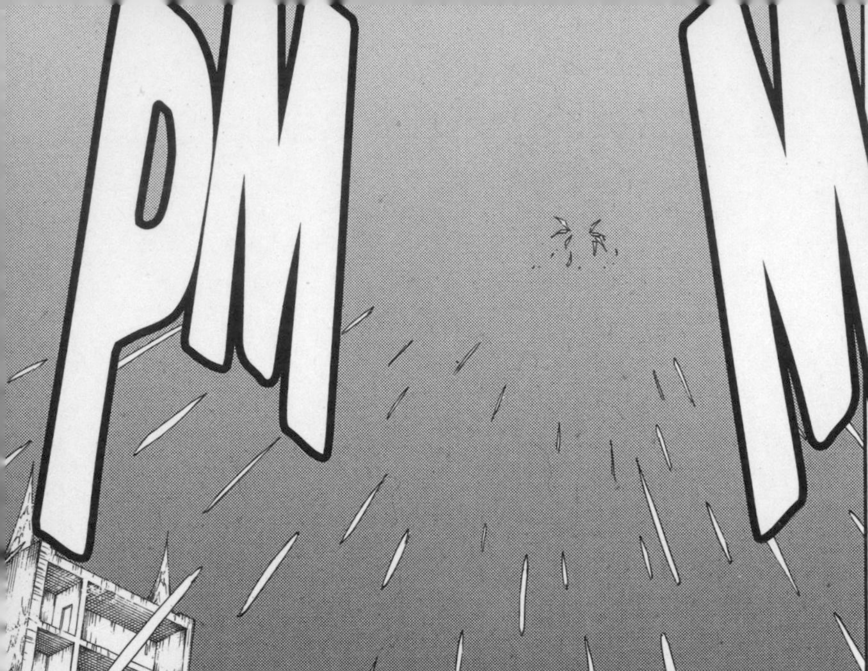
PM

654. DEADMAN STANDING

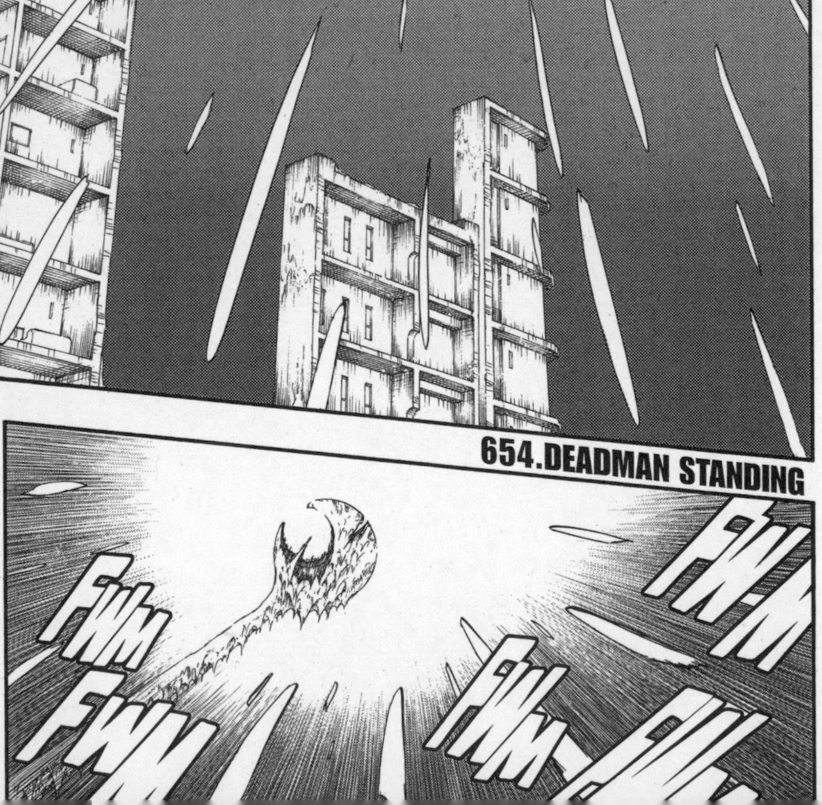
FWM
FWM
FWM

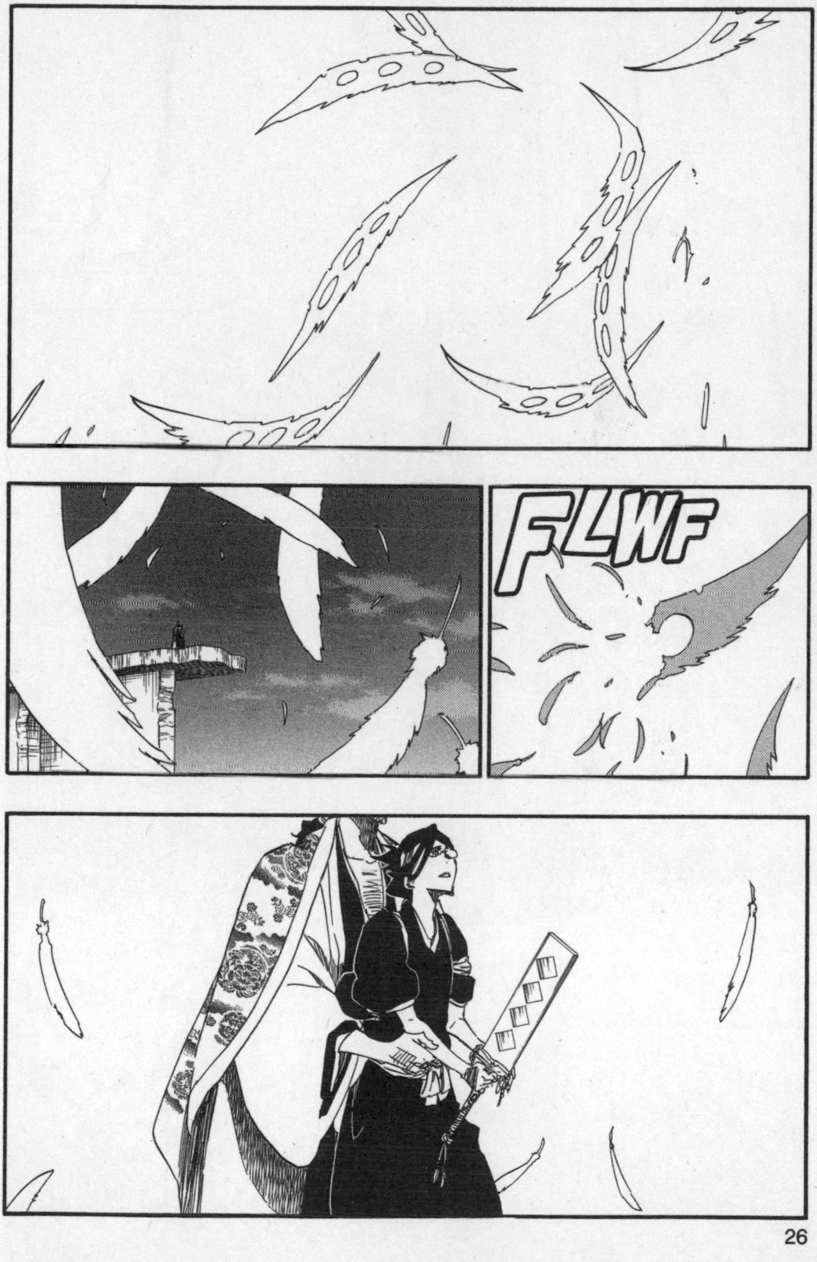
FLWF

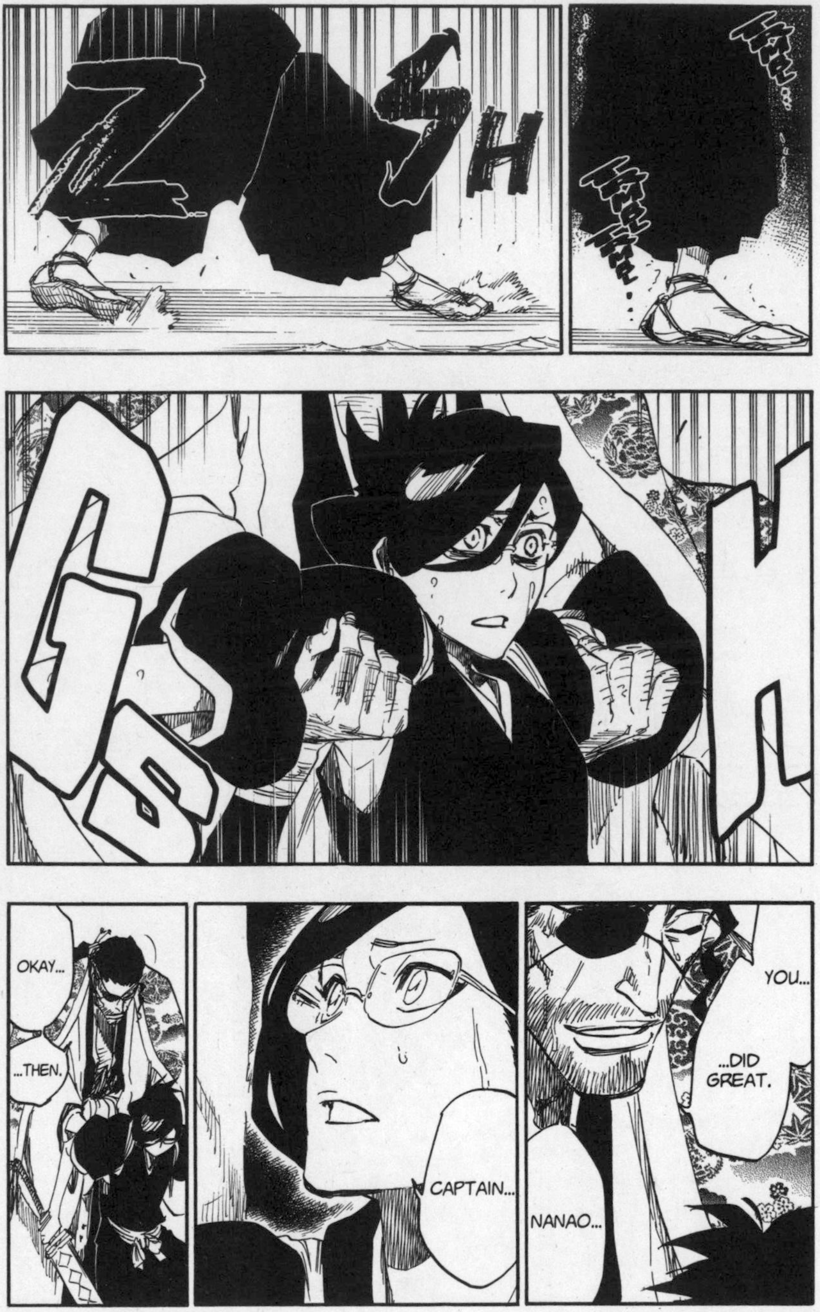
ZSHH
YOU...
...DID GREAT.
NANAO...
CAPTAIN...
OKAY...
...THEN.

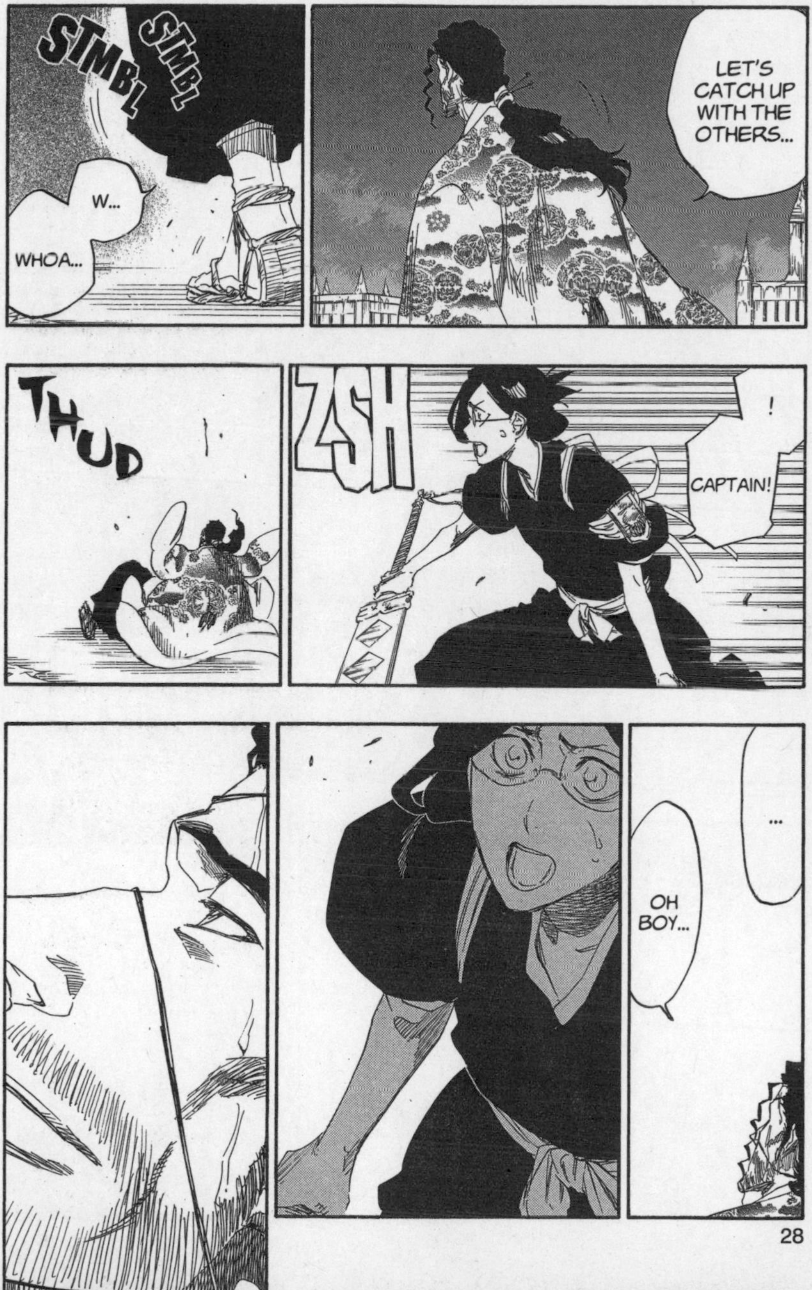
LET'S CATCH UP WITH THE OTHERS...
STMBL
STMBL
W...
WHOA...
ZSH
!
CAPTAIN!
THUD
...
OH BOY...

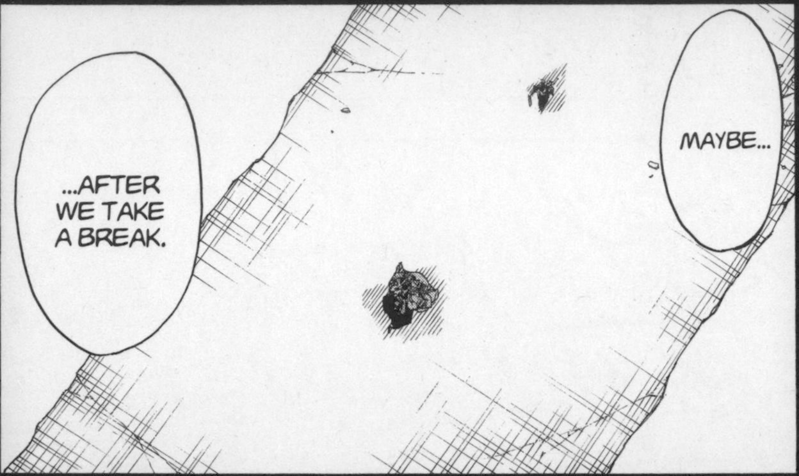
MAYBE...
...AFTER WE TAKE A BREAK.

BLEACH 654.
Deadman Standing

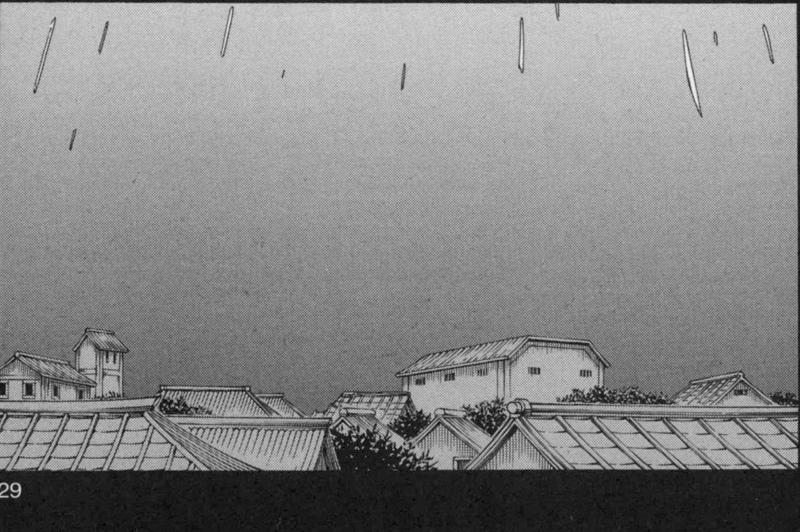

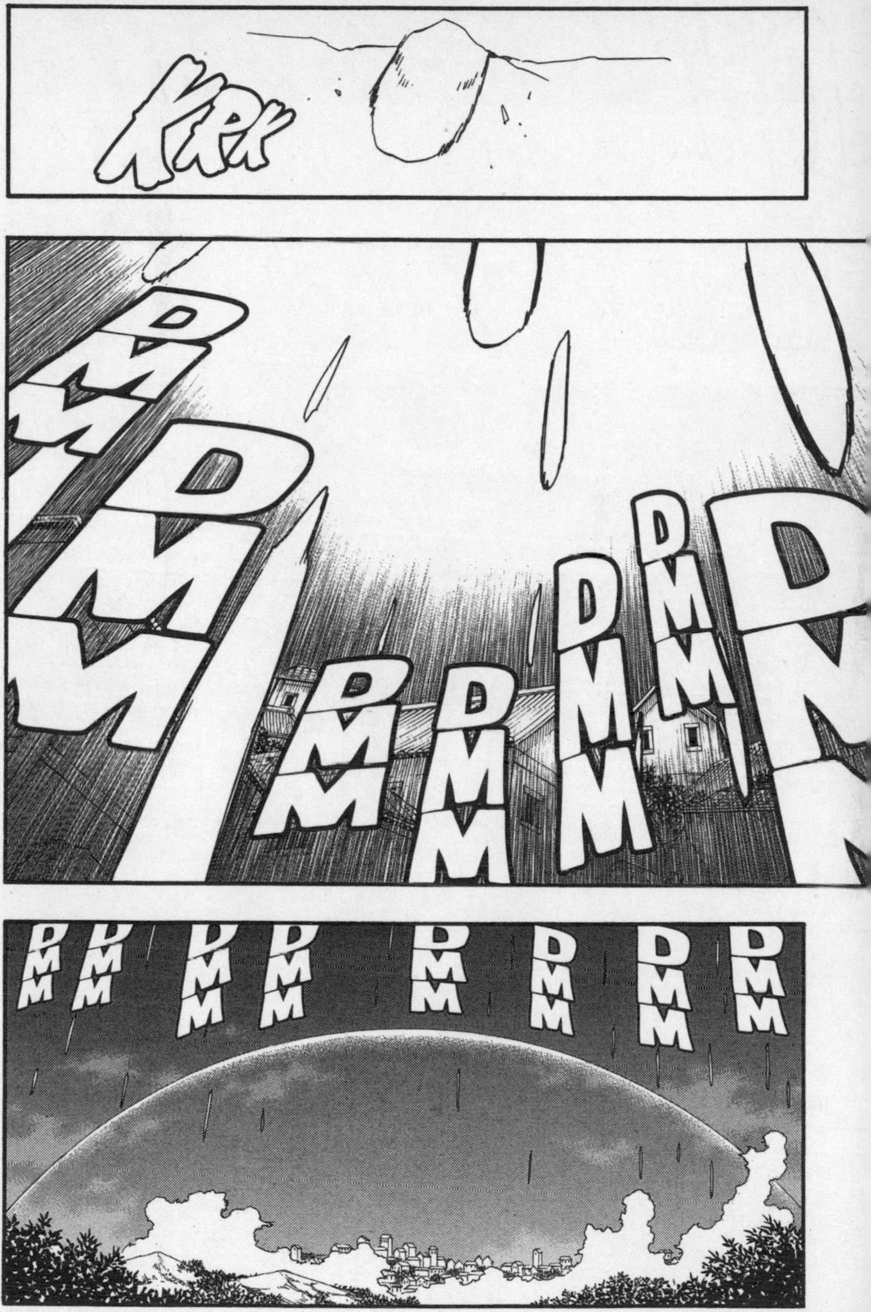
KREK
DMMM
DMM
DMMM
DMMM
DMMM
DMM
DMM
DMM
DMM
DMM
DMM
DMMM
DMMM
DMM
DMM
DMM

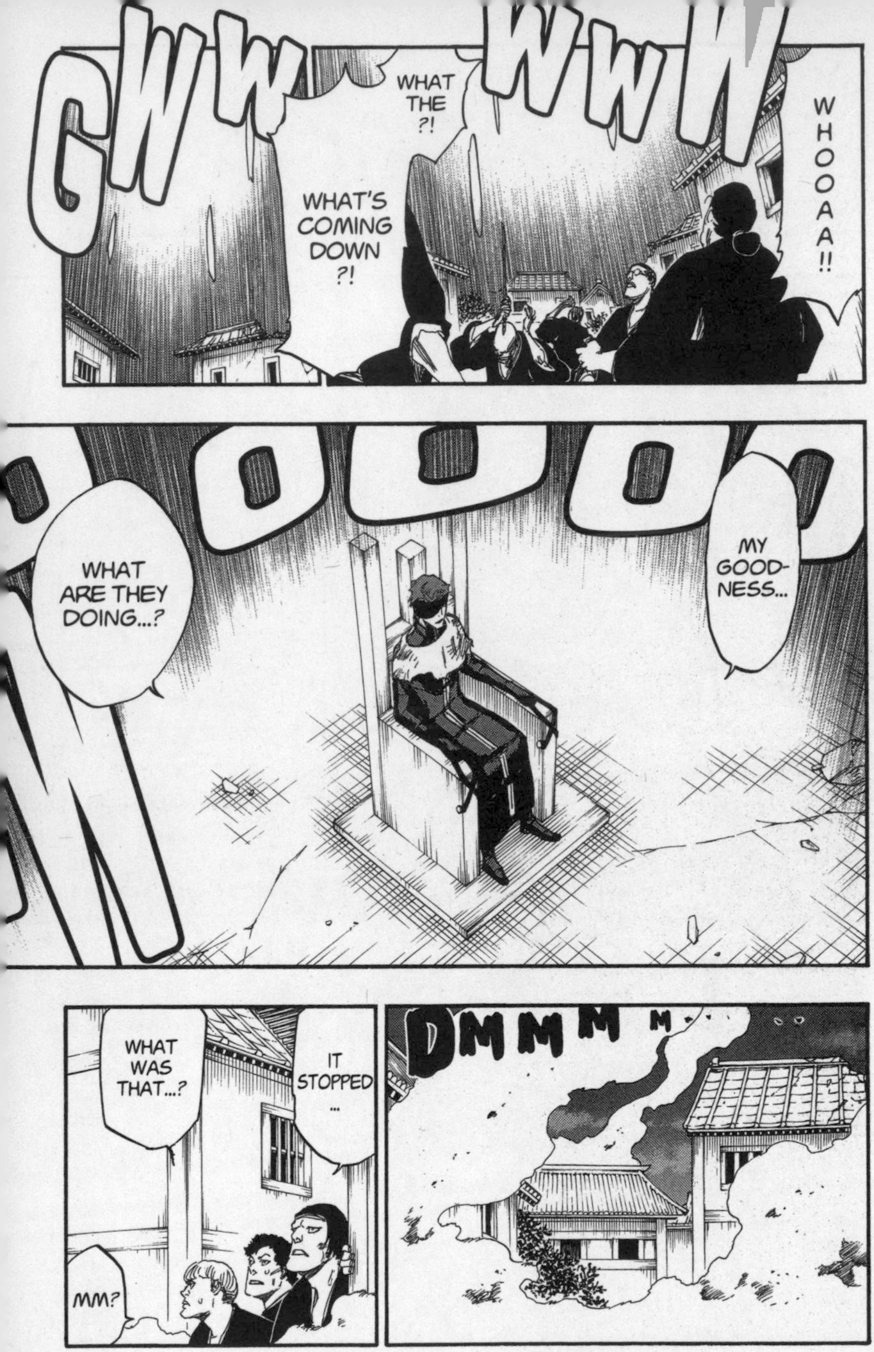
GWW
WWWW
WHOOAAA!!
WHAT THE ?!
WHAT'S COMING DOWN ?!
OOOO
MY GOODNESS...
WHAT ARE THEY DOING...?
DMMMM
IT STOPPED ...
WHAT WAS THAT...?
MM?

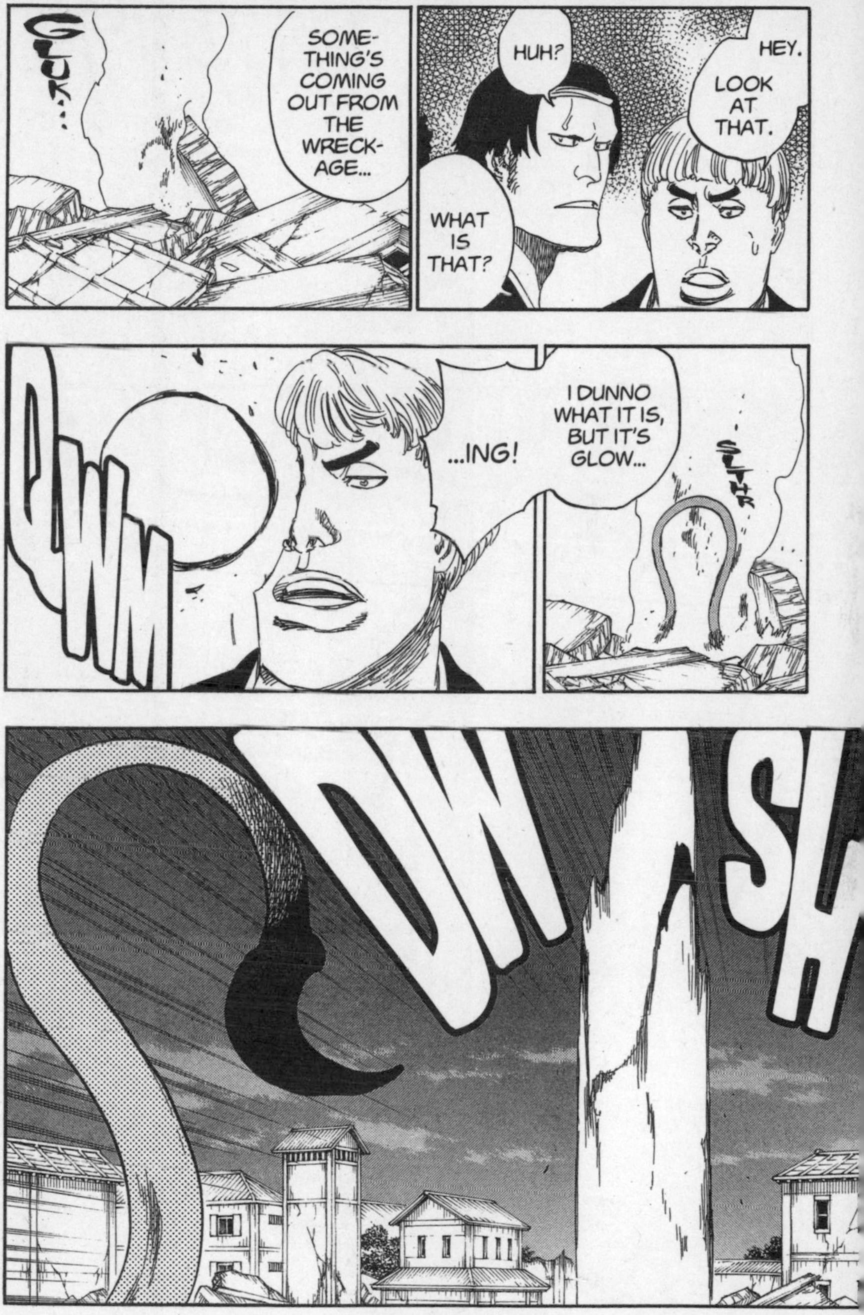
HEY.
LOOK AT THAT.
HUH?
WHAT IS THAT?
SOME-THING'S COMING OUT FROM THE WRECK-AGE...
GLUK...
SLTHR
I DUNNO WHAT IT IS, BUT IT'S GLOW...
...ING!

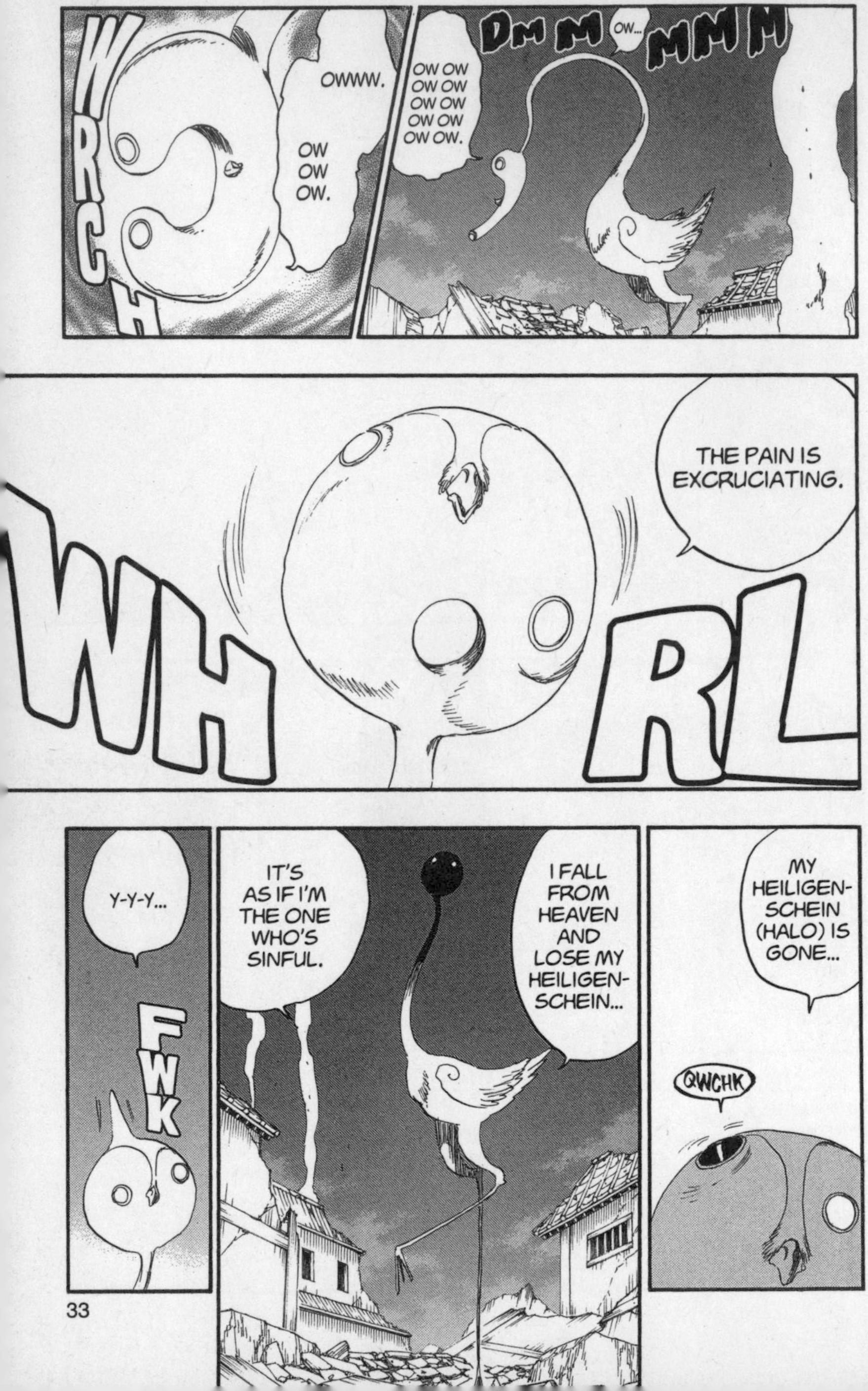
DMMM
OW...
MMMM
OW OW OW OW OW OW OW OW OW OW.
OWWW.
OW OW OW.
WRCH
THE PAIN IS EXCRUCIATING.
WH RL
MY HEILIGEN-SCHEIN (HALO) IS GONE...
QWCHK
I FALL FROM HEAVEN AND LOSE MY HEILIGEN-SCHEIN...
IT'S AS IF I'M THE ONE WHO'S SINFUL.
Y-Y-Y...
FWK

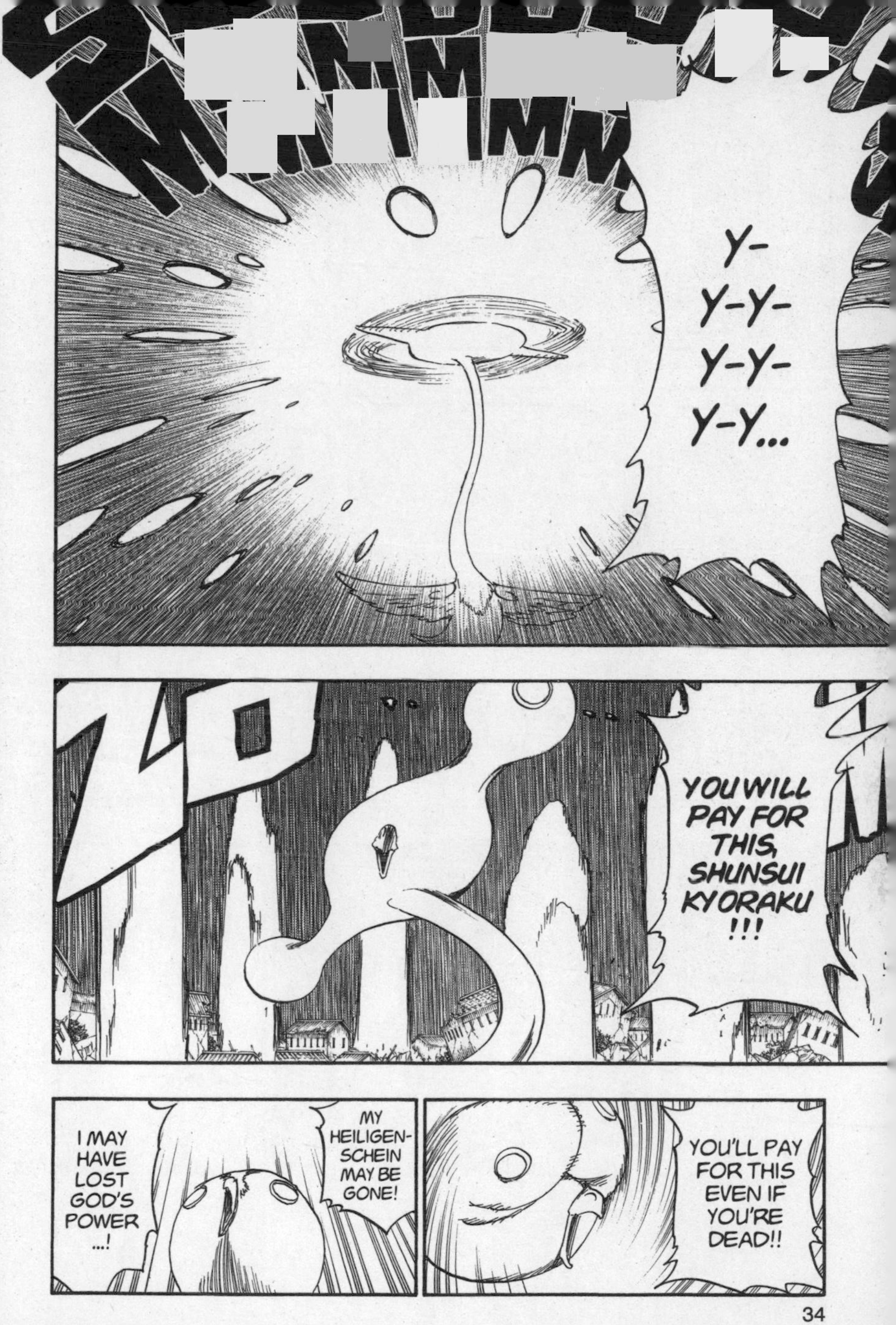
Y-
Y-Y-
Y-Y-
Y-Y...
YOU WILL PAY FOR THIS, SHUNSUI KYORAKU!!!
YOU'LL PAY FOR THIS EVEN IF YOU'RE DEAD!!
MY HEILIGEN-SCHEIN MAY BE GONE!
I MAY HAVE LOST GOD'S POWER...!

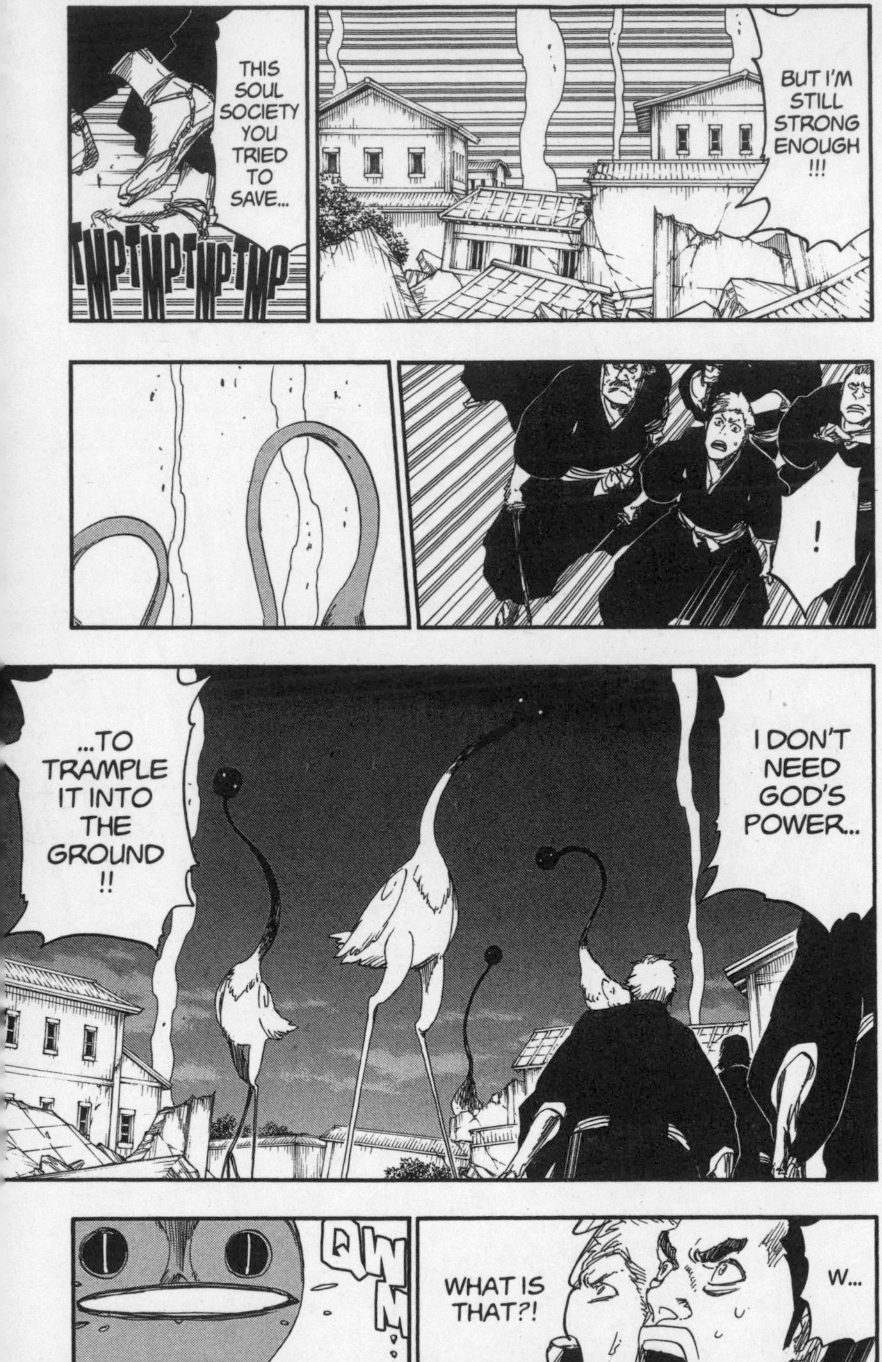
BUT I'M STILL STRONG ENOUGH !!!
THIS SOUL SOCIETY YOU TRIED TO SAVE...
TMPTMPTMPTMP
!
I DON'T NEED GOD'S POWER...
...TO TRAMPLE IT INTO THE GROUND !!
W...
WHAT IS THAT?!
QWM

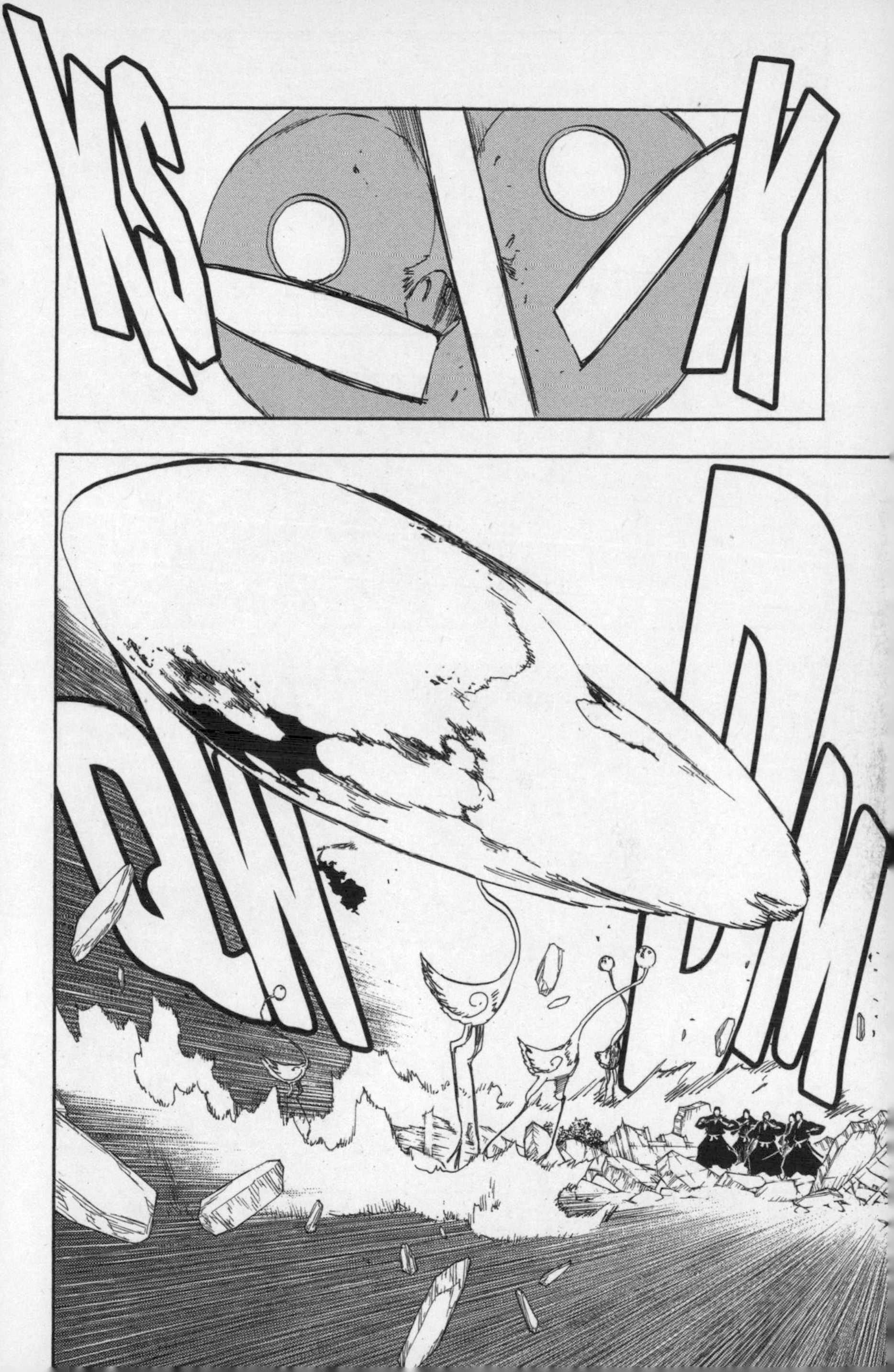

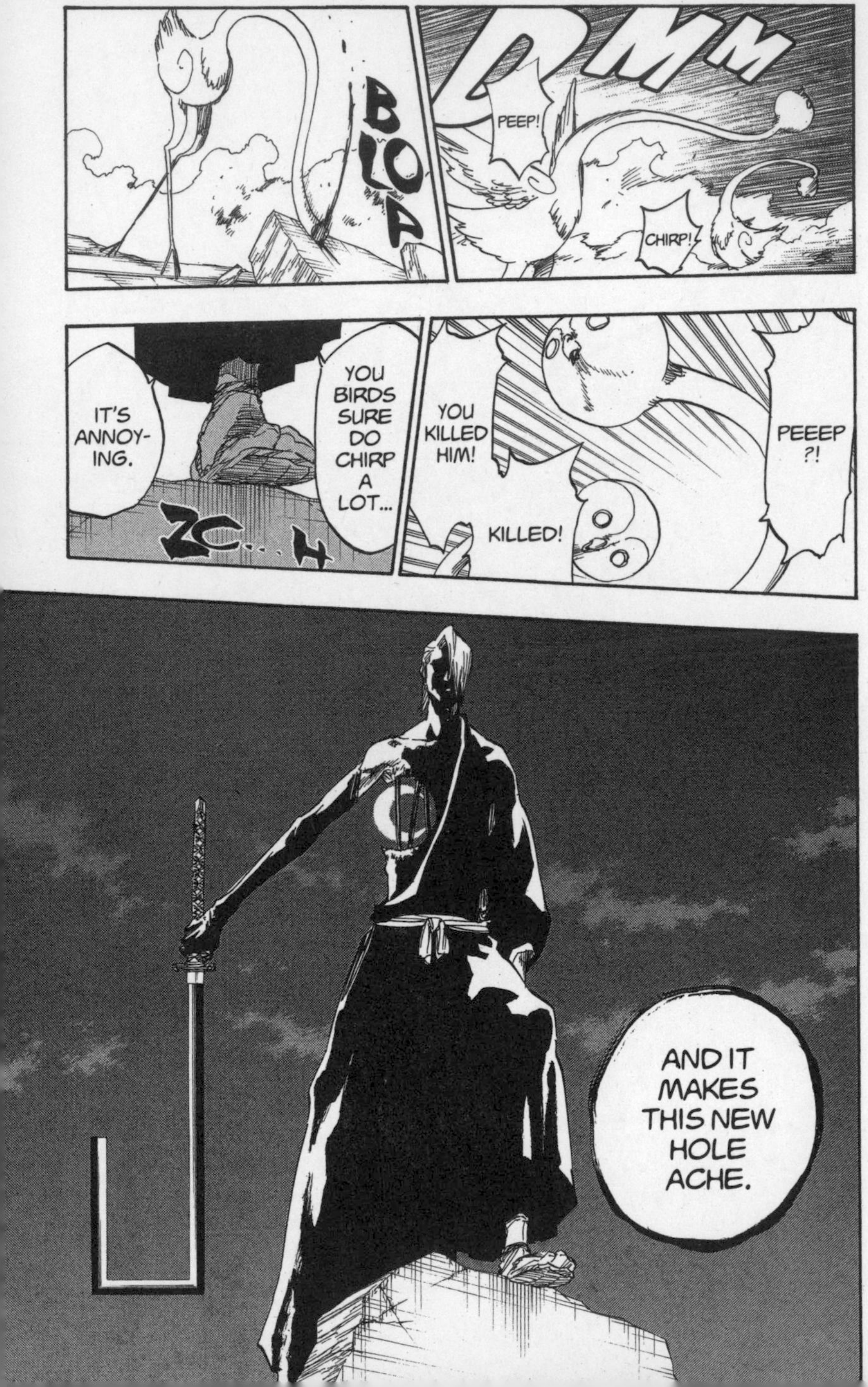
DMM
PEEP!
CHIRP!
BLOP
PEEEP ?!
YOU KILLED HIM!
KILLED!
YOU BIRDS SURE DO CHIRP A LOT...
IT'S ANNOY-ING.
ZC..H
AND IT MAKES THIS NEW HOLE ACHE.

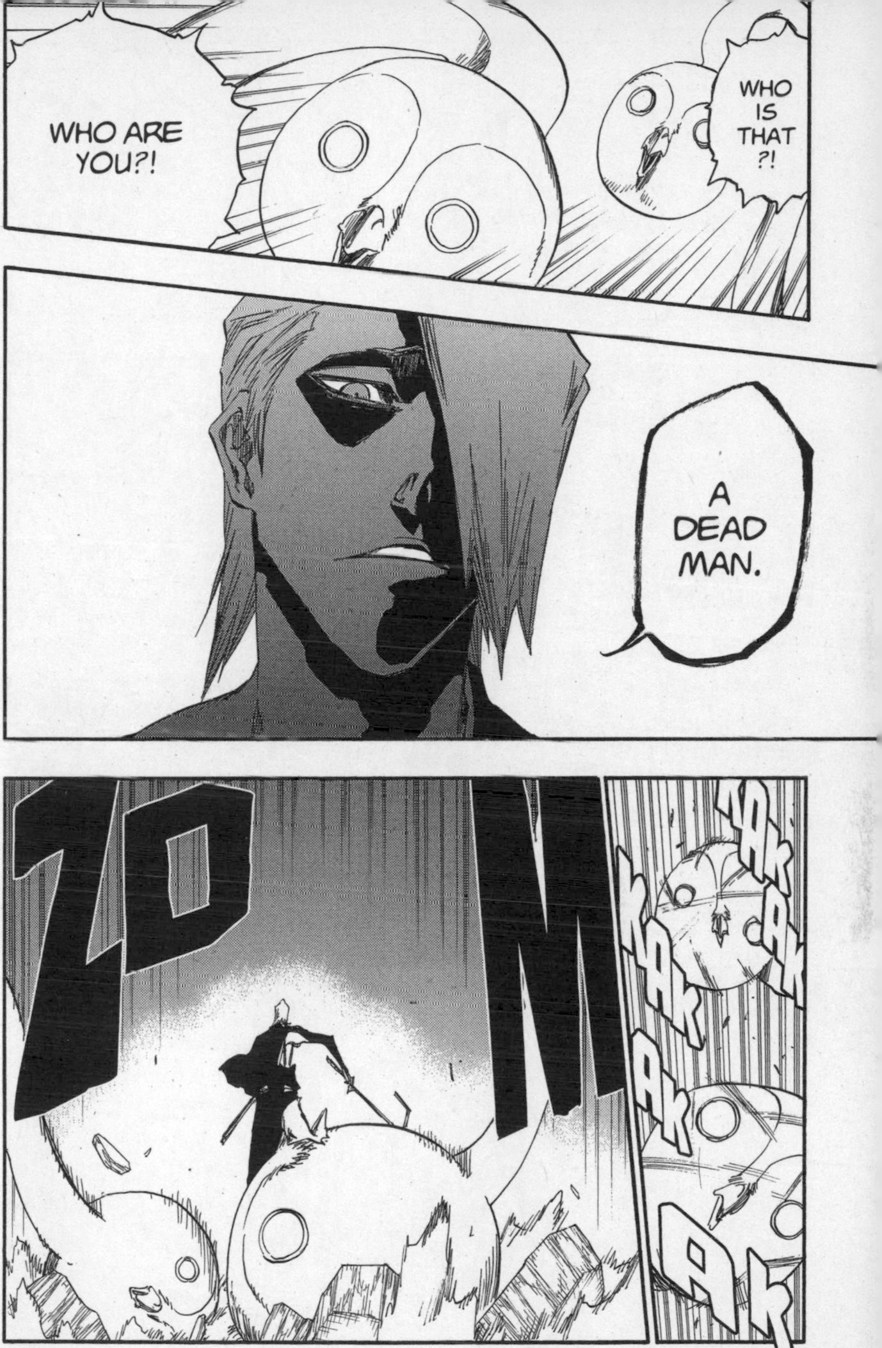
WHO IS THAT ?!
WHO ARE YOU?!
A DEAD MAN.
KAK AK KAK KAK AK AK
ZOM

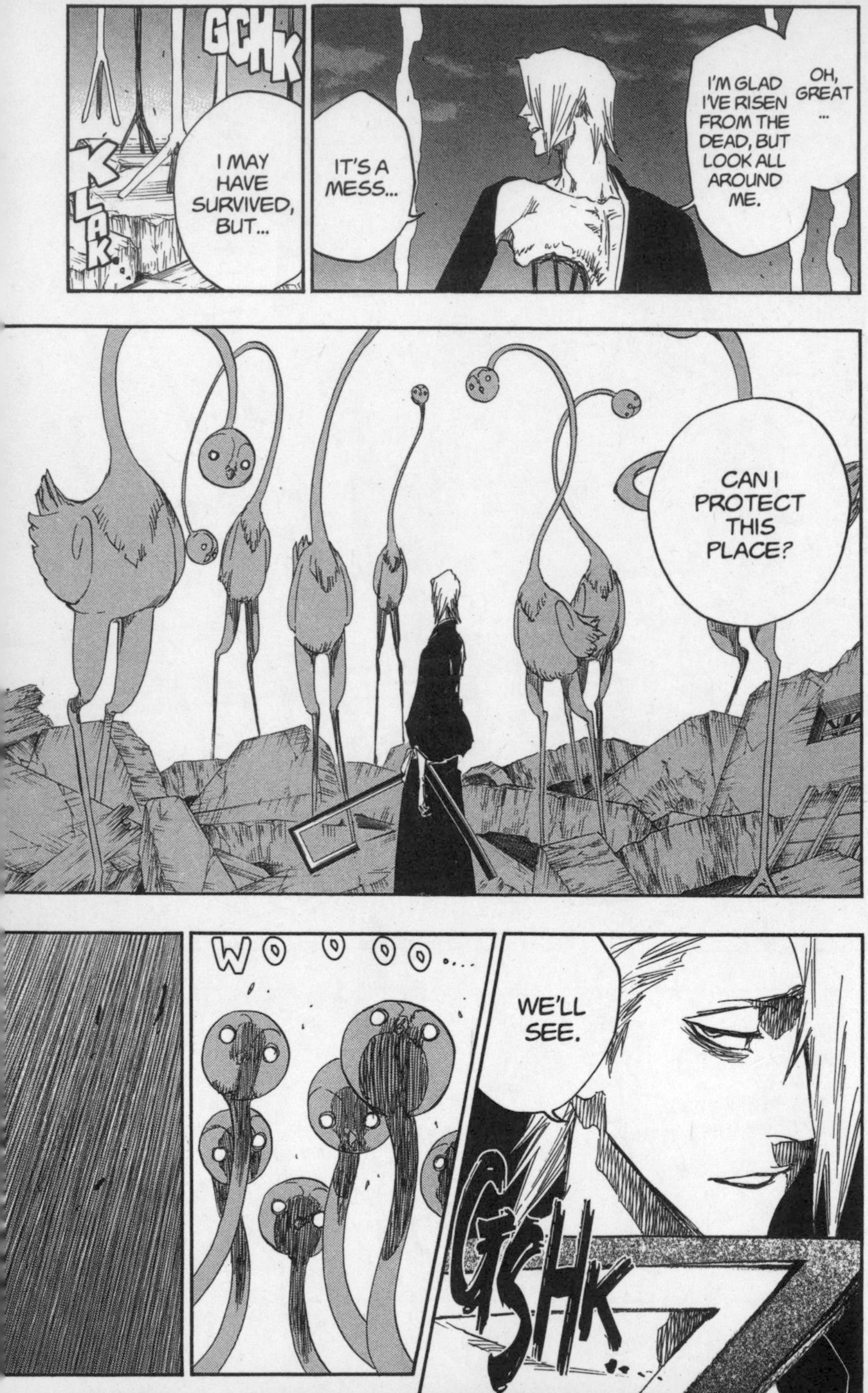
OH, GREAT ...
I'M GLAD I'VE RISEN FROM THE DEAD, BUT LOOK ALL AROUND ME.
IT'S A MESS...
GCHK
KLAK
I MAY HAVE SURVIVED, BUT...
CAN I PROTECT THIS PLACE?
WE'LL SEE.
GSHK
WOOOO...

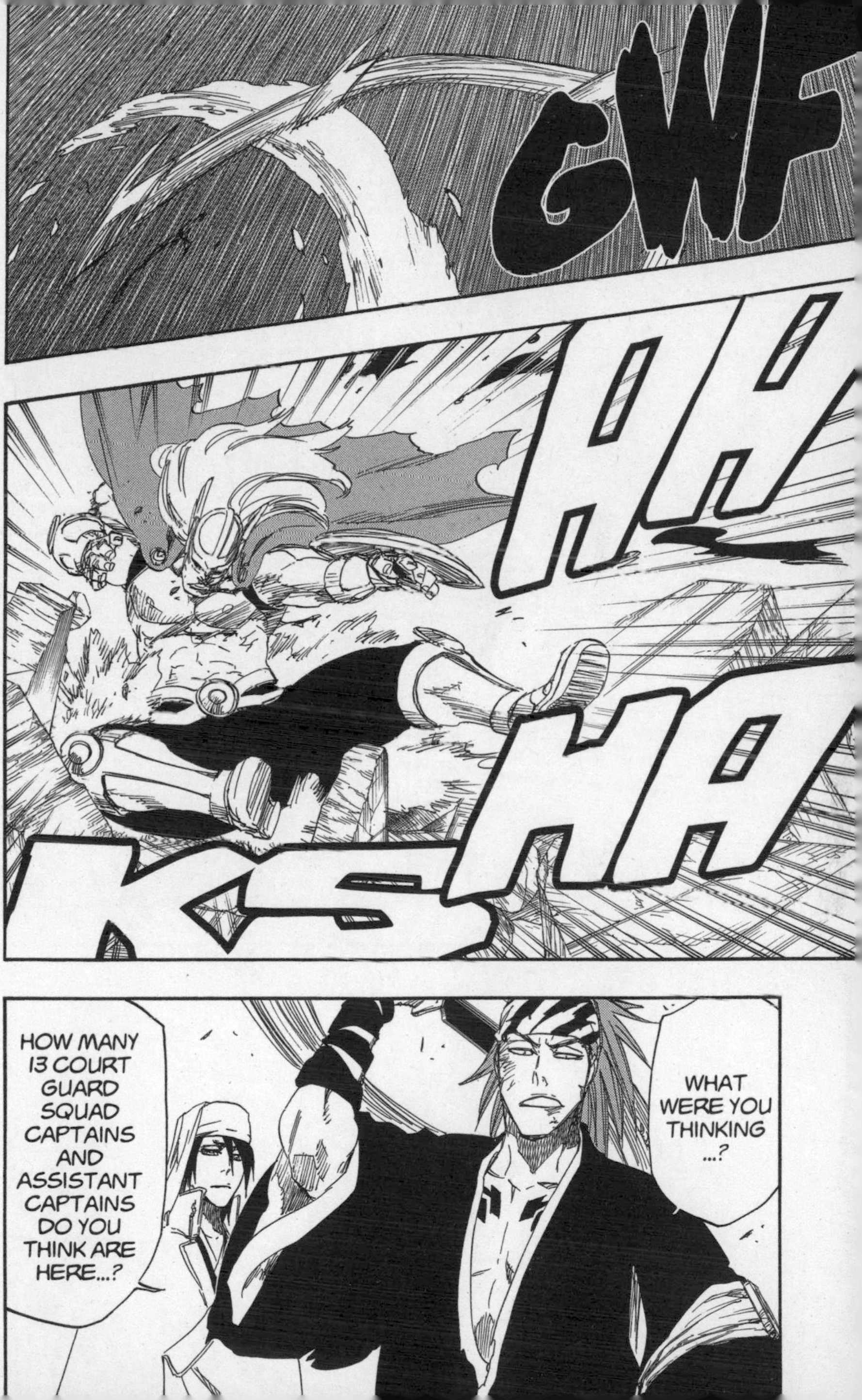
GWF
HA
HA
KS
WHAT WERE YOU THINKING ...?
HOW MANY 13 COURT GUARD SQUAD CAPTAINS AND ASSISTANT CAPTAINS DO YOU THINK ARE HERE...?

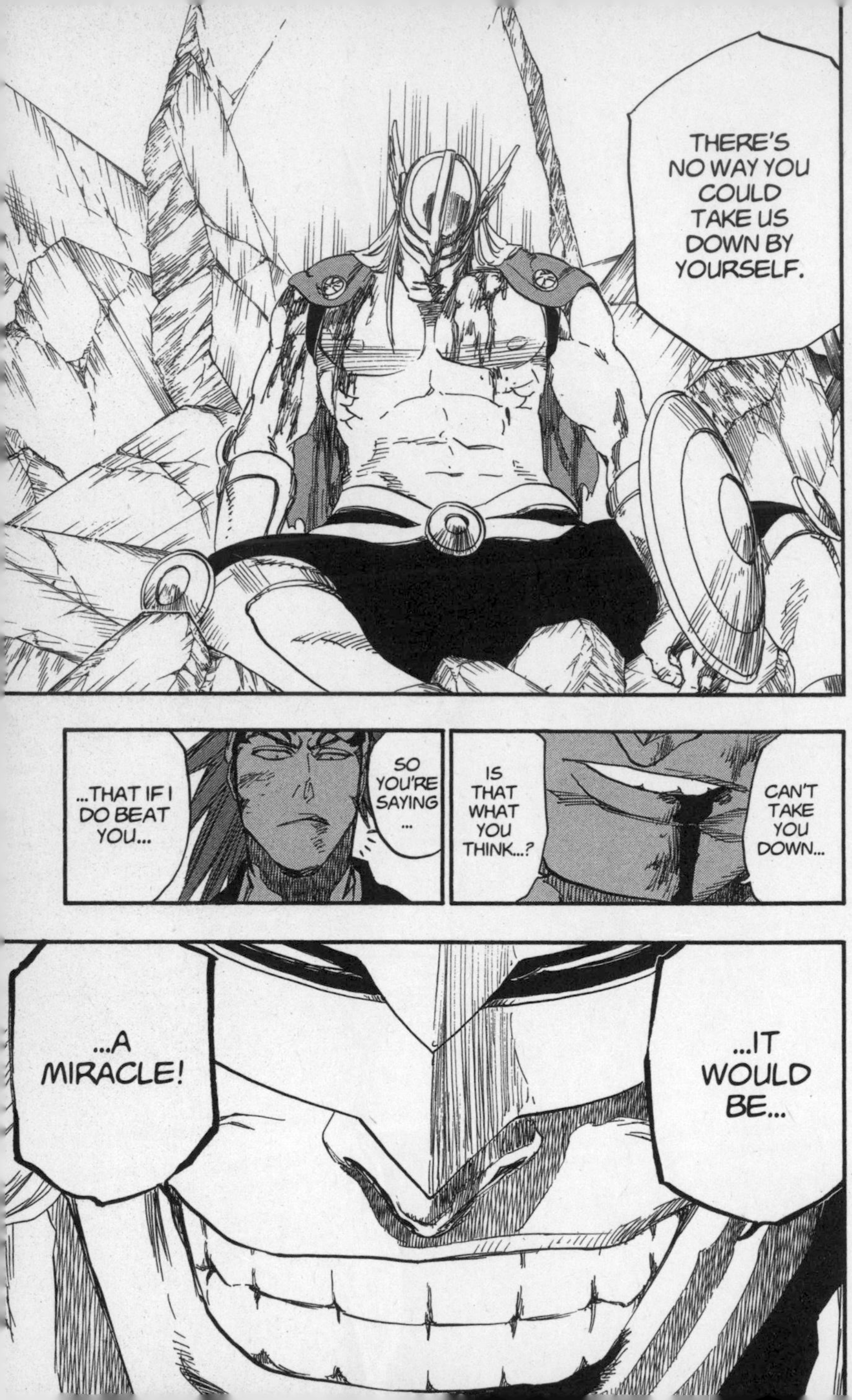
THERE'S NO WAY YOU COULD TAKE US DOWN BY YOURSELF.
CAN'T TAKE YOU DOWN...
IS THAT WHAT YOU THINK...?
SO YOU'RE SAYING ...
...THAT IF I DO BEAT YOU...
...IT WOULD BE...
...A MIRACLE!

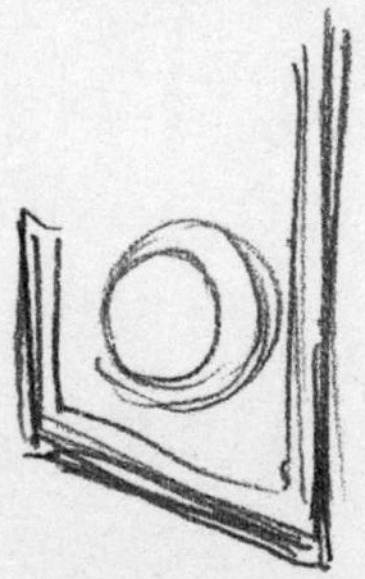

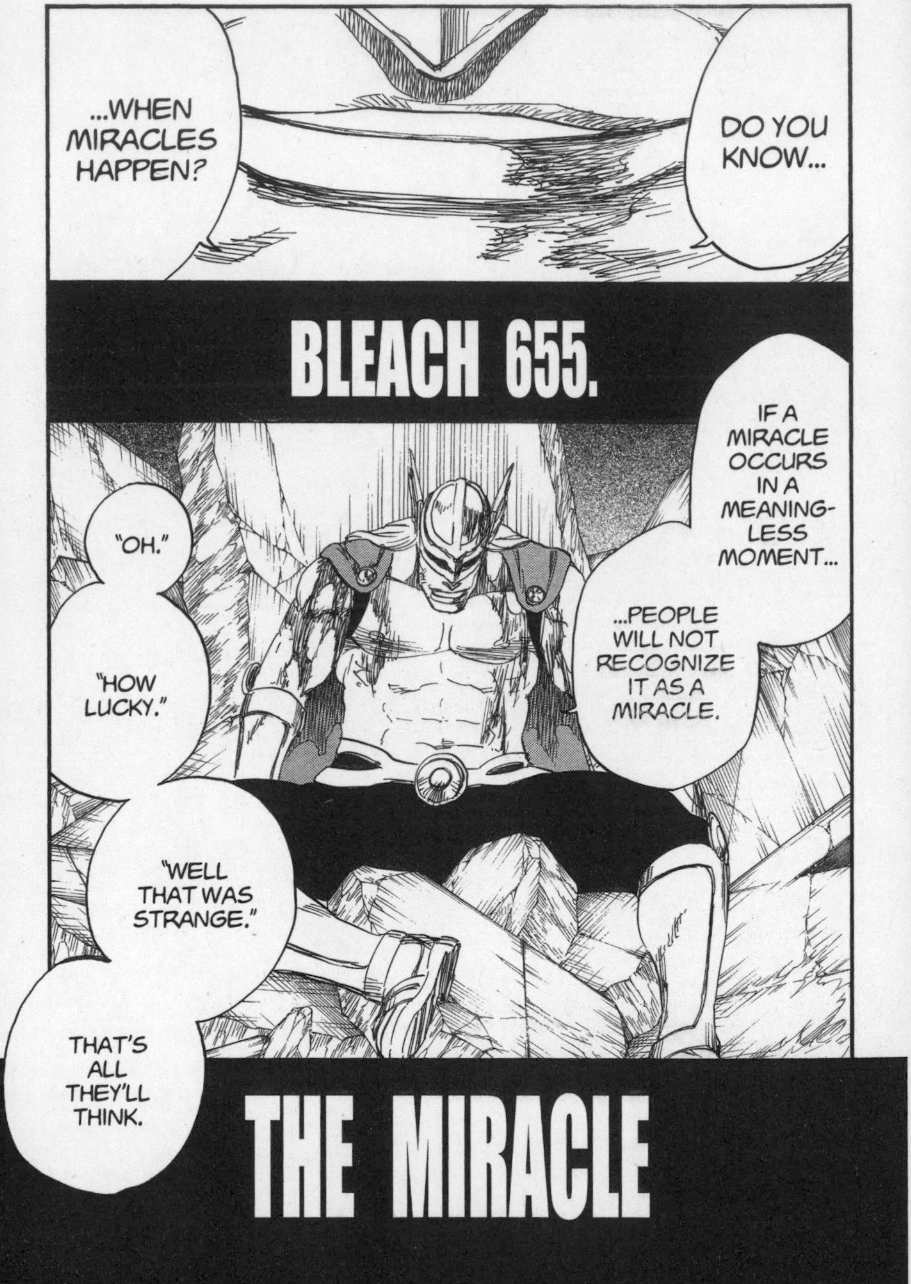
DO YOU KNOW...
...WHEN MIRACLES HAPPEN?
BLEACH 655.
IF A MIRACLE OCCURS IN A MEANING-LESS MOMENT...
...PEOPLE WILL NOT RECOGNIZE IT AS A MIRACLE.
"OH."
"HOW LUCKY."
"WELL THAT WAS STRANGE."
THAT'S ALL THEY'LL THINK.
THE MIRACLE

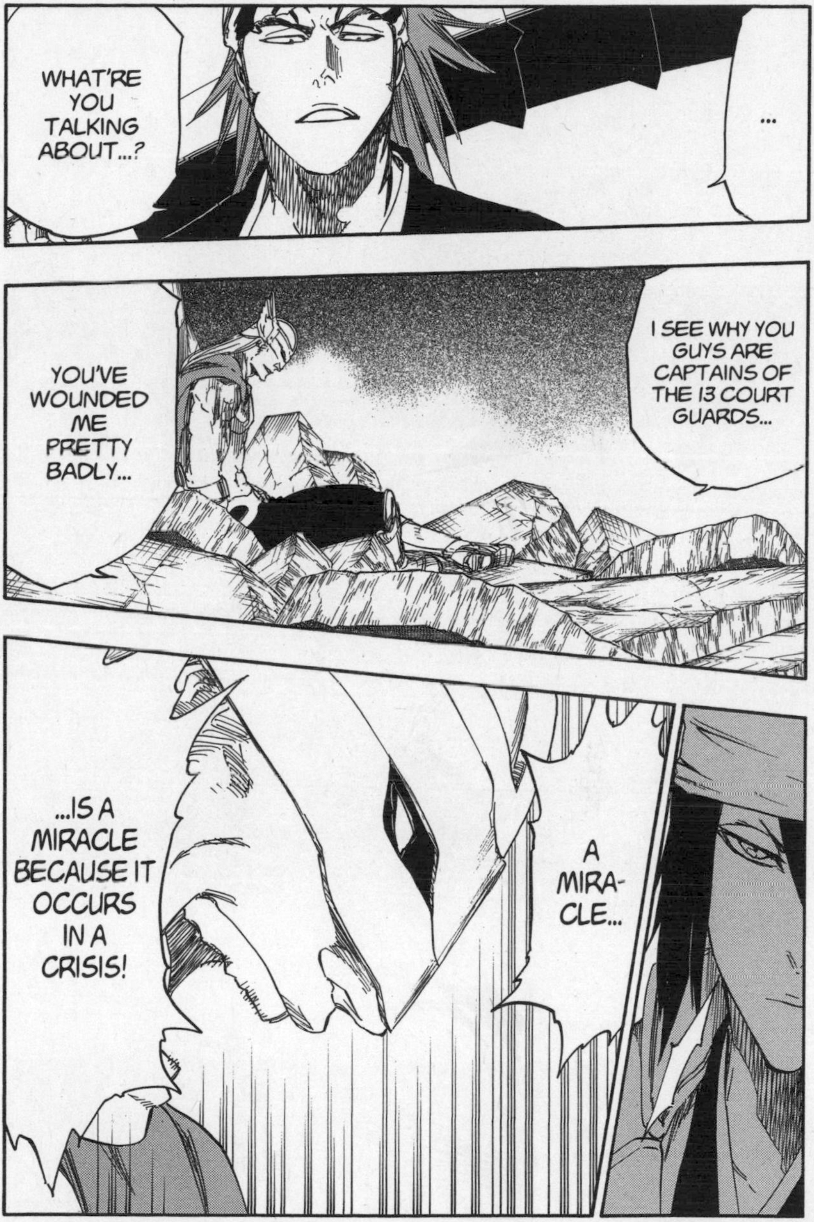
...
WHAT'RE YOU TALKING ABOUT...?
I SEE WHY YOU GUYS ARE CAPTAINS OF THE 13 COURT GUARDS...
YOU'VE WOUNDED ME PRETTY BADLY...
A MIRA-CLE...
...IS A MIRACLE BECAUSE IT OCCURS IN A CRISIS!

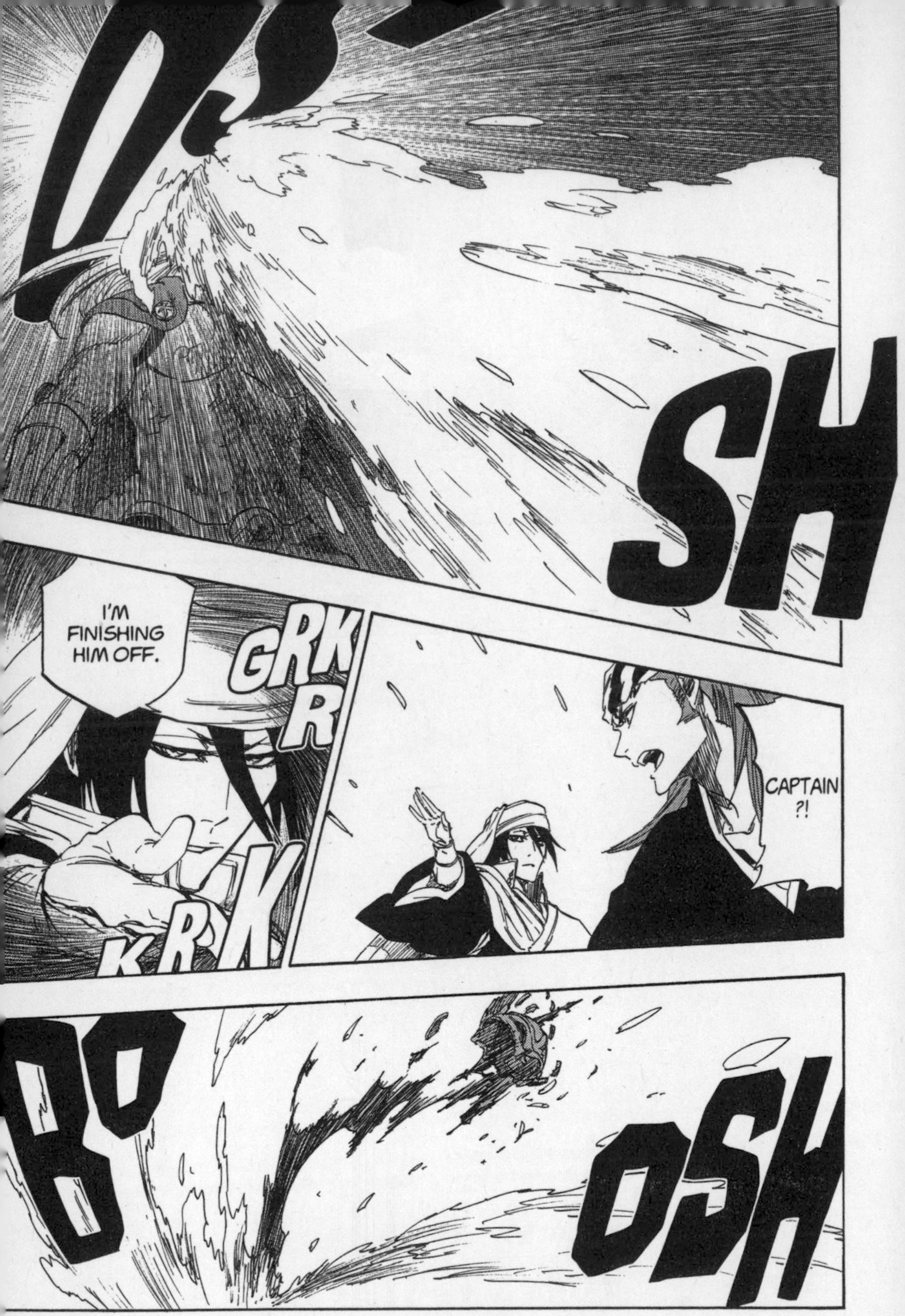
SH
CAPTAIN ?!
I'M FINISHING HIM OFF.
GRK R
KRK
BO
OSH

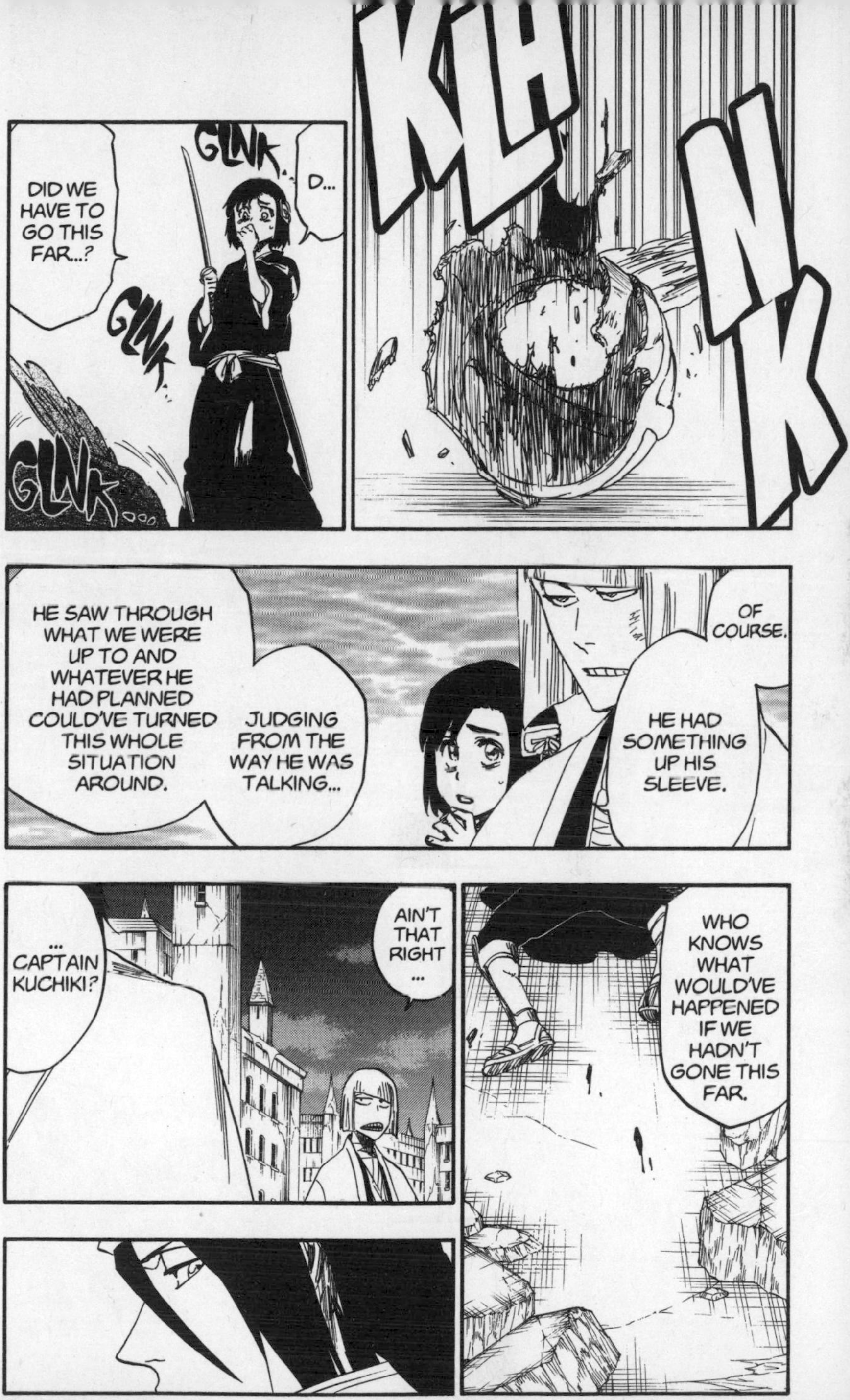
KLANK
D...
DID WE HAVE TO GO THIS FAR...?
GLNK
GLNK
GLNK
OF COURSE.
HE HAD SOMETHING UP HIS SLEEVE.
JUDGING FROM THE WAY HE WAS TALKING...
HE SAW THROUGH WHAT WE WERE UP TO AND WHATEVER HE HAD PLANNED COULD'VE TURNED THIS WHOLE SITUATION AROUND.
WHO KNOWS WHAT WOULD'VE HAPPENED IF WE HADN'T GONE THIS FAR.
AIN'T THAT RIGHT ...
... CAPTAIN KUCHIKI?

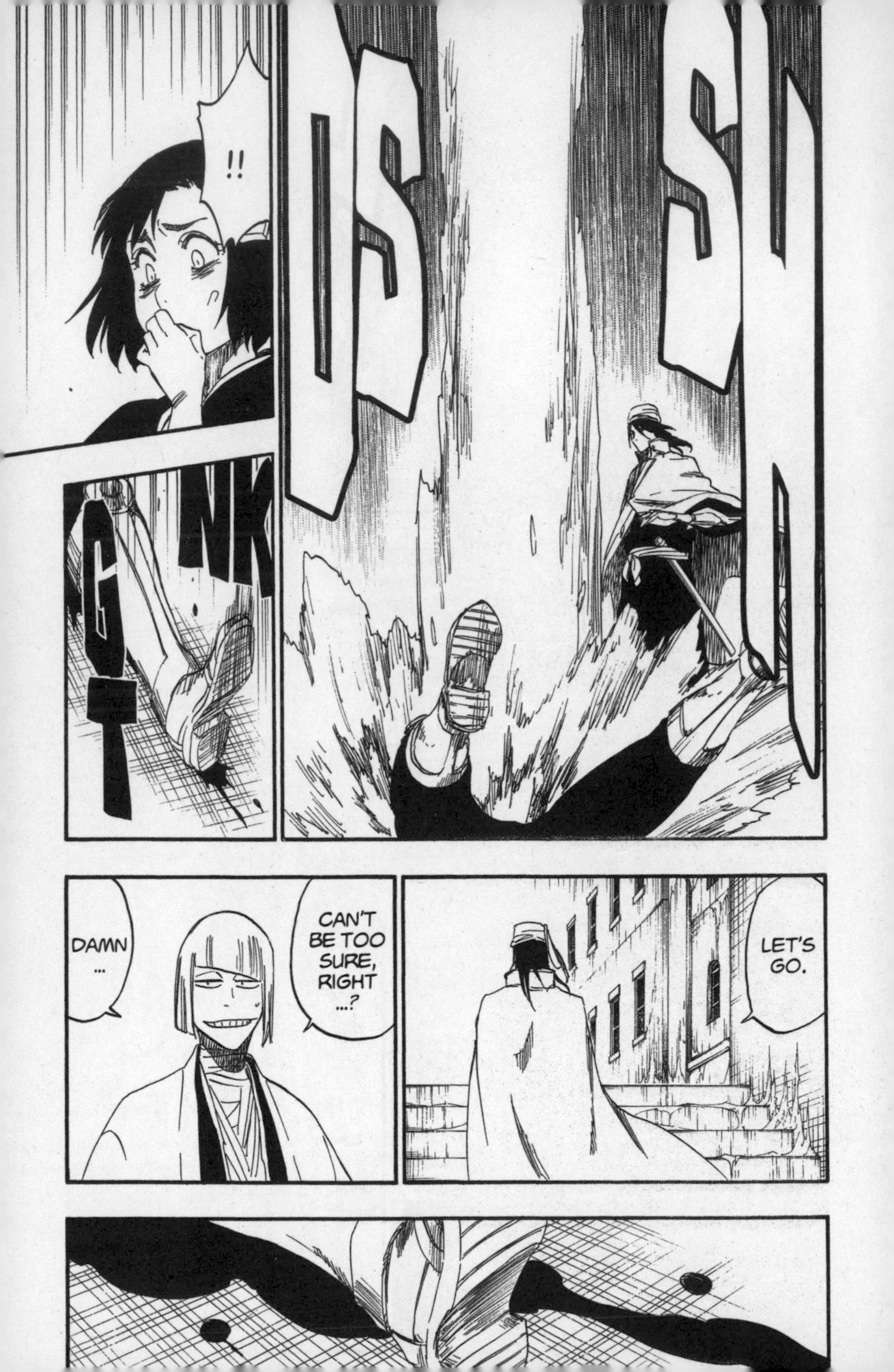
DS
SH
!!
G
NK
T
LET'S GO.
CAN'T BE TOO SURE, RIGHT ...?
DAMN ...

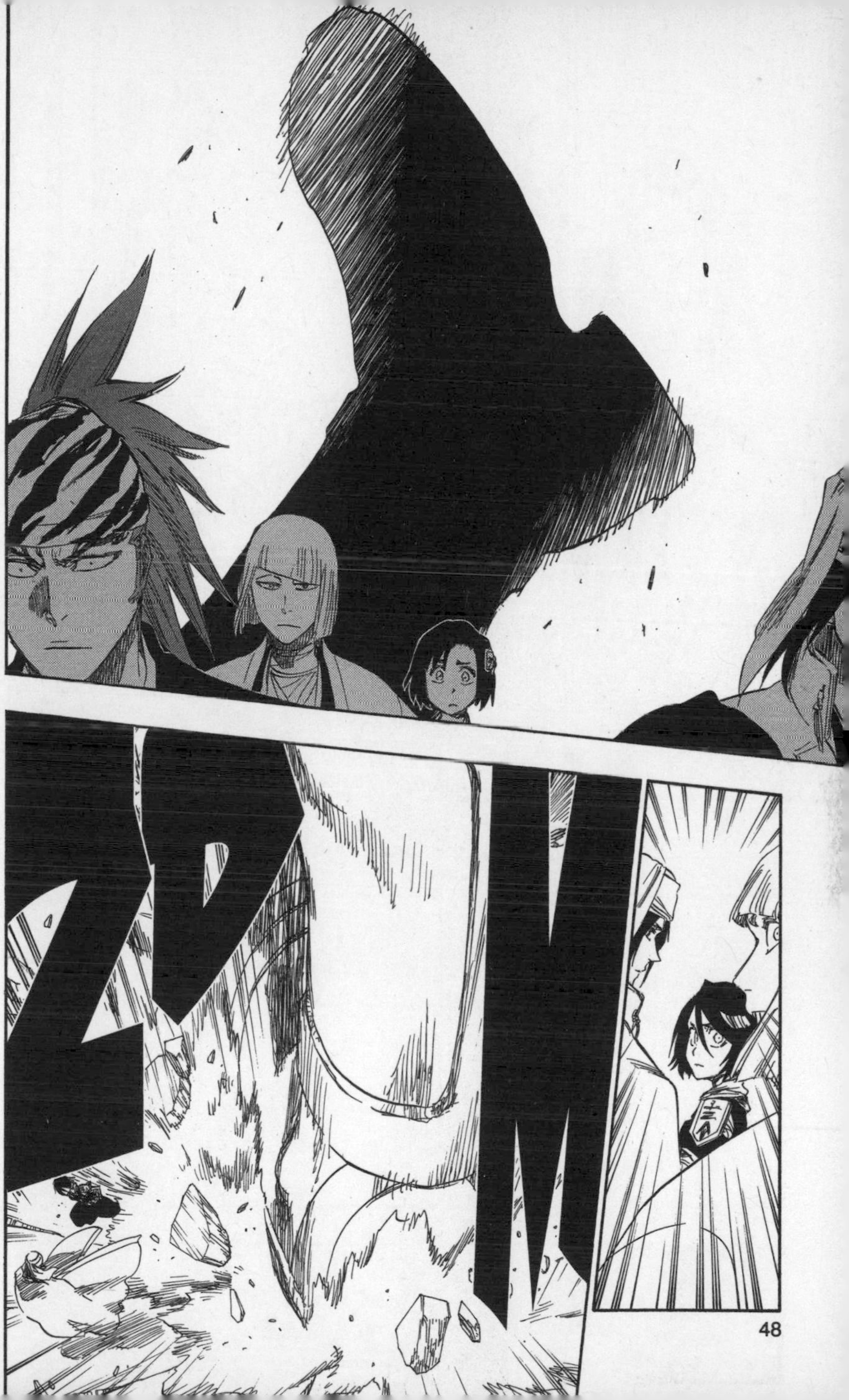

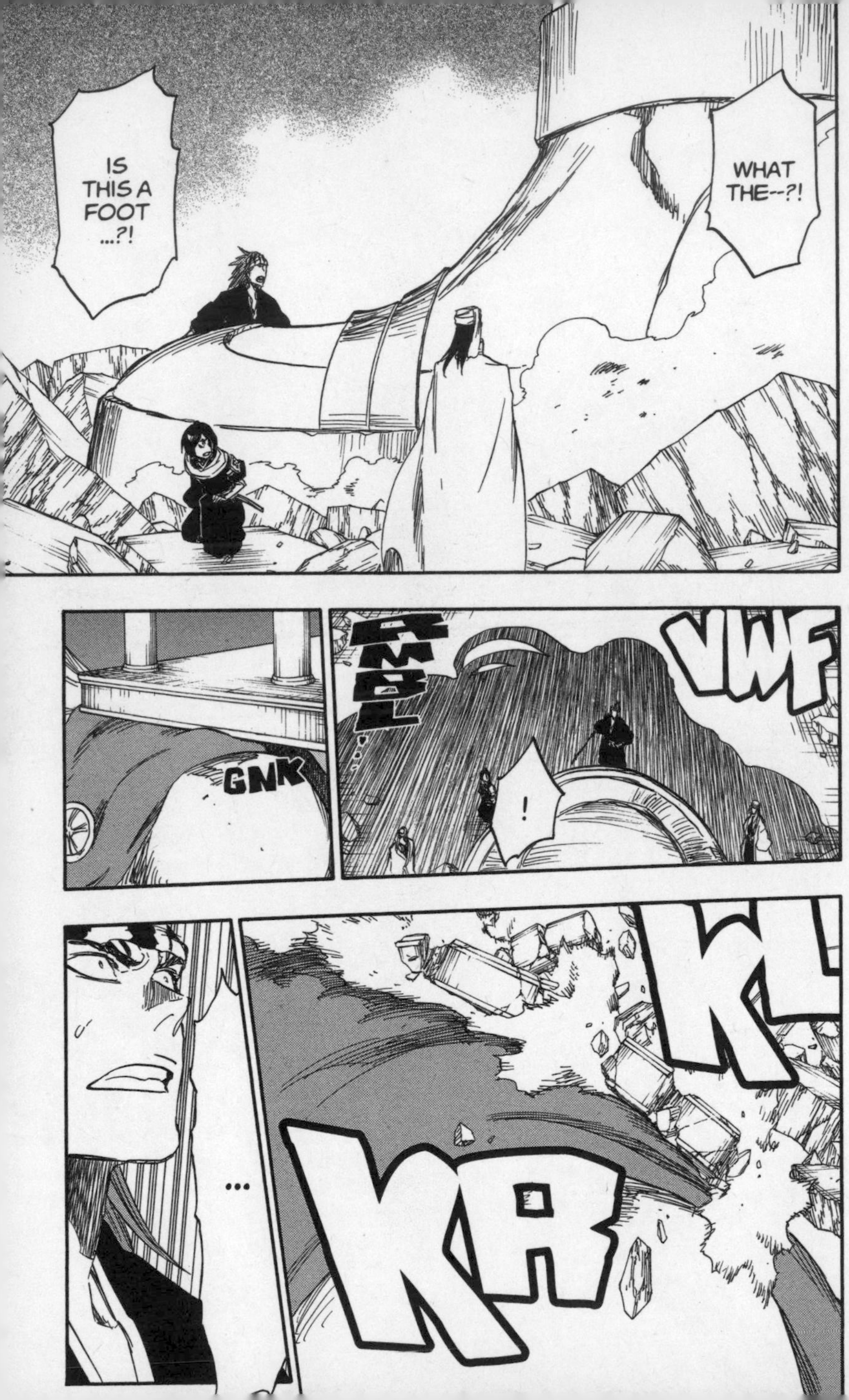
WHAT THE--?!
IS THIS A FOOT ...?!
VWF
RMBL...
!
GNK
KR
...

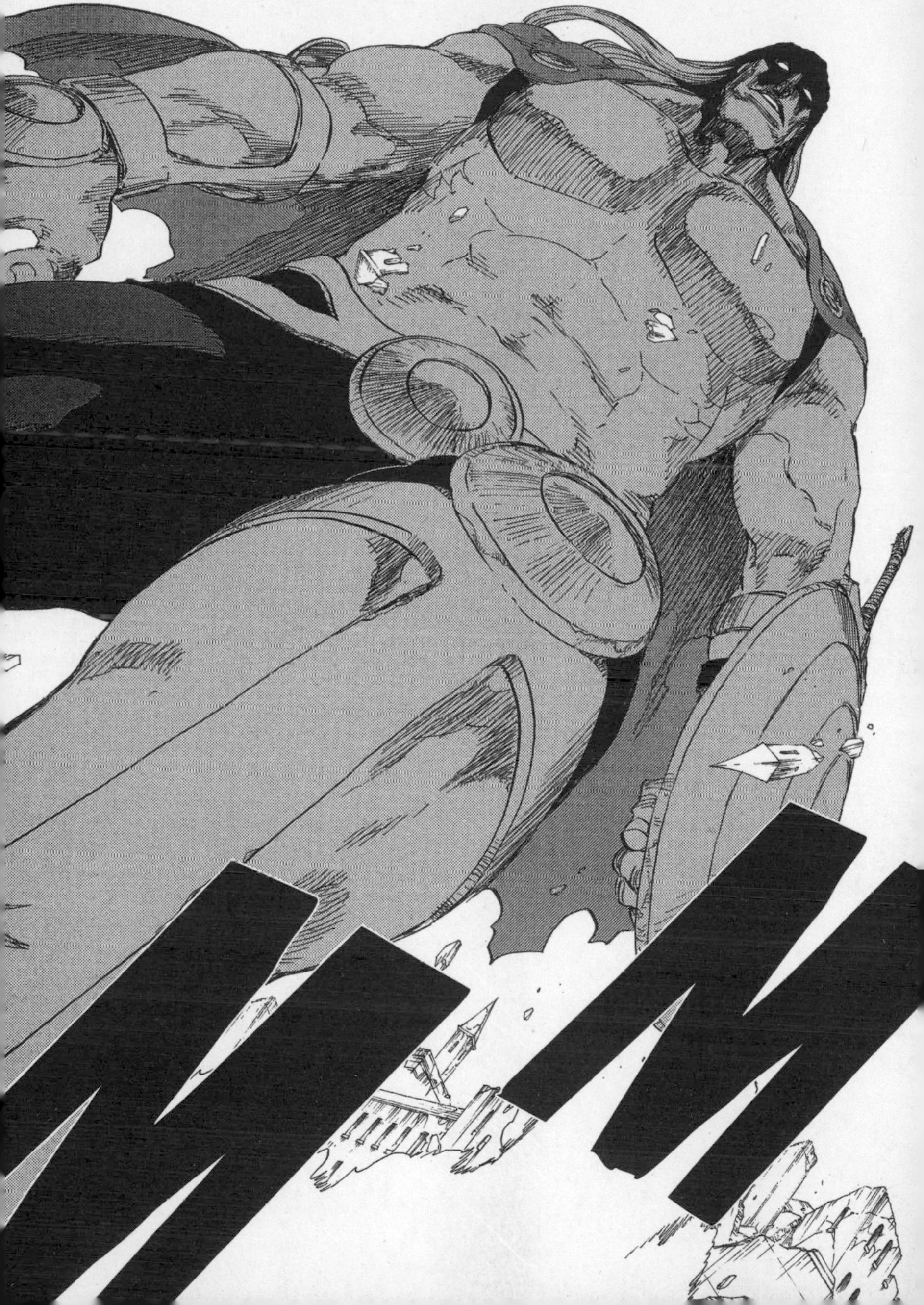

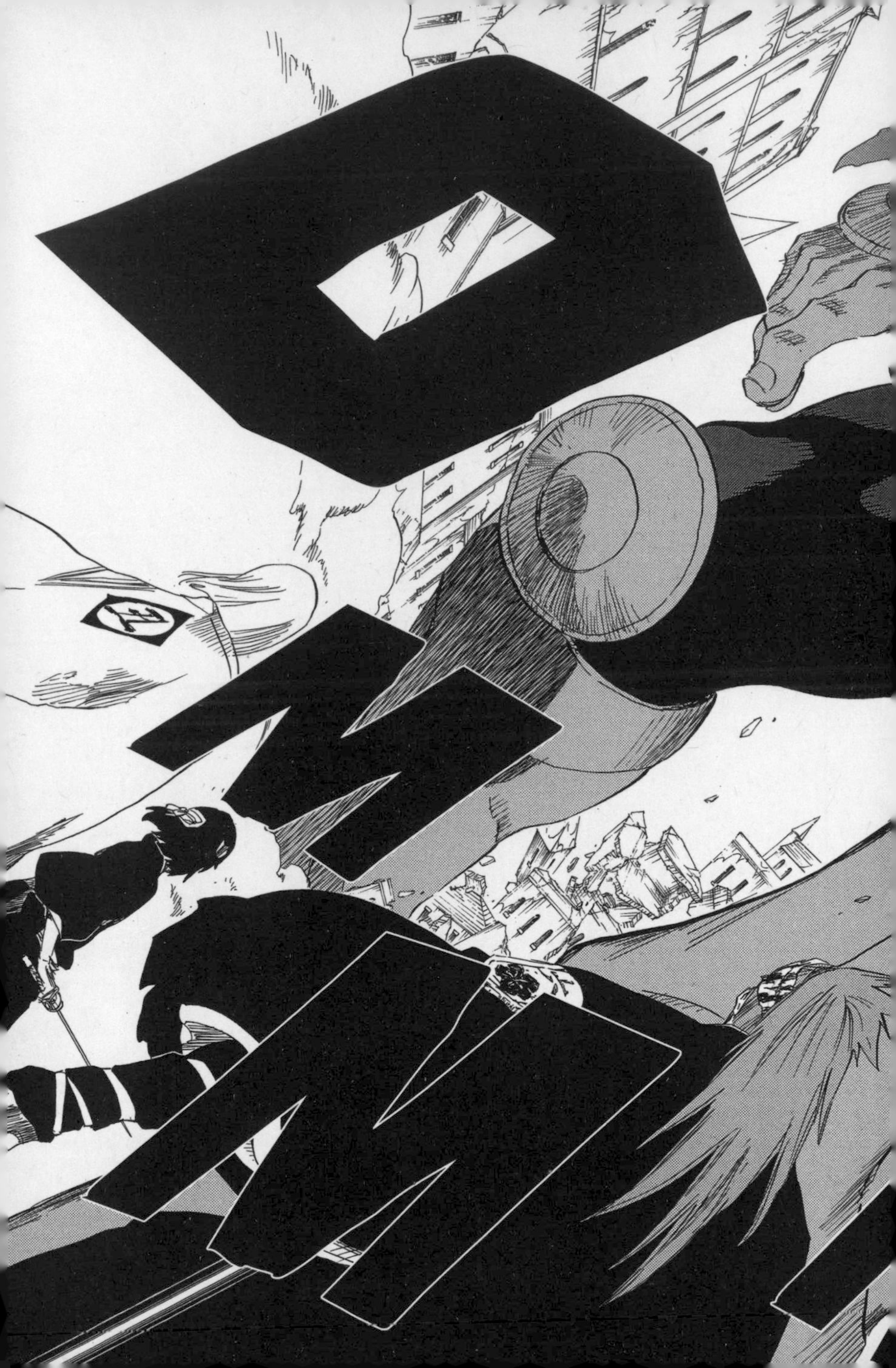

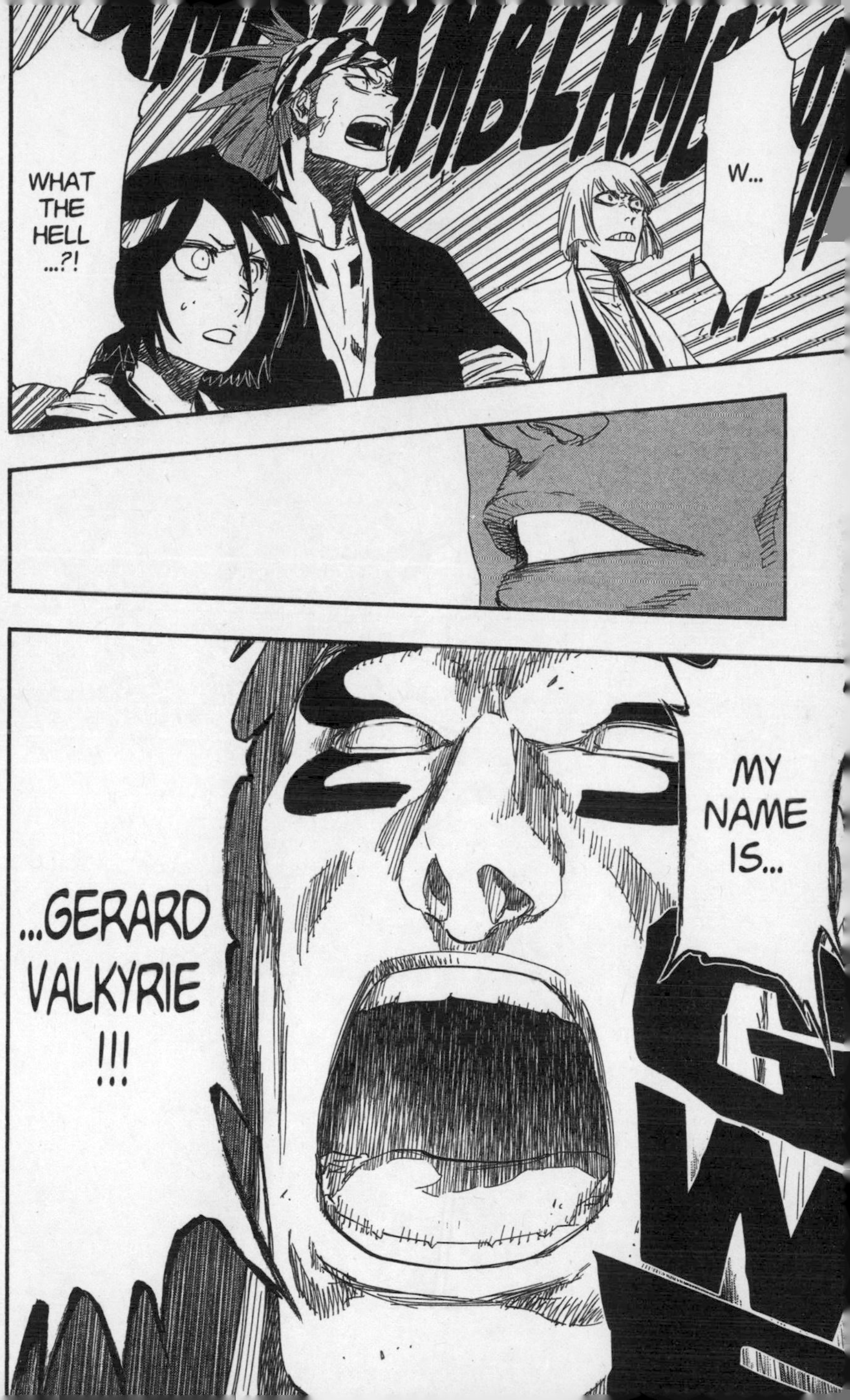
W...
WHAT THE HELL ...?!
MY NAME IS...
...GERARD VALKYRIE !!!

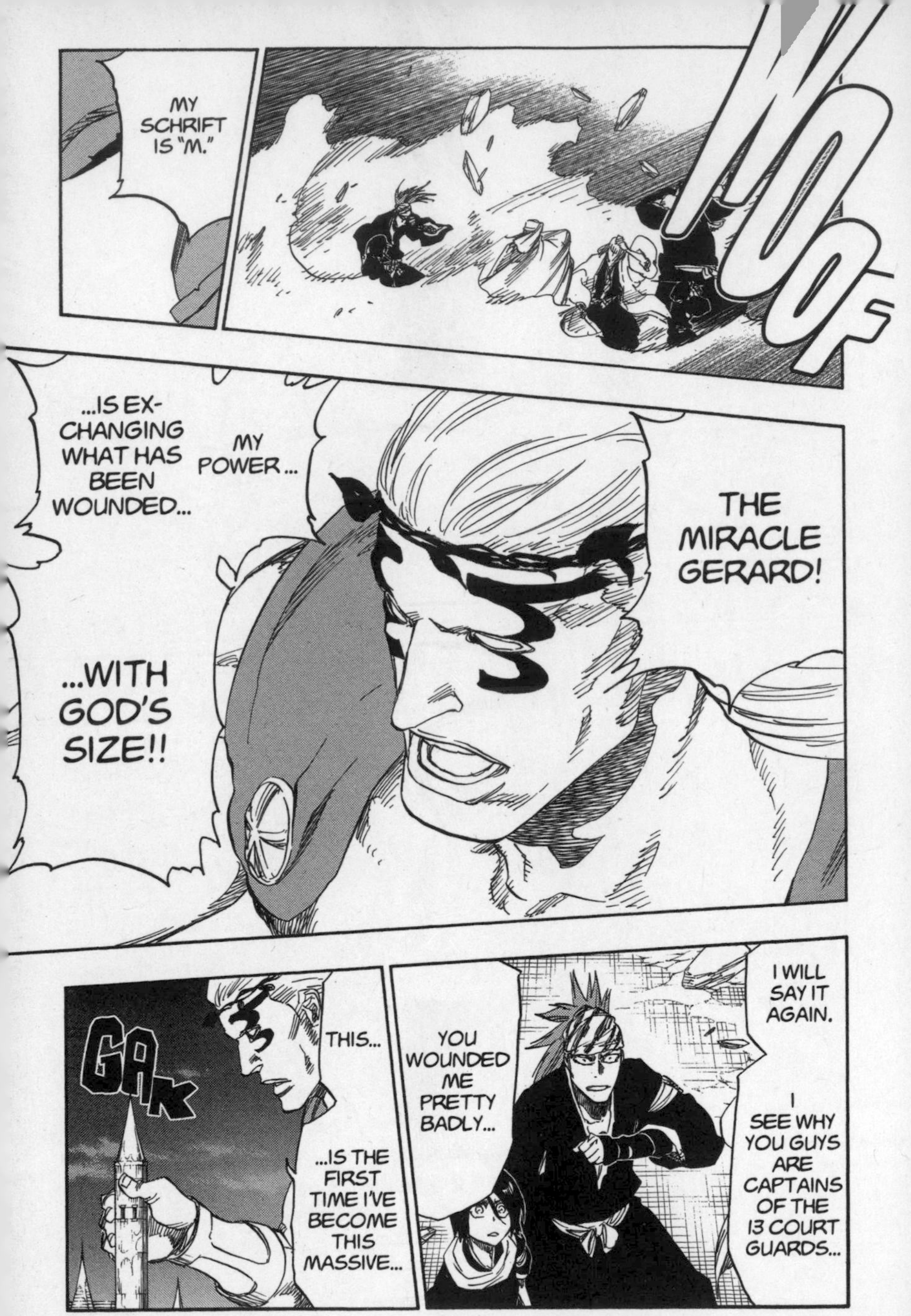
VOOF
MY SCHRIFT IS "M."
THE MIRACLE GERARD!
MY POWER...
...IS EX-CHANGING WHAT HAS BEEN WOUNDED...
...WITH GOD'S SIZE!!
I WILL SAY IT AGAIN.
I SEE WHY YOU GUYS ARE CAPTAINS OF THE 13 COURT GUARDS...
YOU WOUNDED ME PRETTY BADLY...
THIS...
...IS THE FIRST TIME I'VE BECOME THIS MASSIVE...
GAK

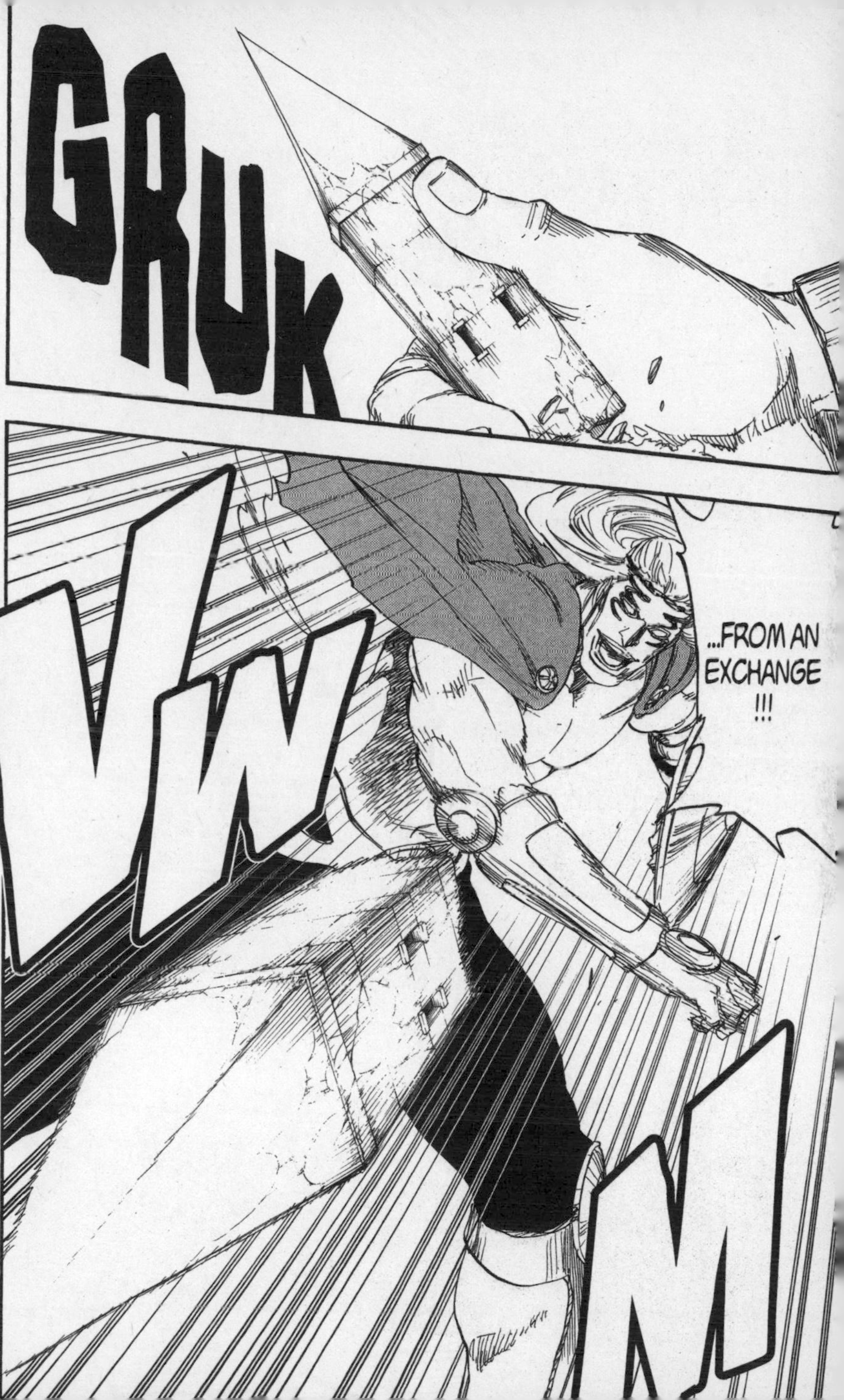
GRUK
...FROM AN EXCHANGE !!!
VWM

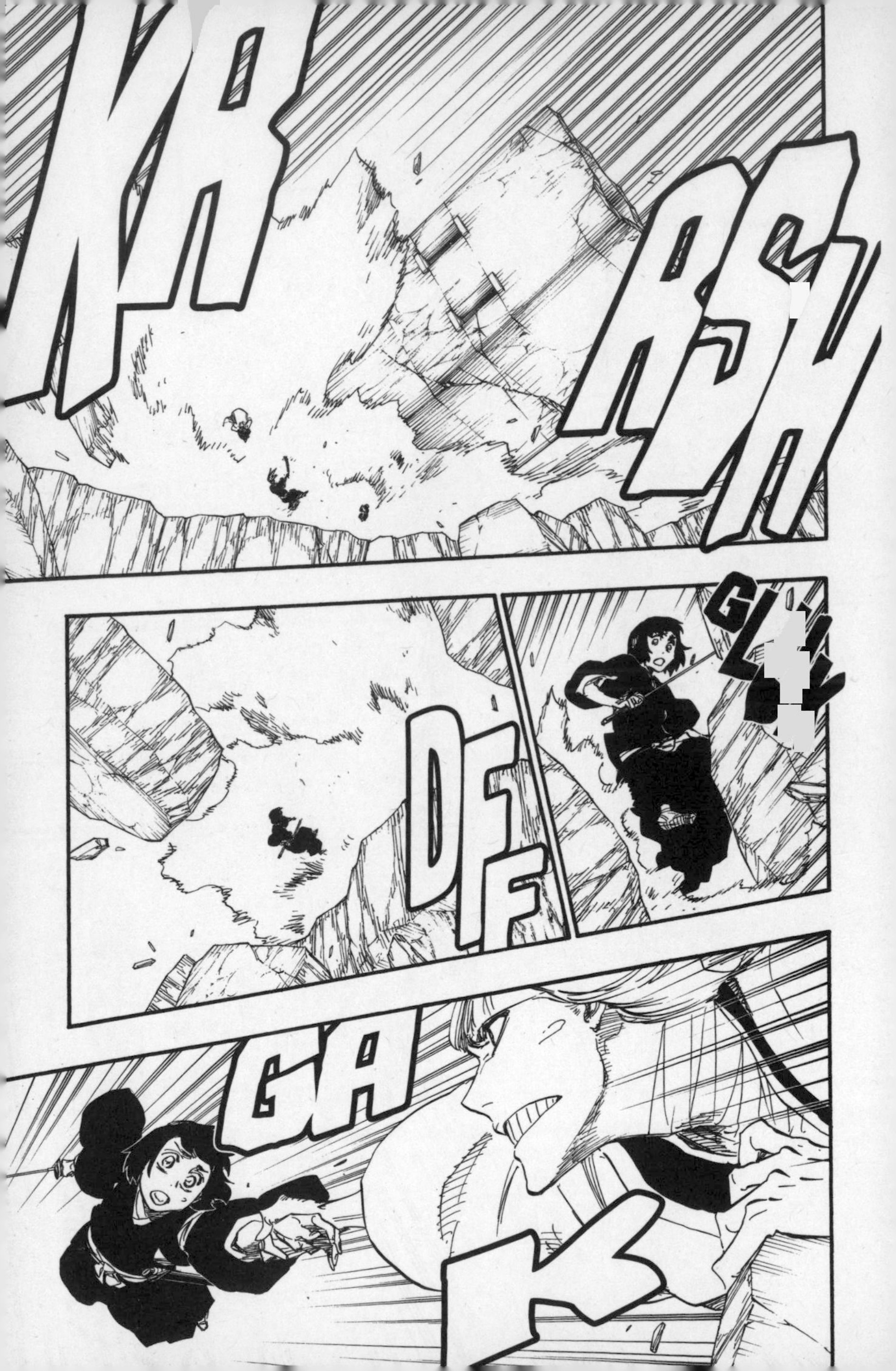
KARASH
GL
DFF
GAK

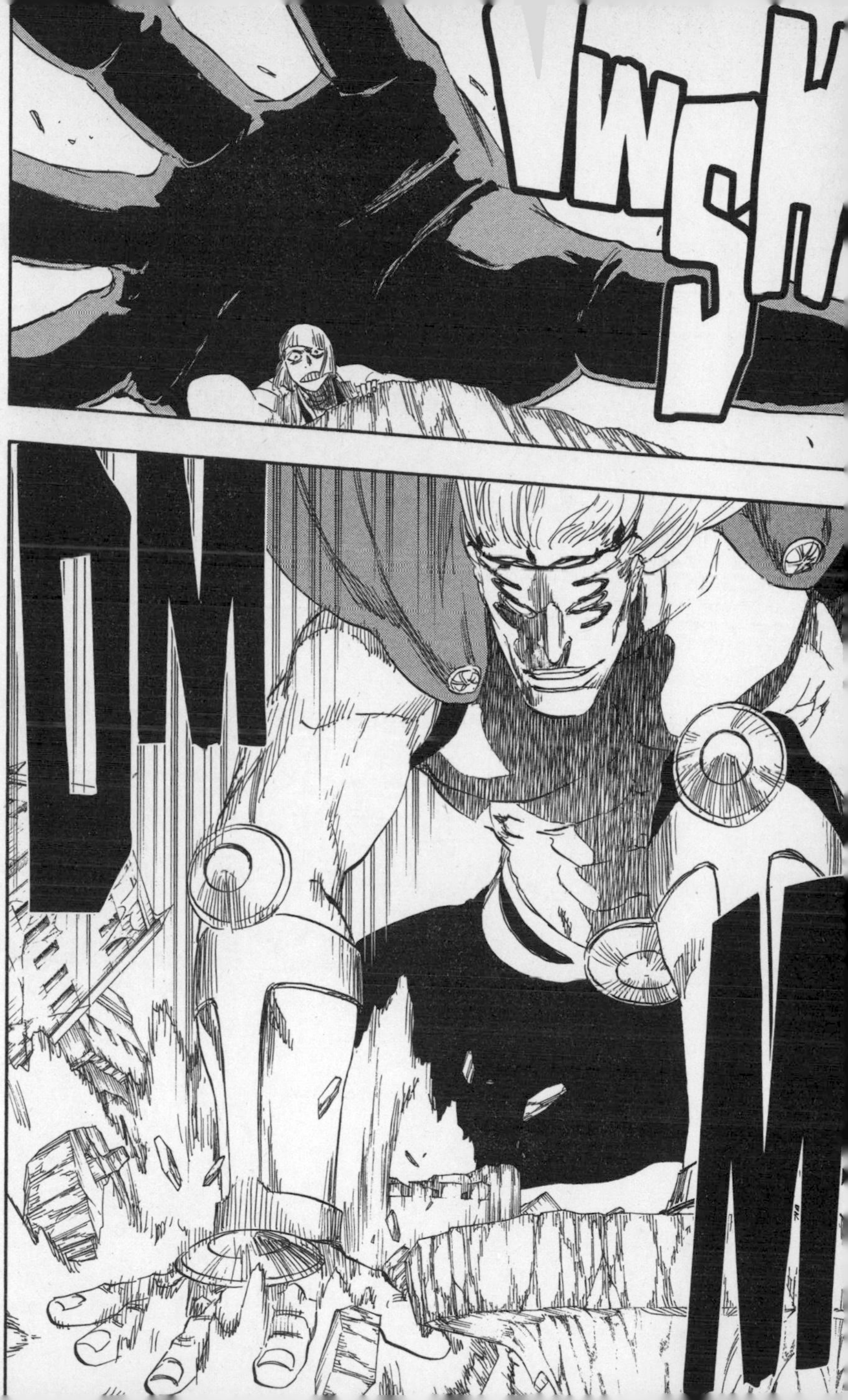

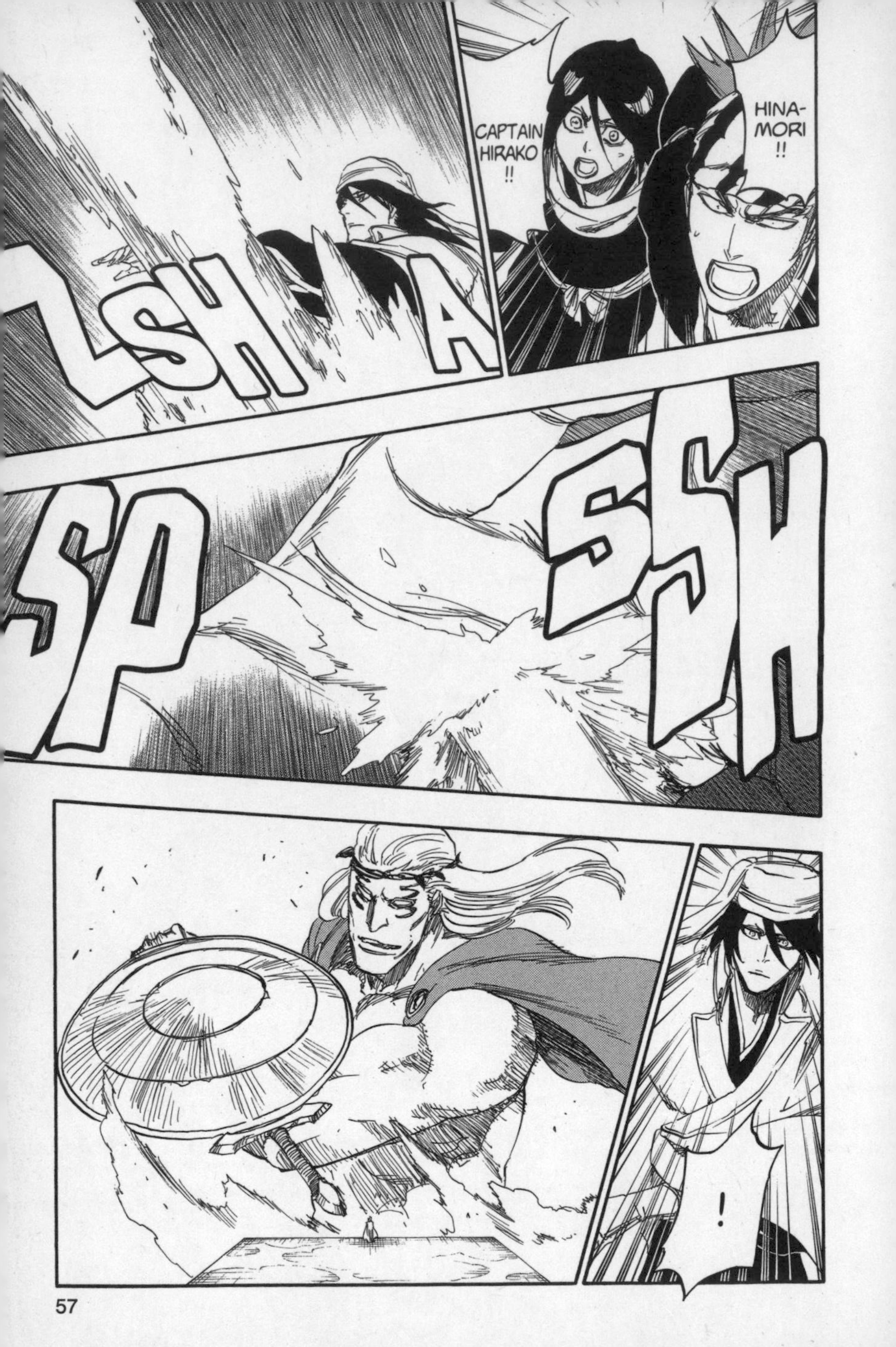
HINA-
MORI
!!
CAPTAIN
HIRAKO
!!
SHA
SSH
SP
!

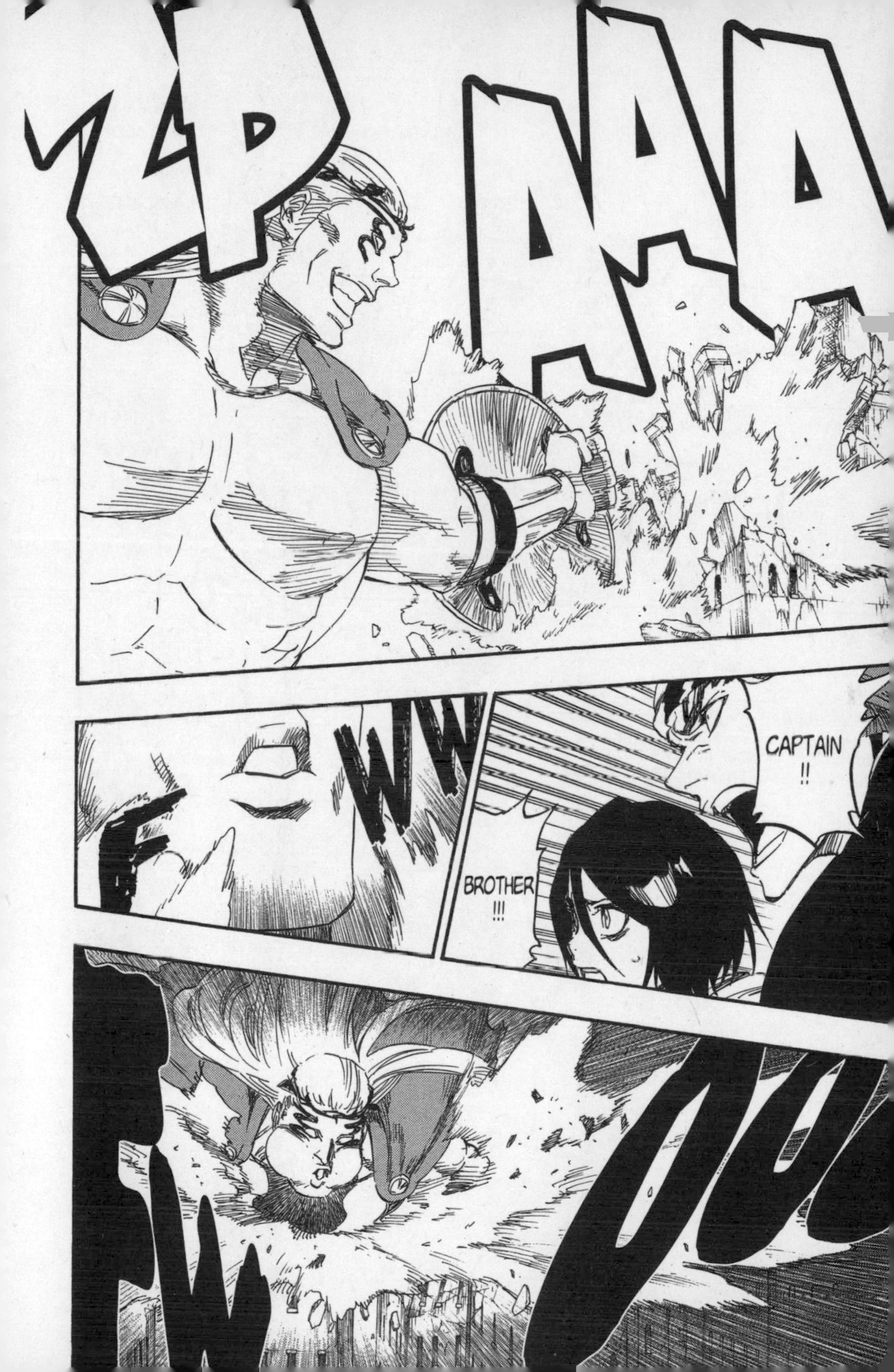
CAPTAIN !!
BROTHER !!!

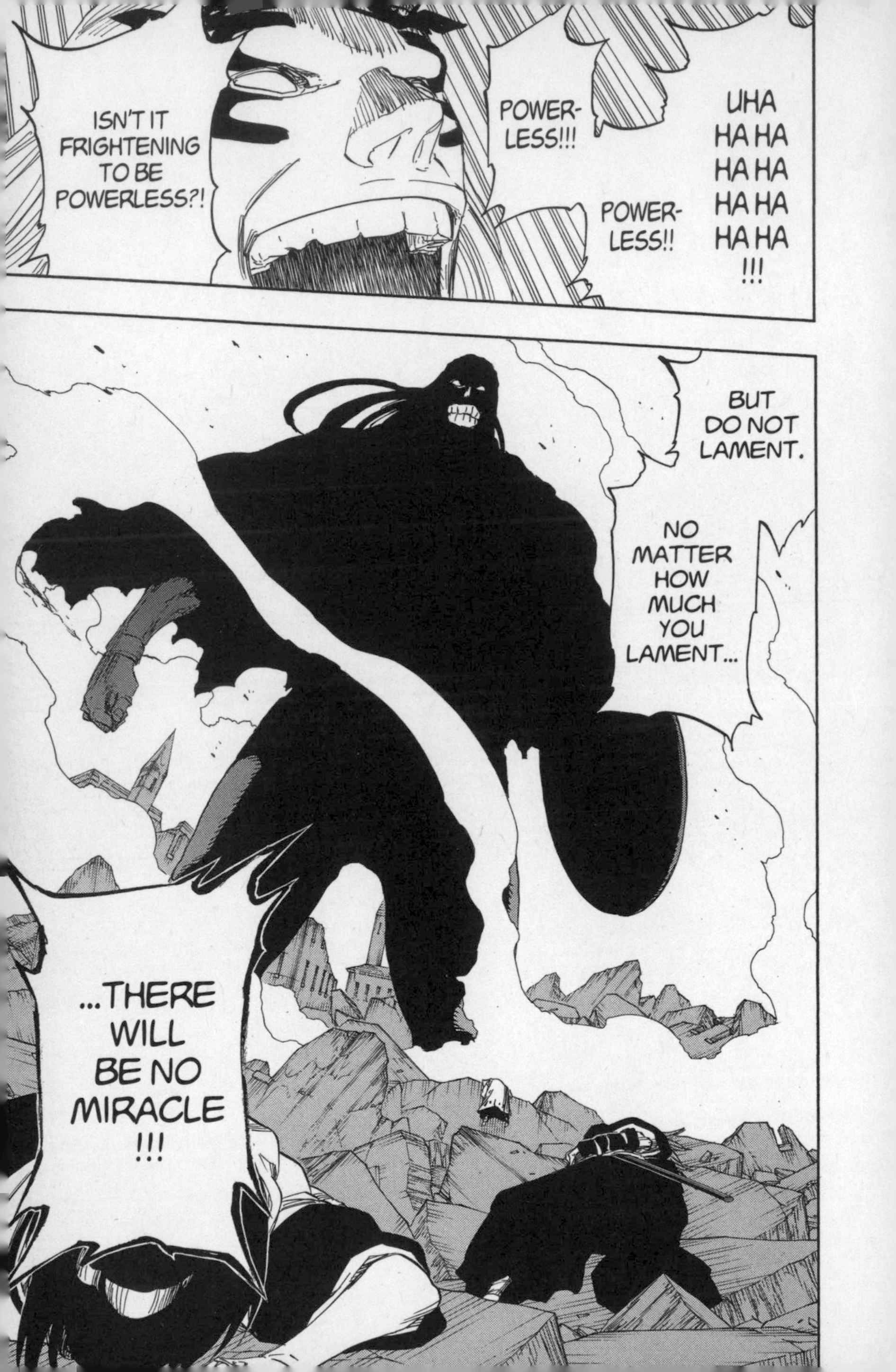
UHA HA HA HA HA HA HA HA HA !!!
POWER-LESS!!!
POWER-LESS!!
ISN'T IT FRIGHTENING TO BE POWERLESS?!
BUT DO NOT LAMENT.
NO MATTER HOW MUCH YOU LAMENT...
...THERE WILL BE NO MIRACLE !!!

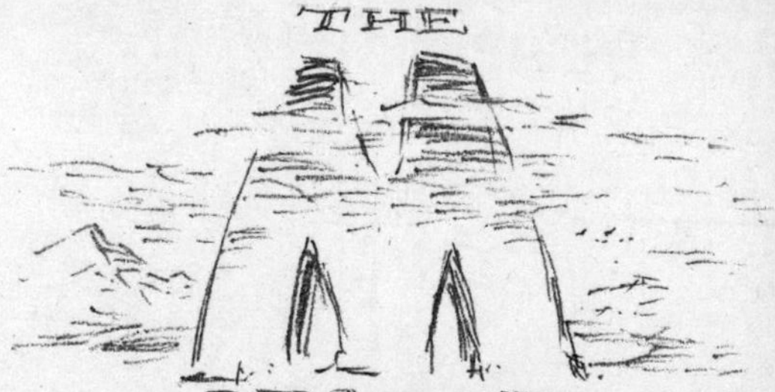

THE

ORACLE

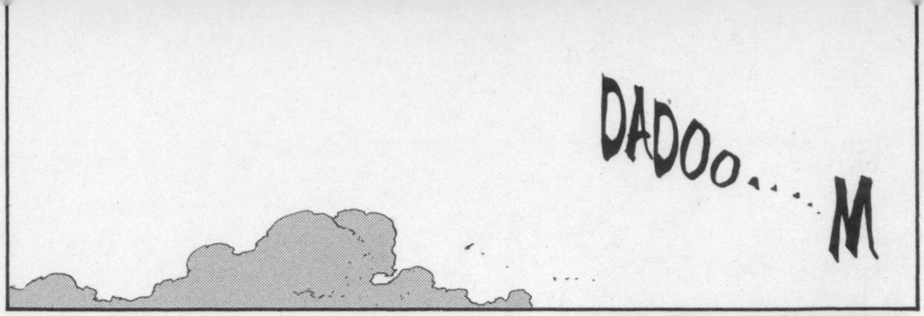
DADOO....M

656.GOD OF THUNDER

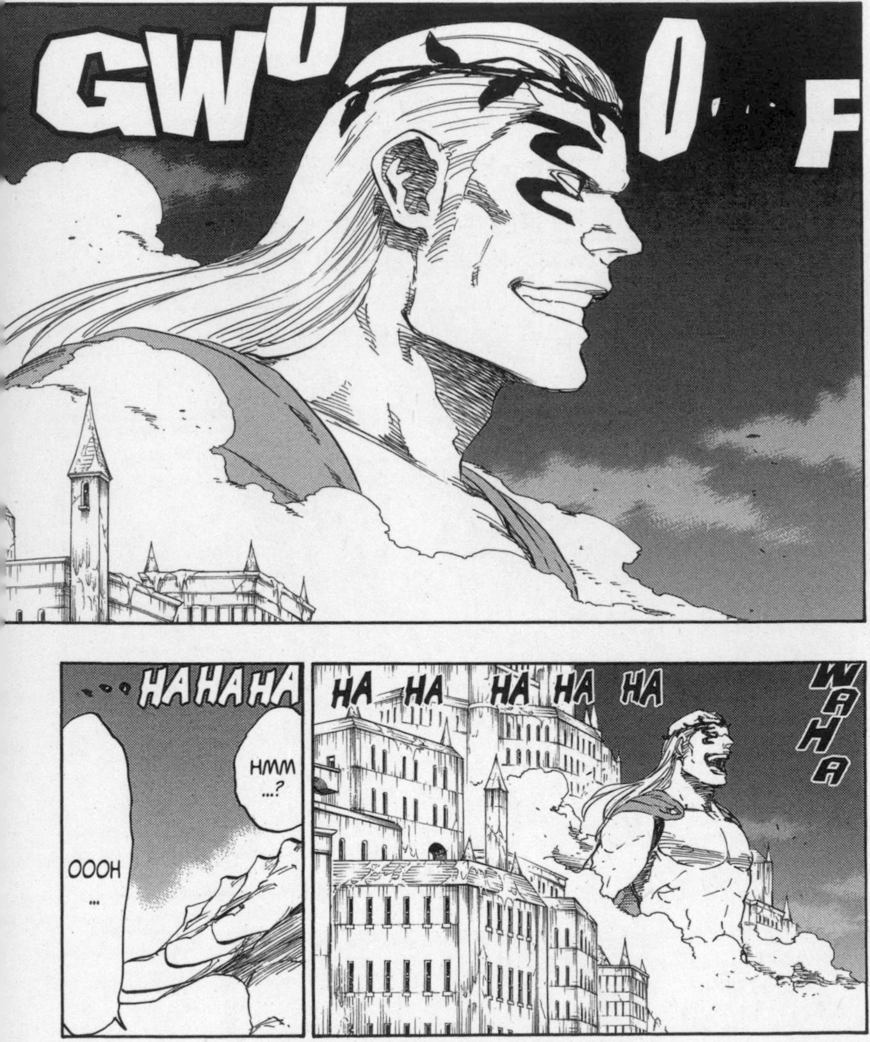
GWUO..F
HA HA HA HA HA
WAHAHA
...HAHAHA
HMM ...?
OOOH ...

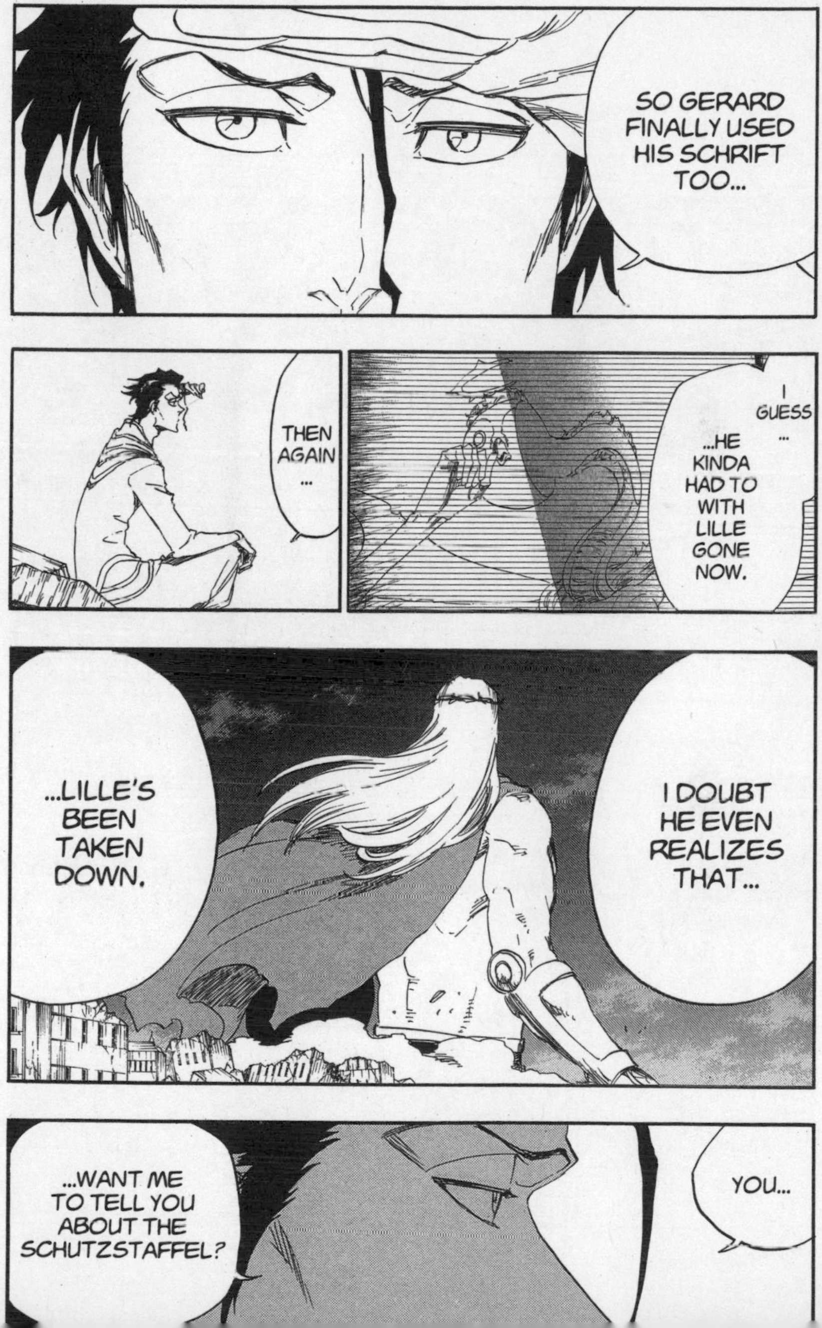
SO GERARD FINALLY USED HIS SCHRIFT TOO...
I GUESS...
...HE KINDA HAD TO WITH LILLE GONE NOW.
THEN AGAIN...
I DOUBT HE EVEN REALIZES THAT...
...LILLE'S BEEN TAKEN DOWN.
YOU...
...WANT ME TO TELL YOU ABOUT THE SCHUTZSTAFFEL?

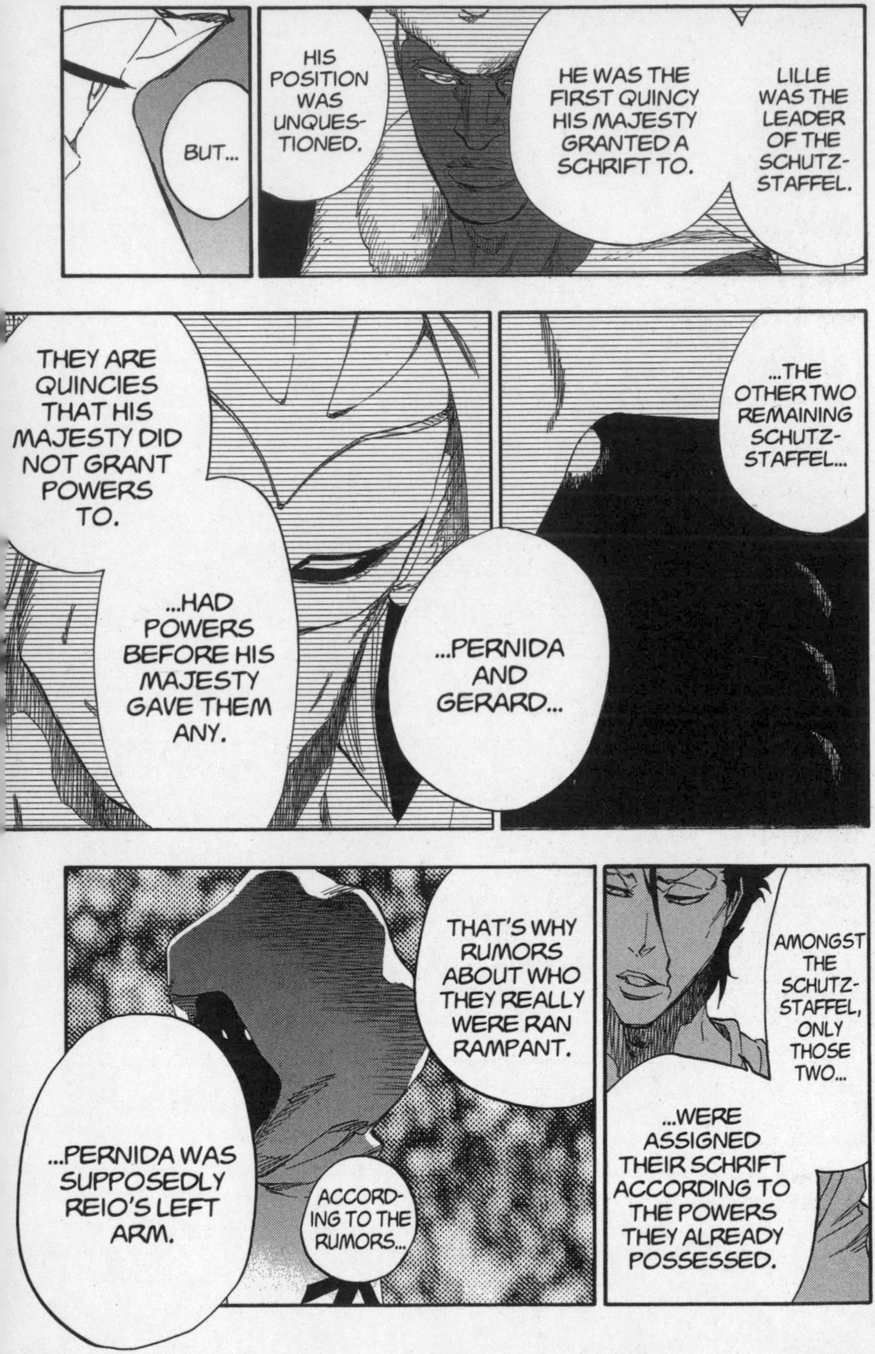
LILLE WAS THE LEADER OF THE SCHUTZ-STAFFEL.
HE WAS THE FIRST QUINCY HIS MAJESTY GRANTED A SCHRIFT TO.
HIS POSITION WAS UNQUES-TIONED.
BUT...
...THE OTHER TWO REMAINING SCHUTZ-STAFFEL...
...PERNIDA AND GERARD...
THEY ARE QUINCIES THAT HIS MAJESTY DID NOT GRANT POWERS TO.
...HAD POWERS BEFORE HIS MAJESTY GAVE THEM ANY.
AMONGST THE SCHUTZ-STAFFEL, ONLY THOSE TWO...
...WERE ASSIGNED THEIR SCHRIFT ACCORDING TO THE POWERS THEY ALREADY POSSESSED.
THAT'S WHY RUMORS ABOUT WHO THEY REALLY WERE RAN RAMPANT.
ACCORD-ING TO THE RUMORS...
...PERNIDA WAS SUPPOSEDLY REIO'S LEFT ARM.

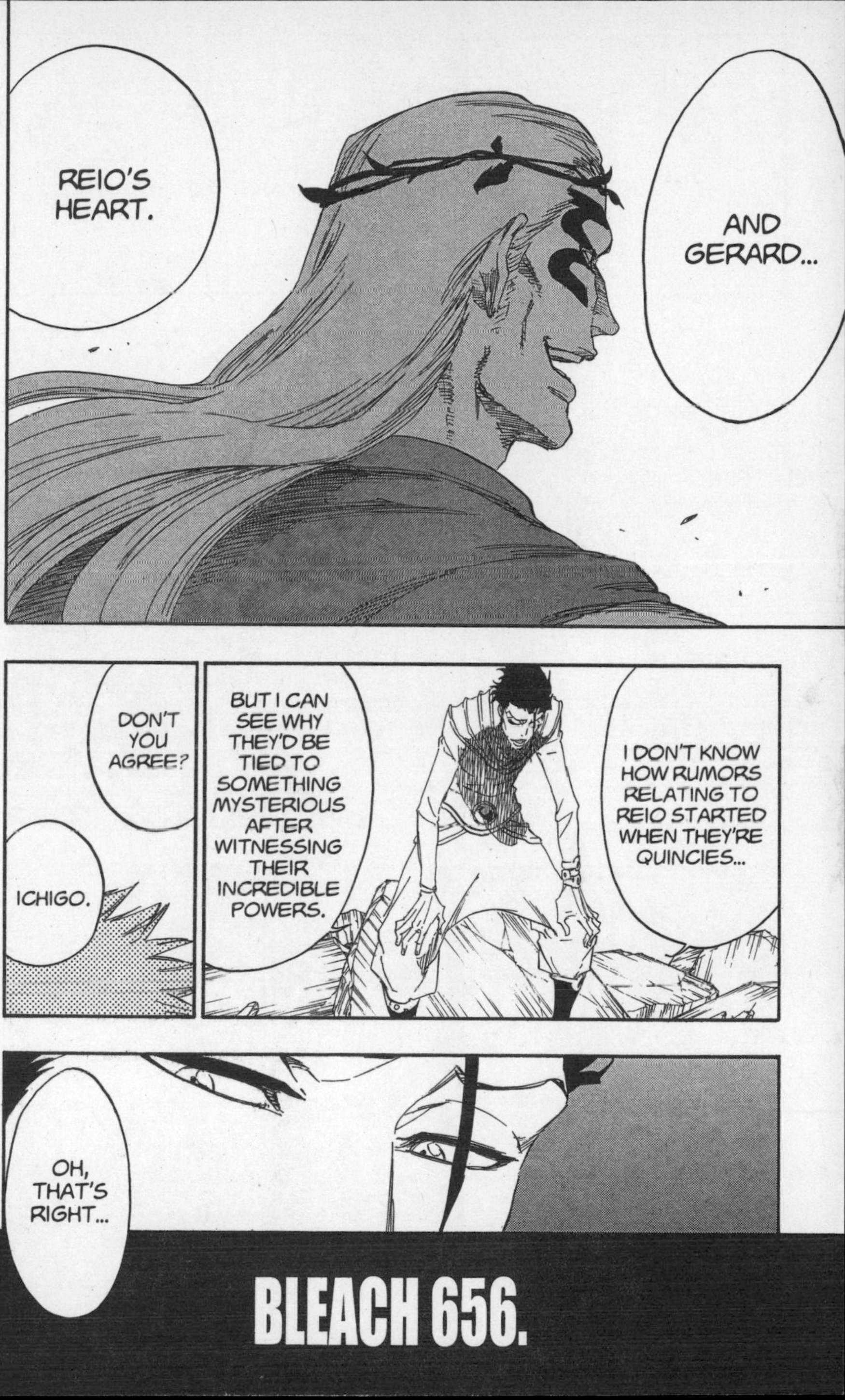
AND GERARD...
REIO'S HEART.
I DON'T KNOW HOW RUMORS RELATING TO REIO STARTED WHEN THEY'RE QUINCIES...
BUT I CAN SEE WHY THEY'D BE TIED TO SOMETHING MYSTERIOUS AFTER WITNESSING THEIR INCREDIBLE POWERS.
DON'T YOU AGREE?
ICHIGO.
OH, THAT'S RIGHT...
BLEACH 656.

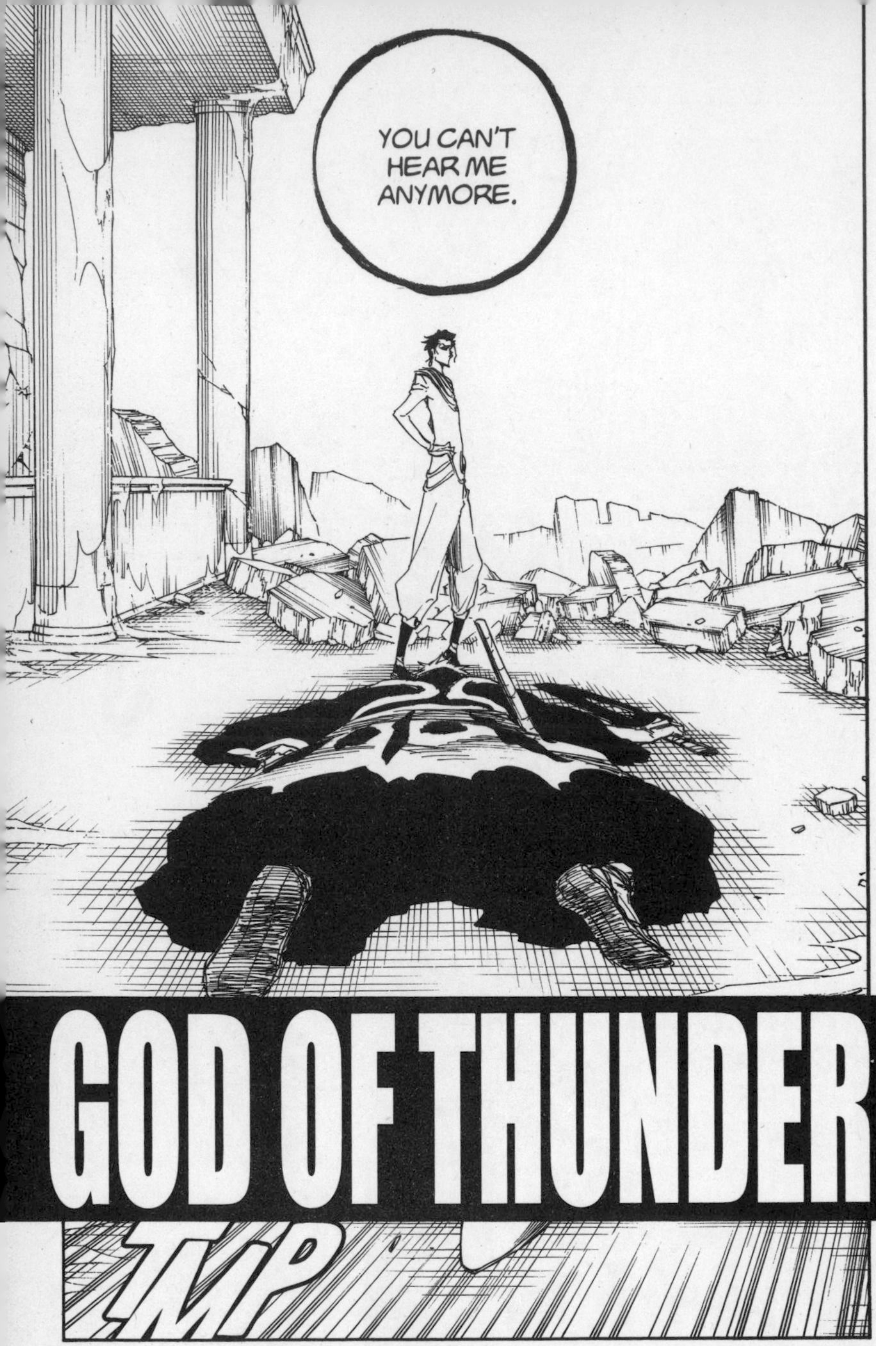
YOU CAN'T HEAR ME ANYMORE.
GOD OF THUNDER
TMP

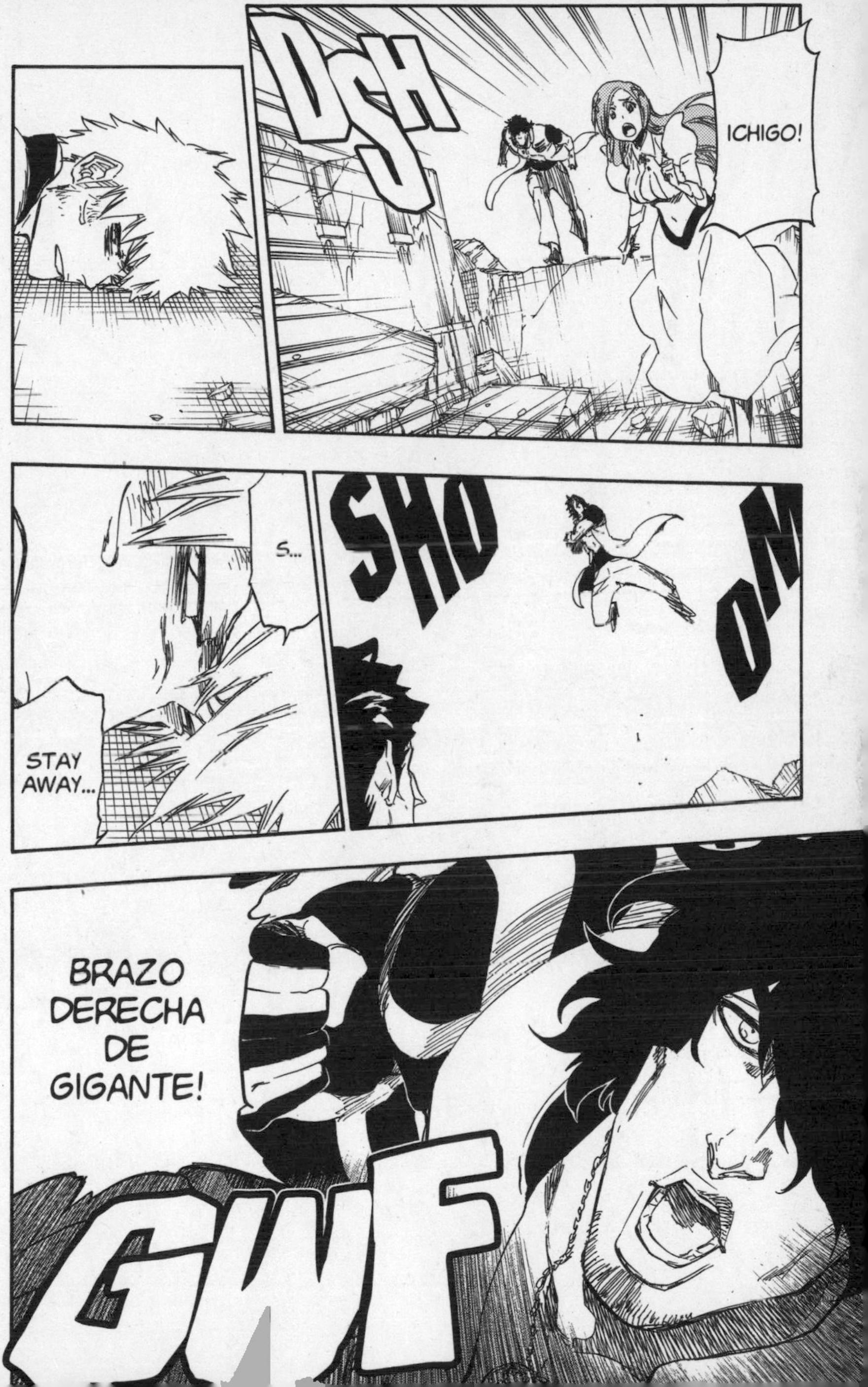
DSH
ICHIGO!
SHOOM
S...
STAY AWAY...
BRAZO DERECHA DE GIGANTE!
GWF

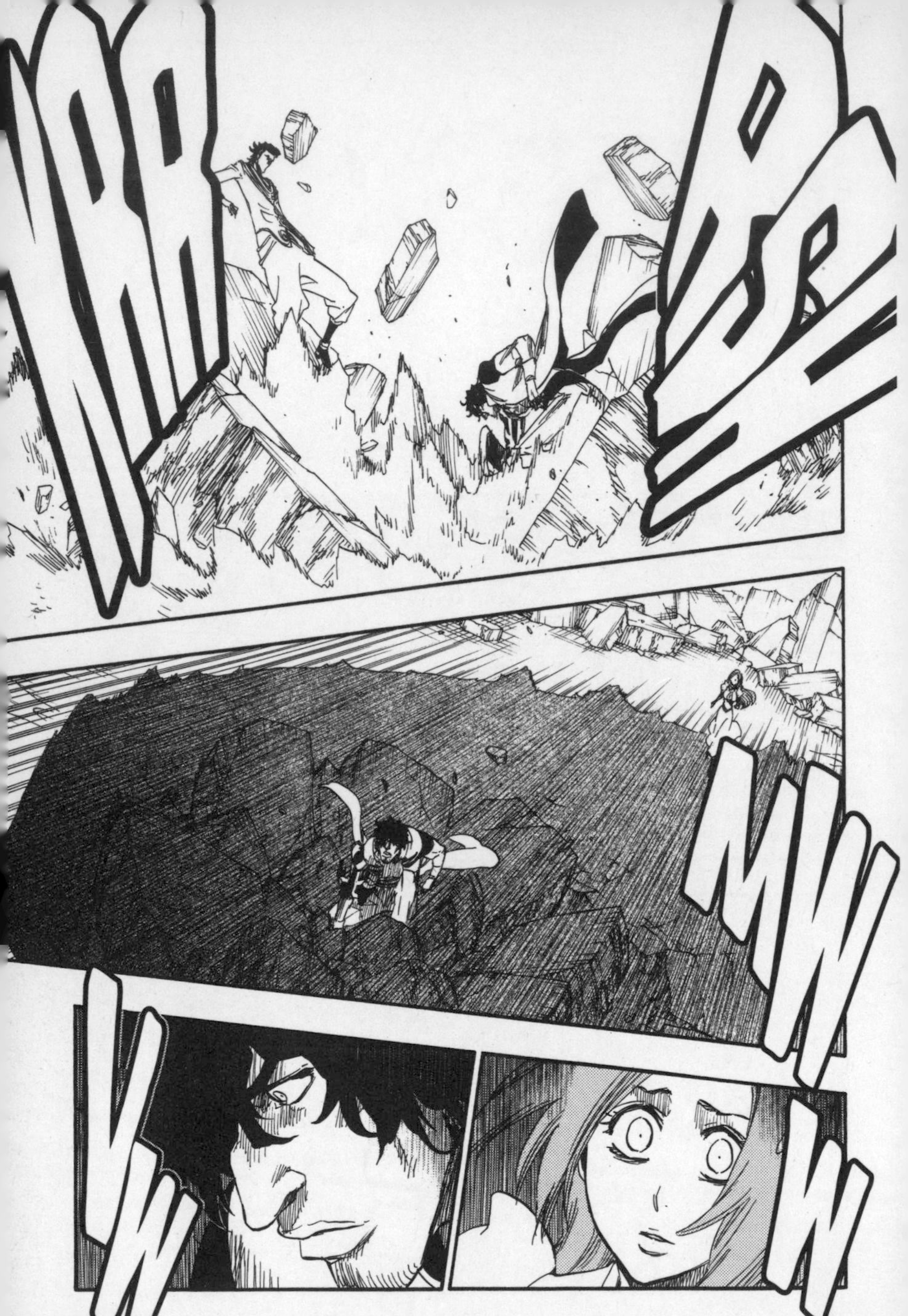

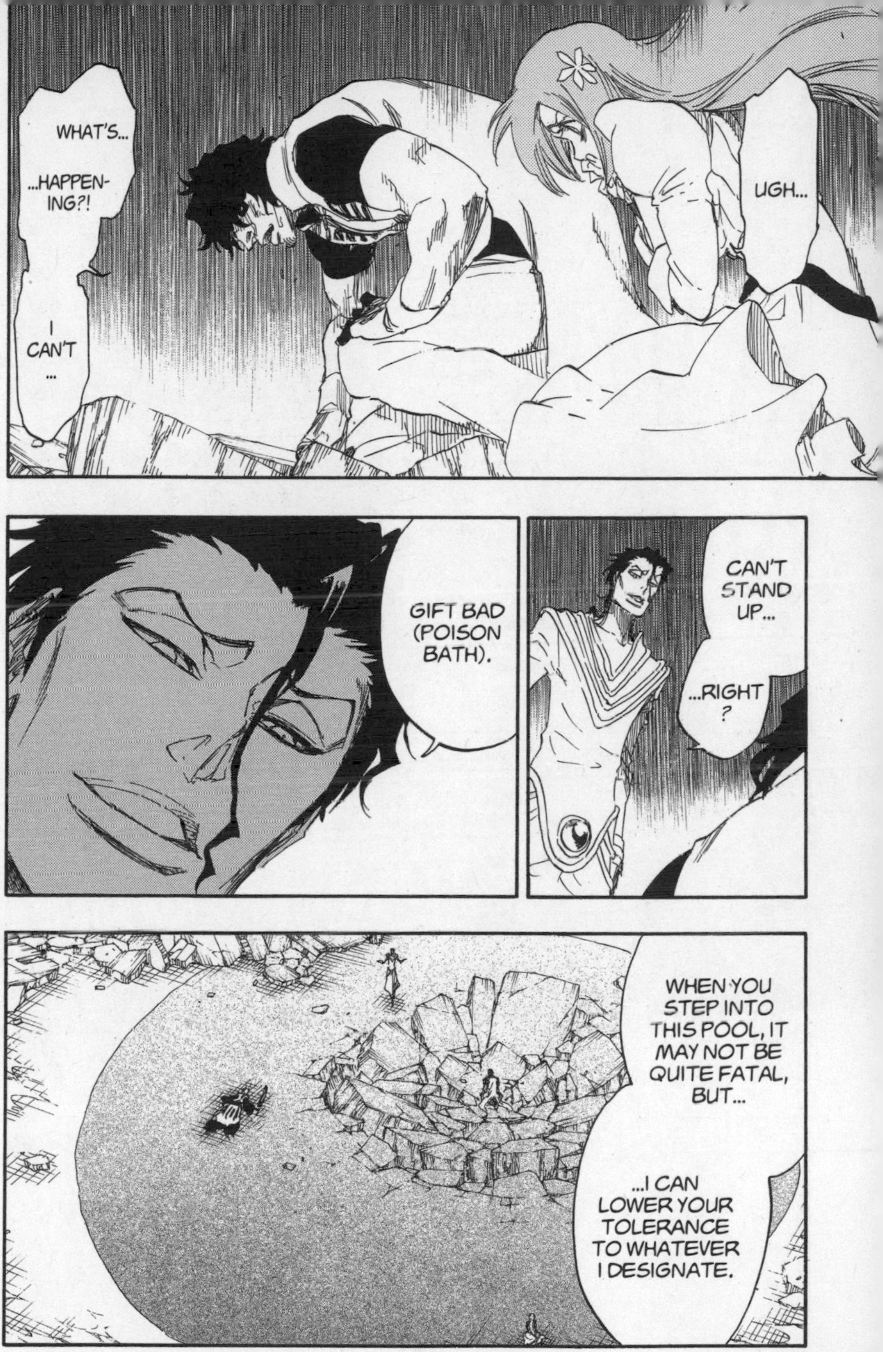
UGH...
WHAT'S...
...HAPPEN-ING?!
I CAN'T ...
CAN'T STAND UP...
...RIGHT ?
GIFT BAD (POISON BATH).
WHEN YOU STEP INTO THIS POOL, IT MAY NOT BE QUITE FATAL, BUT...
...I CAN LOWER YOUR TOLERANCE TO WHATEVER I DESIGNATE.

READ THIS WAY

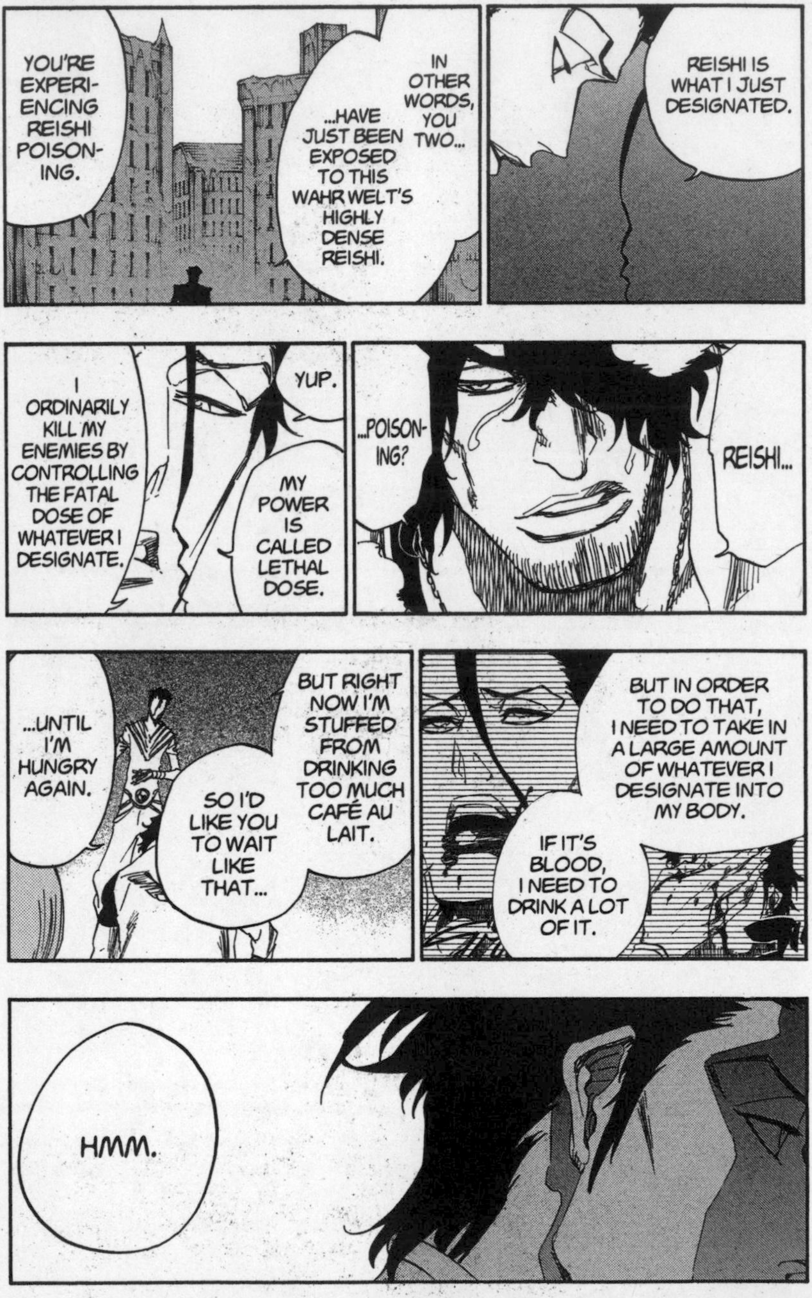
REISHI IS WHAT I JUST DESIGNATED.
IN OTHER WORDS, YOU TWO...
...HAVE JUST BEEN EXPOSED TO THIS WAHRWELT'S HIGHLY DENSE REISHI.
YOU'RE EXPERIENCING REISHI POISONING.
REISHI...
...POISONING?
YUP.
MY POWER IS CALLED LETHAL DOSE.
I ORDINARILY KILL MY ENEMIES BY CONTROLLING THE FATAL DOSE OF WHATEVER I DESIGNATE.
BUT IN ORDER TO DO THAT, I NEED TO TAKE IN A LARGE AMOUNT OF WHATEVER I DESIGNATE INTO MY BODY.
IF IT'S BLOOD, I NEED TO DRINK A LOT OF IT.
BUT RIGHT NOW I'M STUFFED FROM DRINKING TOO MUCH CAFÉ AU LAIT.
SO I'D LIKE YOU TO WAIT LIKE THAT...
...UNTIL I'M HUNGRY AGAIN.
HMM.

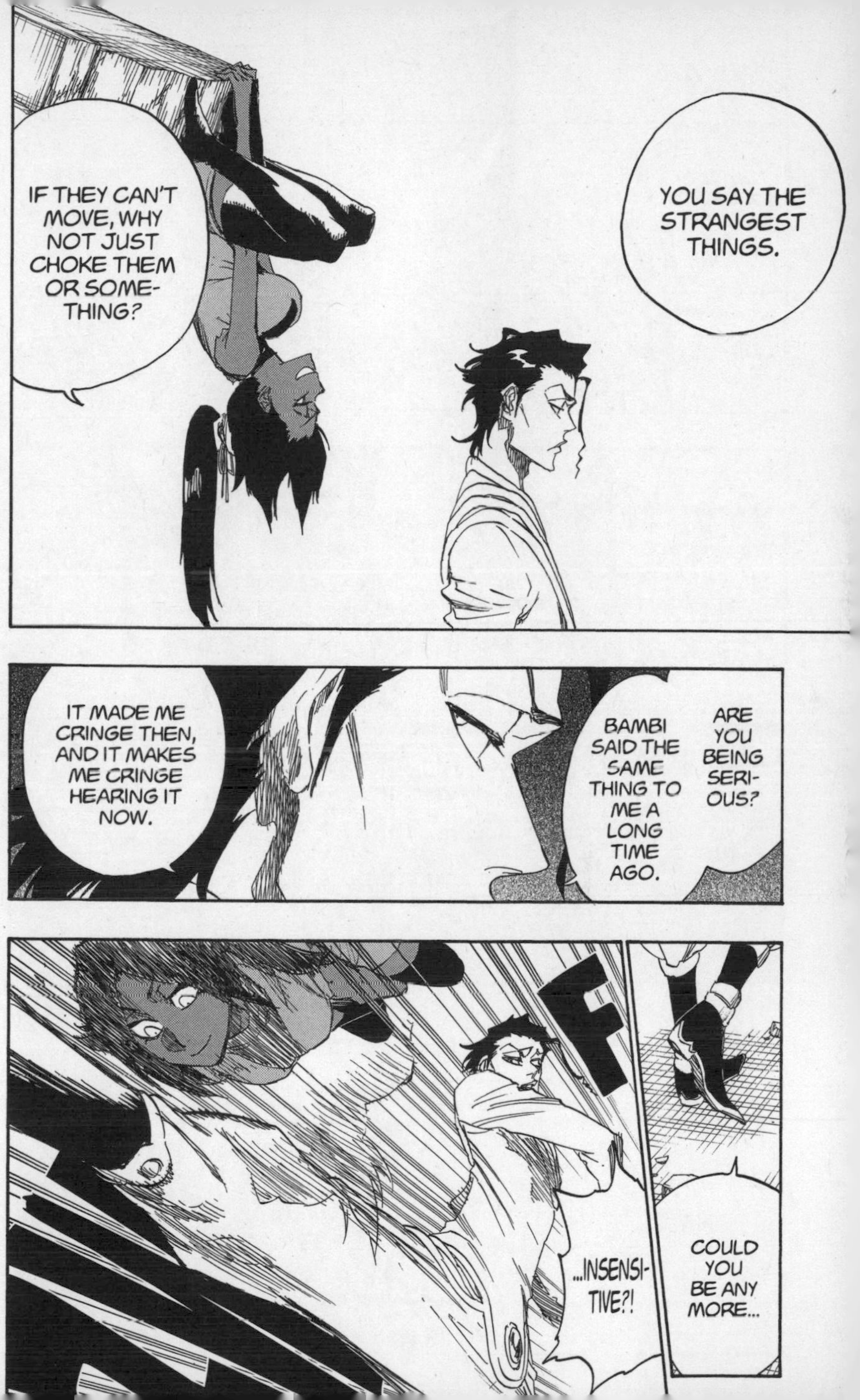
YOU SAY THE STRANGEST THINGS.
IF THEY CAN'T MOVE, WHY NOT JUST CHOKE THEM OR SOME-THING?
ARE YOU BEING SERI-OUS?
BAMBI SAID THE SAME THING TO ME A LONG TIME AGO.
IT MADE ME CRINGE THEN, AND IT MAKES ME CRINGE HEARING IT NOW.
COULD YOU BE ANY MORE...
...INSENSI-TIVE?!
F

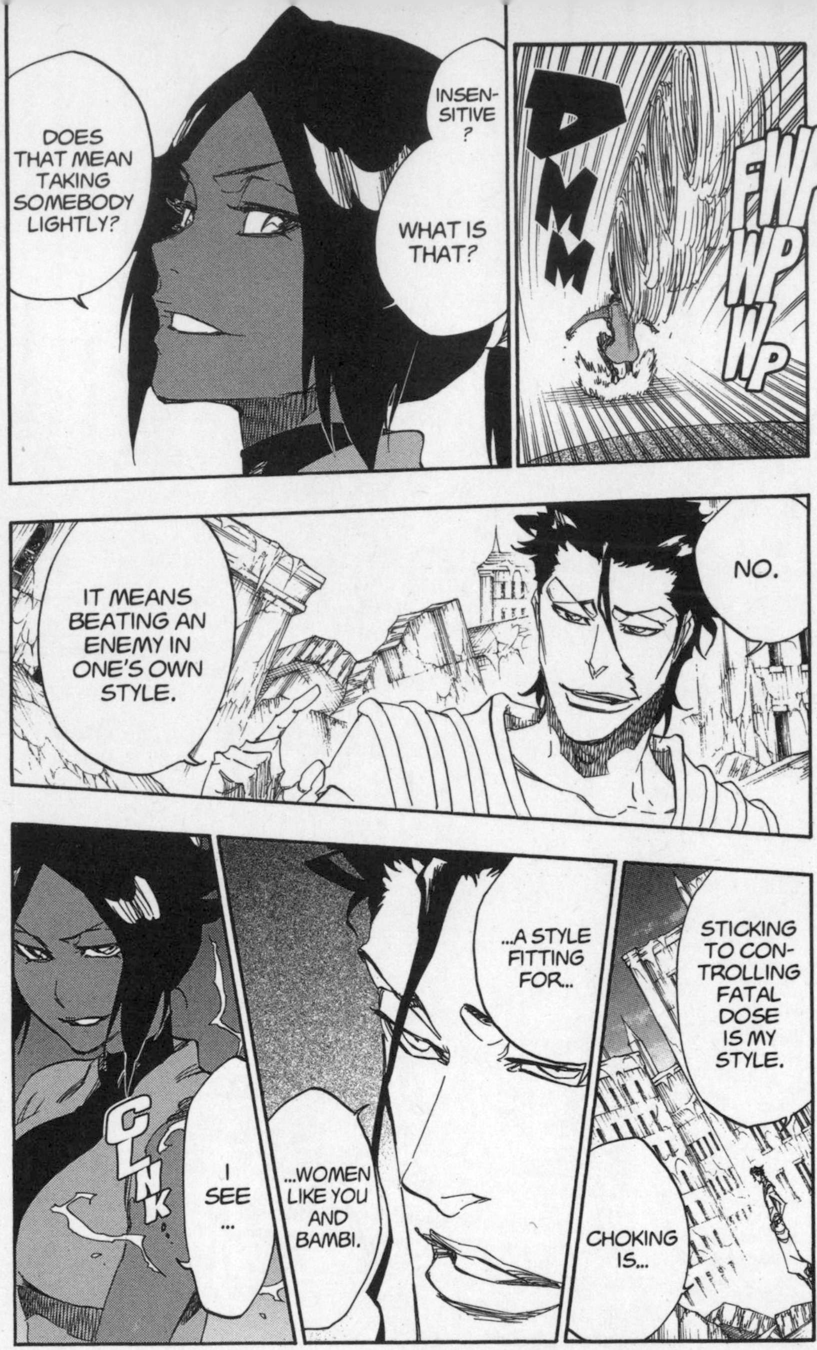
FWP WP WP WP
DMM
INSENSITIVE?
WHAT IS THAT?
DOES THAT MEAN TAKING SOMEBODY LIGHTLY?
NO.
IT MEANS BEATING AN ENEMY IN ONE'S OWN STYLE.
STICKING TO CONTROLLING FATAL DOSE IS MY STYLE.
CHOKING IS...
...A STYLE FITTING FOR...
...WOMEN LIKE YOU AND BAMBI.
I SEE...
CLNK

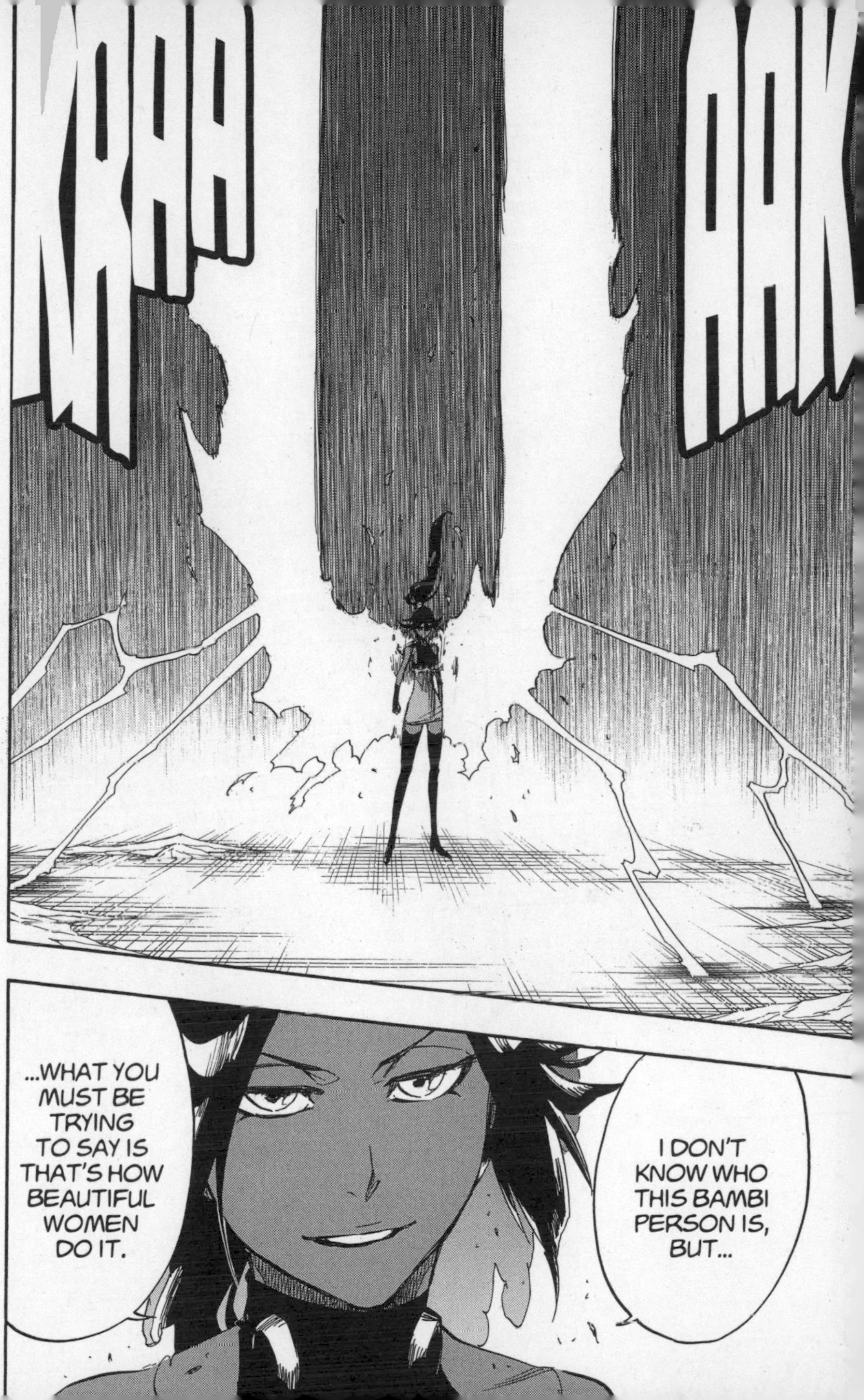
KRAA
AAK
I DON'T KNOW WHO THIS BAMBI PERSON IS, BUT...
...WHAT YOU MUST BE TRYING TO SAY IS THAT'S HOW BEAUTIFUL WOMEN DO IT.

READ THIS WAY

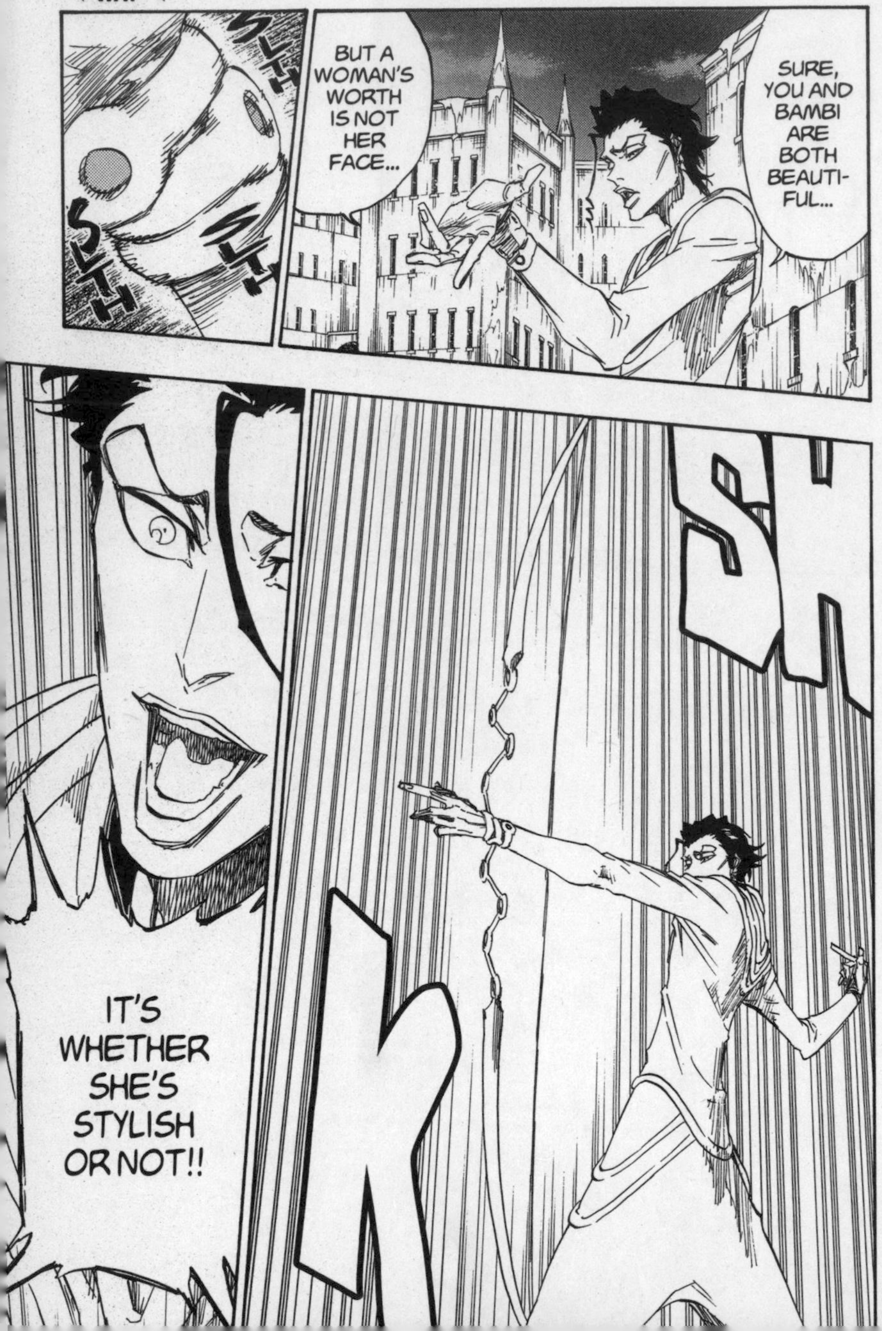
SURE, YOU AND BAMBI ARE BOTH BEAUTIFUL...
BUT A WOMAN'S WORTH IS NOT HER FACE...
SLTH
SLTH
SLTH
SHK
IT'S WHETHER SHE'S STYLISH OR NOT!!

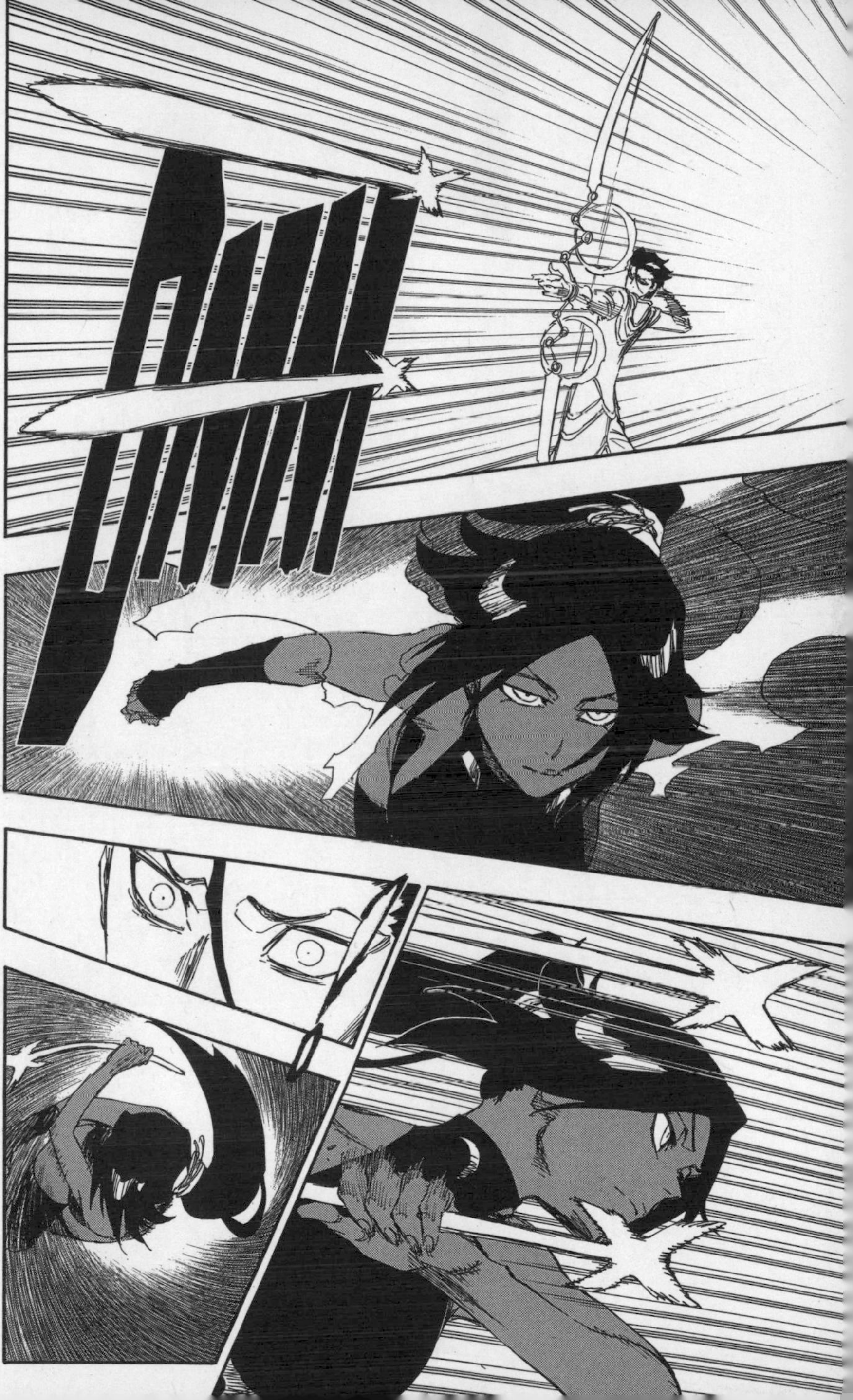

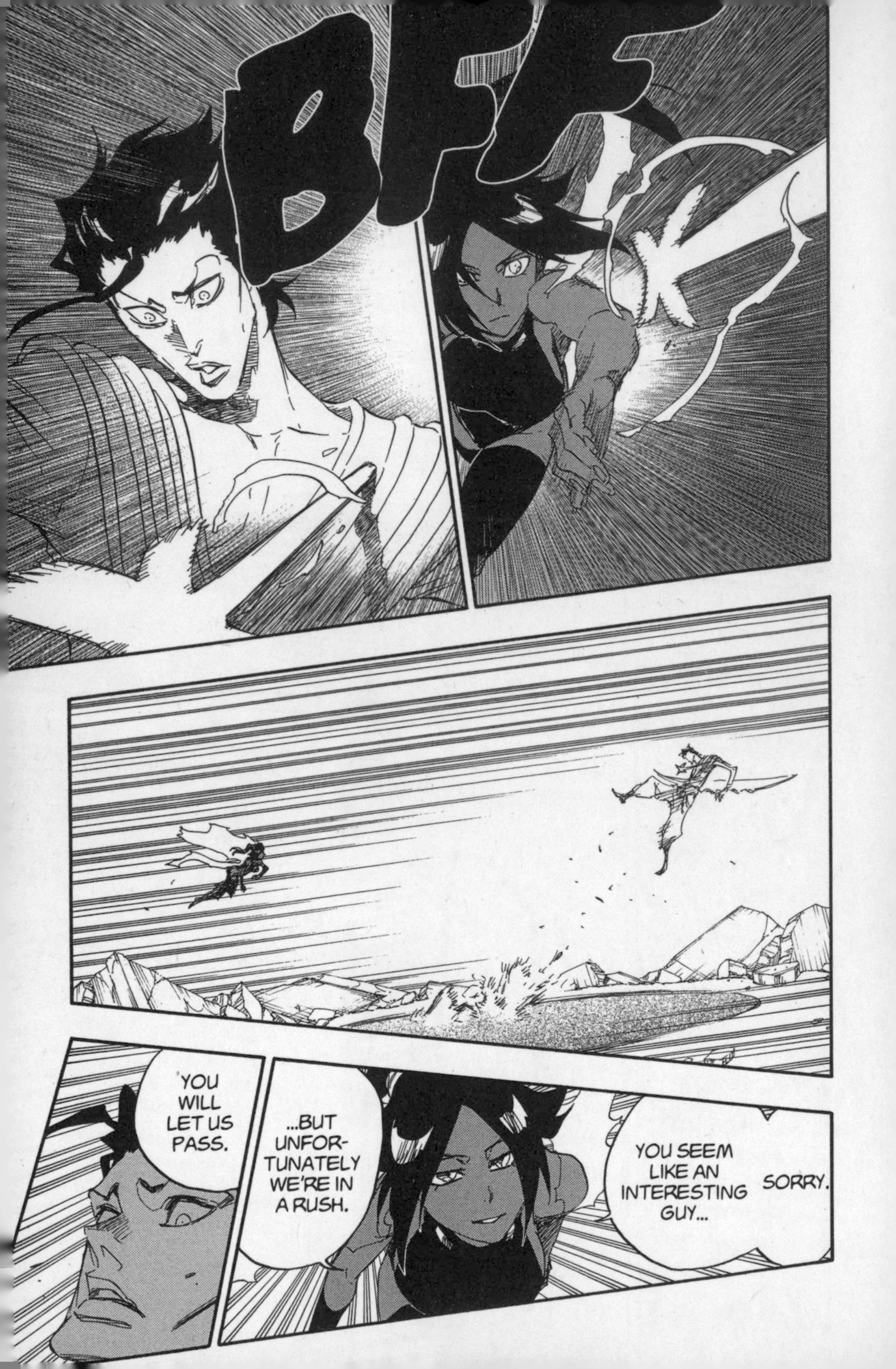
SORRY.
YOU SEEM LIKE AN INTERESTING GUY...
...BUT UNFORTUNATELY WE'RE IN A RUSH.
YOU WILL LET US PASS.

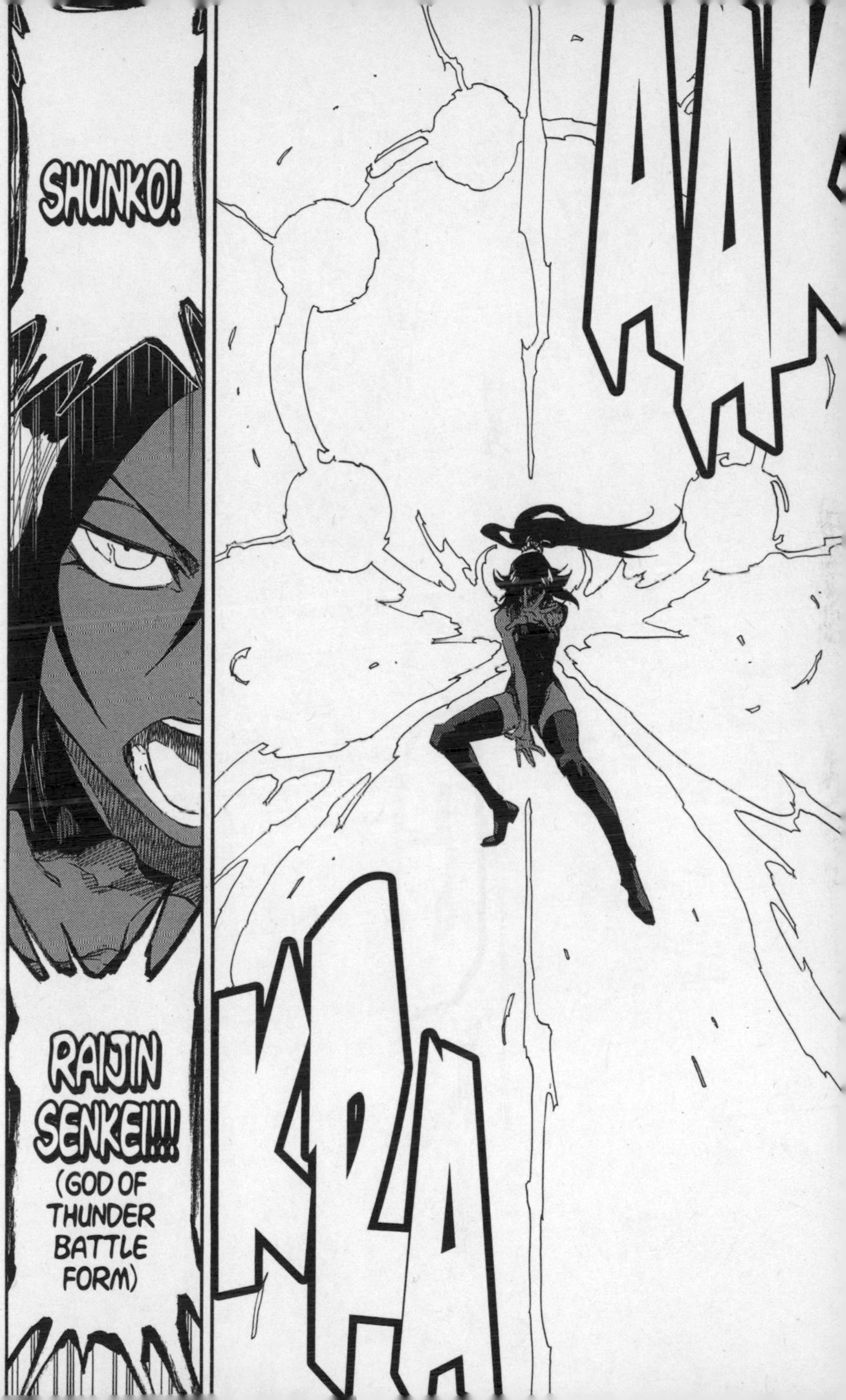
KRA
AAK
SHUNKO!
RAIJIN SENKEI!!!!
(GOD OF THUNDER BATTLE FORM)

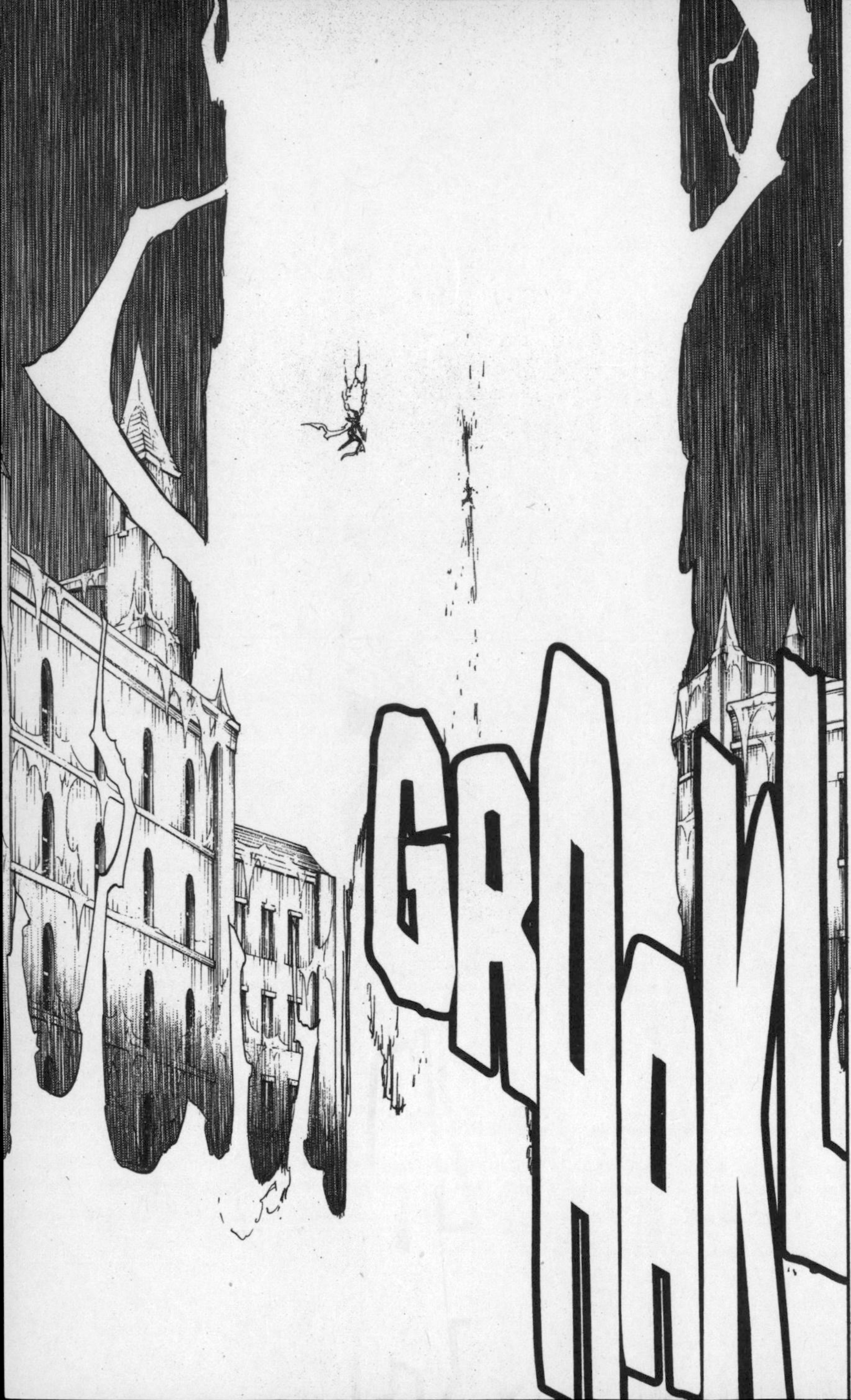
GRAAKL

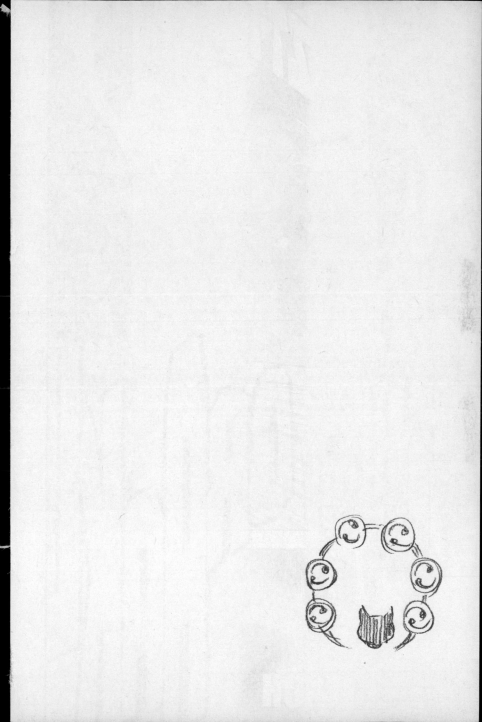

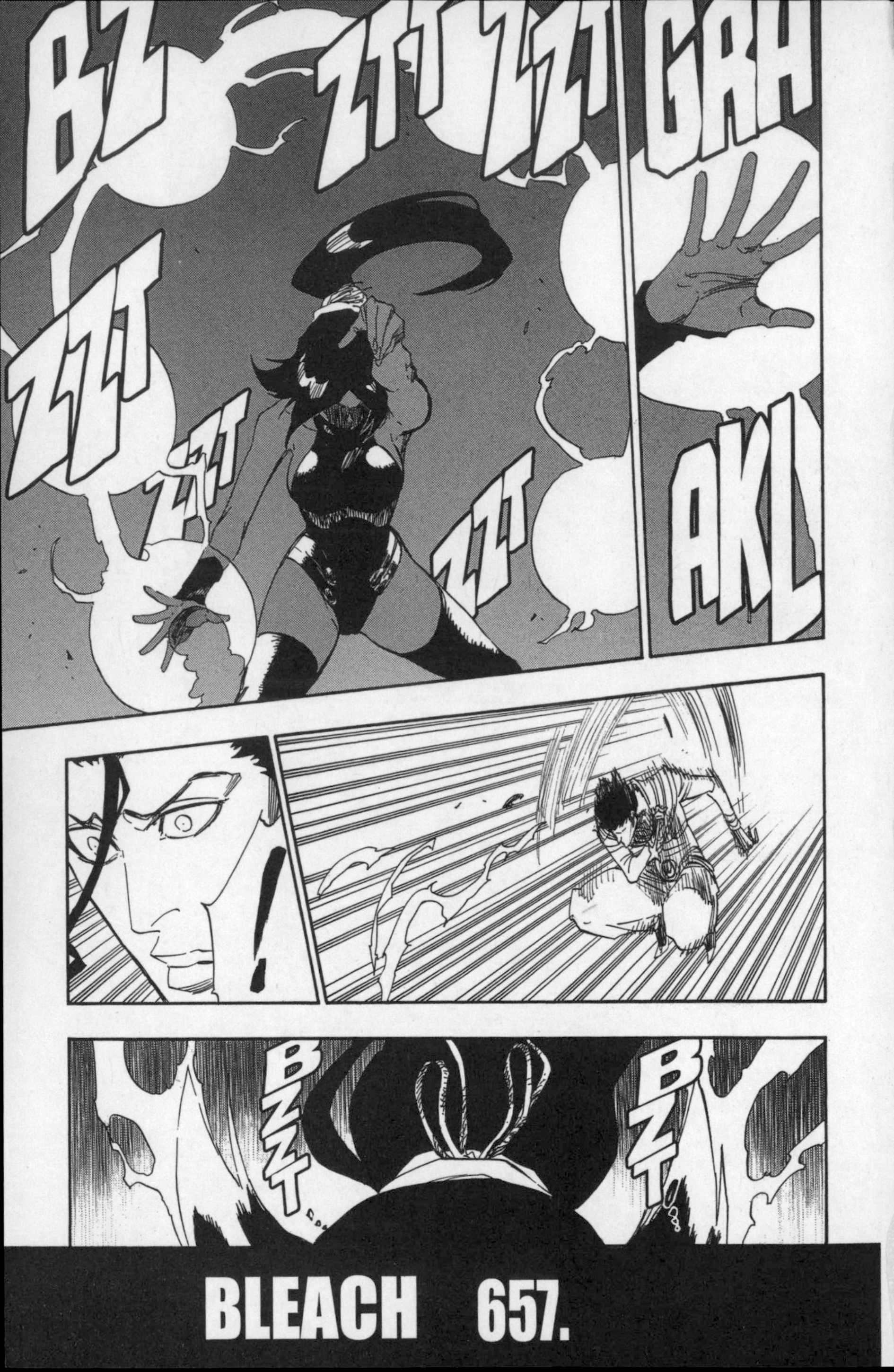
GRAH
BZ
ZZT
ZZT
ZZT
ZZT
BZZT
BZZZT

BLEACH 657.

GOD OF THUNDER 2

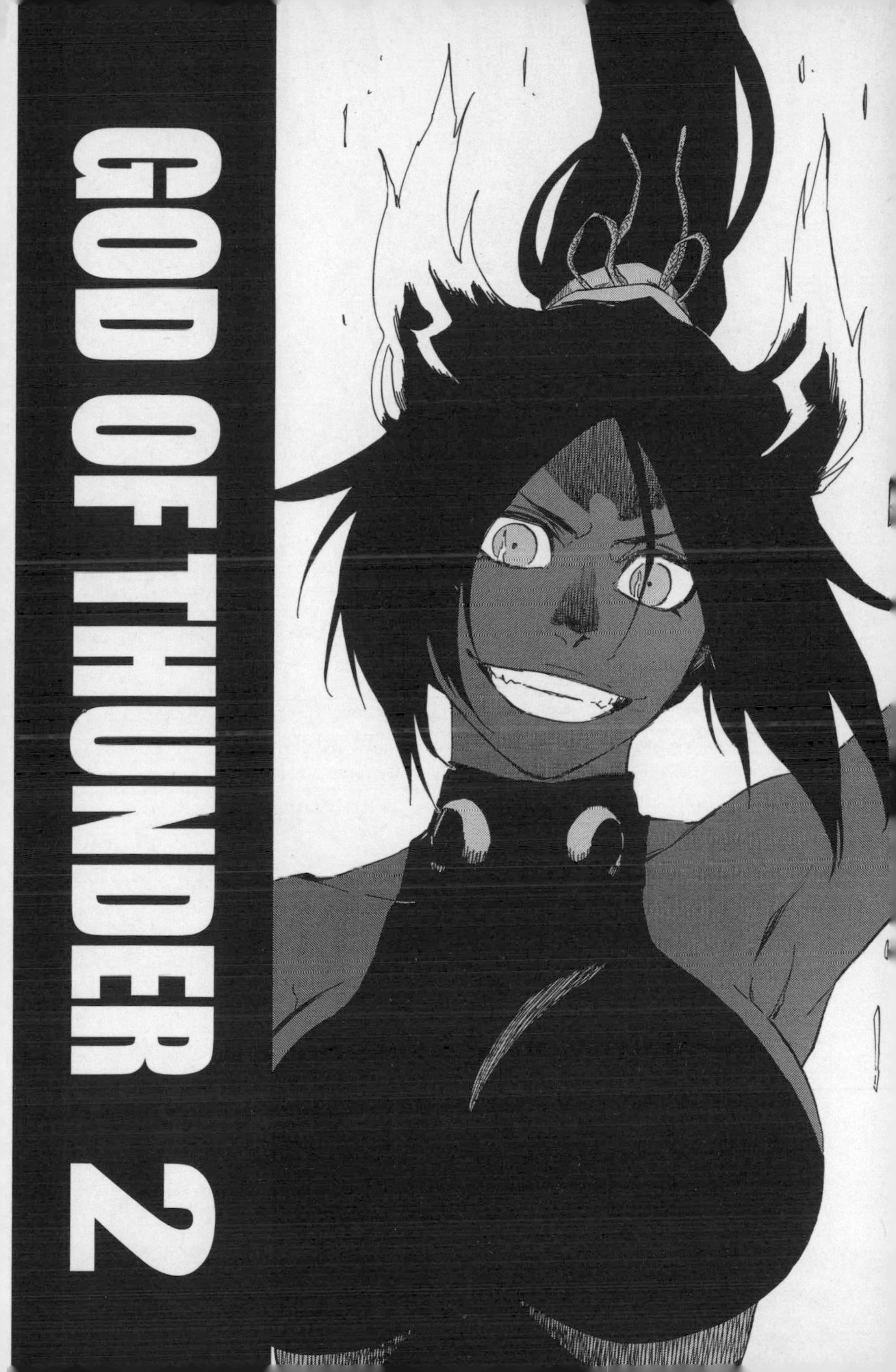

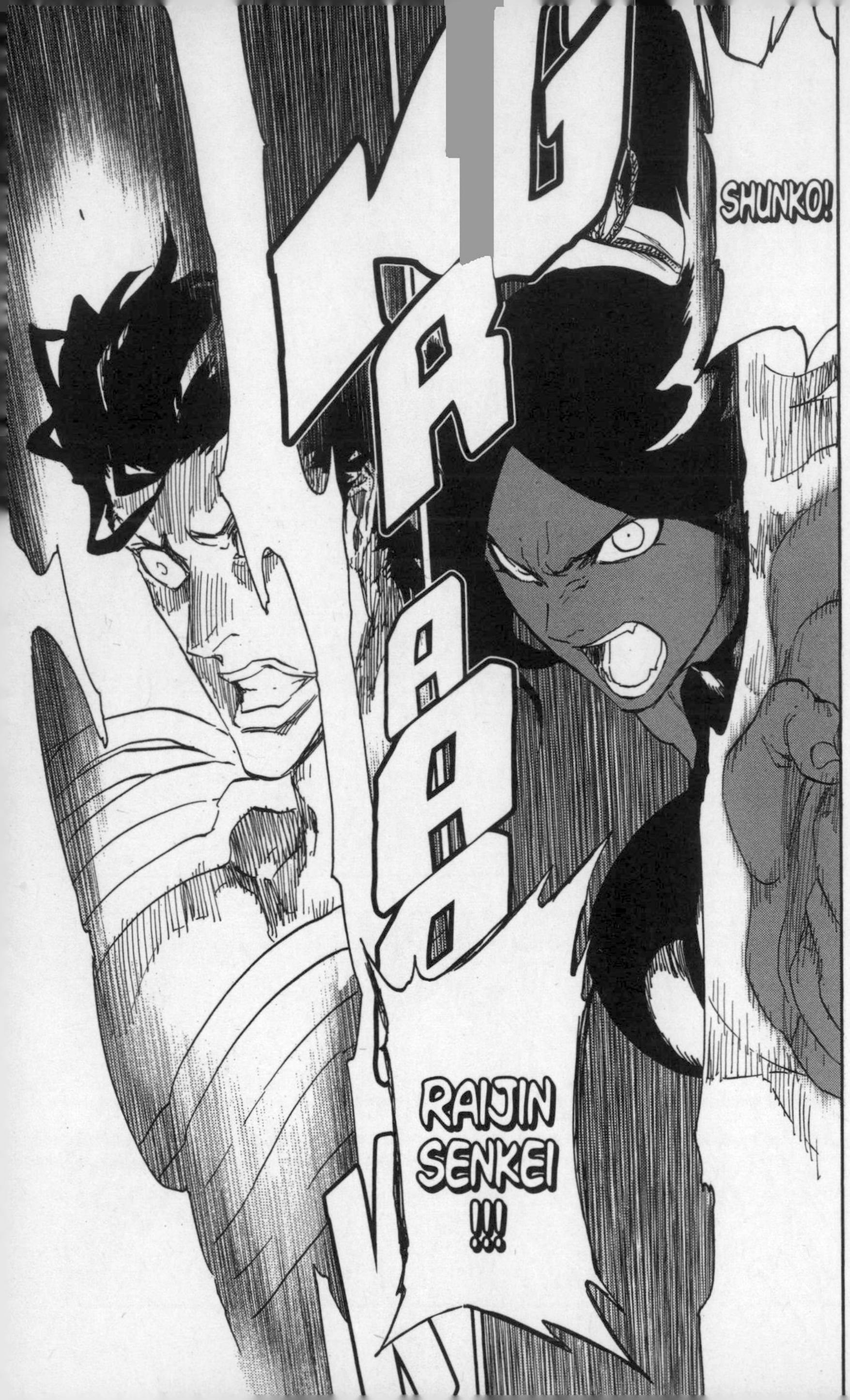
SHUNKO!
RAIJIN SENKEI!!!

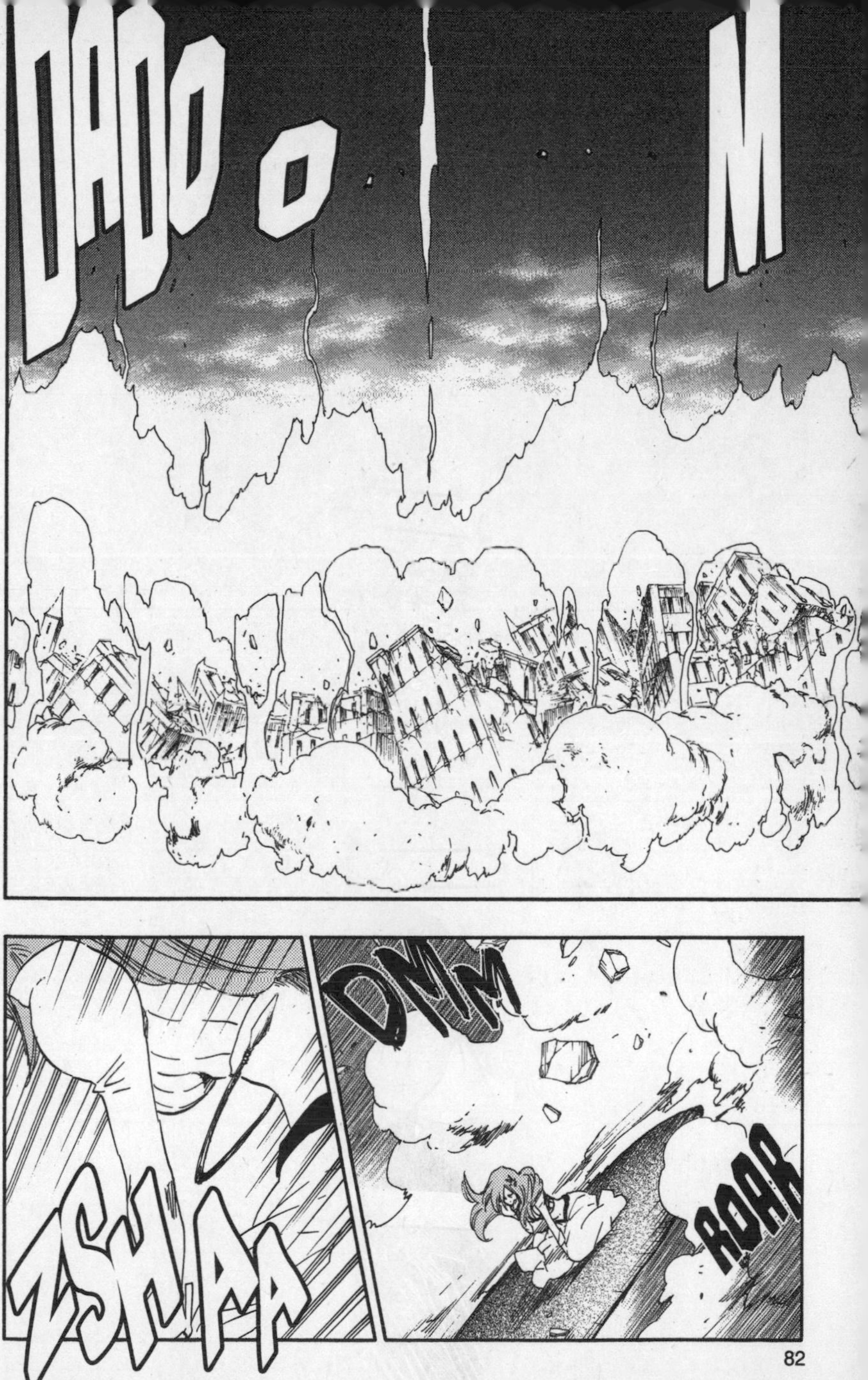
DADOOM
DMM
ROAR
ZSHAA

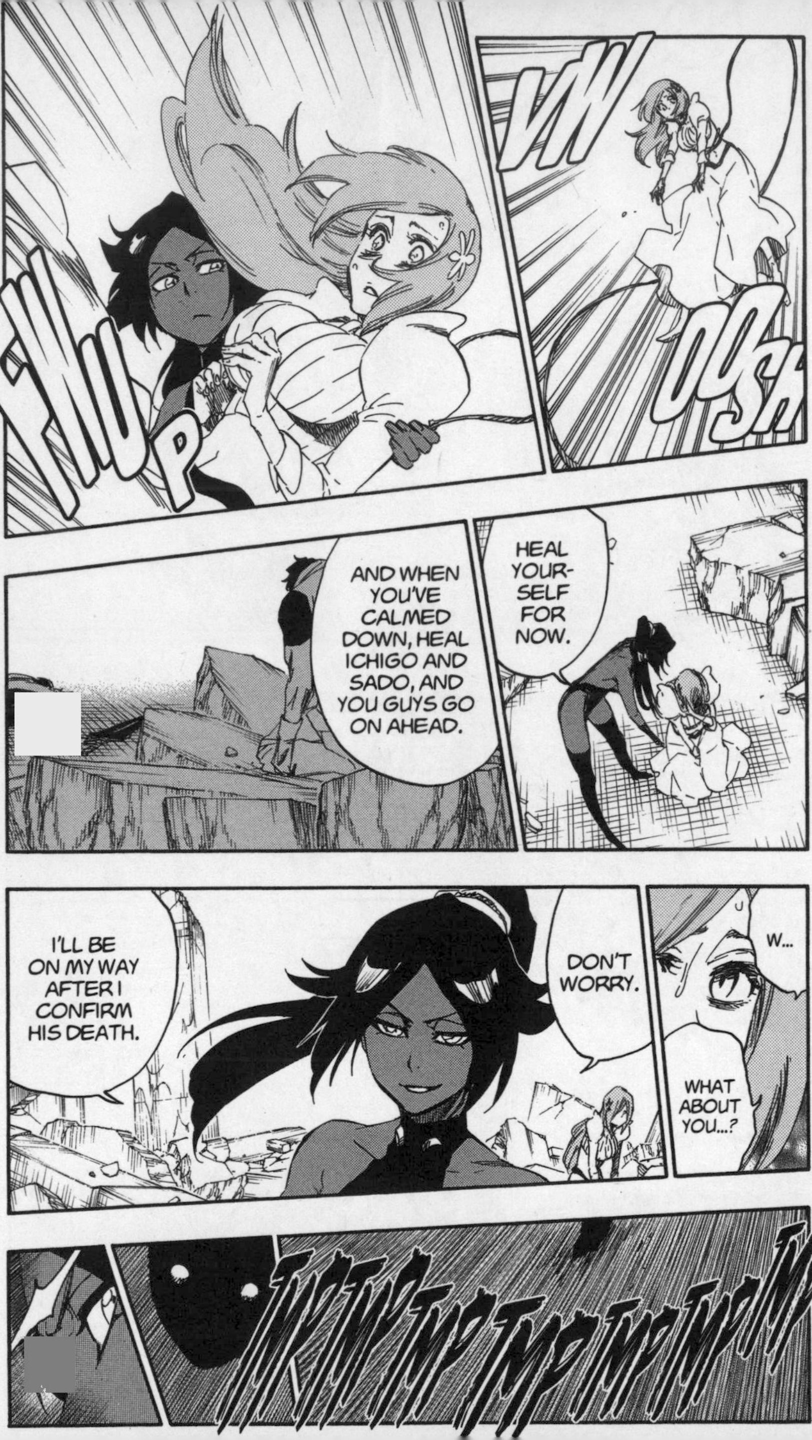
VN
OOSH
FWUP
HEAL YOUR-SELF FOR NOW.
AND WHEN YOU'VE CALMED DOWN, HEAL ICHIGO AND SADO, AND YOU GUYS GO ON AHEAD.
W...
WHAT ABOUT YOU...?
DON'T WORRY.
I'LL BE ON MY WAY AFTER I CONFIRM HIS DEATH.
TMP TMP TMP TMP TMP TMP

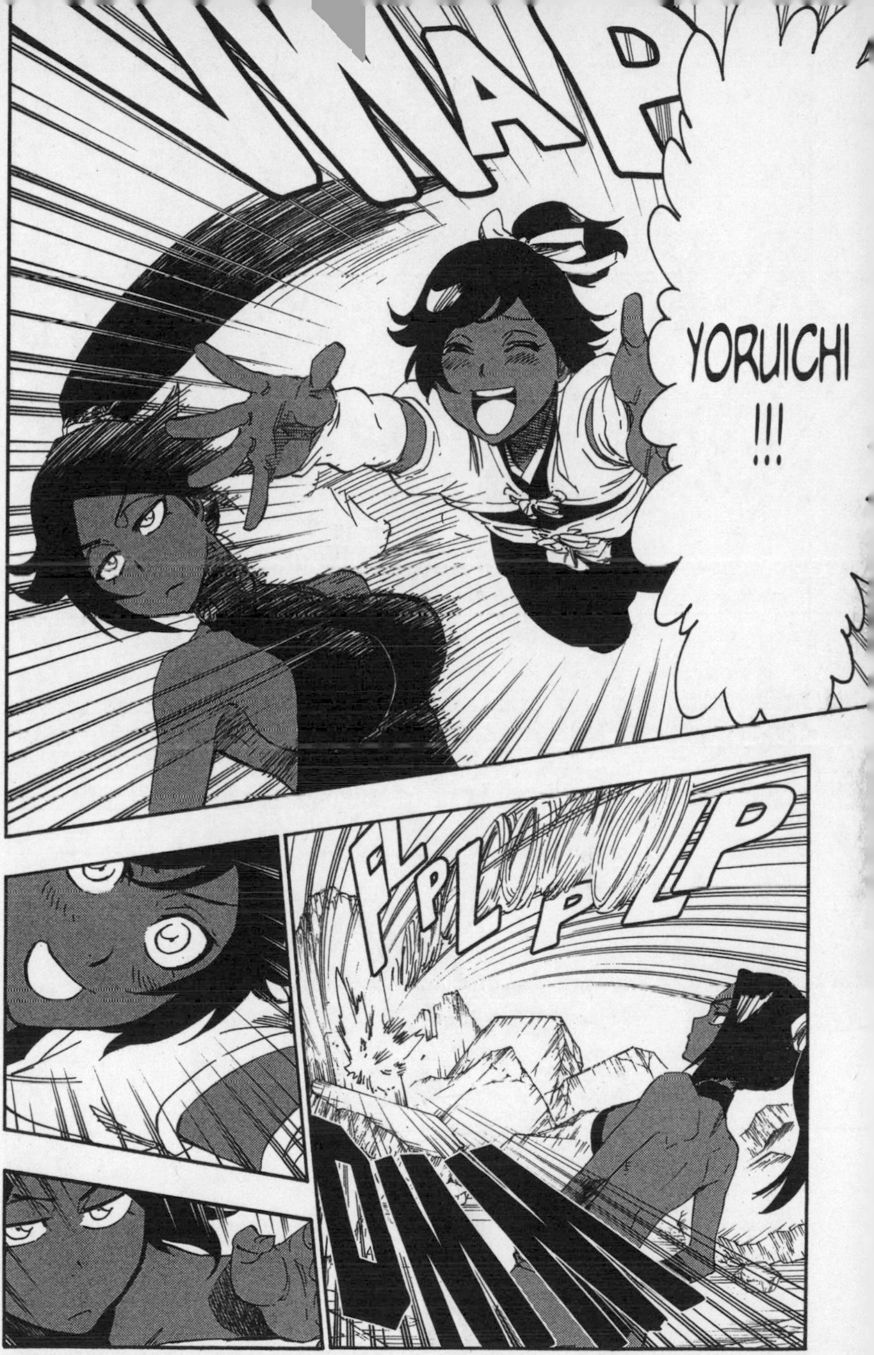
WHAP
YORUICHI !!!

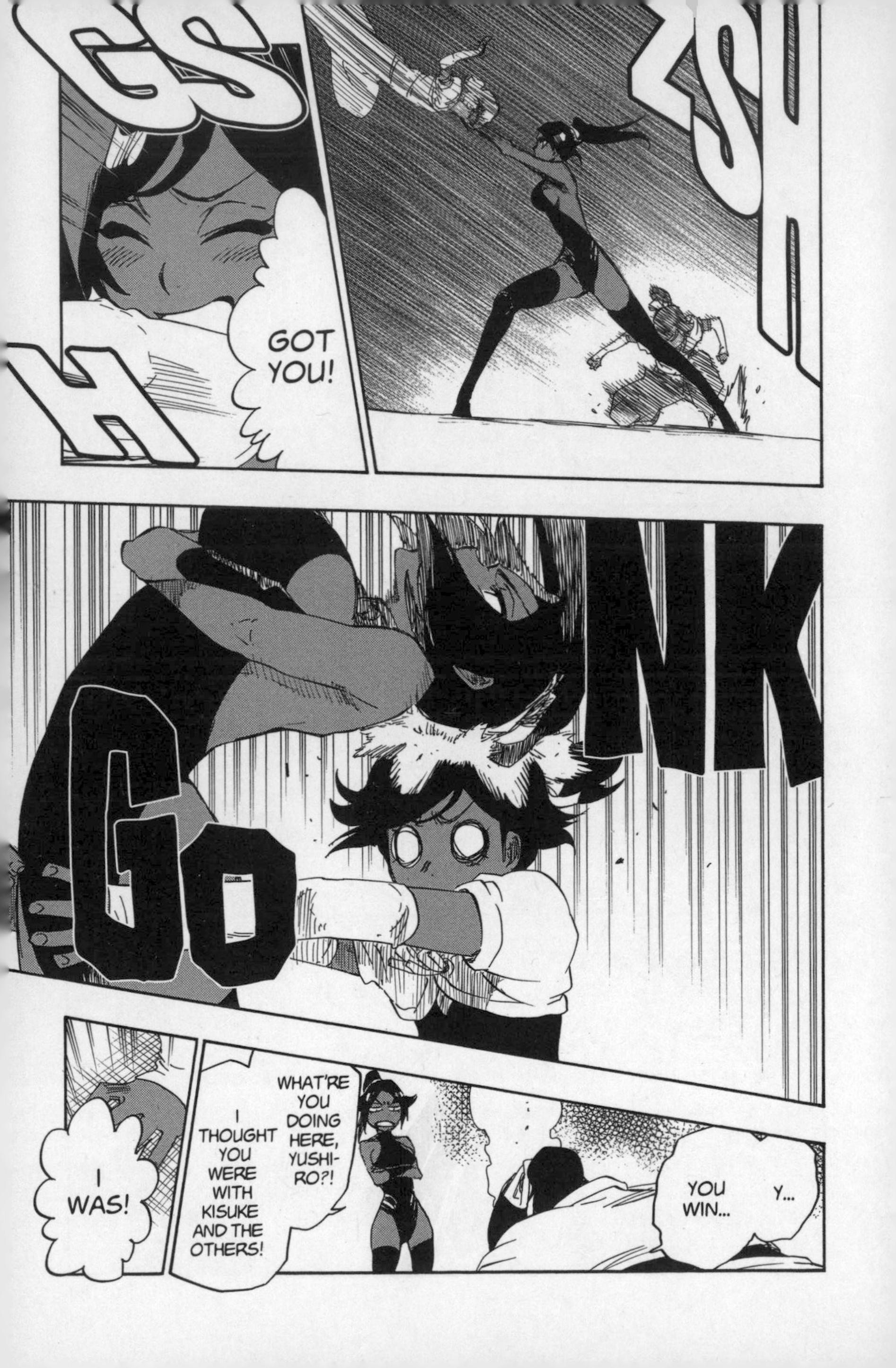
GOT YOU!
Y...
YOU WIN...
WHAT'RE YOU DOING HERE, YUSHIRO?!
I THOUGHT YOU WERE WITH KISUKE AND THE OTHERS!
I WAS!

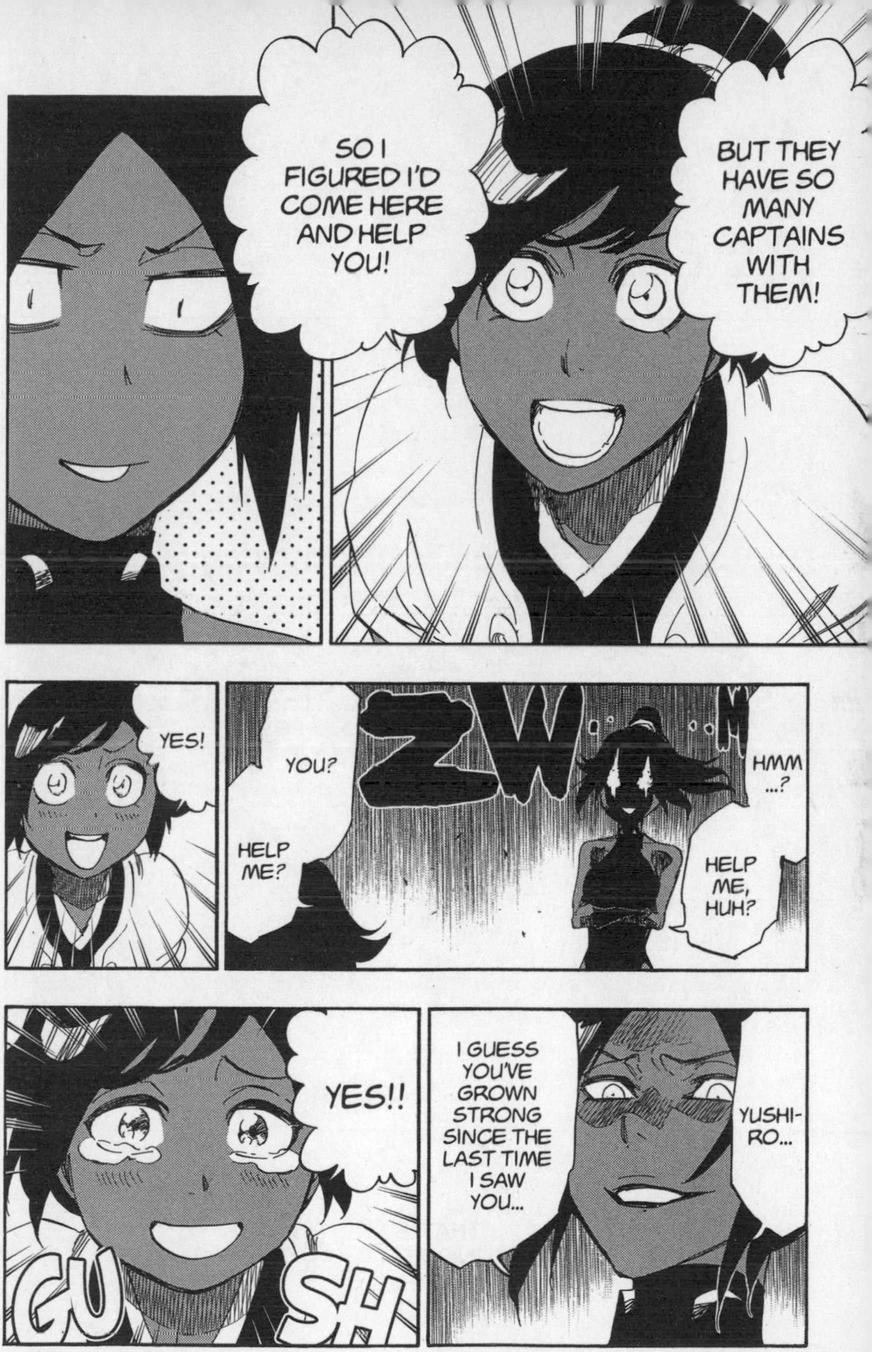
BUT THEY HAVE SO MANY CAPTAINS WITH THEM!
SO I FIGURED I'D COME HERE AND HELP YOU!
HMM ...?
ZW...M
HELP ME, HUH?
YOU?
HELP ME?
YES!
YUSHIRO...
I GUESS YOU'VE GROWN STRONG SINCE THE LAST TIME I SAW YOU...
YES!!
GUSH

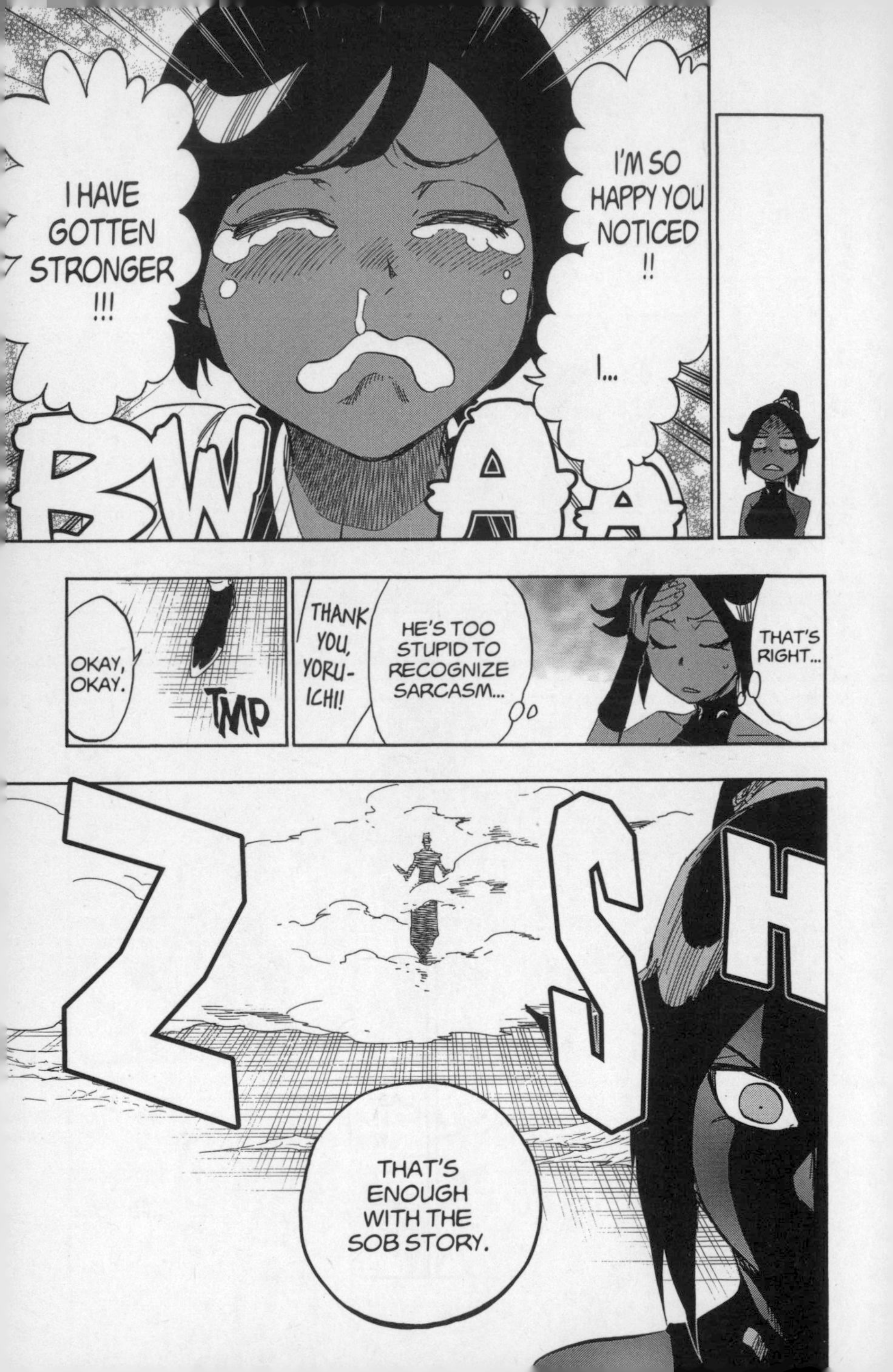
I'M SO HAPPY YOU NOTICED !!
I...
I HAVE GOTTEN STRONGER !!!
BWAA
THAT'S RIGHT...
HE'S TOO STUPID TO RECOGNIZE SARCASM...
THANK YOU, YORU-ICHI!
OKAY, OKAY.
TMP
ZSH
THAT'S ENOUGH WITH THE SOB STORY.

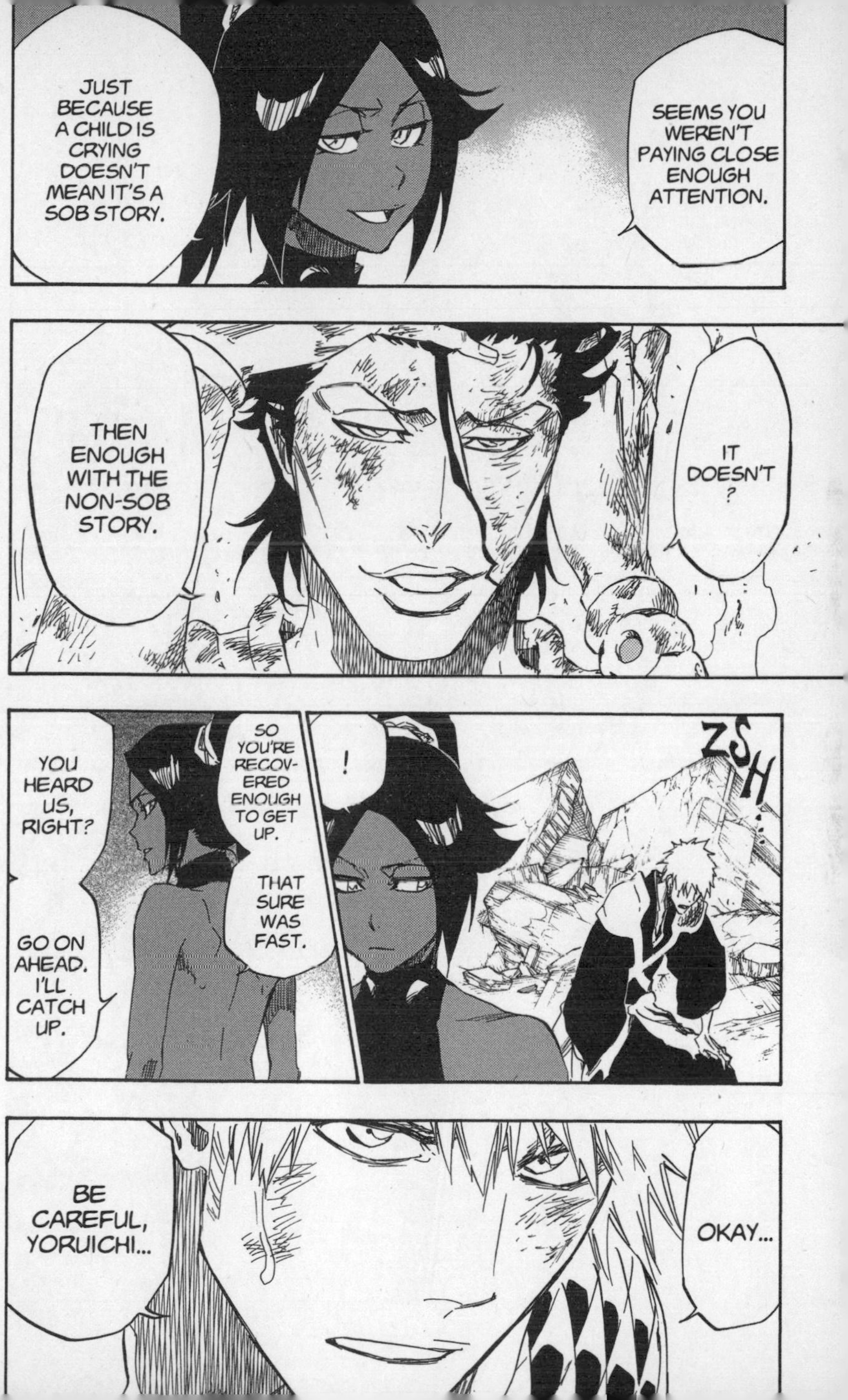
SEEMS YOU WEREN'T PAYING CLOSE ENOUGH ATTENTION.
JUST BECAUSE A CHILD IS CRYING DOESN'T MEAN IT'S A SOB STORY.
IT DOESN'T ?
THEN ENOUGH WITH THE NON-SOB STORY.
ZSH
!
SO YOU'RE RECOVERED ENOUGH TO GET UP.
THAT SURE WAS FAST.
YOU HEARD US, RIGHT?
GO ON AHEAD. I'LL CATCH UP.
OKAY...
BE CAREFUL, YORUICHI...

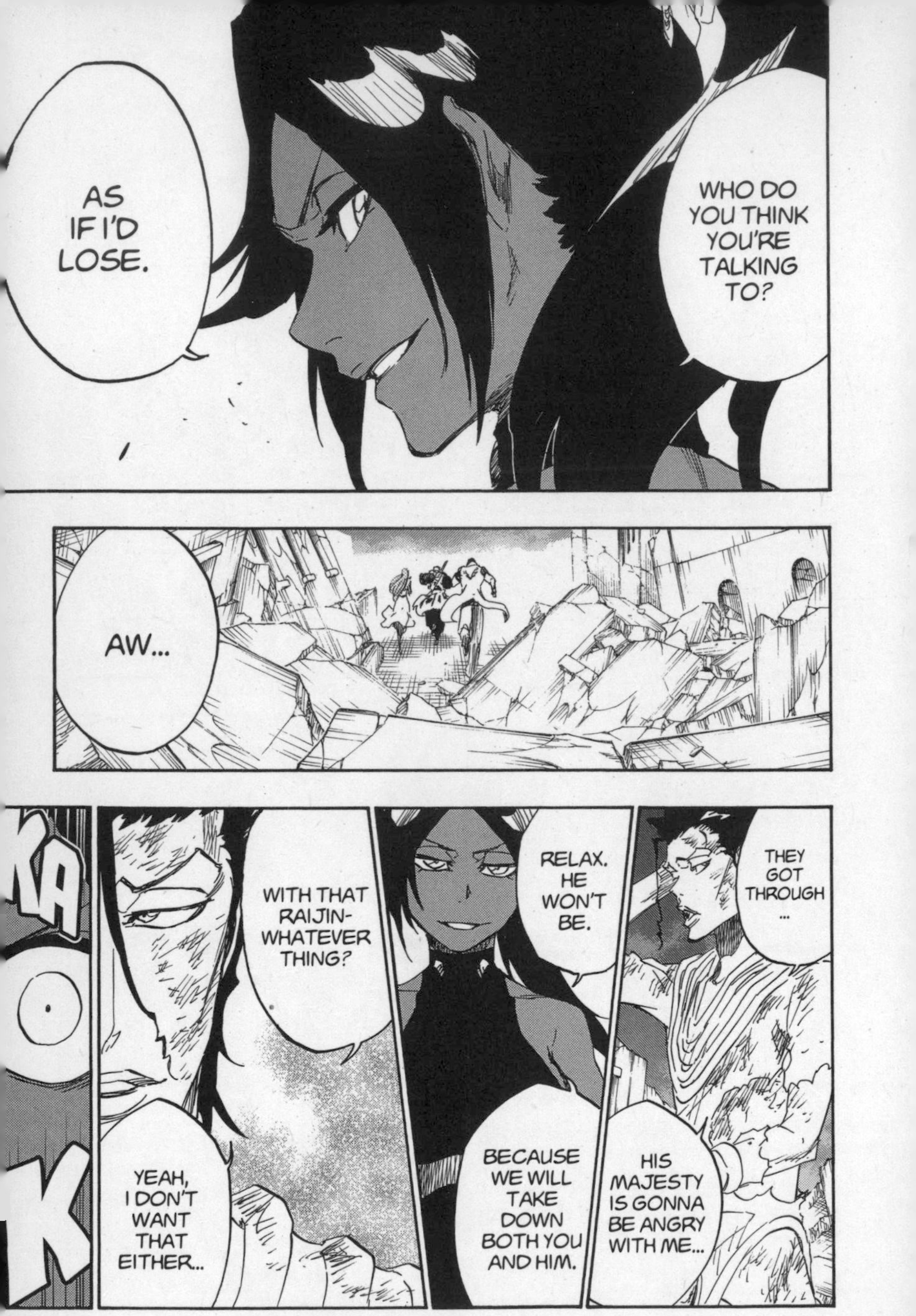
WHO DO YOU THINK YOU'RE TALKING TO?
AS IF I'D LOSE.
AW...
THEY GOT THROUGH ...
HIS MAJESTY IS GONNA BE ANGRY WITH ME...
RELAX. HE WON'T BE.
BECAUSE WE WILL TAKE DOWN BOTH YOU AND HIM.
WITH THAT RAIJIN-WHATEVER THING?
YEAH, I DON'T WANT THAT EITHER...

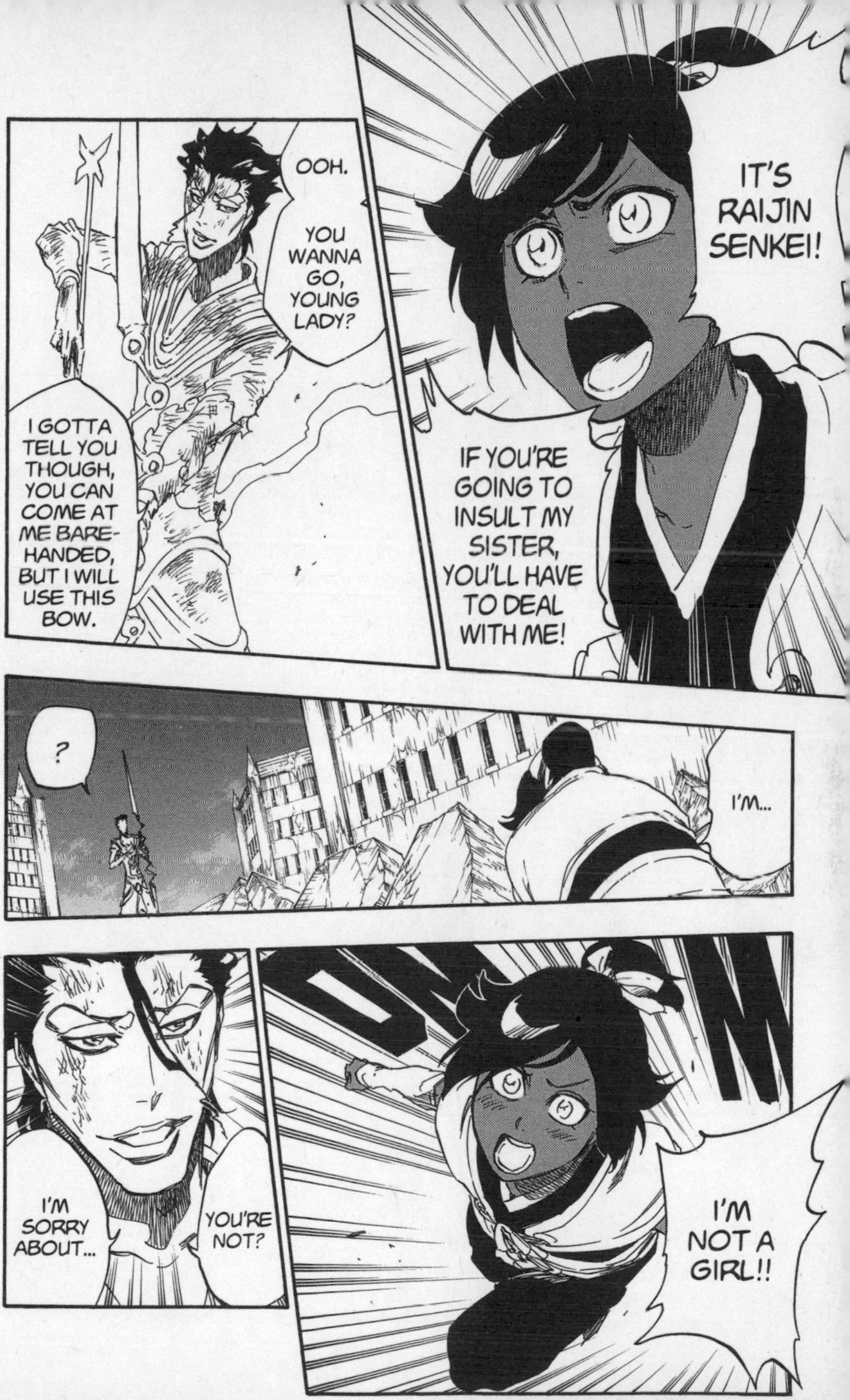
IT'S RAIJIN SENKEI!
IF YOU'RE GOING TO INSULT MY SISTER, YOU'LL HAVE TO DEAL WITH ME!
OOH.
YOU WANNA GO, YOUNG LADY?
I GOTTA TELL YOU THOUGH, YOU CAN COME AT ME BARE-HANDED, BUT I WILL USE THIS BOW.
I'M...
?
I'M NOT A GIRL!!
YOU'RE NOT?
I'M SORRY ABOUT...

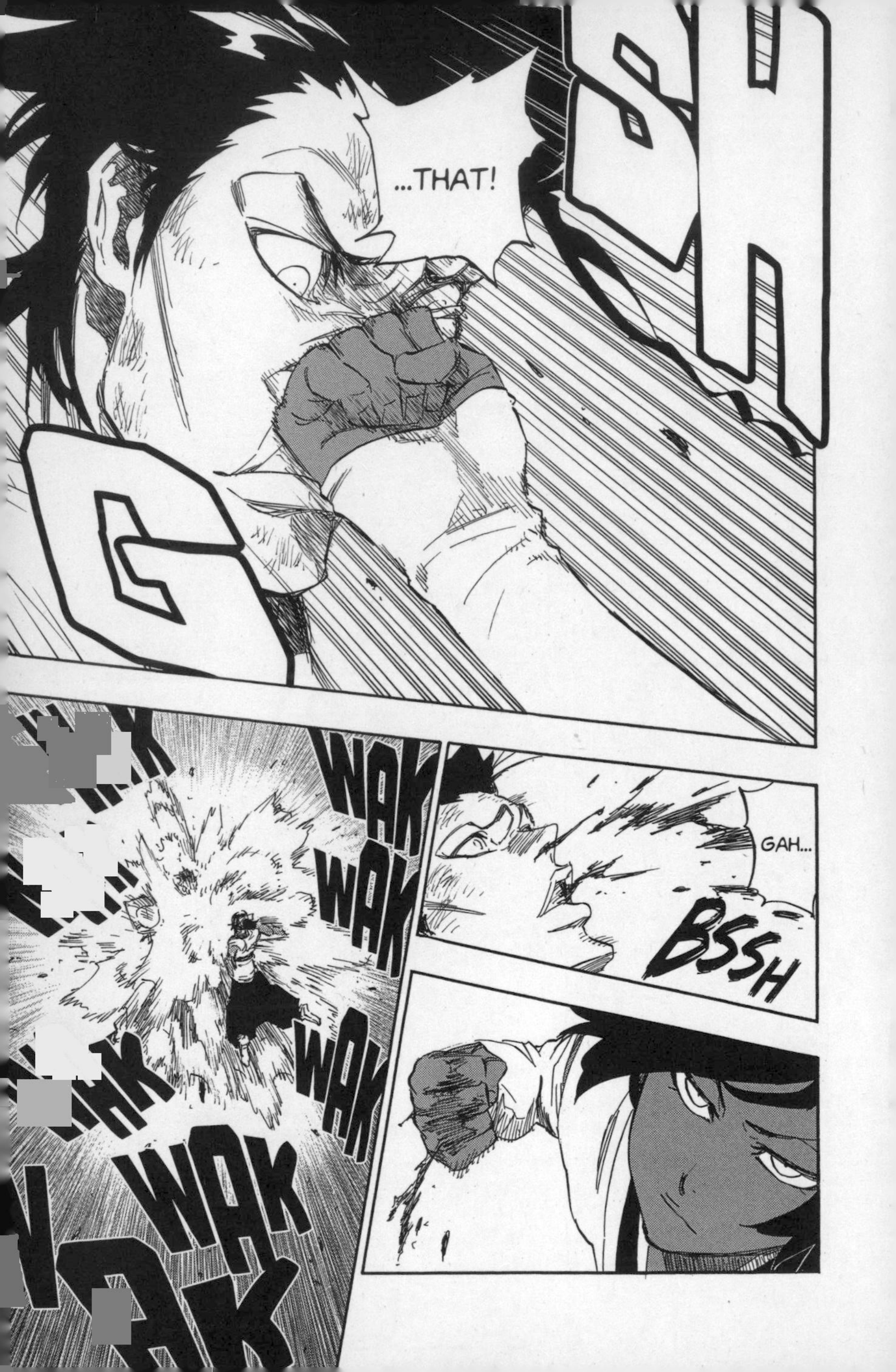
...THAT!
GAH...
BSSH
WAK
WAK
WAK
WAK
WAK

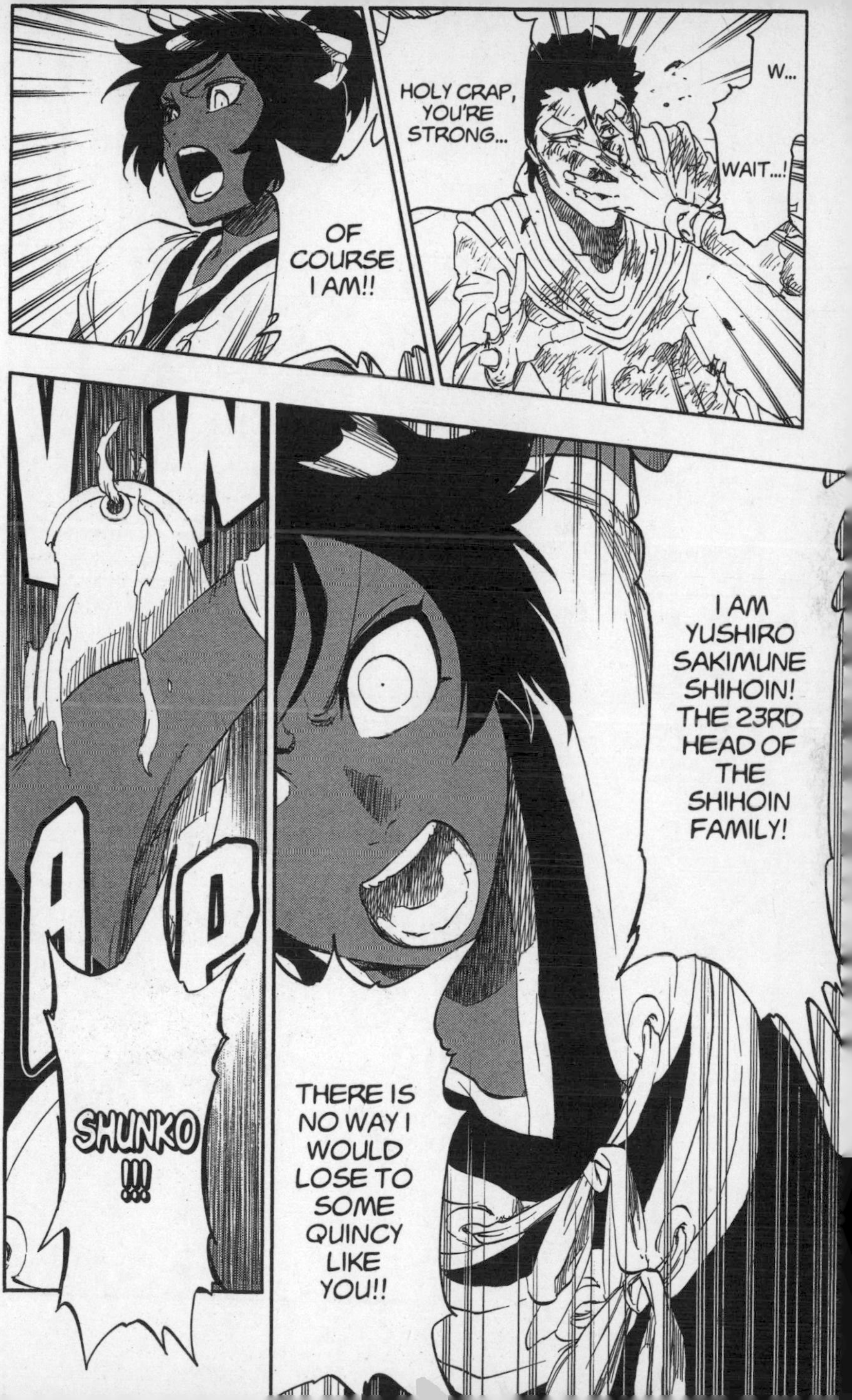
W...
WAIT...!
HOLY CRAP, YOU'RE STRONG...
OF COURSE I AM!!
I AM YUSHIRO SAKIMUNE SHIHOIN! THE 23RD HEAD OF THE SHIHOIN FAMILY!
THERE IS NO WAY I WOULD LOSE TO SOME QUINCY LIKE YOU!!
SHUNKO!!!

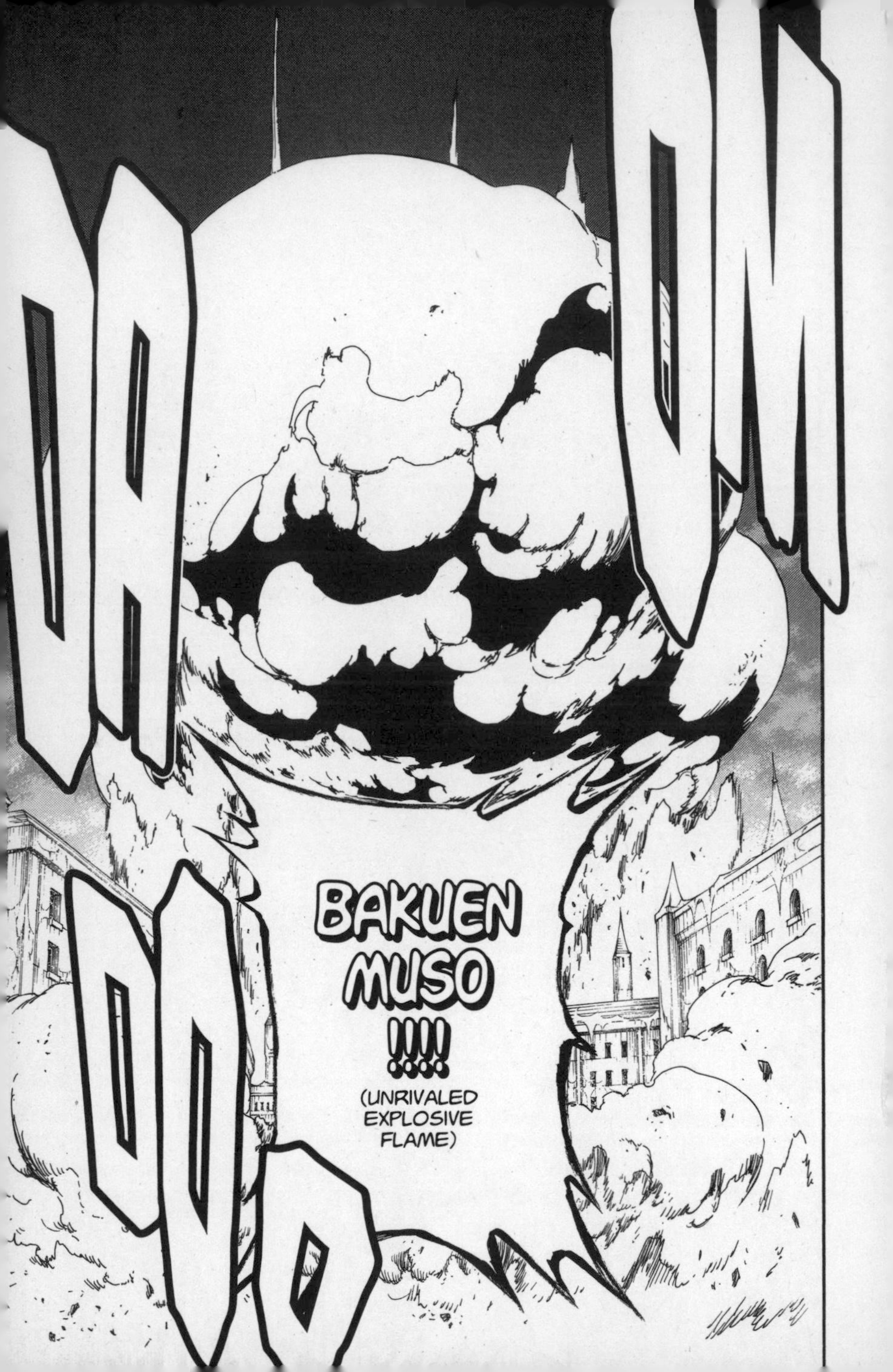
BAKUEN MUSO !!!!
(UNRIVALED EXPLOSIVE FLAME)

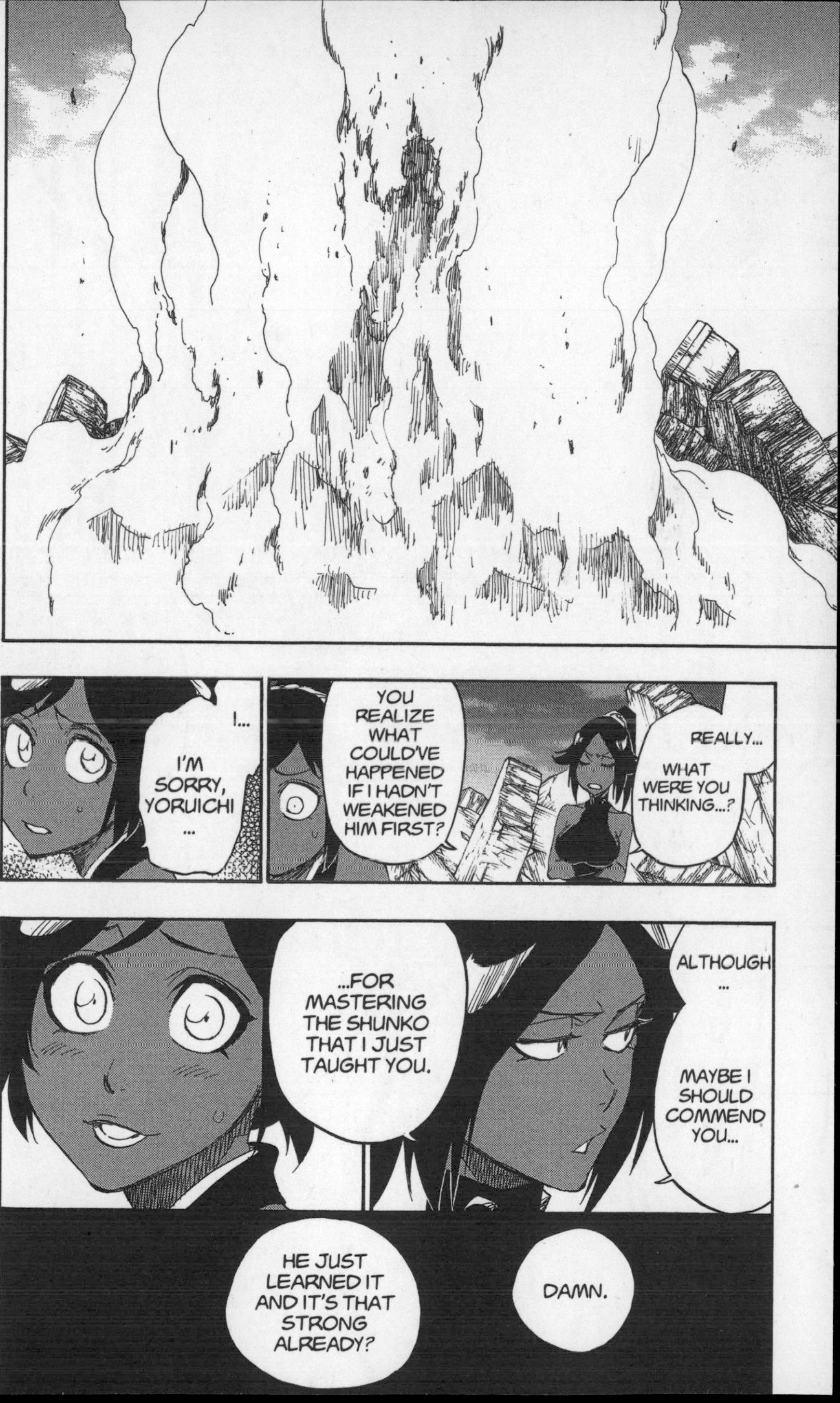
REALLY...
WHAT WERE YOU THINKING...?
YOU REALIZE WHAT COULD'VE HAPPENED IF I HADN'T WEAKENED HIM FIRST?
I...
I'M SORRY, YORUICHI...
ALTHOUGH...
MAYBE I SHOULD COMMEND YOU...
...FOR MASTERING THE SHUNKO THAT I JUST TAUGHT YOU.
DAMN.
HE JUST LEARNED IT AND IT'S THAT STRONG ALREADY?

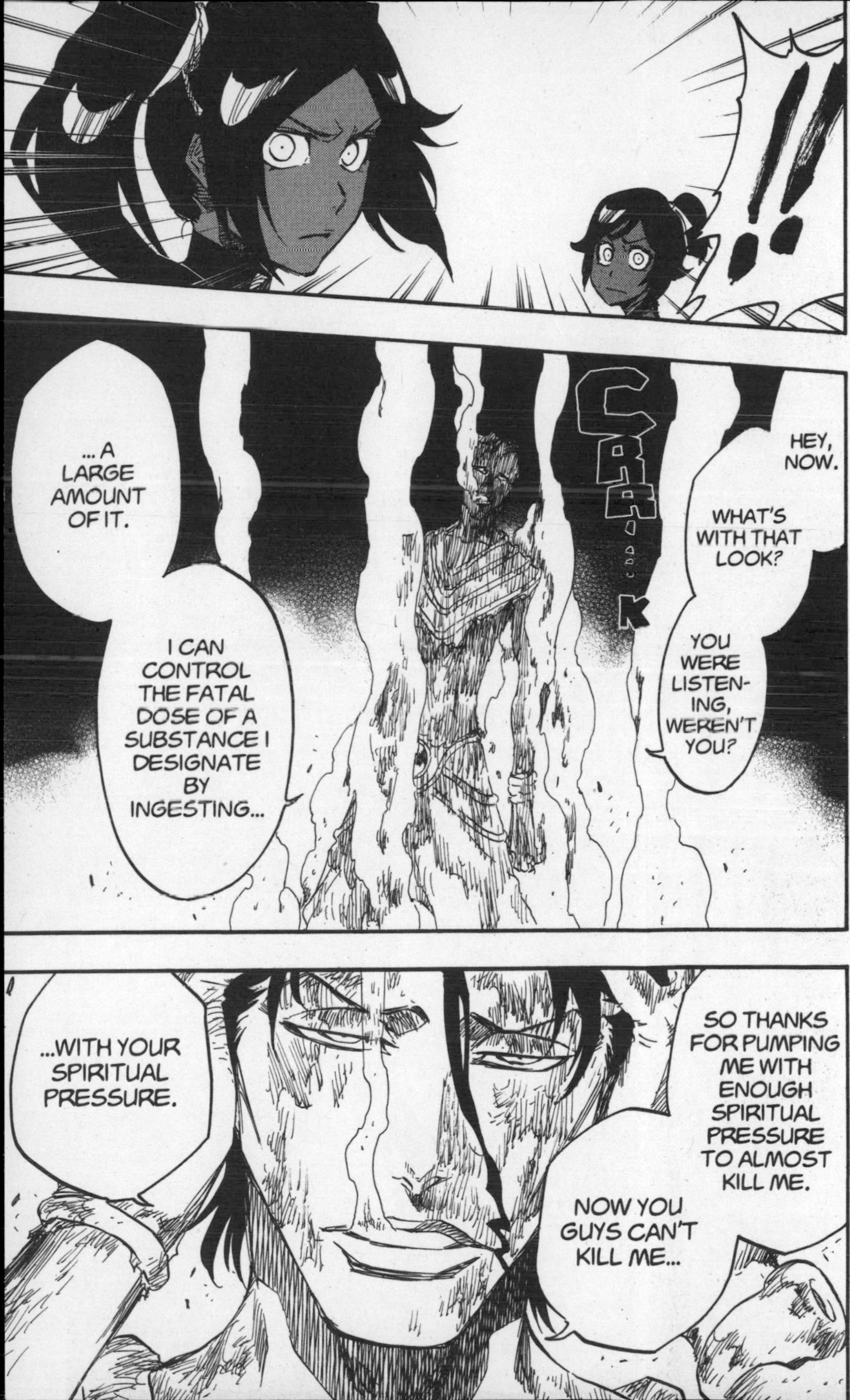
!!
HEY, NOW.
WHAT'S WITH THAT LOOK?
YOU WERE LISTENING, WEREN'T YOU?
CRA...K
I CAN CONTROL THE FATAL DOSE OF A SUBSTANCE I DESIGNATE BY INGESTING...
...A LARGE AMOUNT OF IT.
SO THANKS FOR PUMPING ME WITH ENOUGH SPIRITUAL PRESSURE TO ALMOST KILL ME.
NOW YOU GUYS CAN'T KILL ME...
...WITH YOUR SPIRITUAL PRESSURE.

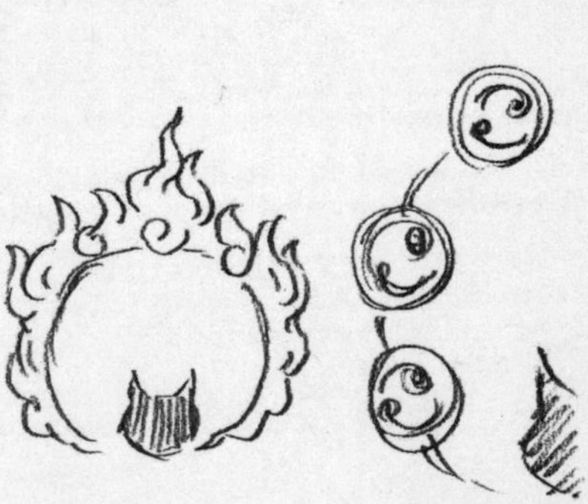

658.FATAL MATTERS ARE COLD

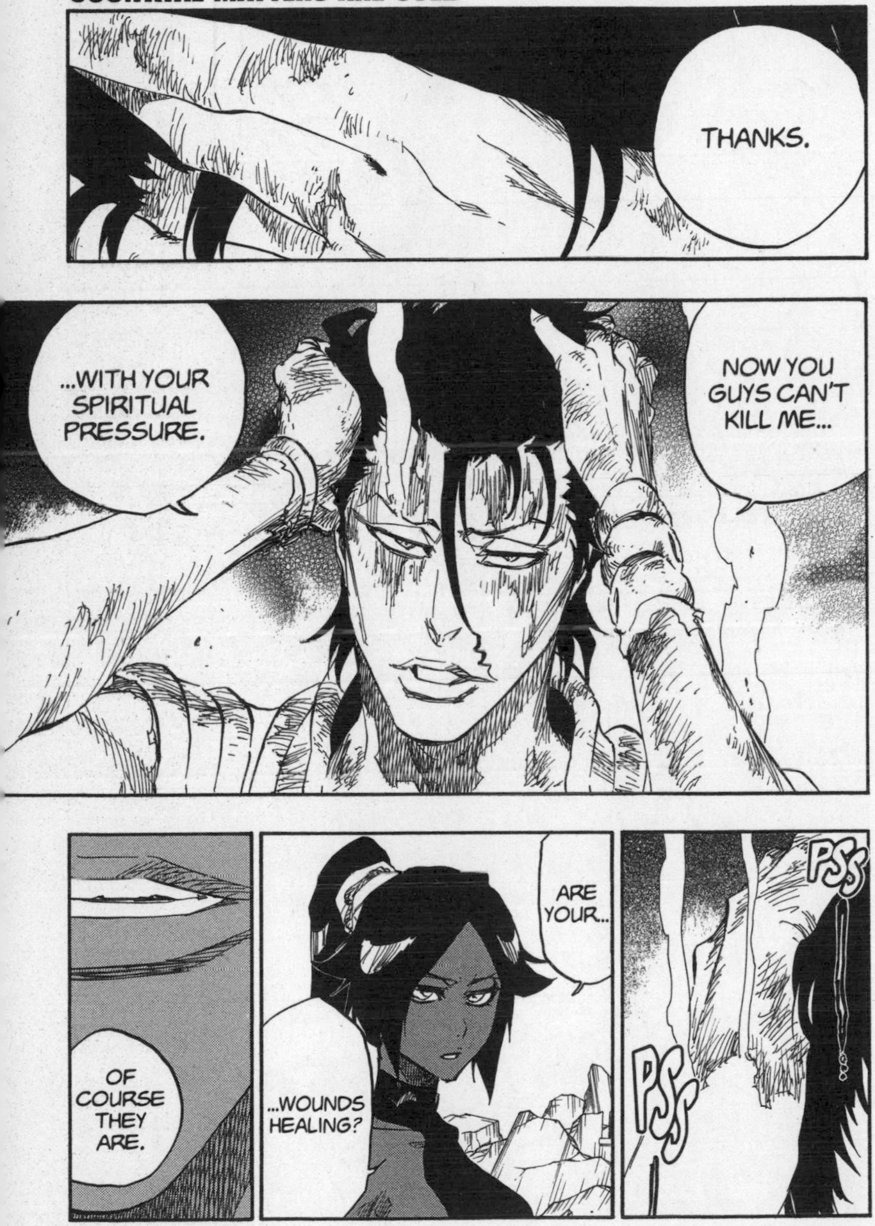
THANKS.
NOW YOU GUYS CAN'T KILL ME...
...WITH YOUR SPIRITUAL PRESSURE.
PSS
PSS
ARE YOUR...
...WOUNDS HEALING?
OF COURSE THEY ARE.

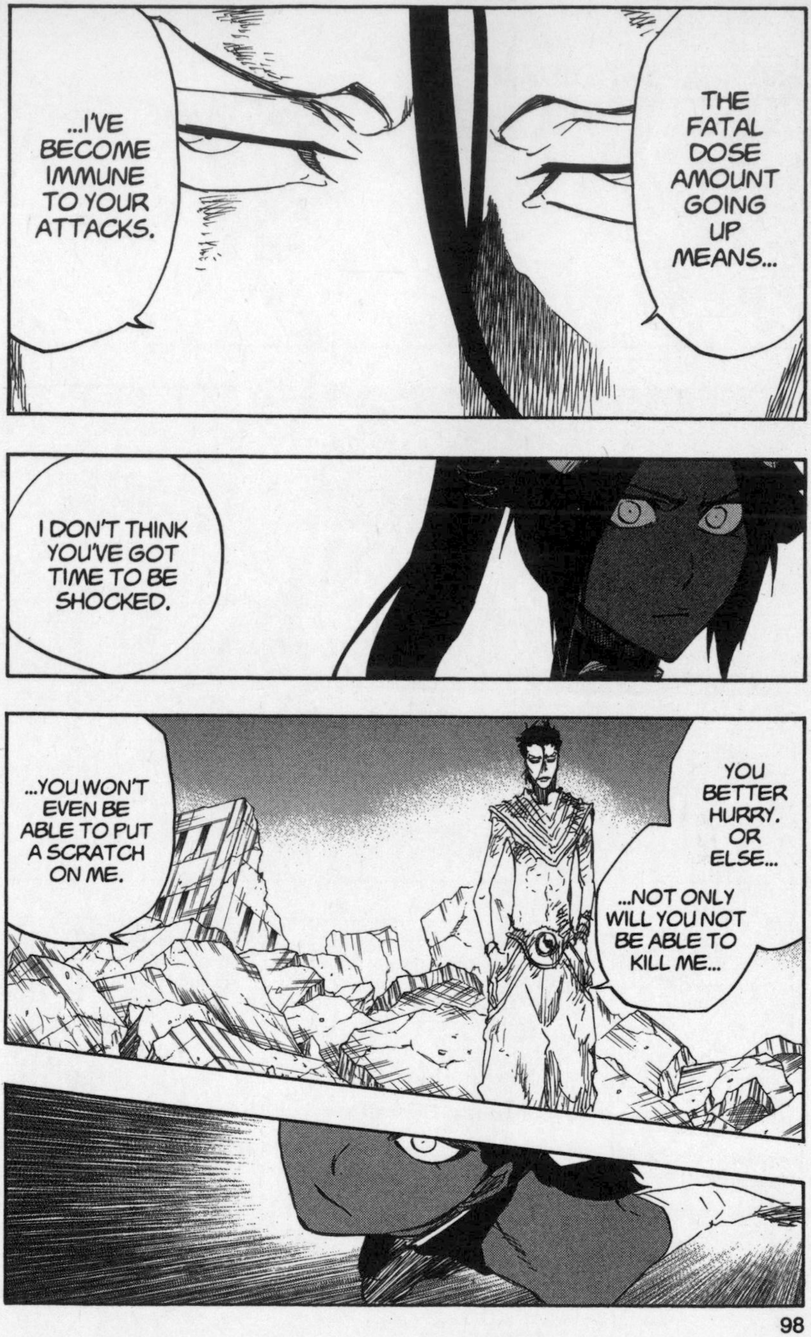
THE FATAL DOSE AMOUNT GOING UP MEANS...
...I'VE BECOME IMMUNE TO YOUR ATTACKS.
I DON'T THINK YOU'VE GOT TIME TO BE SHOCKED.
YOU BETTER HURRY. OR ELSE...
...NOT ONLY WILL YOU NOT BE ABLE TO KILL ME...
...YOU WON'T EVEN BE ABLE TO PUT A SCRATCH ON ME.

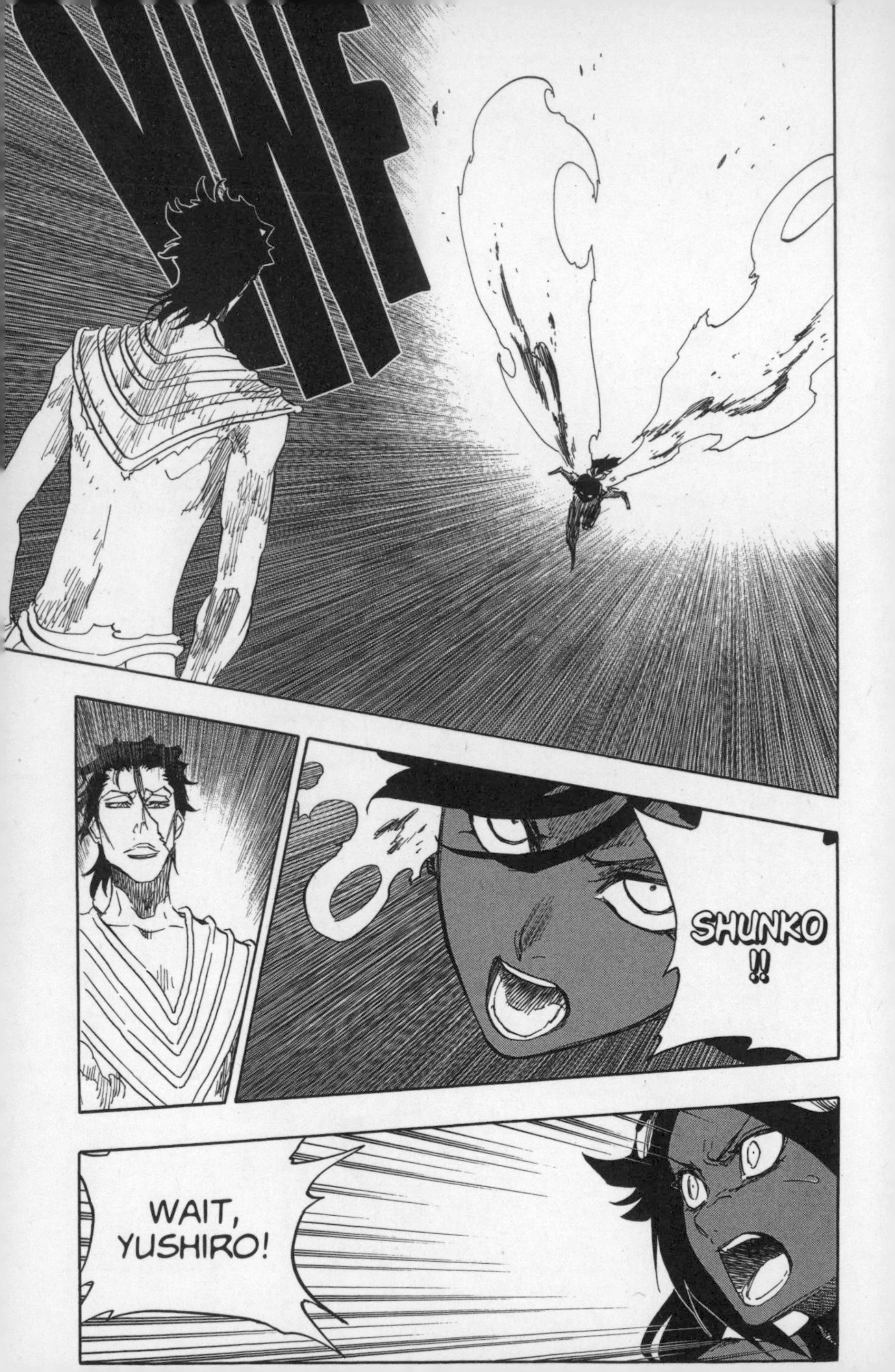
SHUNKO !!
WAIT, YUSHIRO!

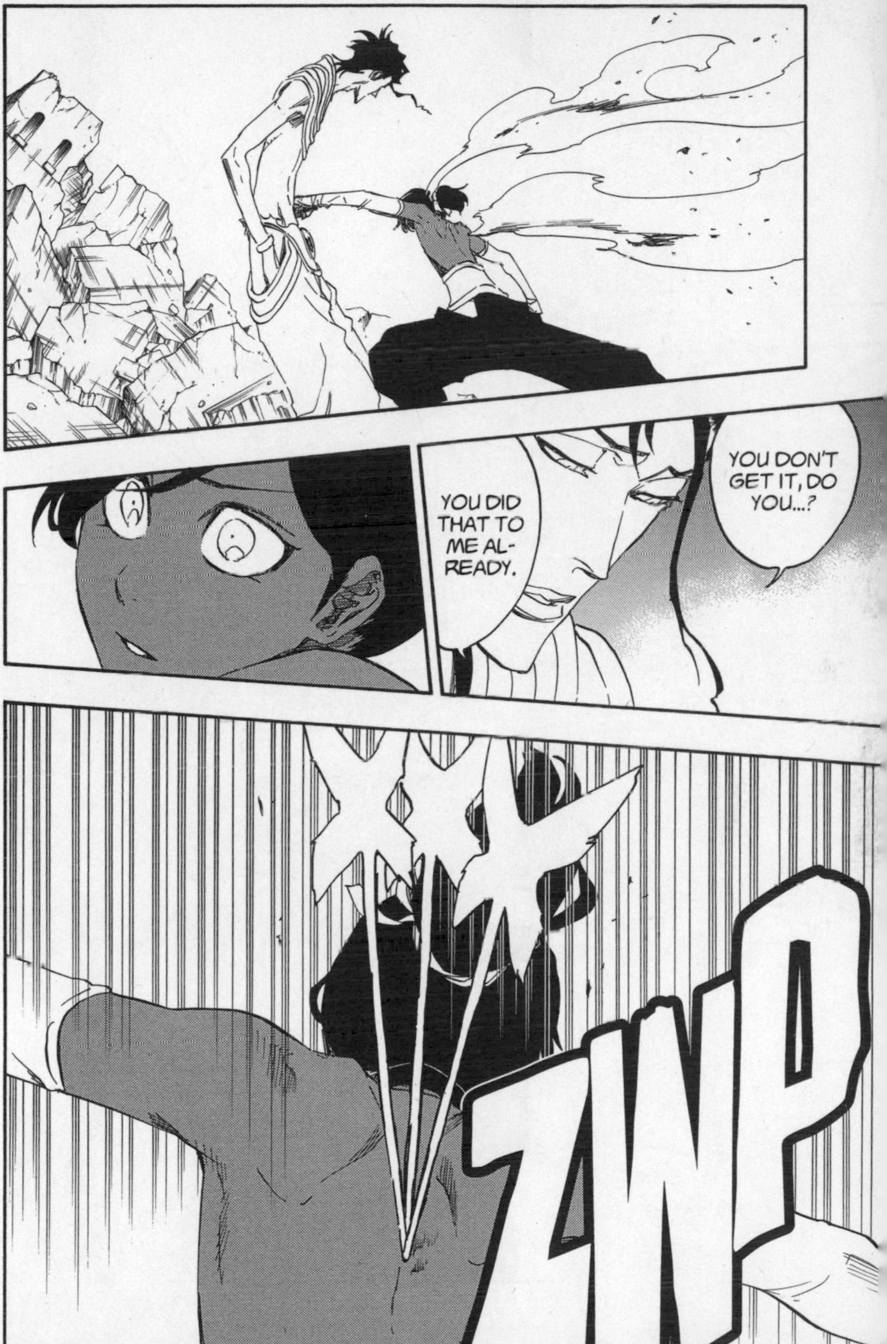
YOU DON'T GET IT, DO YOU...?
YOU DID THAT TO ME AL-READY.
ZWIP

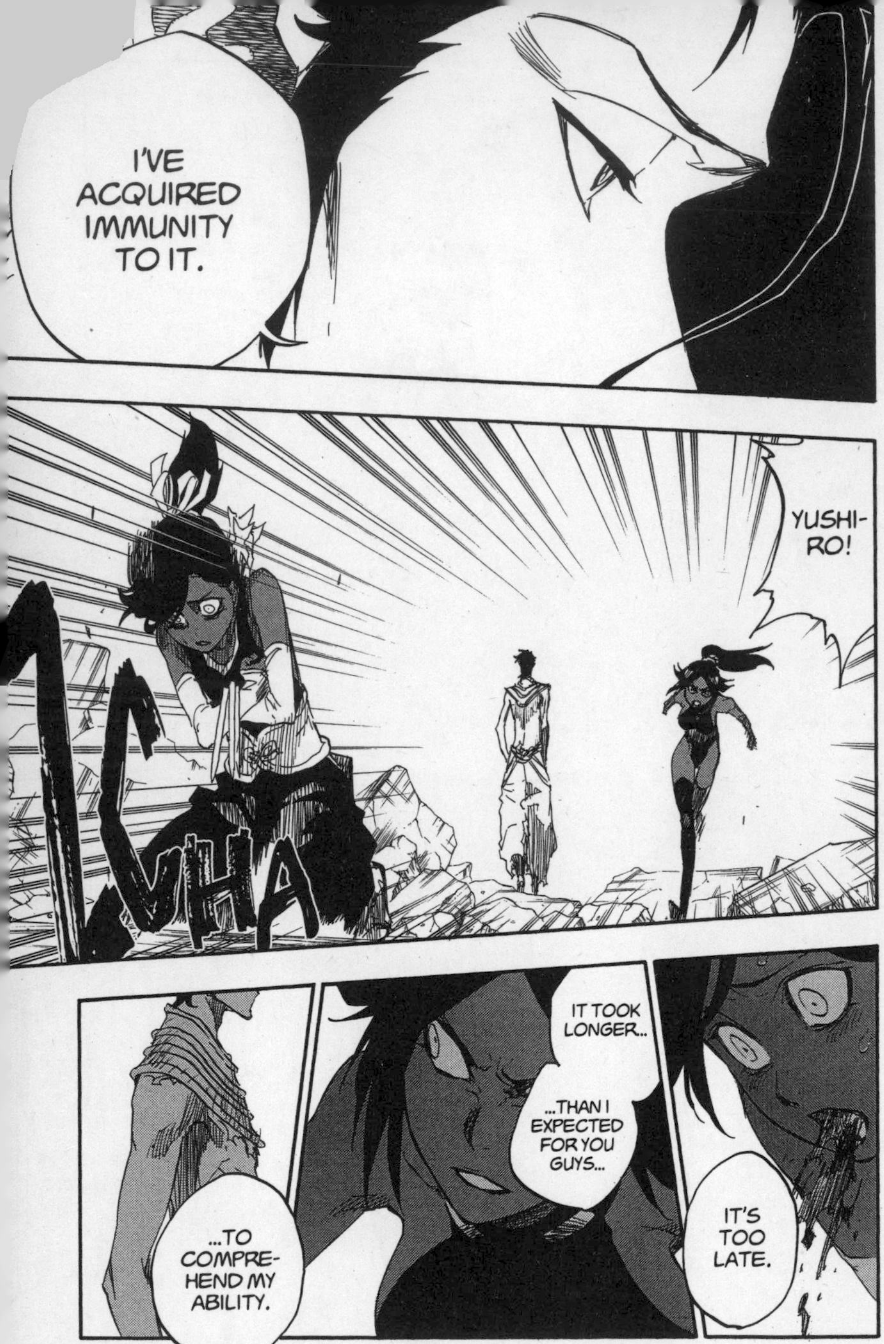
I'VE ACQUIRED IMMUNITY TO IT.
YUSHIRO!
WHA
IT'S TOO LATE.
IT TOOK LONGER...
...THAN I EXPECTED FOR YOU GUYS...
...TO COMPREHEND MY ABILITY.

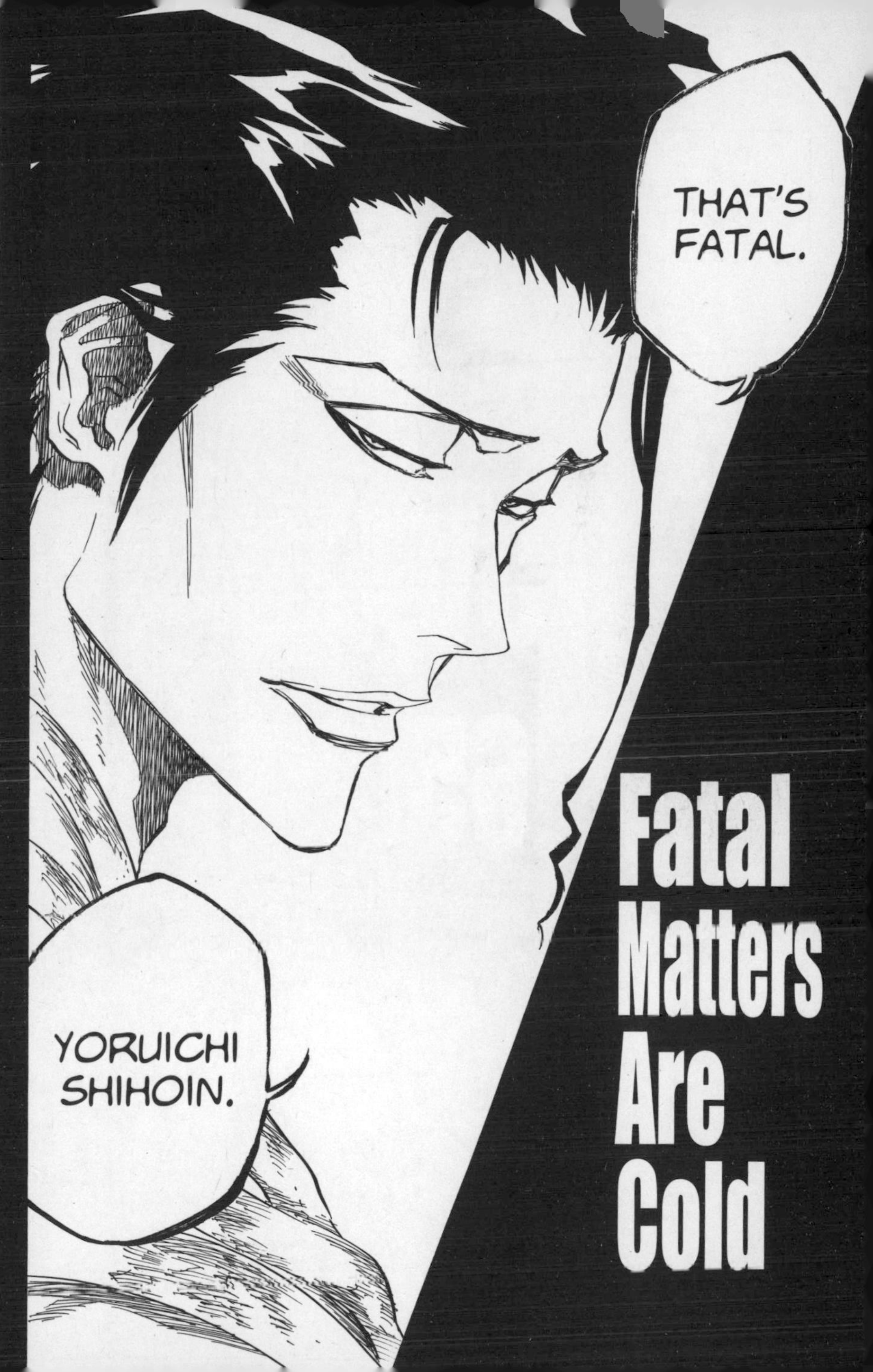
THAT'S FATAL.
Fatal Matters Are Cold
YORUICHI SHIHOIN.

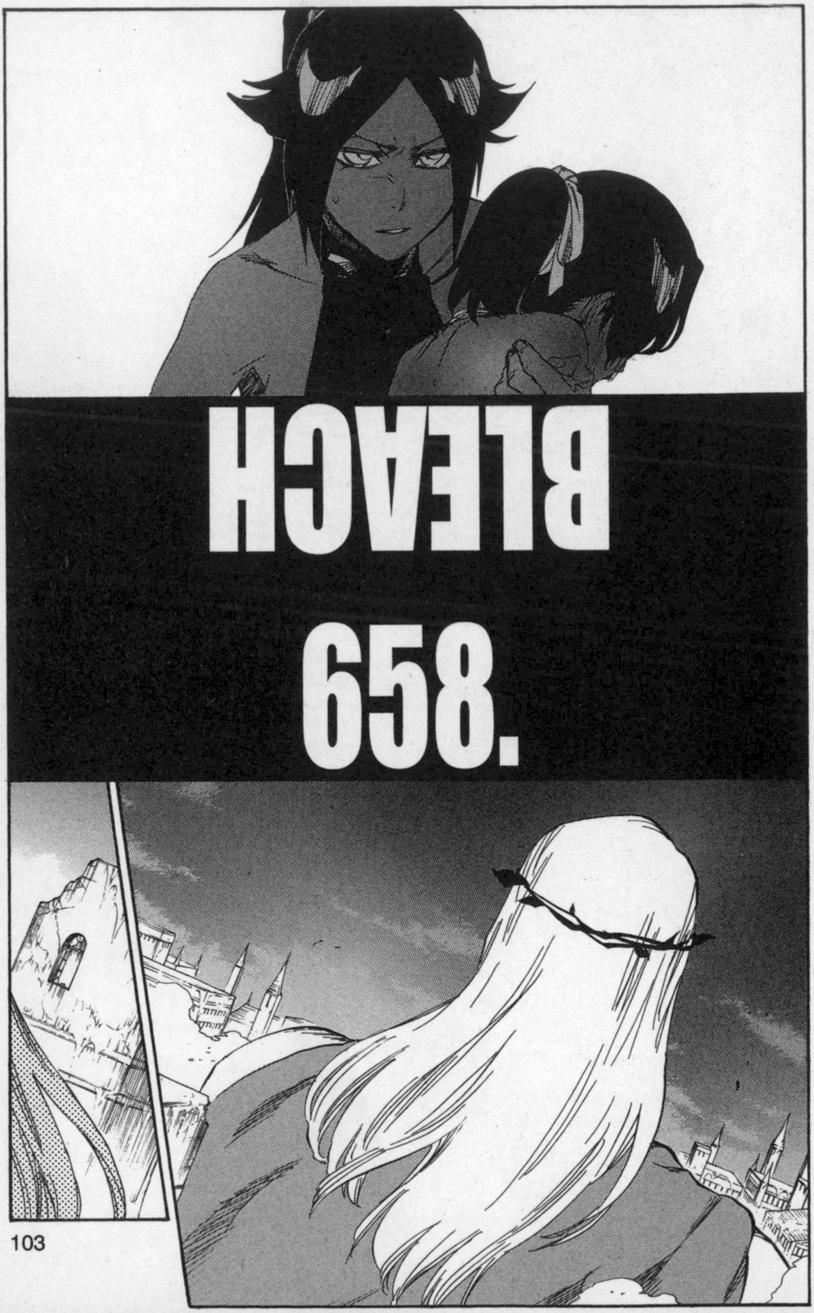
BLEACH
658.

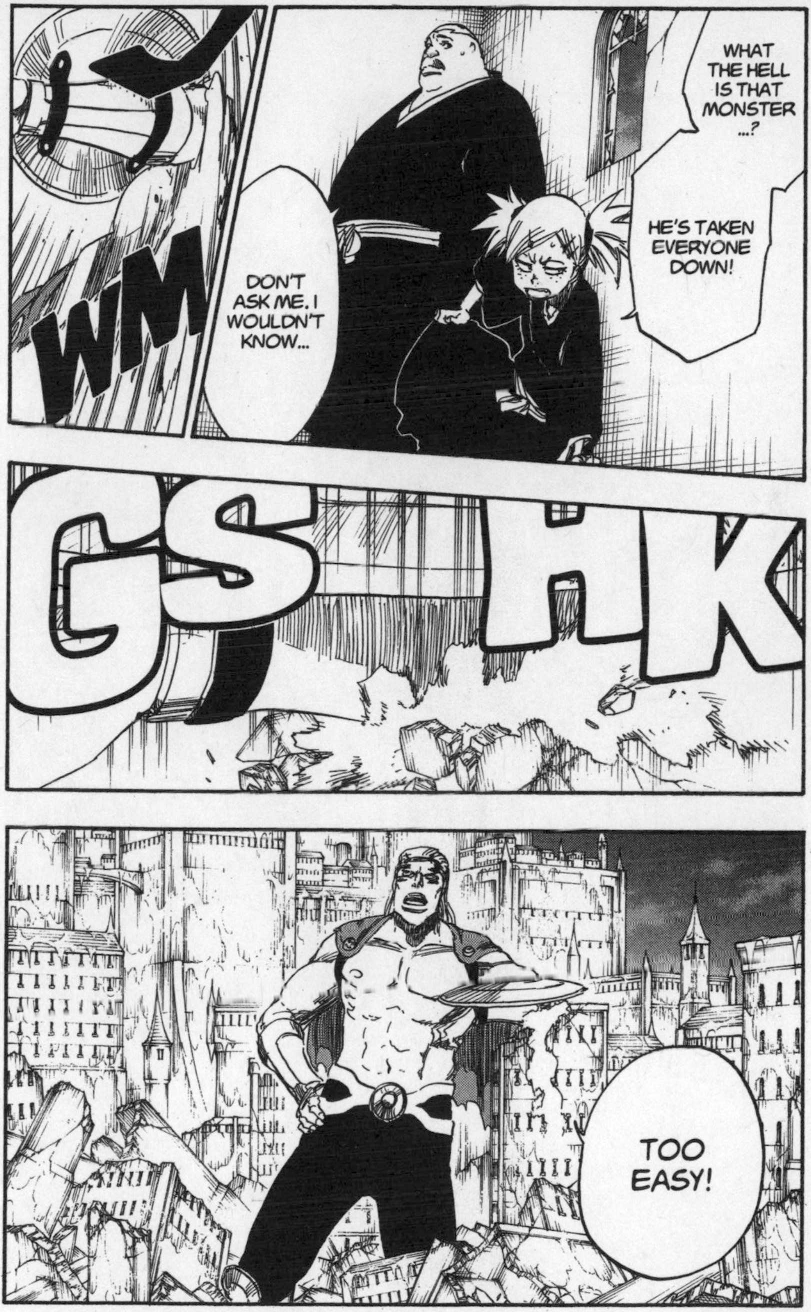
WHAT THE HELL IS THAT MONSTER ...?
HE'S TAKEN EVERYONE DOWN!
DON'T ASK ME. I WOULDN'T KNOW...
WM
GSHK
TOO EASY!

READ THIS WAY

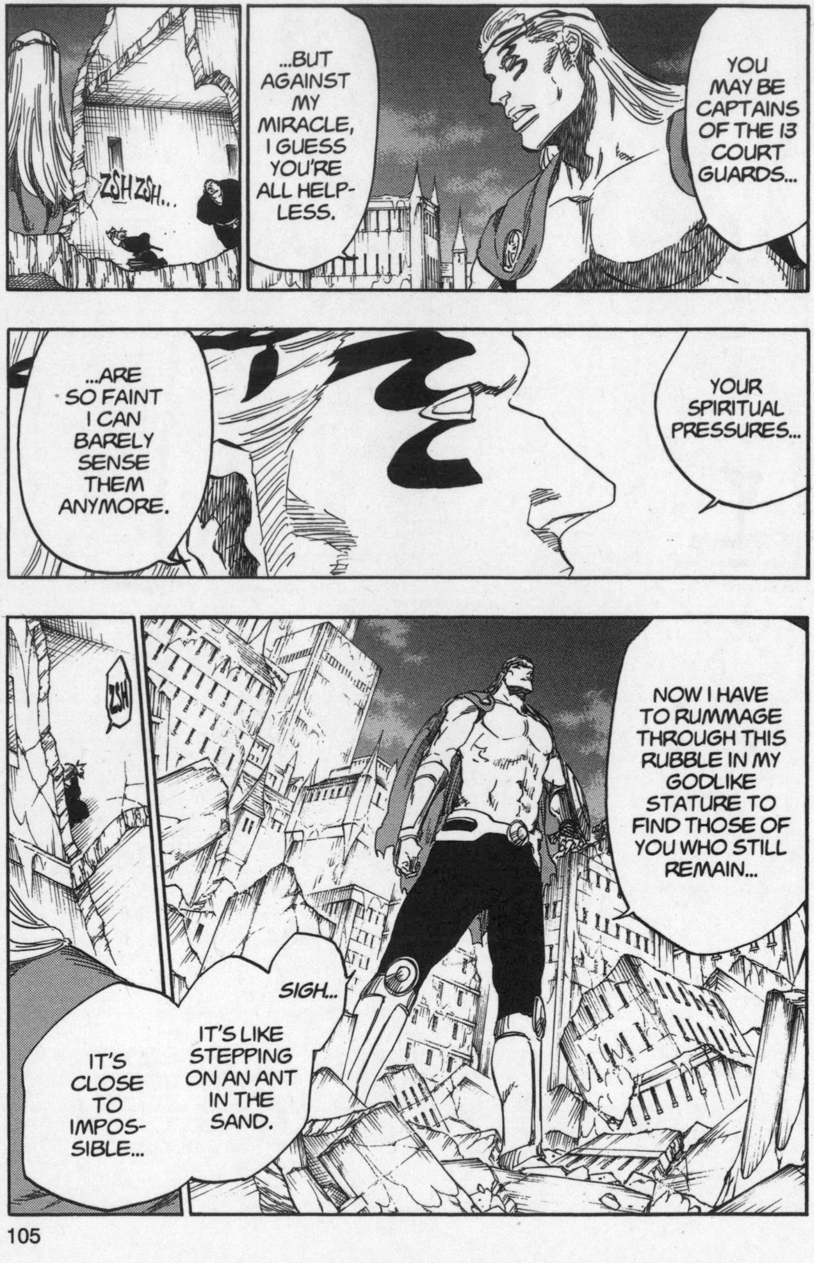
YOU MAY BE CAPTAINS OF THE 13 COURT GUARDS...
...BUT AGAINST MY MIRACLE, I GUESS YOU'RE ALL HELPLESS.
ZSH ZSH...
YOUR SPIRITUAL PRESSURES...
...ARE SO FAINT I CAN BARELY SENSE THEM ANYMORE.
NOW I HAVE TO RUMMAGE THROUGH THIS RUBBLE IN MY GODLIKE STATURE TO FIND THOSE OF YOU WHO STILL REMAIN...
SIGH...
IT'S LIKE STEPPING ON AN ANT IN THE SAND.
IT'S CLOSE TO IMPOSSIBLE...
ZSH

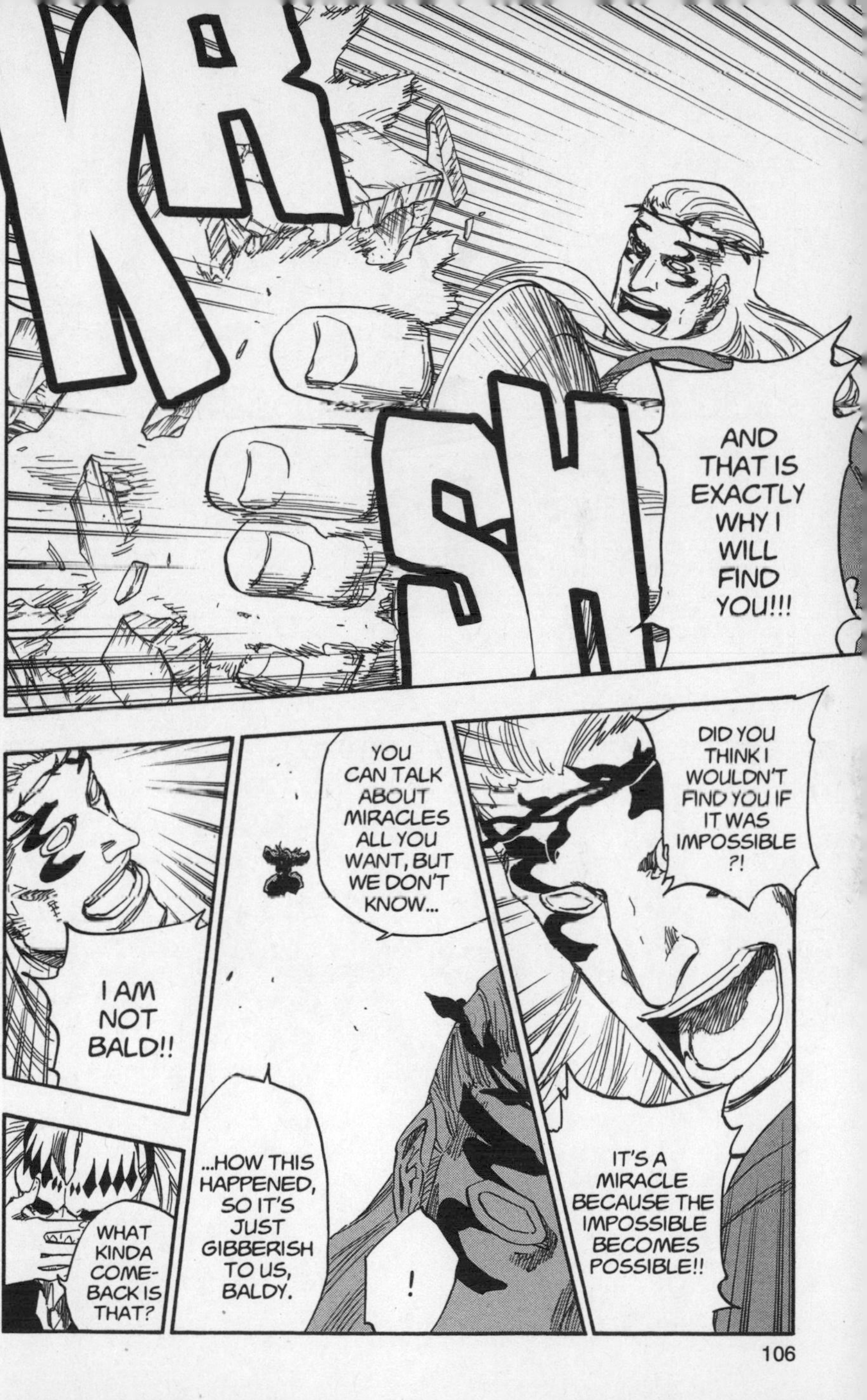
KRASH
AND THAT IS EXACTLY WHY I WILL FIND YOU!!!
DID YOU THINK I WOULDN'T FIND YOU IF IT WAS IMPOSSIBLE?!
IT'S A MIRACLE BECAUSE THE IMPOSSIBLE BECOMES POSSIBLE!!
YOU CAN TALK ABOUT MIRACLES ALL YOU WANT, BUT WE DON'T KNOW...
...HOW THIS HAPPENED, SO IT'S JUST GIBBERISH TO US, BALDY.
!
I AM NOT BALD!!
WHAT KINDA COME-BACK IS THAT?

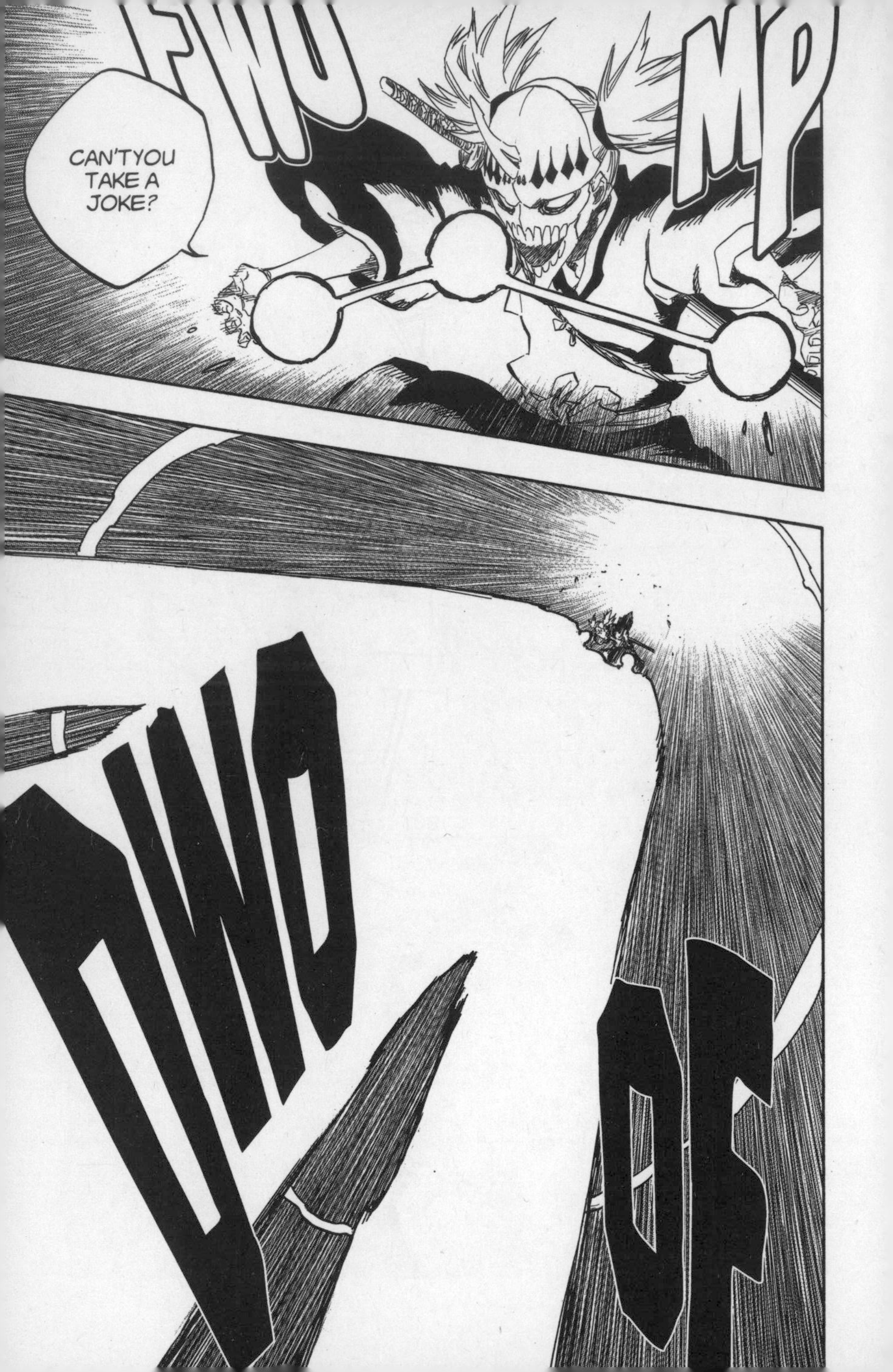
FWOMP
CAN'T YOU TAKE A JOKE?

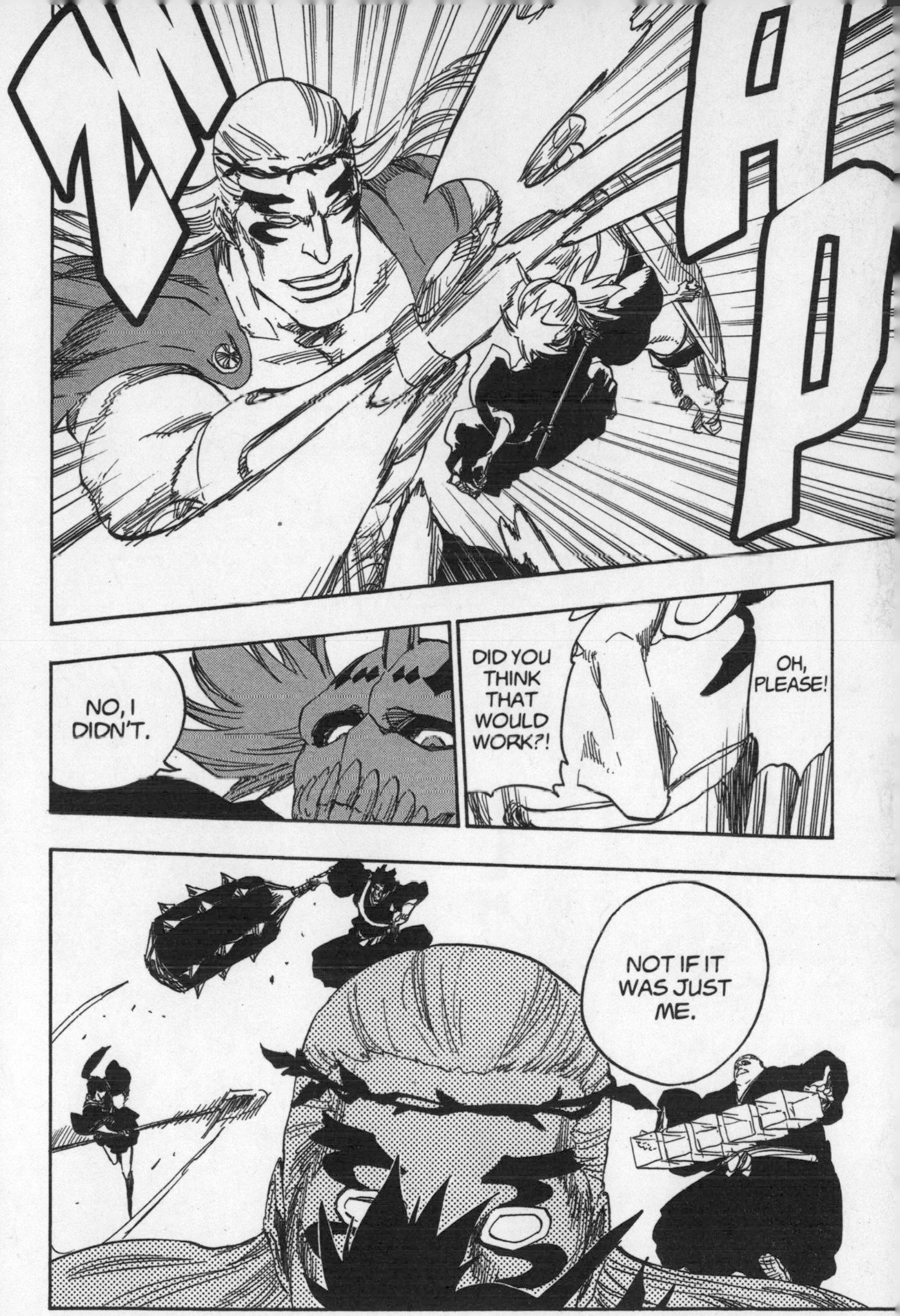
OH, PLEASE!
DID YOU THINK THAT WOULD WORK?!
NO, I DIDN'T.
NOT IF IT WAS JUST ME.

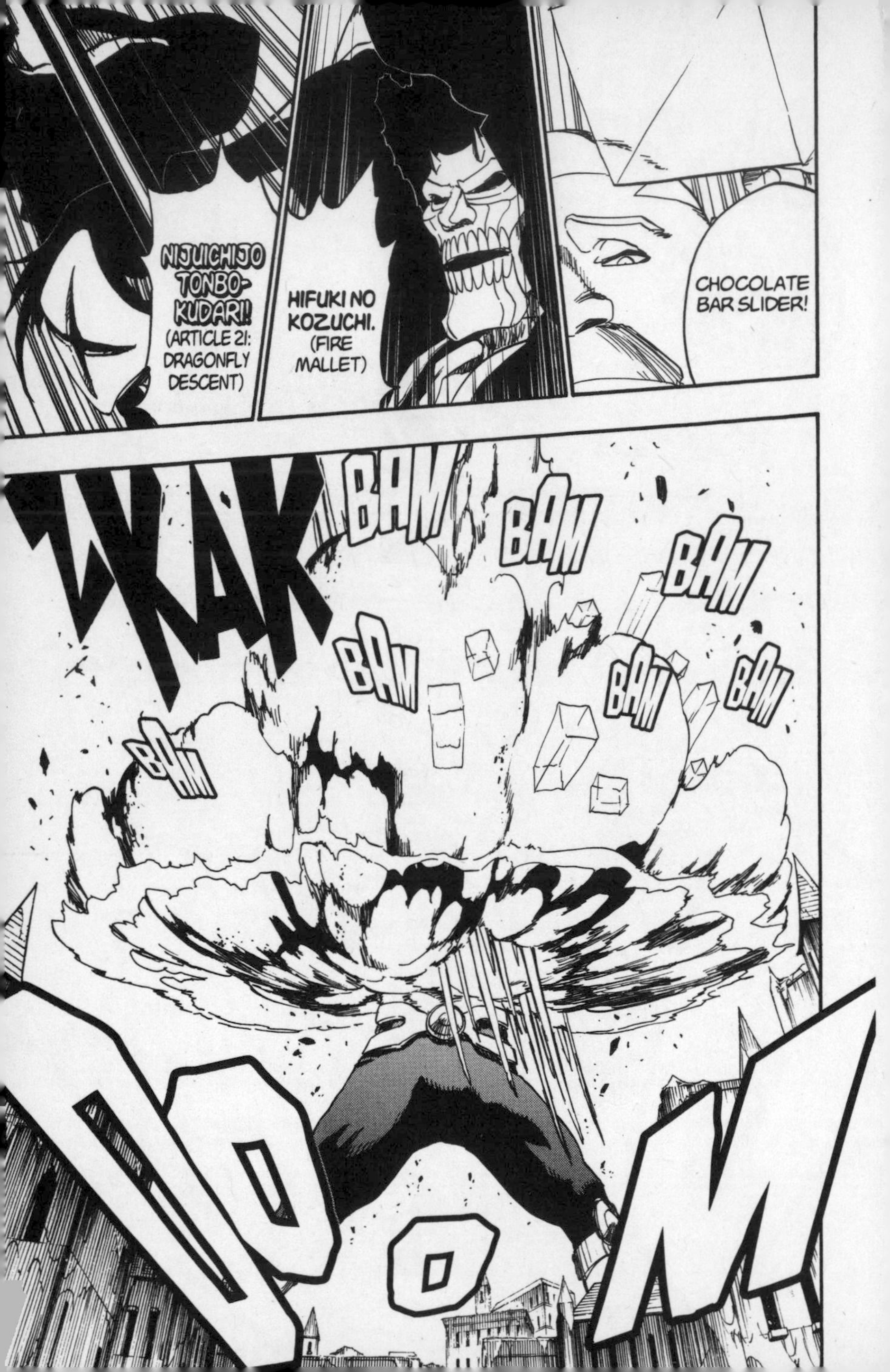
CHOCOLATE BAR SLIDER!
HIFUKI NO KOZUCHI. (FIRE MALLET)
NIJUICHIJO TONBO-KUDARI!! (ARTICLE 21: DRAGONFLY DESCENT)
BAM
BAM
BAM
BAM
BAM
BAM
ZKAK
BAM
BAM
DOOM!

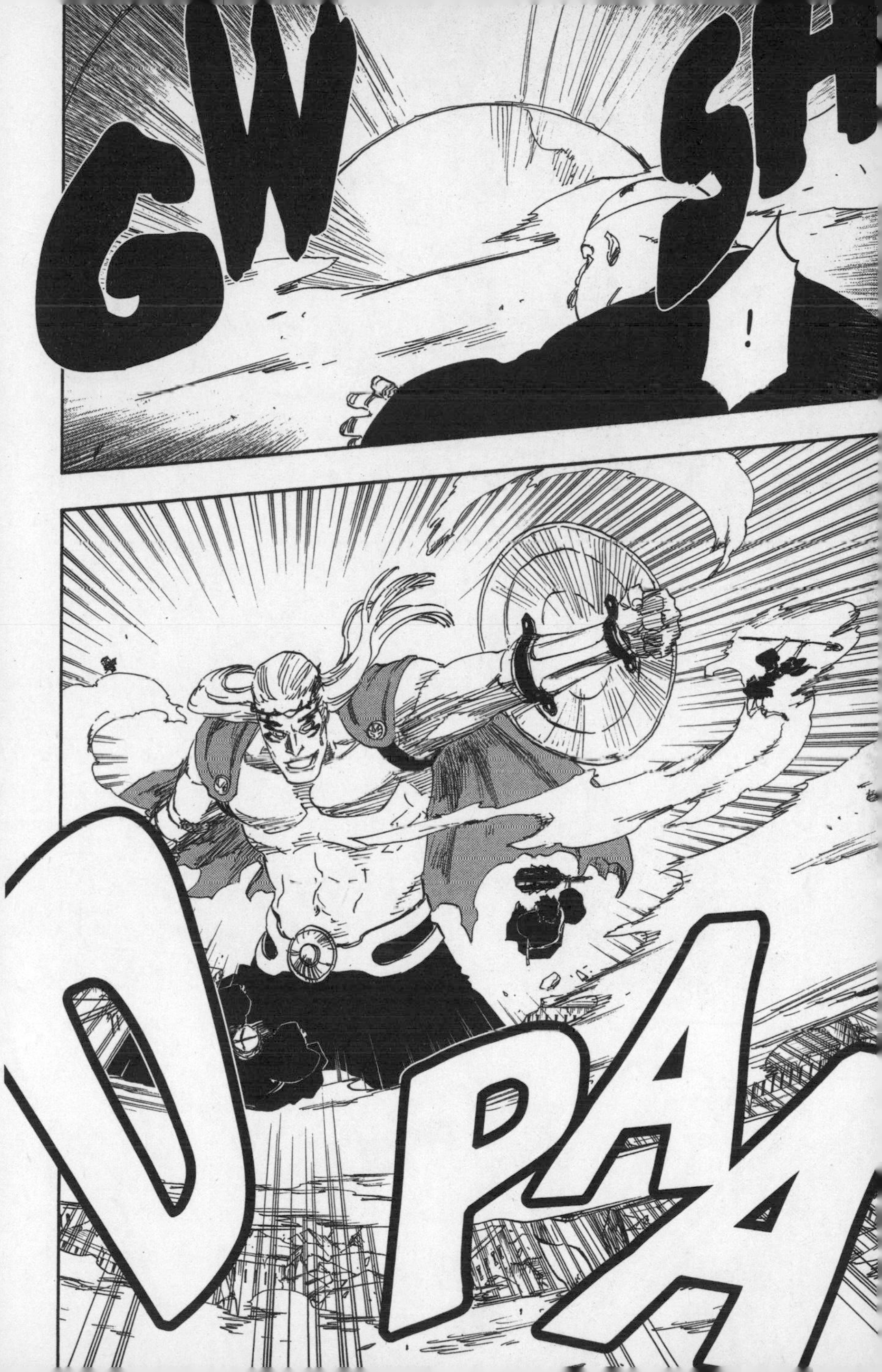
GWSH
!
DPA

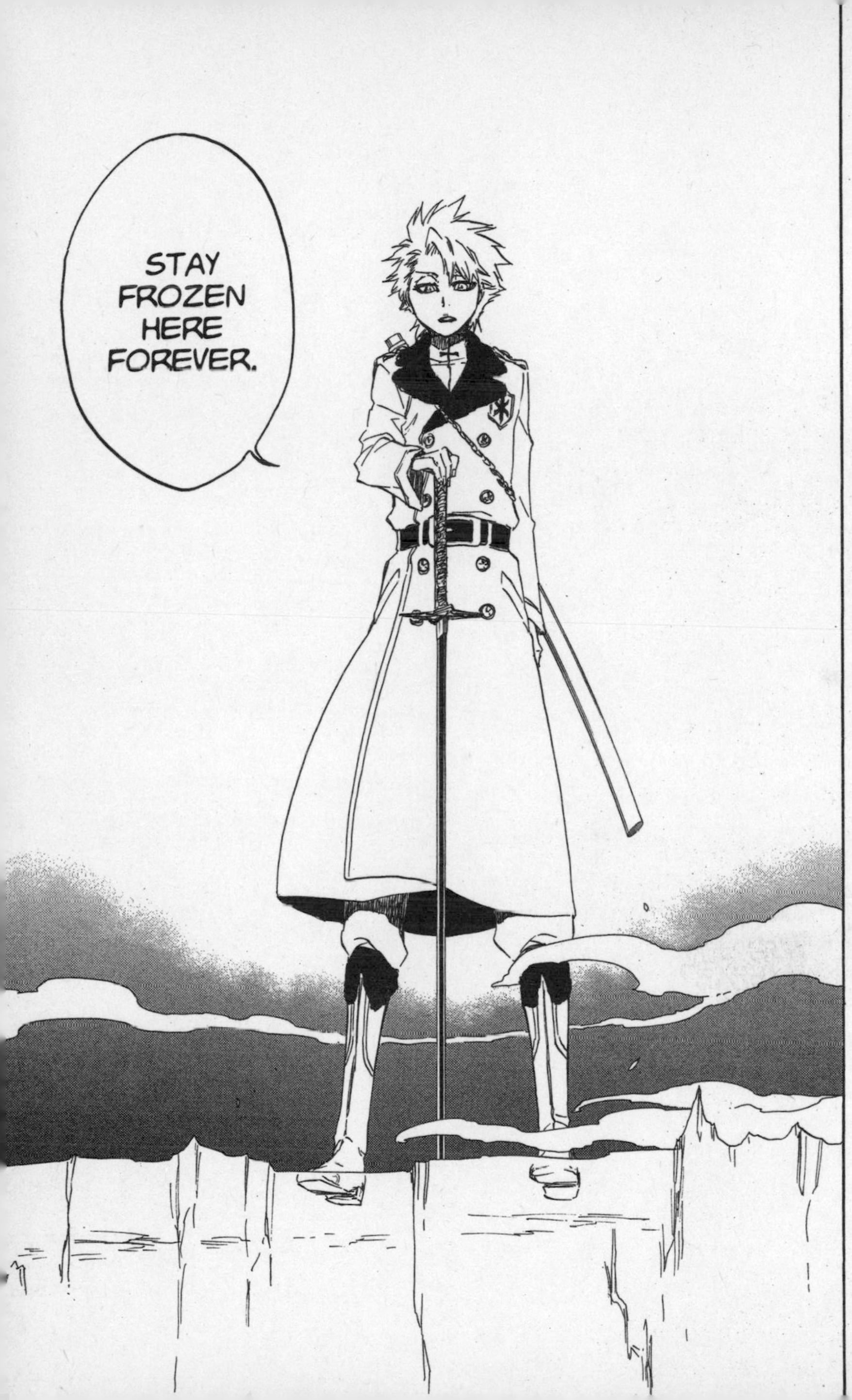
STAY FROZEN HERE FOREVER.

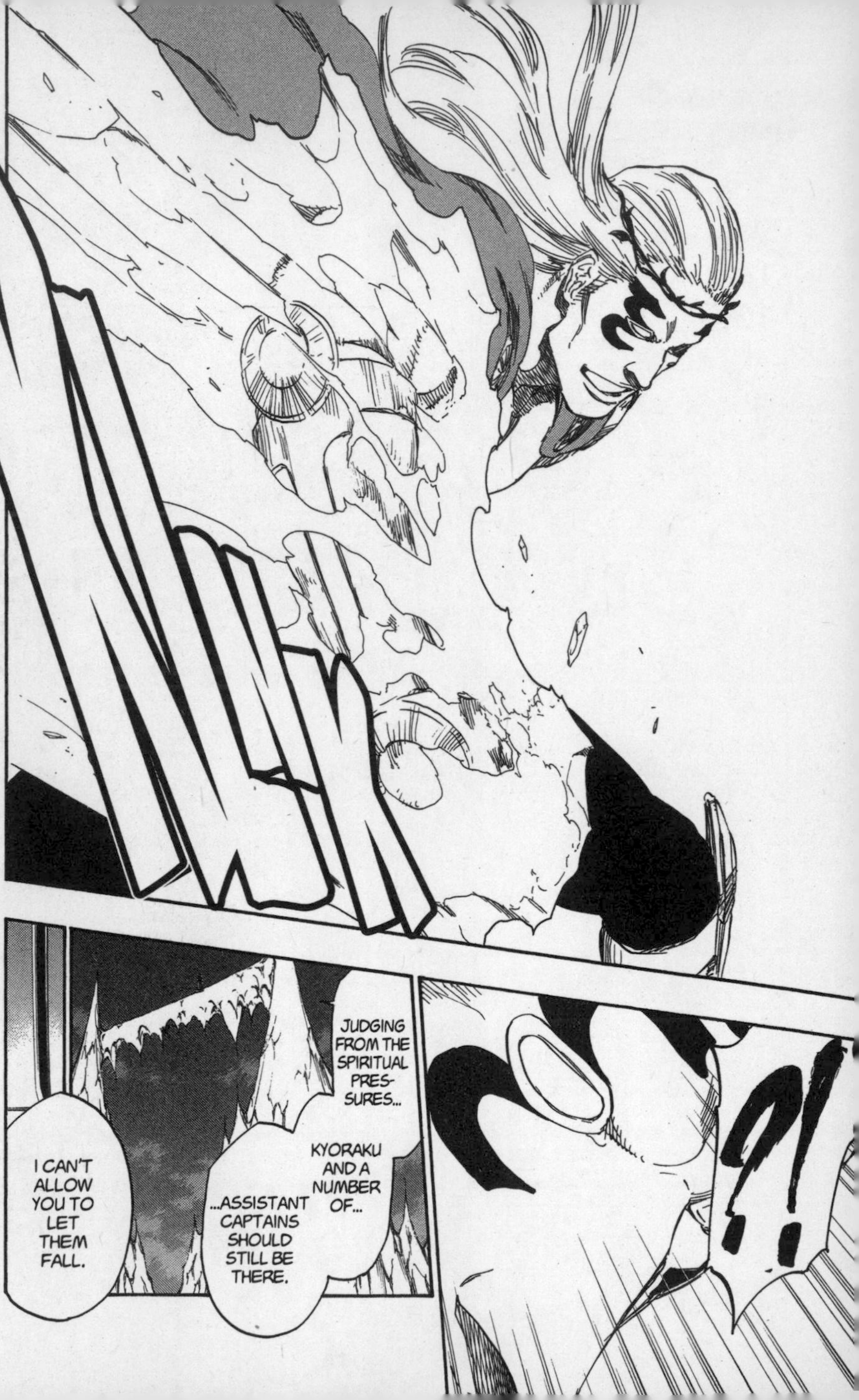
?!
JUDGING FROM THE SPIRITUAL PRES-SURES...
KYORAKU AND A NUMBER OF...
...ASSISTANT CAPTAINS SHOULD STILL BE THERE.
I CAN'T ALLOW YOU TO LET THEM FALL.

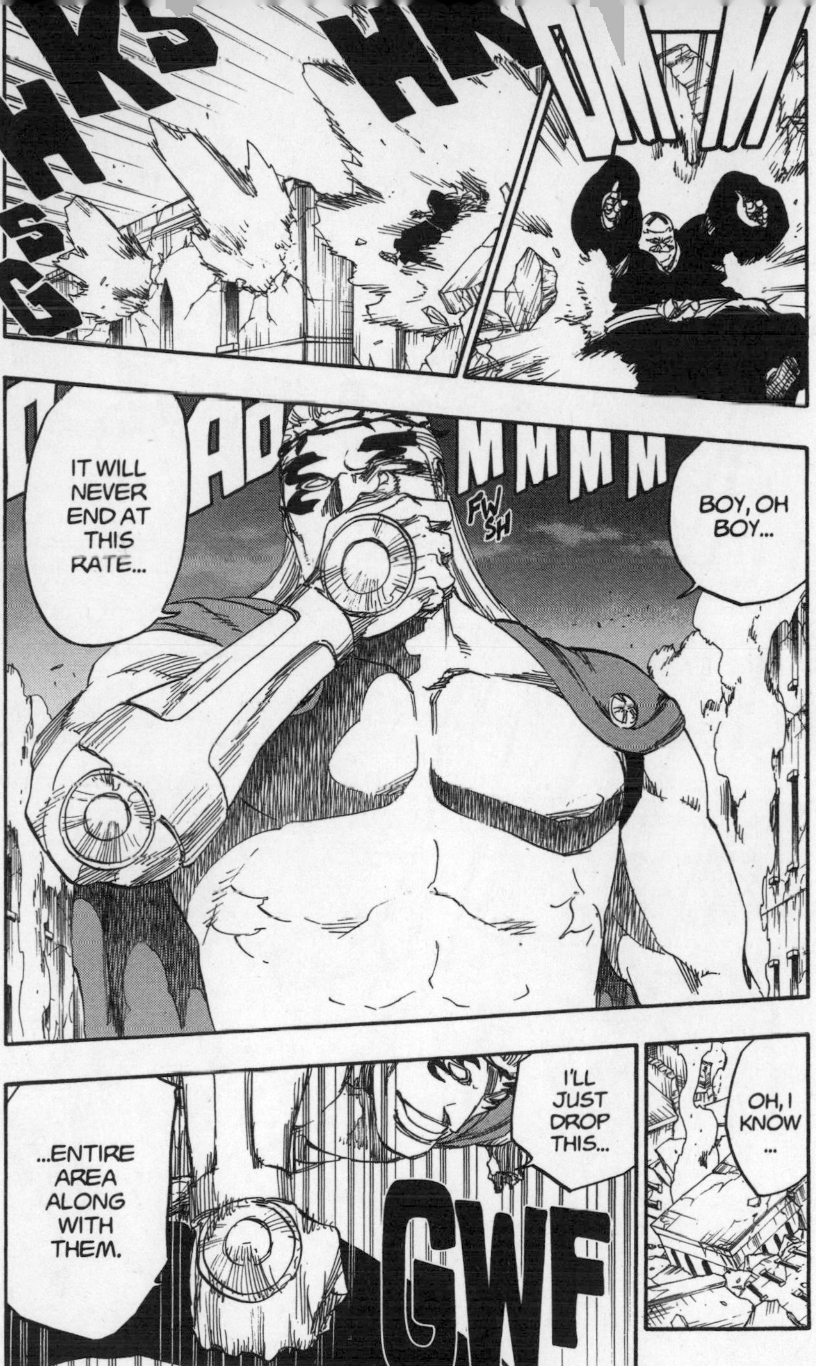
BOY, OH BOY...
FWSH
MMMM
IT WILL NEVER END AT THIS RATE...
OH, I KNOW ...
I'LL JUST DROP THIS...
...ENTIRE AREA ALONG WITH THEM.
GWF

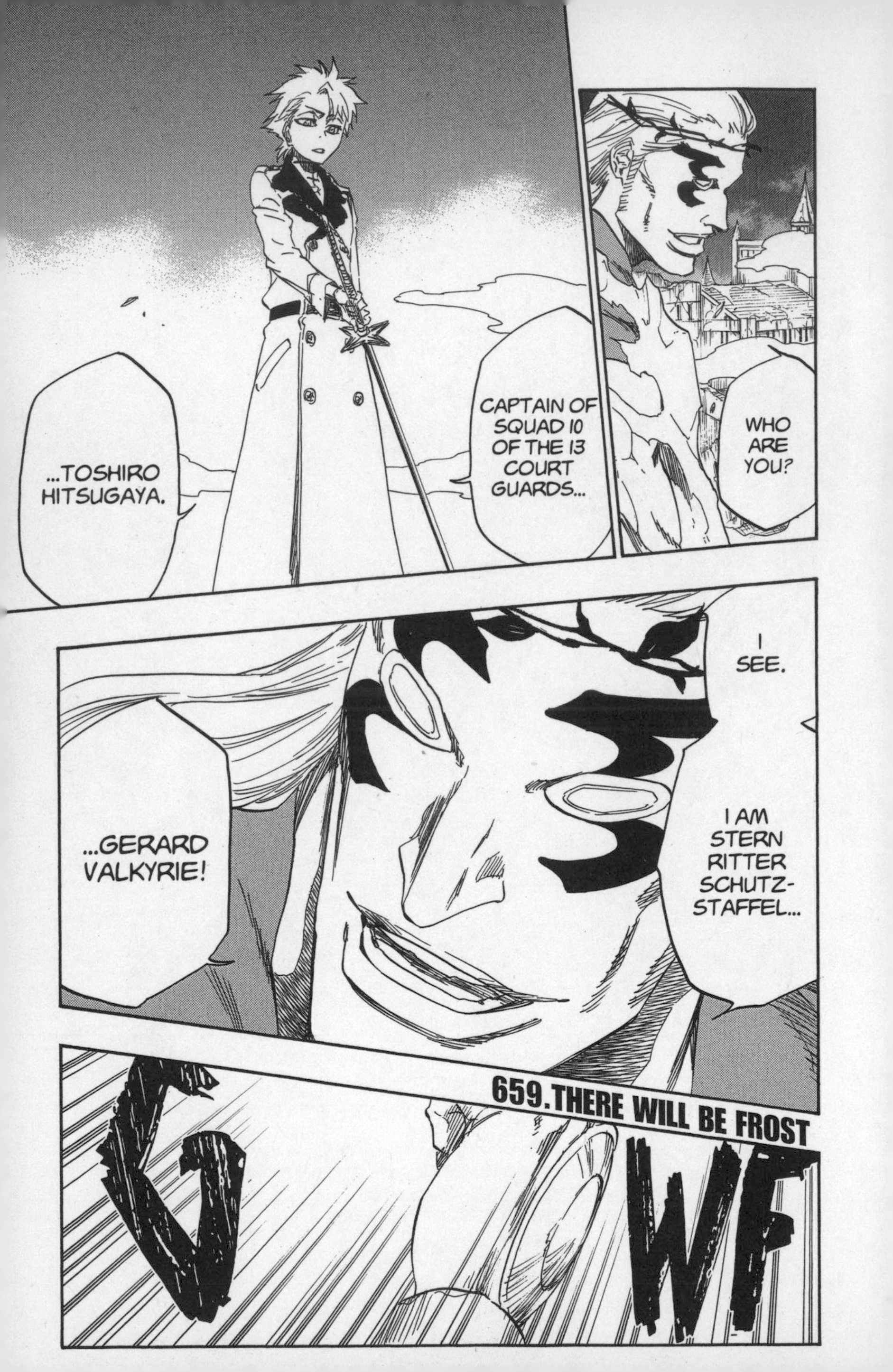
WHO ARE YOU?
CAPTAIN OF SQUAD 10 OF THE 13 COURT GUARDS...
...TOSHIRO HITSUGAYA.
I SEE.
I AM STERN RITTER SCHUTZ-STAFFEL...
...GERARD VALKYRIE!
659. THERE WILL BE FROST
GWF

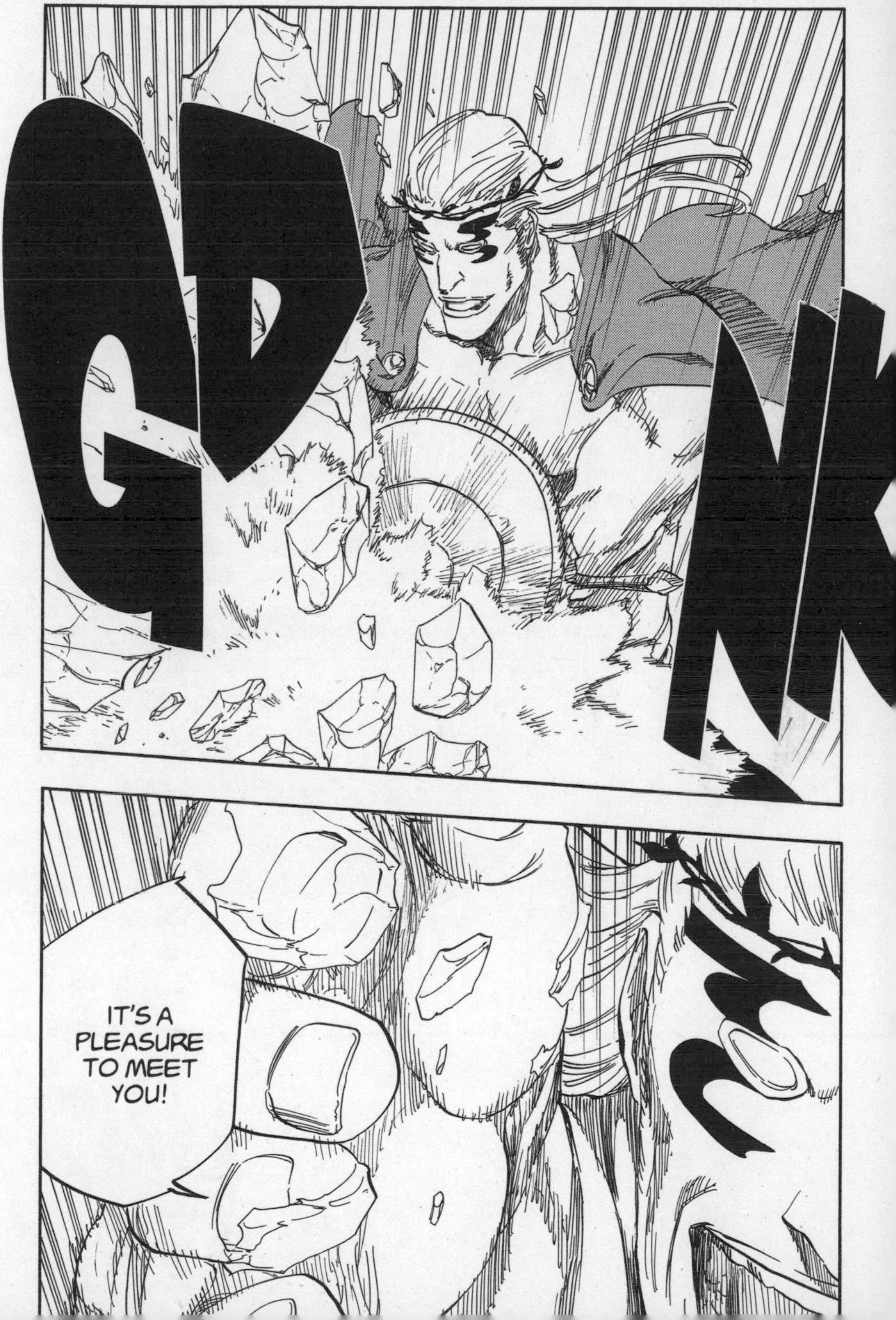
GDNK
IT'S A PLEASURE TO MEET YOU!

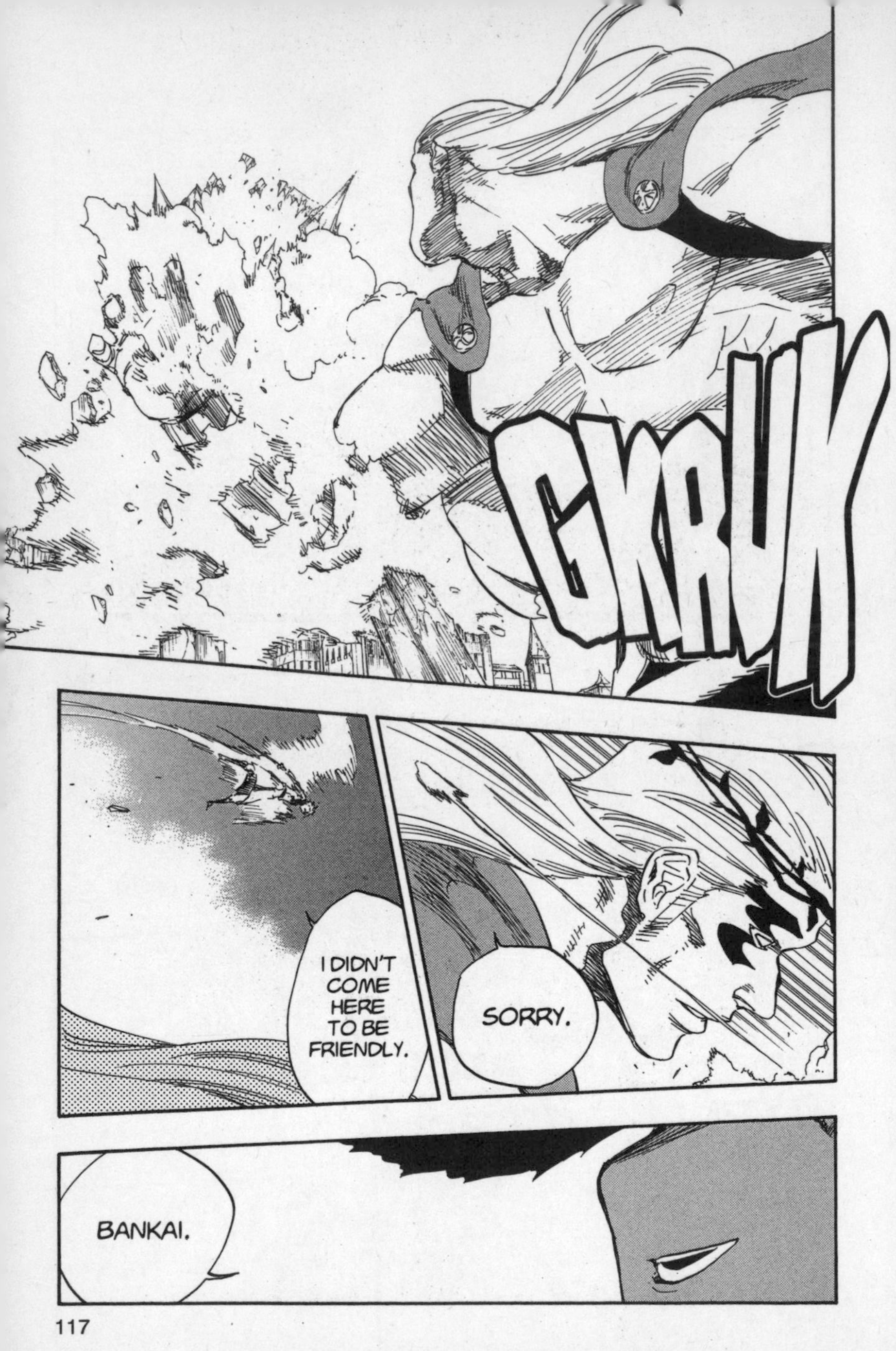
GKRUK
SORRY.
I DIDN'T COME HERE TO BE FRIENDLY.
BANKAI.

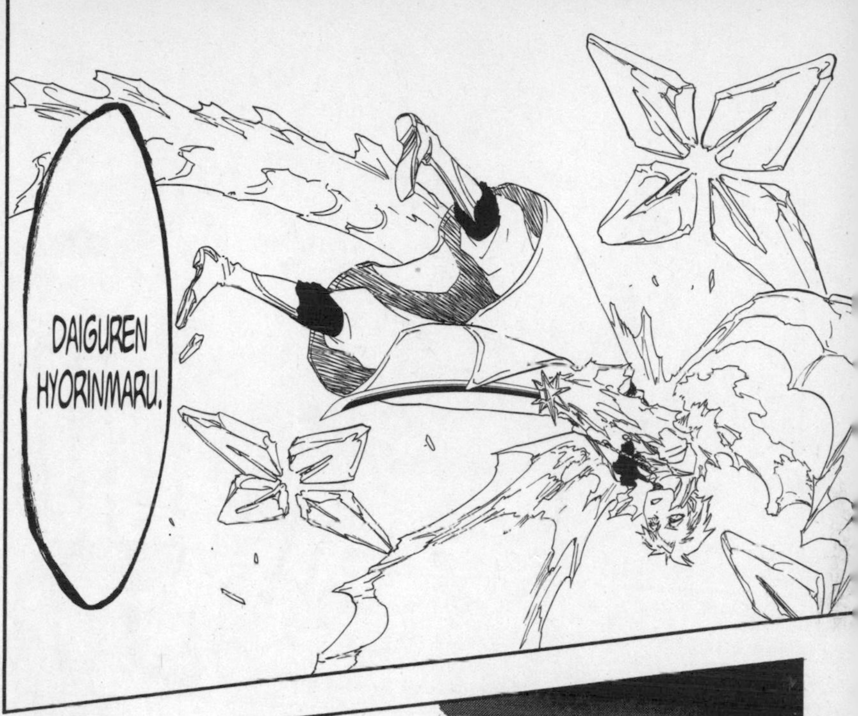
DAIGUREN HYORINMARU.
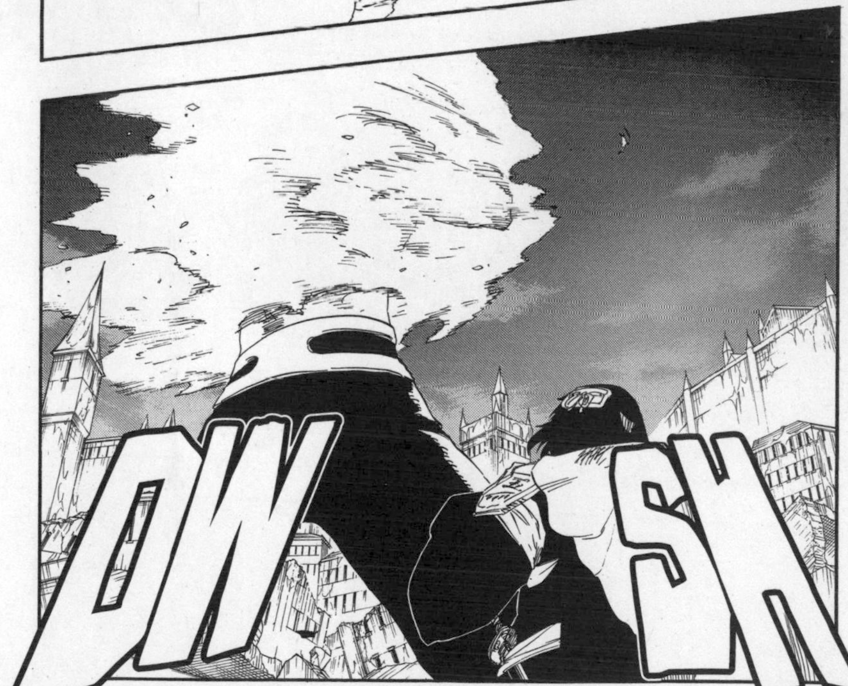
DW
SH

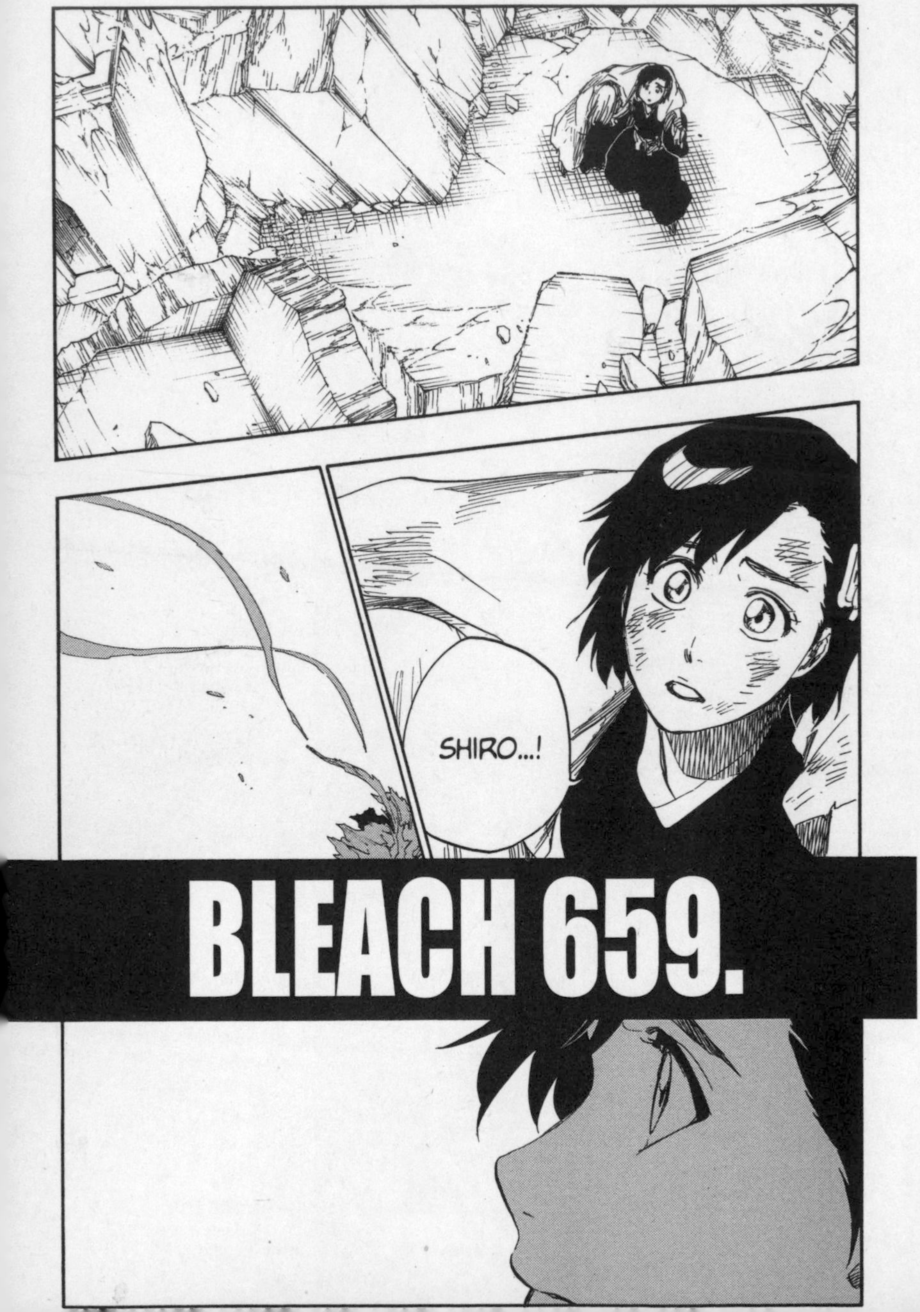
SHIRO...!
BLEACH 659.

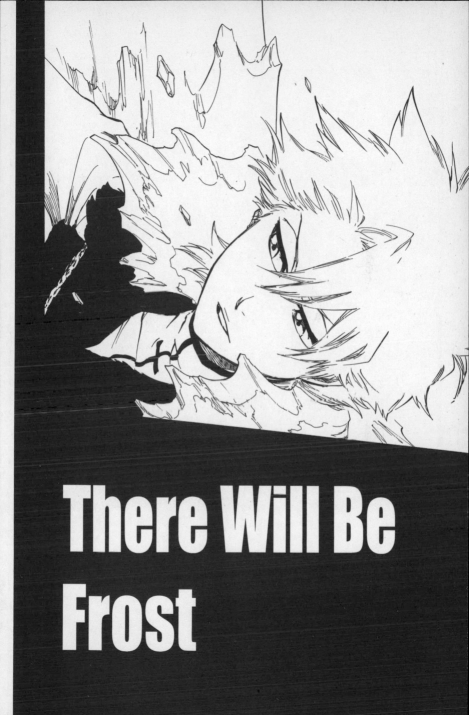

There Will Be Frost

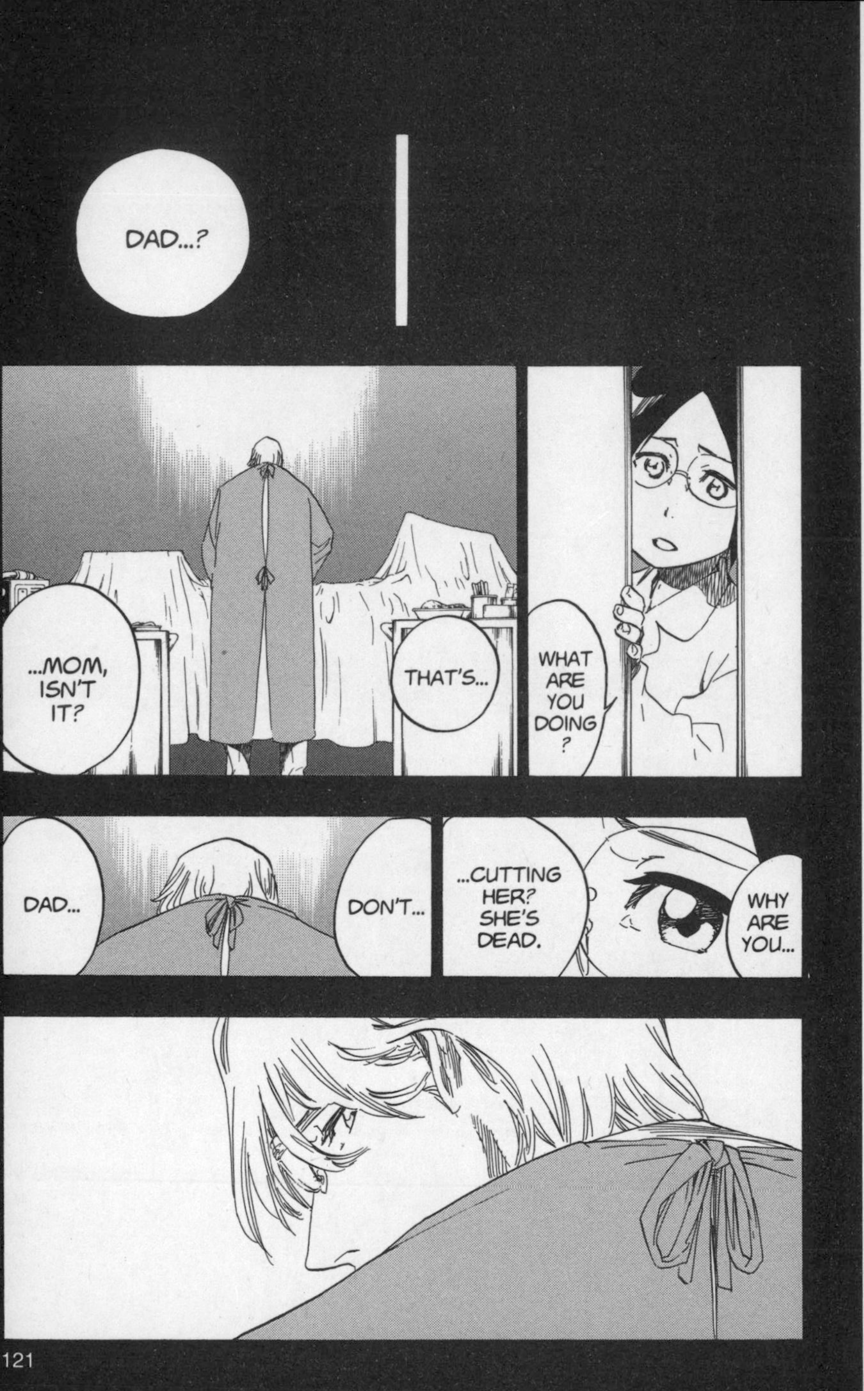
DAD...?
WHAT ARE YOU DOING?
THAT'S...
...MOM, ISN'T IT?
WHY ARE YOU...
...CUTTING HER? SHE'S DEAD.
DON'T...
DAD...

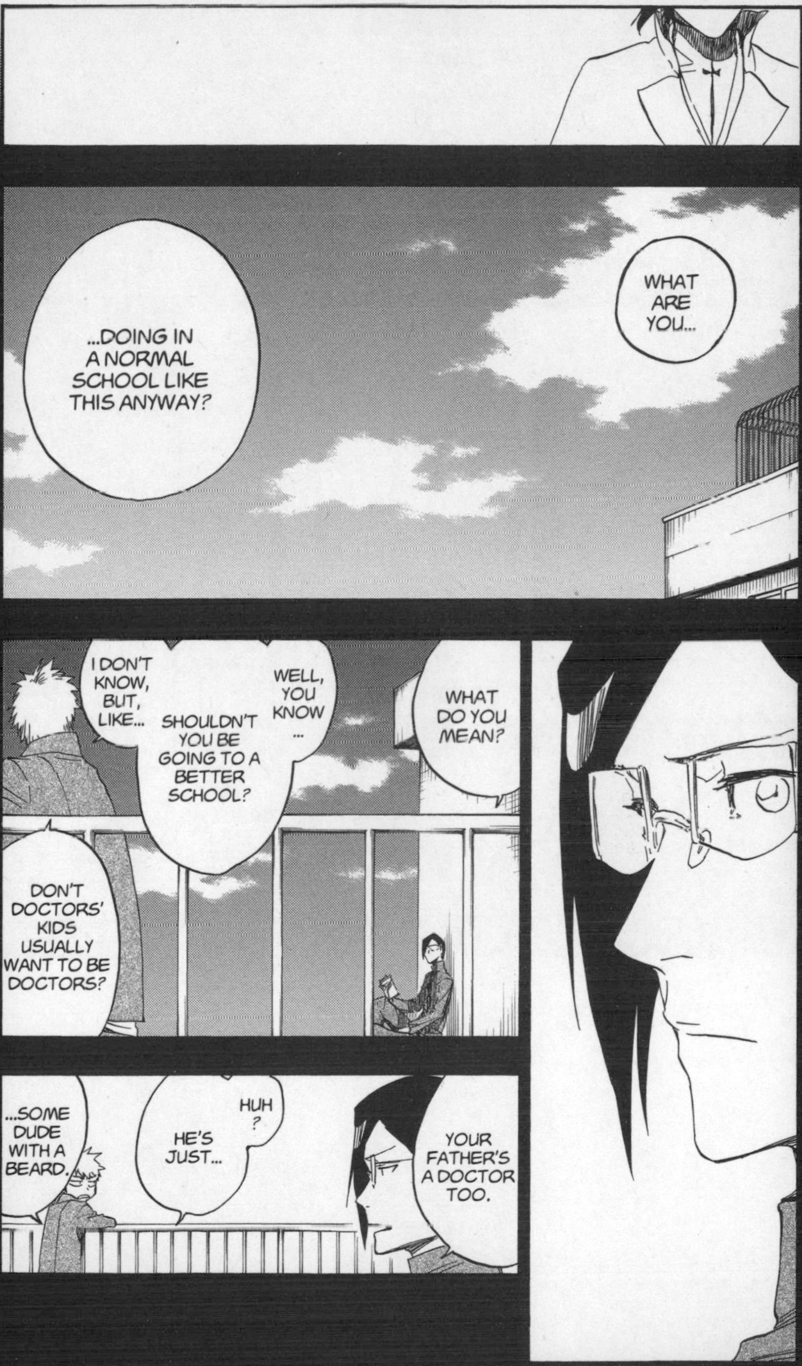
WHAT ARE YOU...
...DOING IN A NORMAL SCHOOL LIKE THIS ANYWAY?
WHAT DO YOU MEAN?
WELL, YOU KNOW ...
I DON'T KNOW, BUT, LIKE...
SHOULDN'T YOU BE GOING TO A BETTER SCHOOL?
DON'T DOCTORS' KIDS USUALLY WANT TO BE DOCTORS?
YOUR FATHER'S A DOCTOR TOO.
HUH?
HE'S JUST...
...SOME DUDE WITH A BEARD.

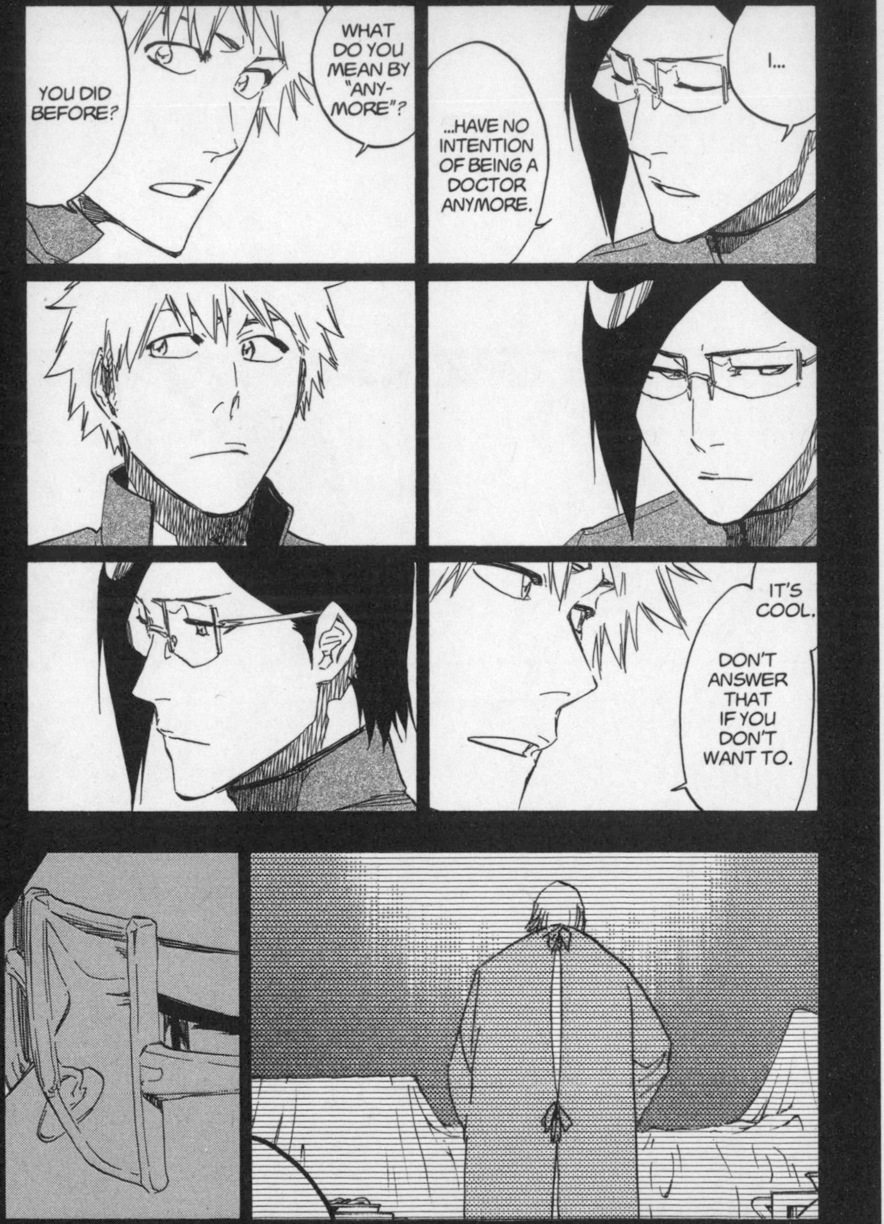
I...
...HAVE NO INTENTION OF BEING A DOCTOR ANYMORE.
WHAT DO YOU MEAN BY "ANY-MORE"?
YOU DID BEFORE?
IT'S COOL.
DON'T ANSWER THAT IF YOU DON'T WANT TO.
THAT'S RIGHT. THAT DAY, I DECIDED I WOULD NOT BE A DOCTOR.

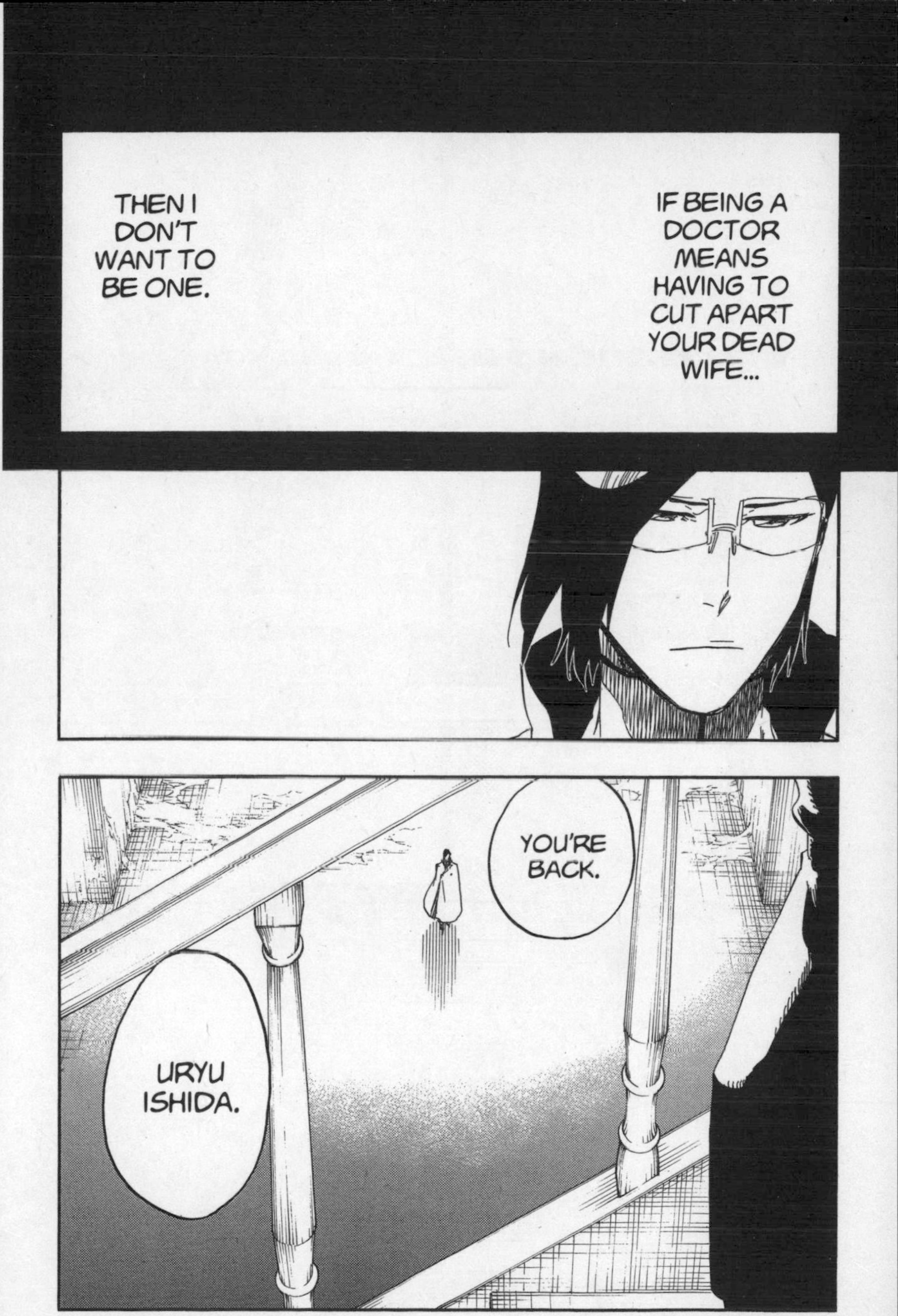
IF BEING A DOCTOR MEANS HAVING TO CUT APART YOUR DEAD WIFE...
THEN I DON'T WANT TO BE ONE.
YOU'RE BACK.
URYU ISHIDA.

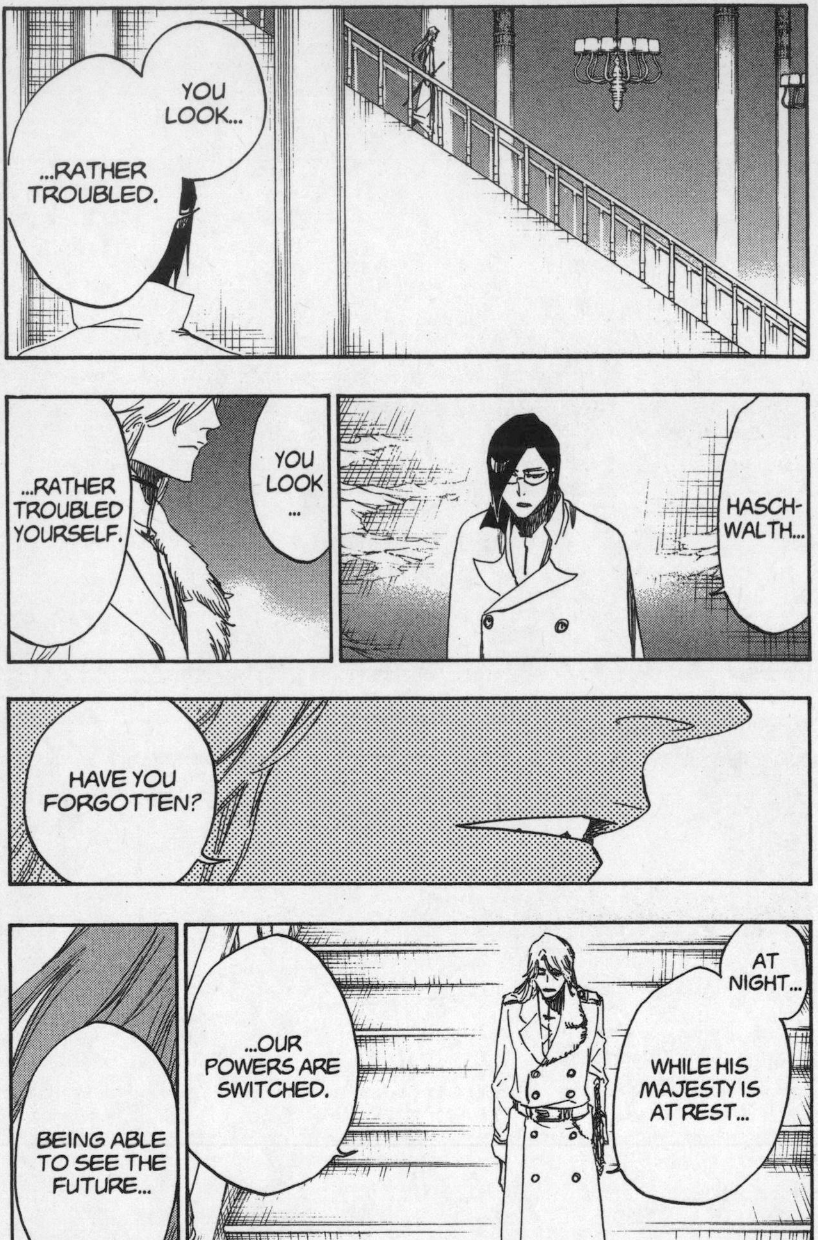
YOU LOOK...
...RATHER TROUBLED.
HASCH-WALTH...
YOU LOOK ...
...RATHER TROUBLED YOURSELF.
HAVE YOU FORGOTTEN?
AT NIGHT...
WHILE HIS MAJESTY IS AT REST...
...OUR POWERS ARE SWITCHED.
BEING ABLE TO SEE THE FUTURE...

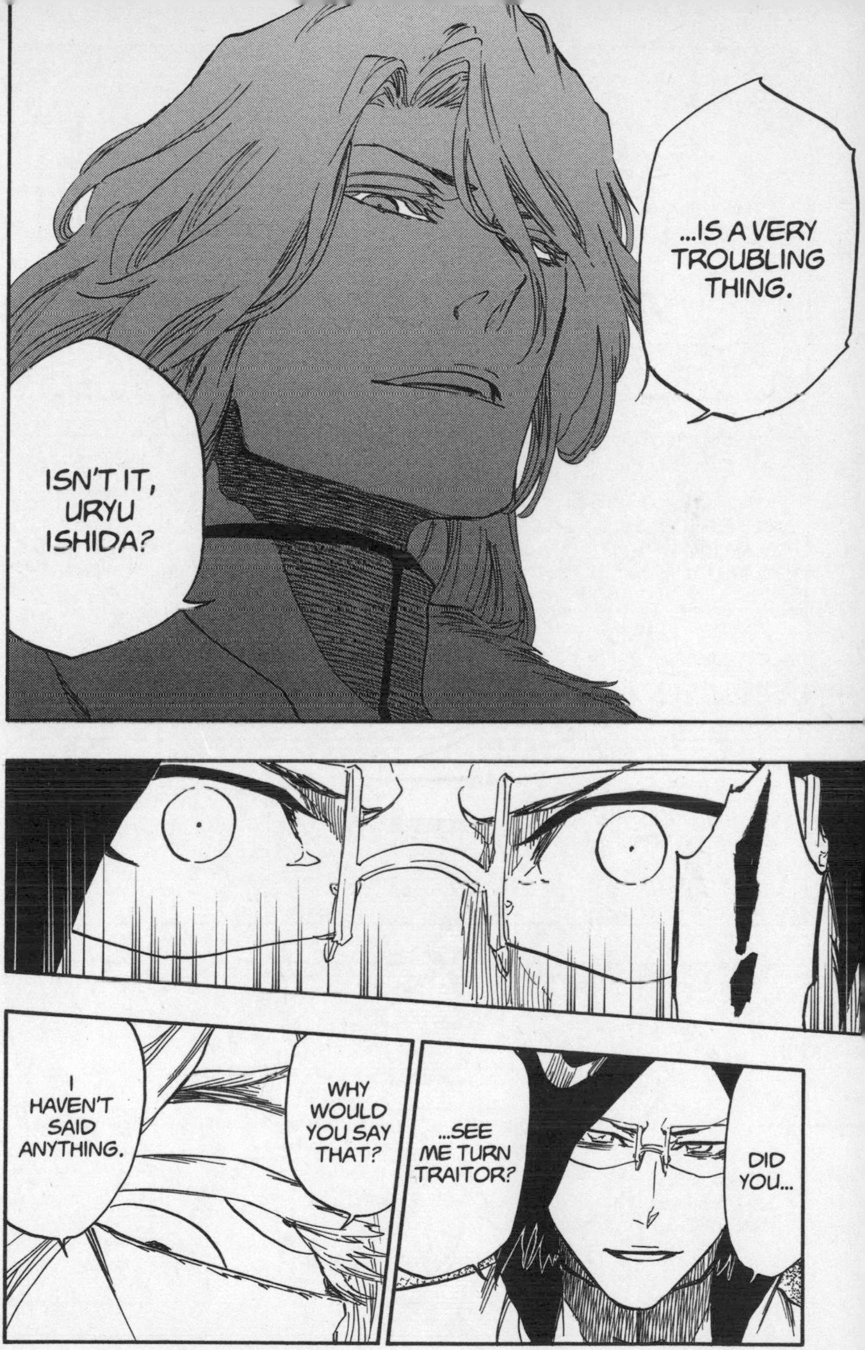
...IS A VERY TROUBLING THING.
ISN'T IT, URYU ISHIDA?
!
DID YOU...
...SEE ME TURN TRAITOR?
WHY WOULD YOU SAY THAT?
I HAVEN'T SAID ANYTHING.

READ THIS WAY

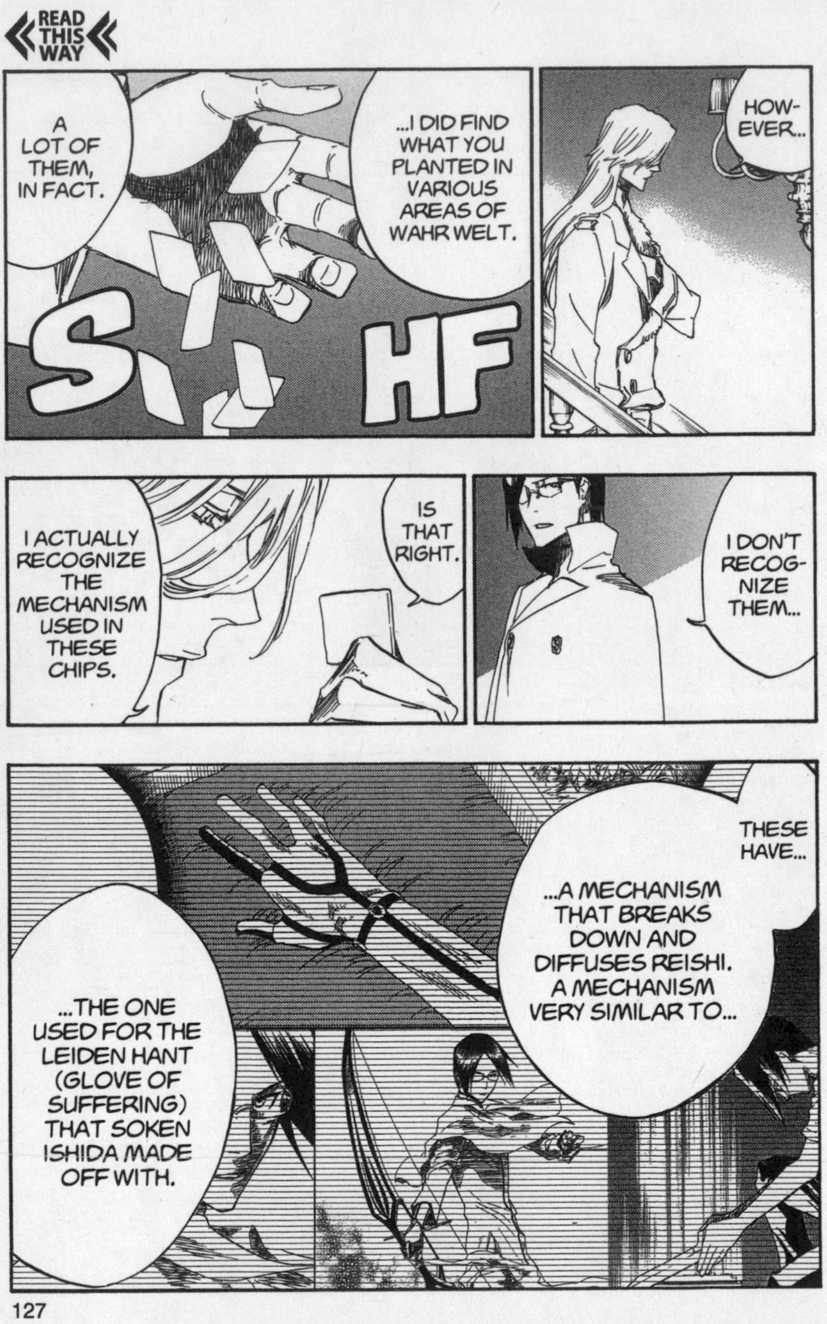
HOW-EVER...
...I DID FIND WHAT YOU PLANTED IN VARIOUS AREAS OF WAHR WELT.
A LOT OF THEM, IN FACT.
SHF
I DON'T RECOG-NIZE THEM...
IS THAT RIGHT.
I ACTUALLY RECOGNIZE THE MECHANISM USED IN THESE CHIPS.
THESE HAVE...
...A MECHANISM THAT BREAKS DOWN AND DIFFUSES REISHI. A MECHANISM VERY SIMILAR TO...
...THE ONE USED FOR THE LEIDEN HANT (GLOVE OF SUFFERING) THAT SOKEN ISHIDA MADE OFF WITH.

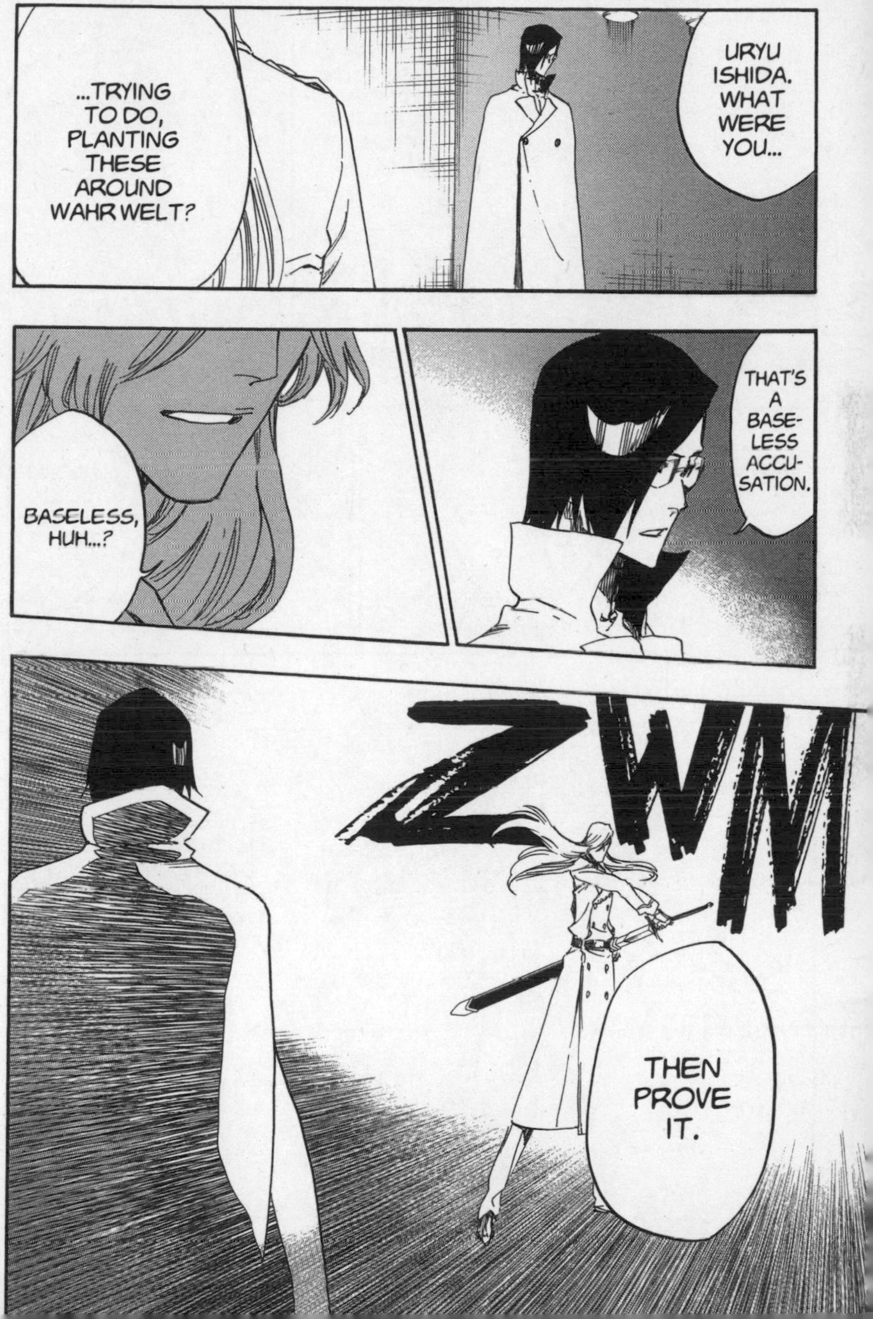
URYU ISHIDA. WHAT WERE YOU...
...TRYING TO DO, PLANTING THESE AROUND WAHR WELT?
THAT'S A BASE-LESS ACCU-SATION.
BASELESS, HUH...?
ZWM
THEN PROVE IT.

The Visible Answer

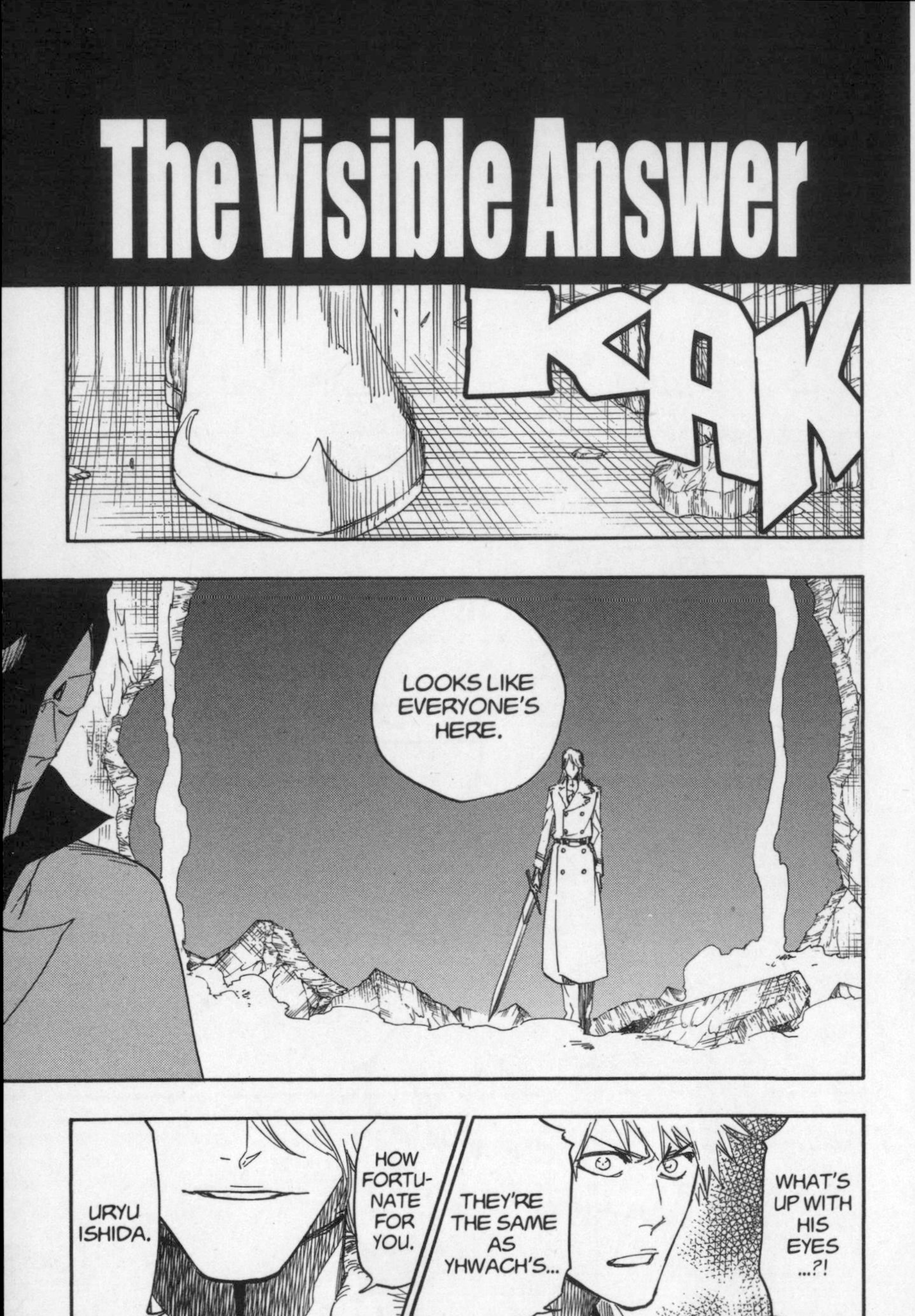

KAK
LOOKS LIKE EVERYONE'S HERE.
WHAT'S UP WITH HIS EYES ...?!
THEY'RE THE SAME AS YHWACH'S...
HOW FORTU-NATE FOR YOU.
URYU ISHIDA.

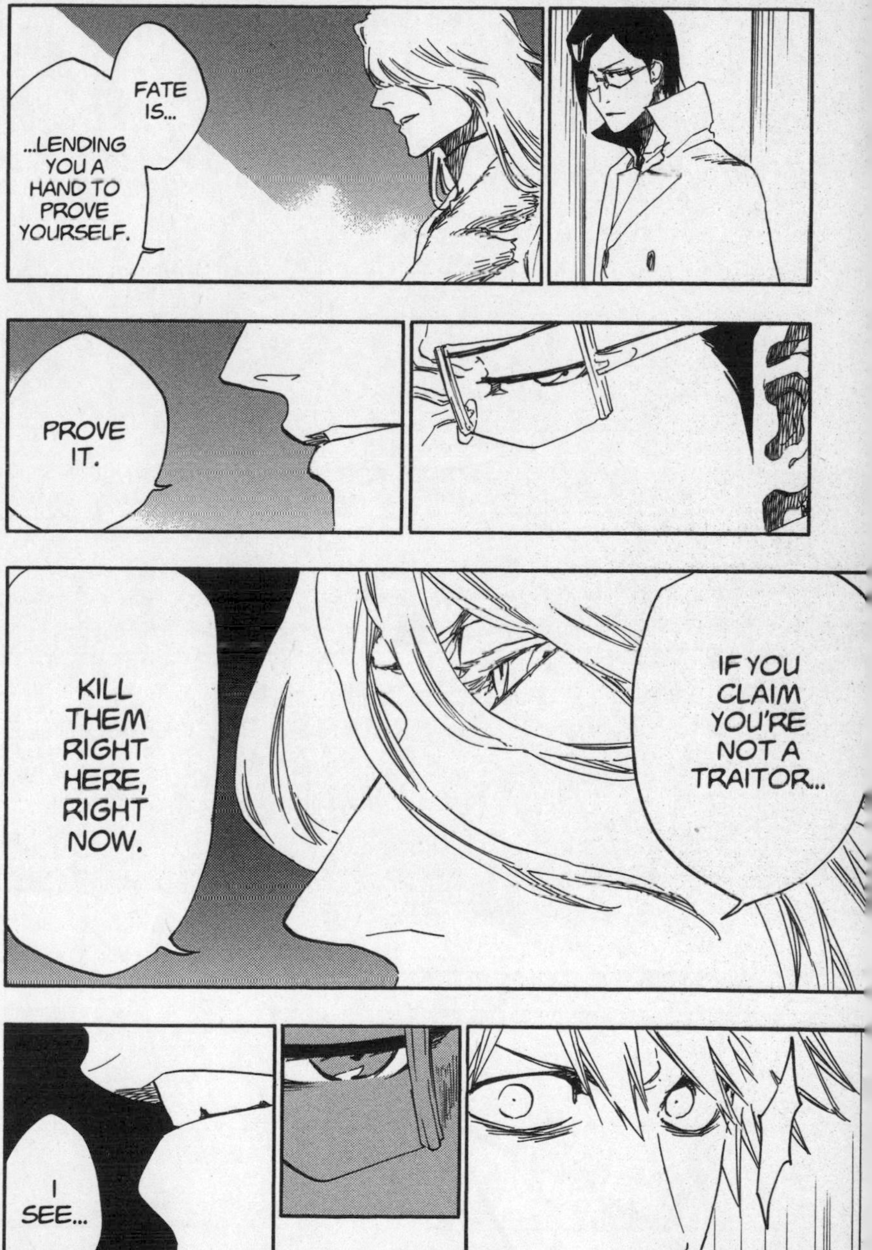
FATE IS...
...LENDING YOU A HAND TO PROVE YOURSELF.
PROVE IT.
IF YOU CLAIM YOU'RE NOT A TRAITOR...
KILL THEM RIGHT HERE, RIGHT NOW.
I SEE...

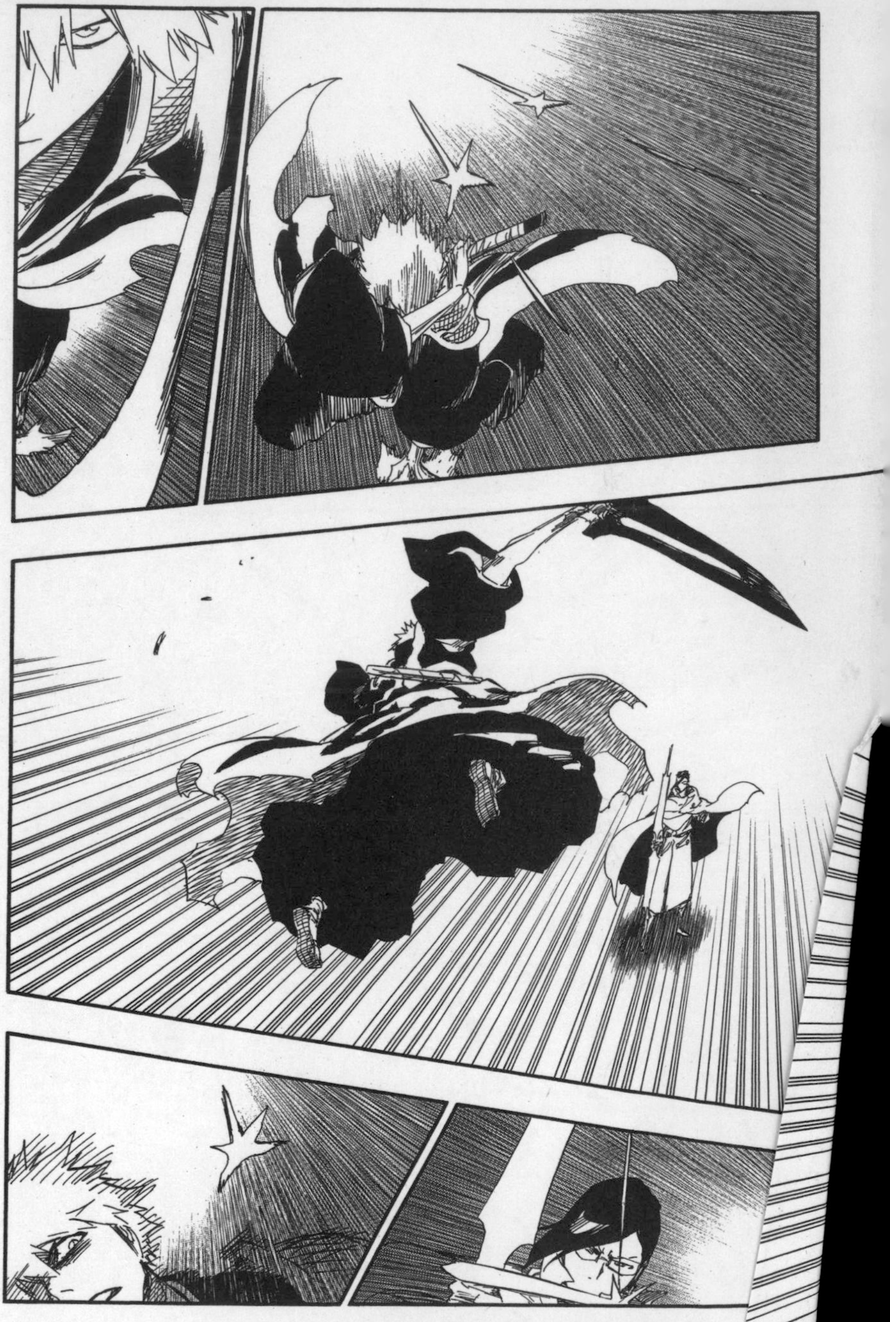

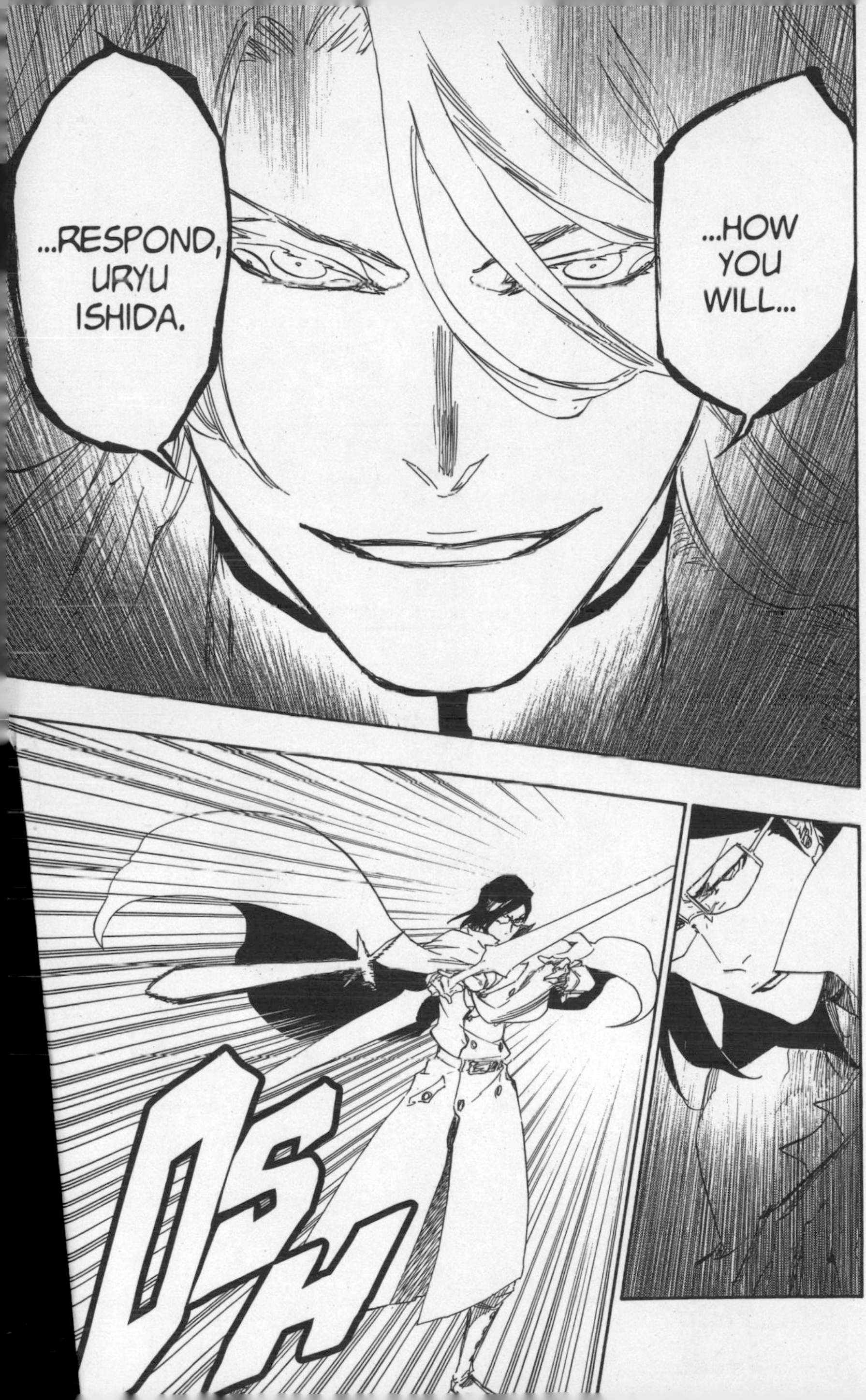
...HOW YOU WILL...
...RESPOND, URYU ISHIDA.

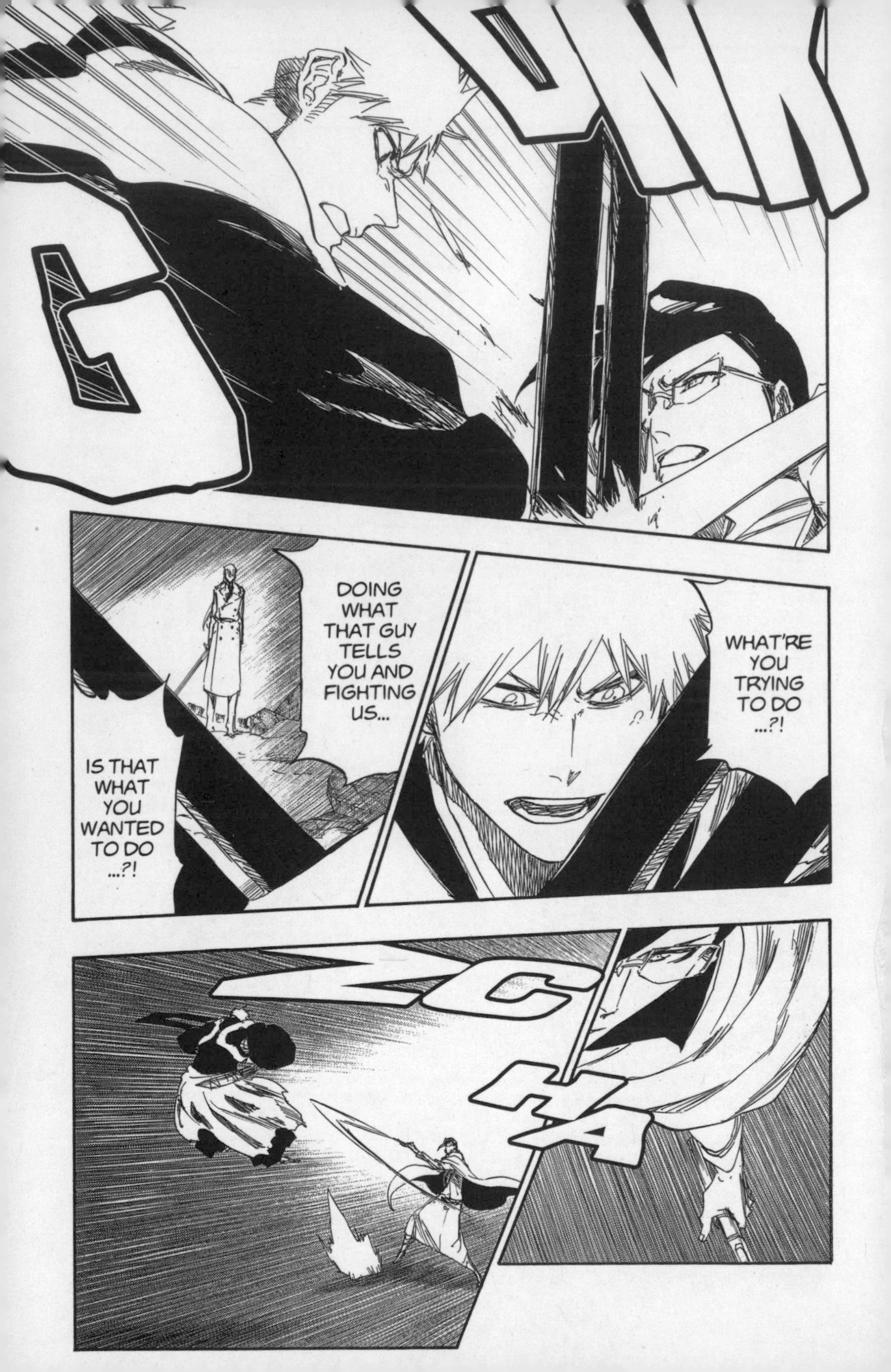
WHAT'RE YOU TRYING TO DO ...?!
DOING WHAT THAT GUY TELLS YOU AND FIGHTING US...
IS THAT WHAT YOU WANTED TO DO ...?!
ZCHA

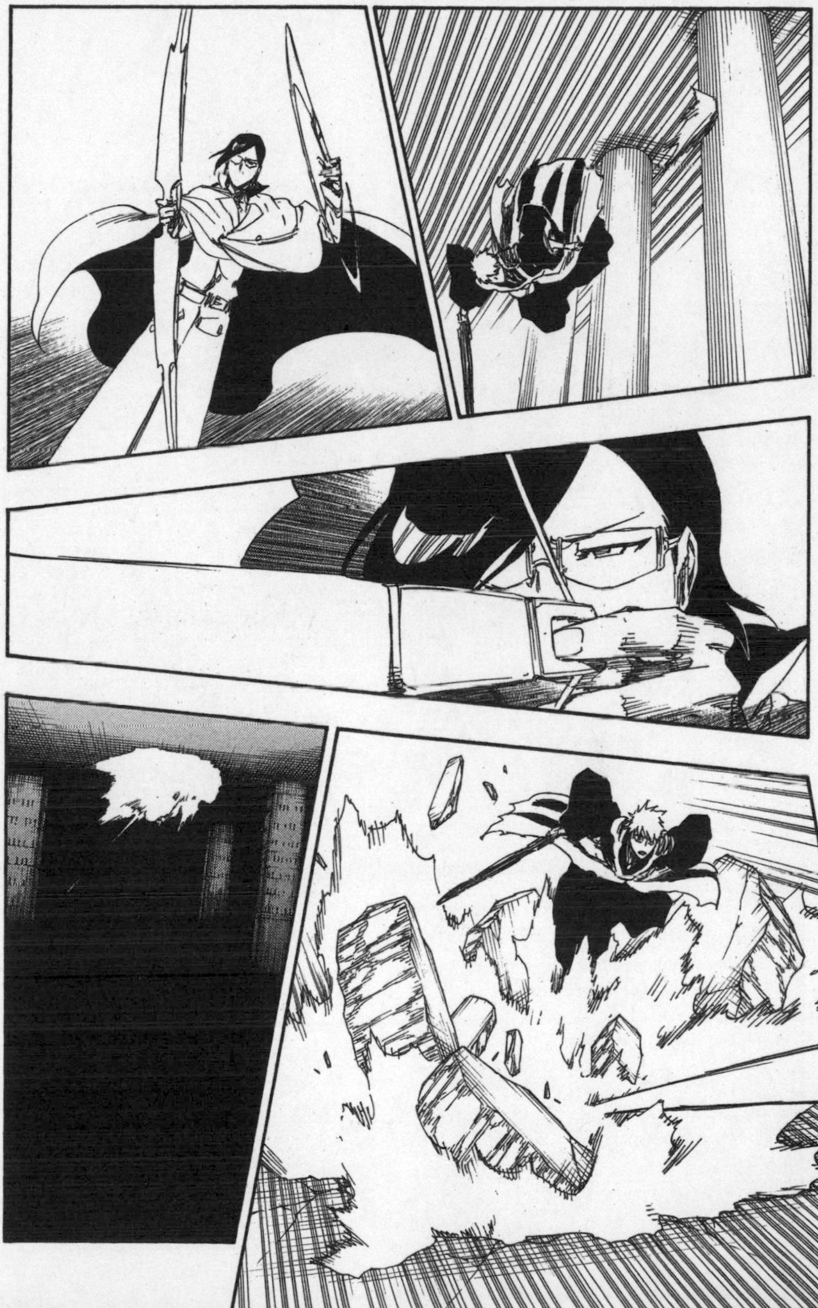

READ THIS WAY

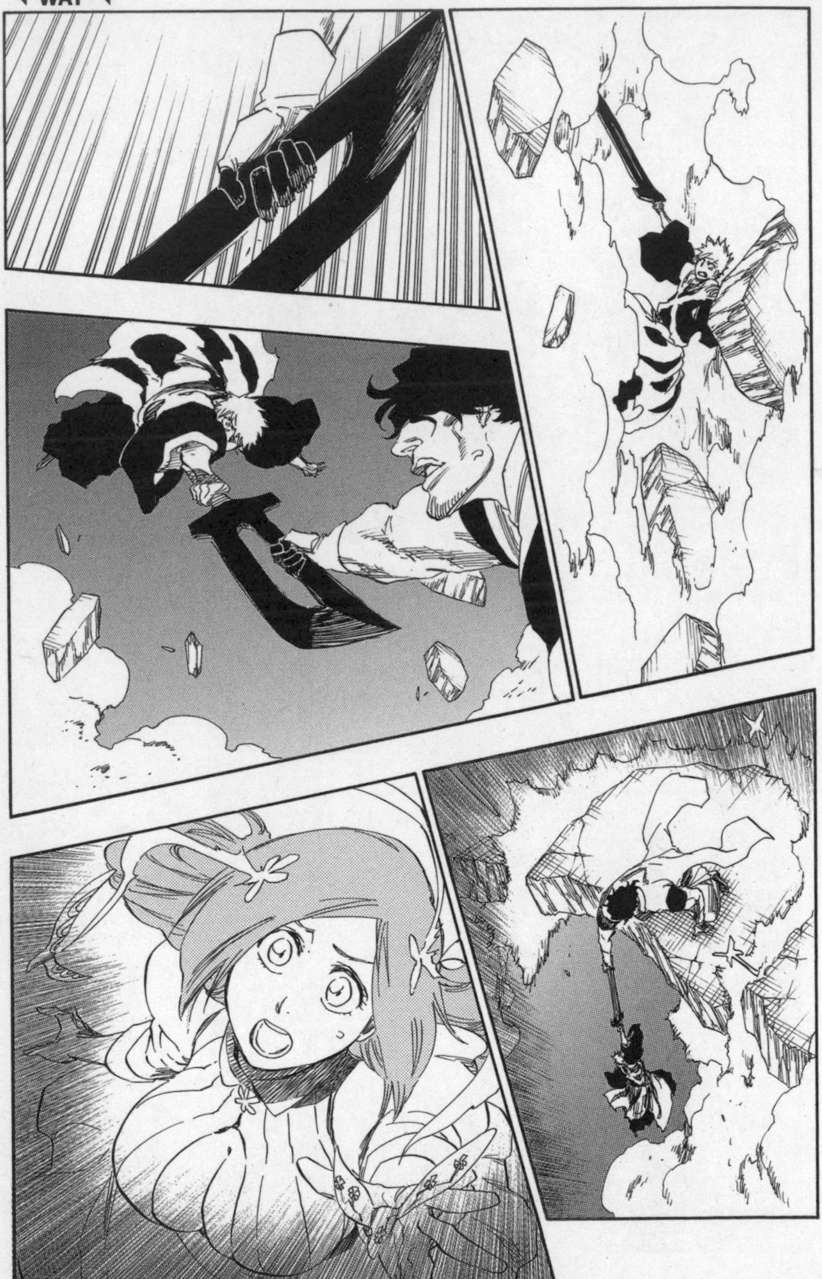

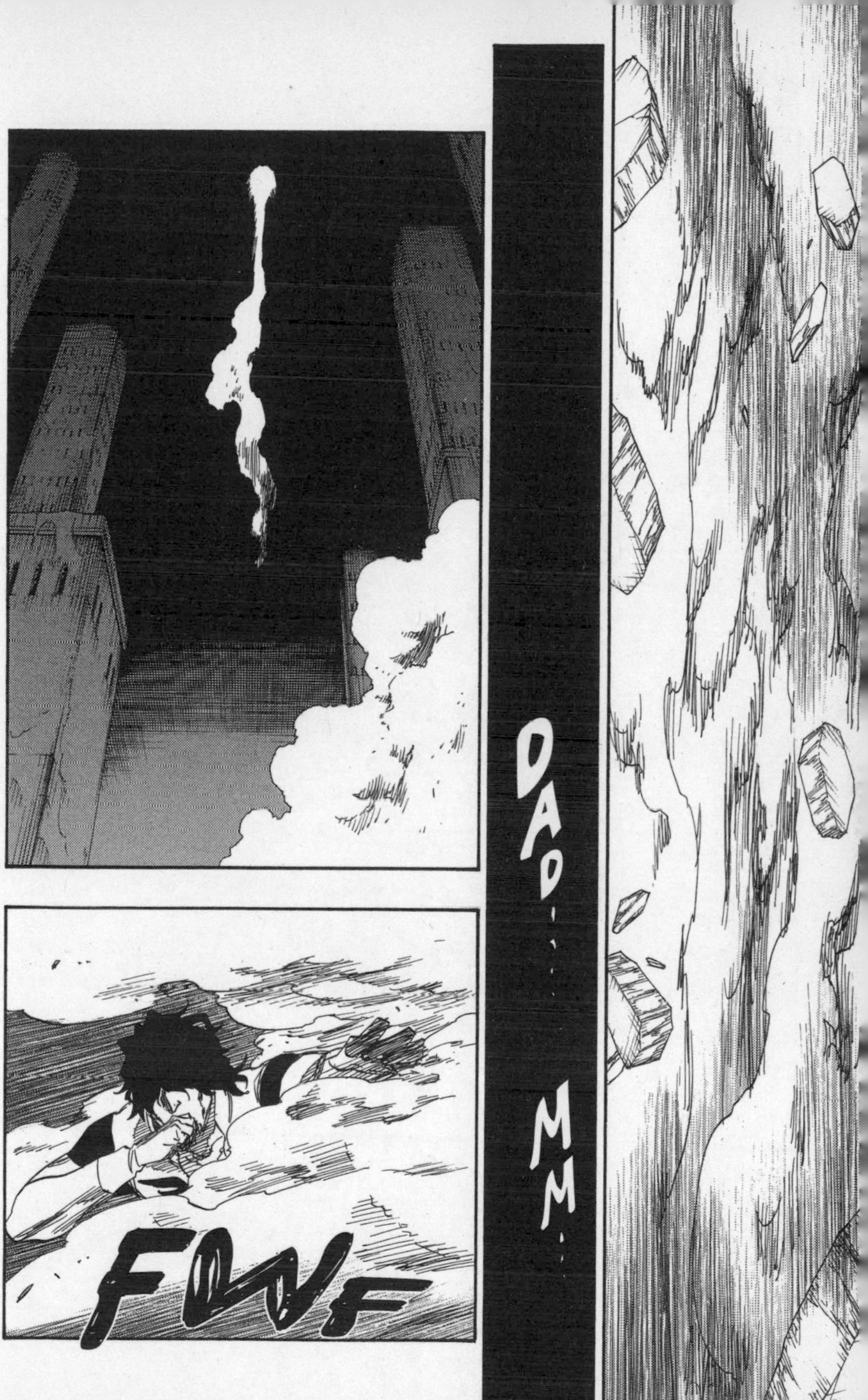
DAD......MM...
FWF

READ THIS WAY

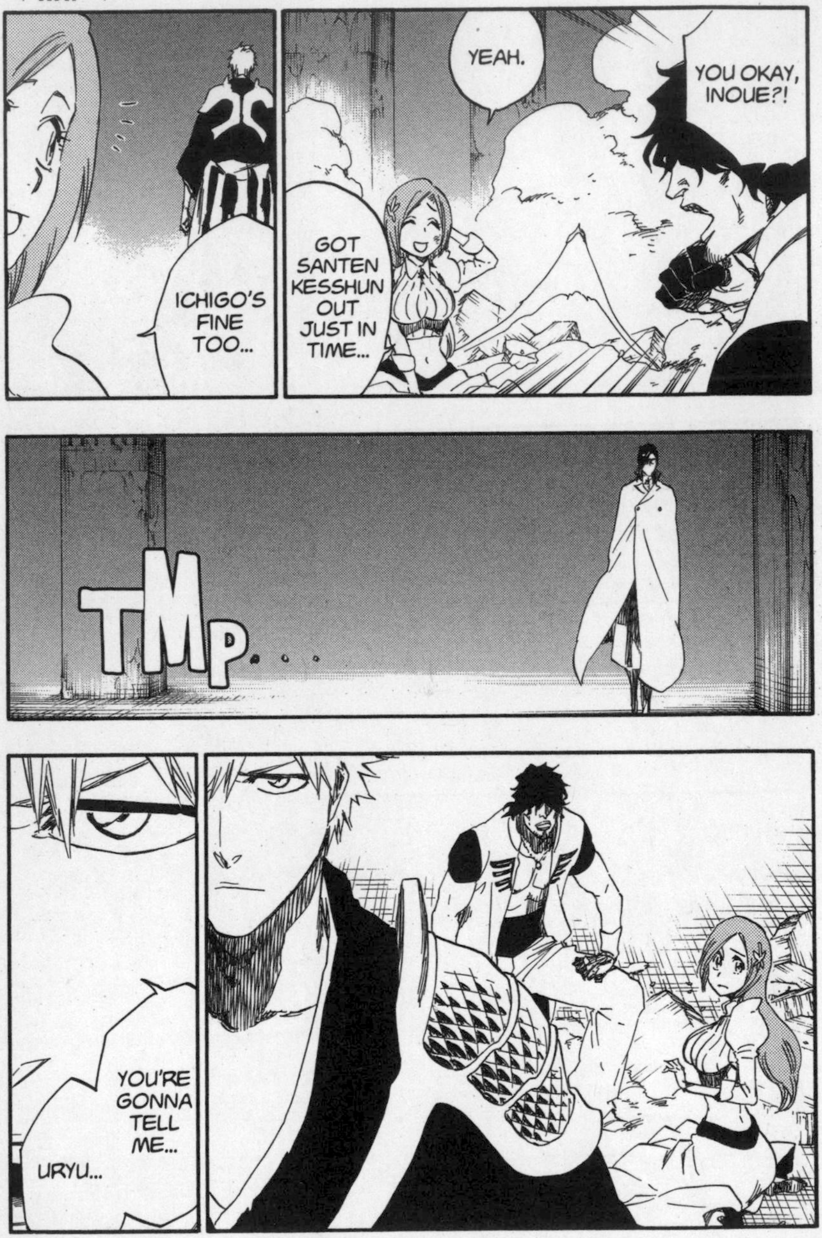
YOU OKAY, INOUE?!
YEAH.
GOT SANTEN KESSHUN OUT JUST IN TIME...
ICHIGO'S FINE TOO...
TMP...
YOU'RE GONNA TELL ME...
URYU...

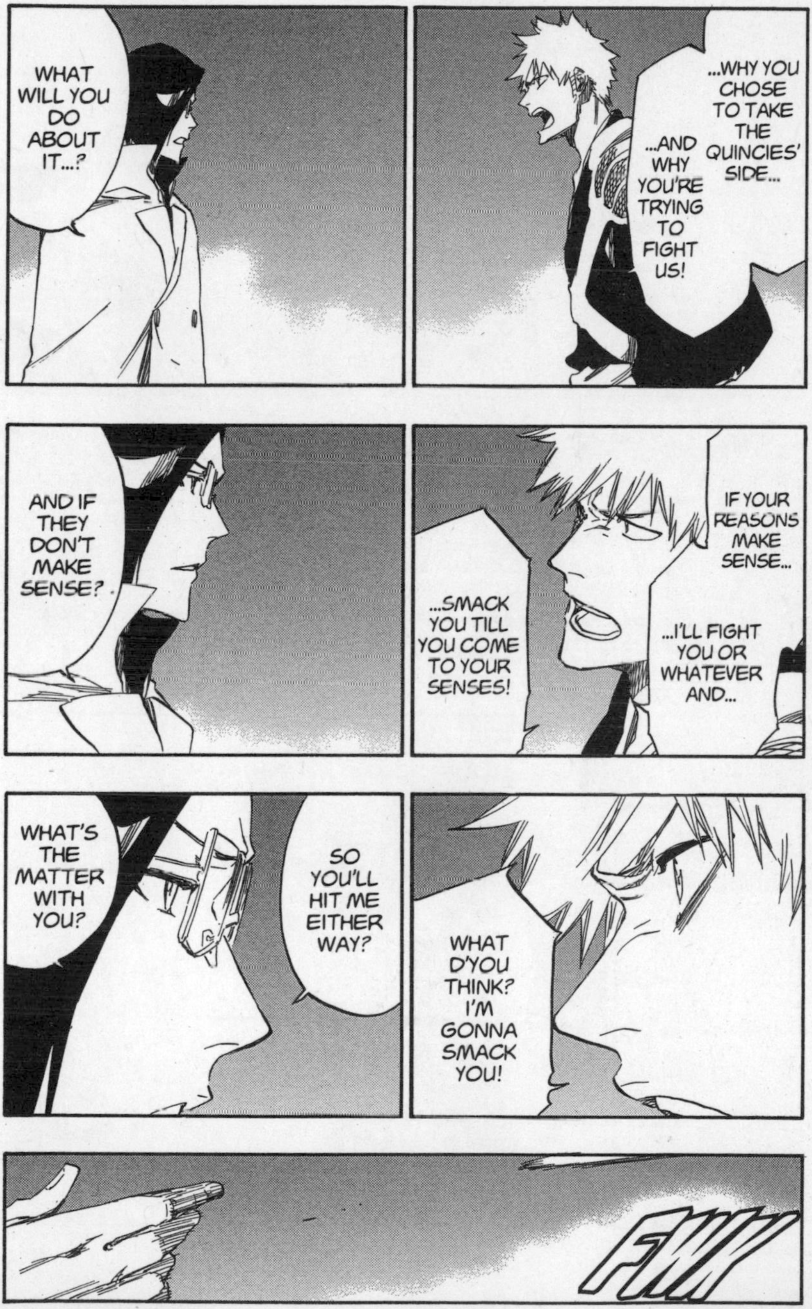
...WHY YOU CHOSE TO TAKE THE QUINCIES' SIDE...
...AND WHY YOU'RE TRYING TO FIGHT US!
WHAT WILL YOU DO ABOUT IT...?
IF YOUR REASONS MAKE SENSE...
...I'LL FIGHT YOU OR WHATEVER AND...
...SMACK YOU TILL YOU COME TO YOUR SENSES!
AND IF THEY DON'T MAKE SENSE?
WHAT D'YOU THINK? I'M GONNA SMACK YOU!
SO YOU'LL HIT ME EITHER WAY?
WHAT'S THE MATTER WITH YOU?
FWX

READ THIS WAY

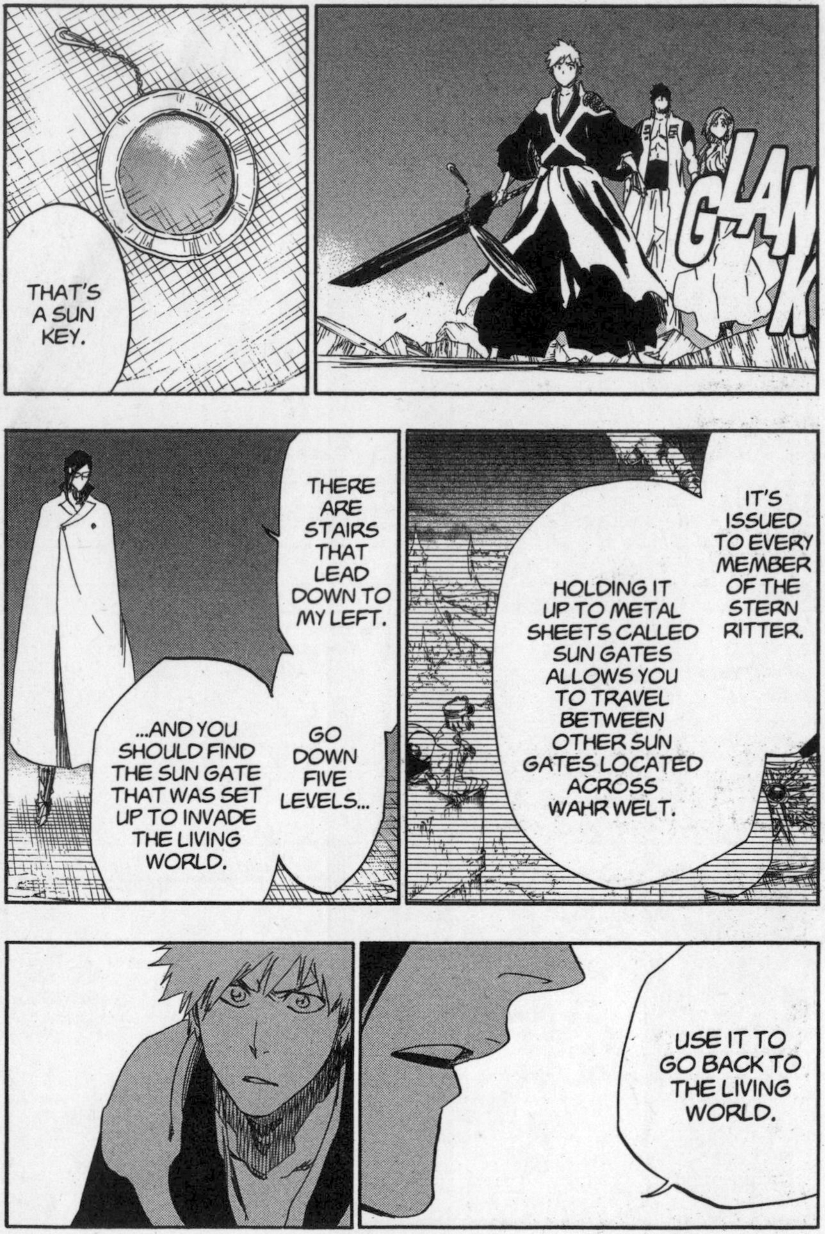
GLANK
THAT'S A SUN KEY.
IT'S ISSUED TO EVERY MEMBER OF THE STERN RITTER.
HOLDING IT UP TO METAL SHEETS CALLED SUN GATES ALLOWS YOU TO TRAVEL BETWEEN OTHER SUN GATES LOCATED ACROSS WAHR WELT.
THERE ARE STAIRS THAT LEAD DOWN TO MY LEFT.
GO DOWN FIVE LEVELS...
...AND YOU SHOULD FIND THE SUN GATE THAT WAS SET UP TO INVADE THE LIVING WORLD.
USE IT TO GO BACK TO THE LIVING WORLD.

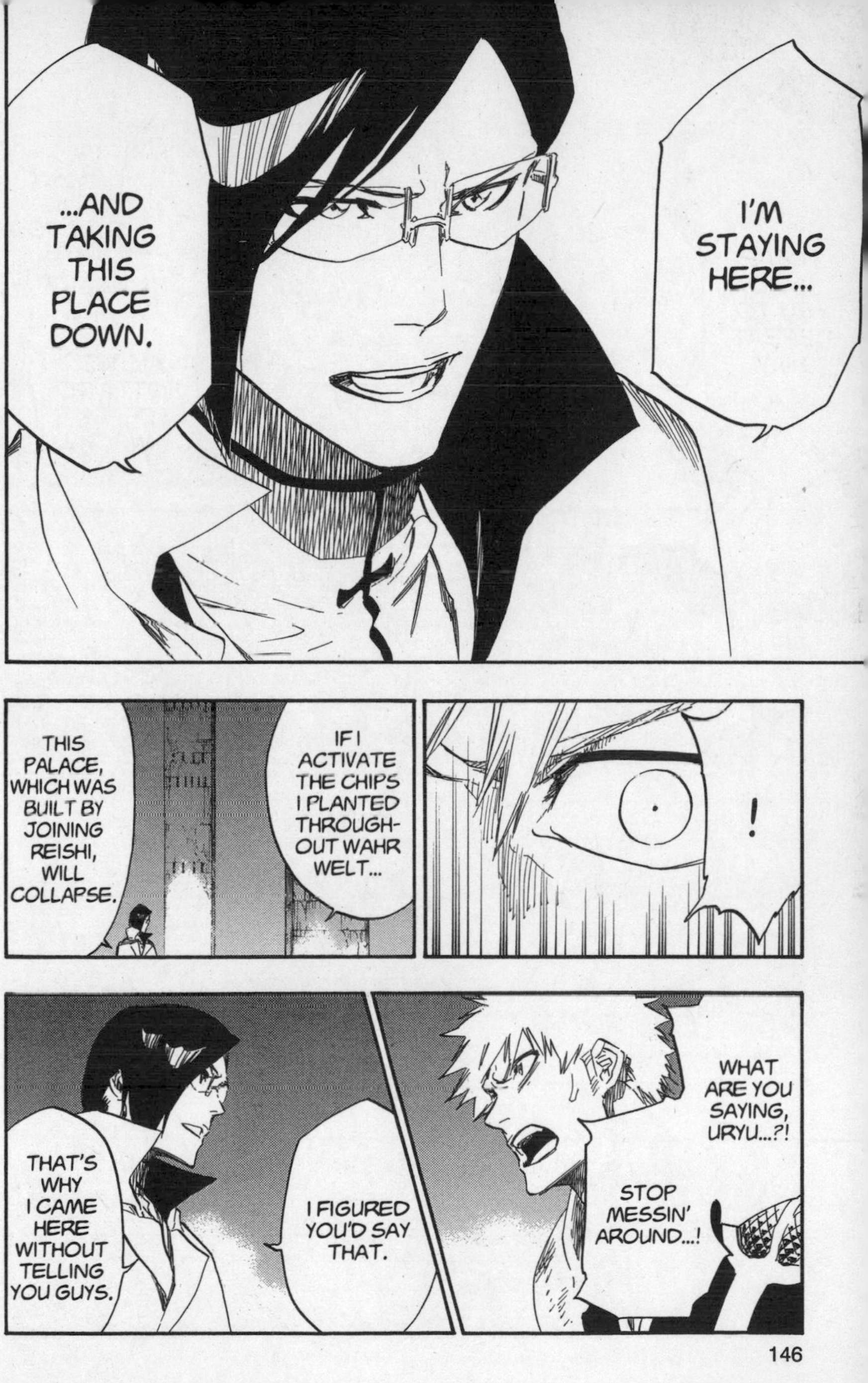
I'M STAYING HERE...
...AND TAKING THIS PLACE DOWN.
!
IF I ACTIVATE THE CHIPS I PLANTED THROUGH-OUT WAHR WELT...
THIS PALACE, WHICH WAS BUILT BY JOINING REISHI, WILL COLLAPSE.
WHAT ARE YOU SAYING, URYU...?!
STOP MESSIN' AROUND...!
I FIGURED YOU'D SAY THAT.
THAT'S WHY I CAME HERE WITHOUT TELLING YOU GUYS.

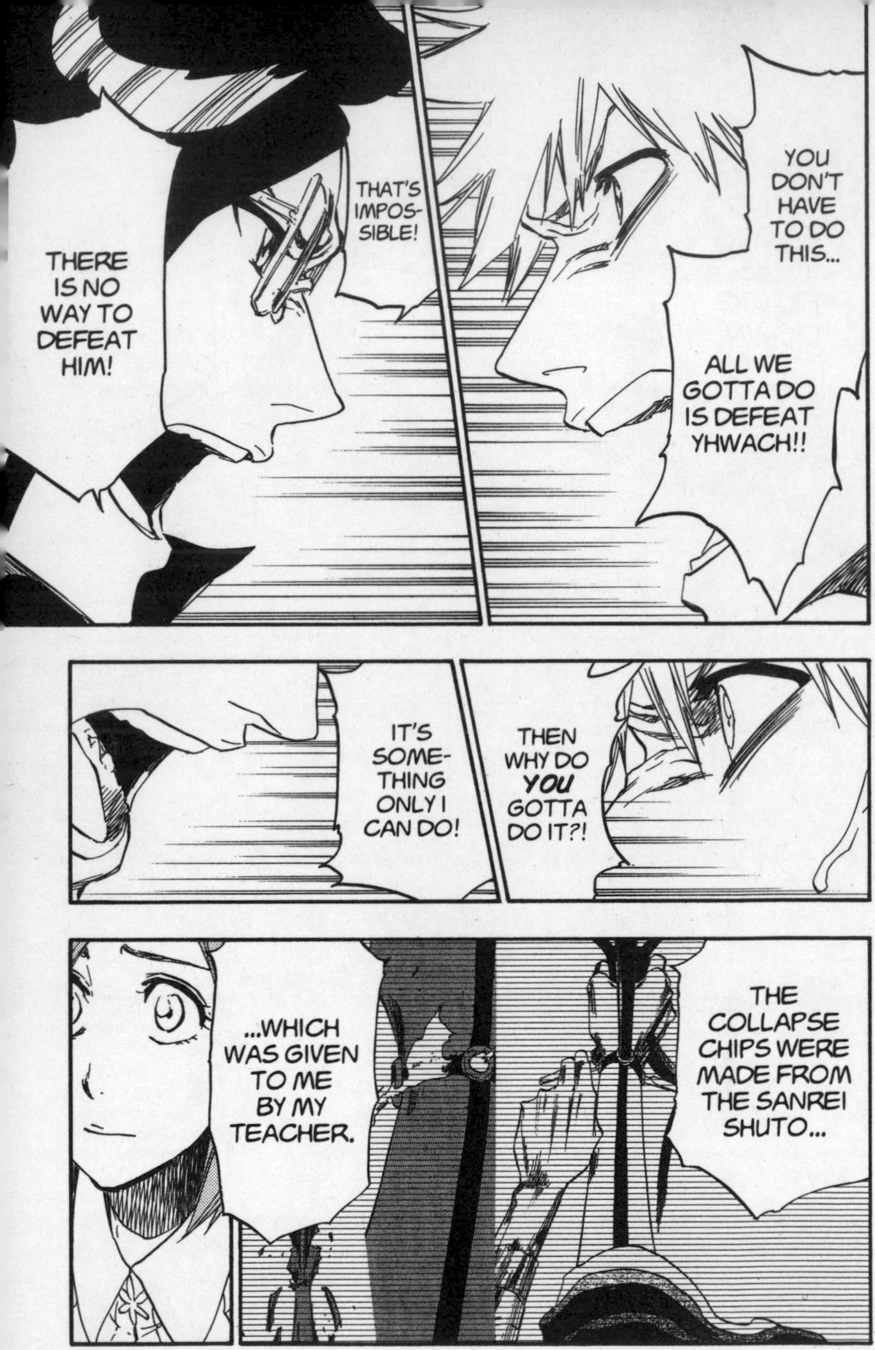
YOU DON'T HAVE TO DO THIS...
ALL WE GOTTA DO IS DEFEAT YHWACH!!
THAT'S IMPOSSIBLE!
THERE IS NO WAY TO DEFEAT HIM!
THEN WHY DO *YOU* GOTTA DO IT?!
IT'S SOMETHING ONLY I CAN DO!
THE COLLAPSE CHIPS WERE MADE FROM THE SANREI SHUTO...
...WHICH WAS GIVEN TO ME BY MY TEACHER.

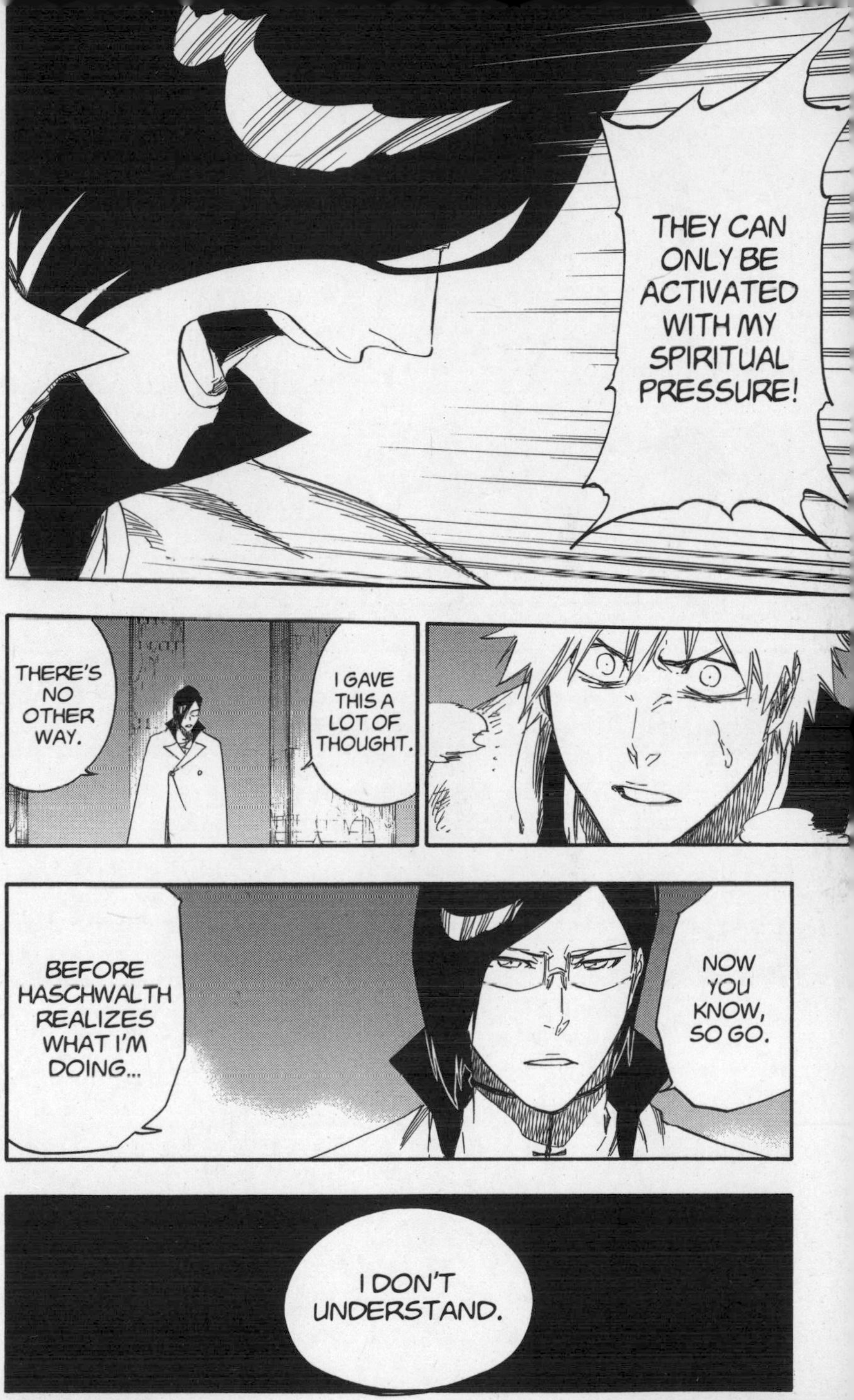
THEY CAN ONLY BE ACTIVATED WITH MY SPIRITUAL PRESSURE!
I GAVE THIS A LOT OF THOUGHT.
THERE'S NO OTHER WAY.
NOW YOU KNOW, SO GO.
BEFORE HASCHWALTH REALIZES WHAT I'M DOING...
I DON'T UNDERSTAND.

READ THIS WAY

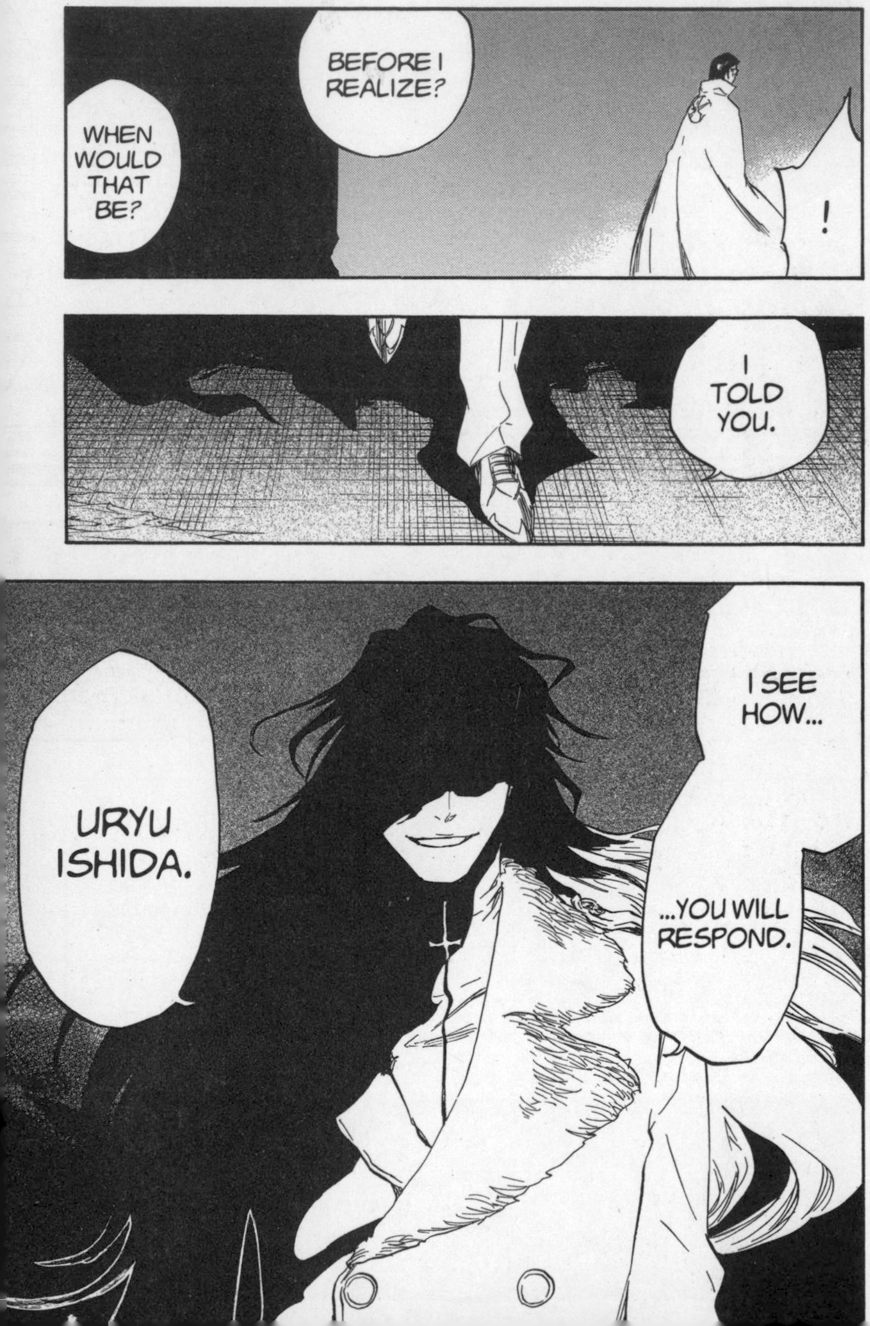
BEFORE I REALIZE?
WHEN WOULD THAT BE?
!
I TOLD YOU.
I SEE HOW...
...YOU WILL RESPOND.
URYU ISHIDA.

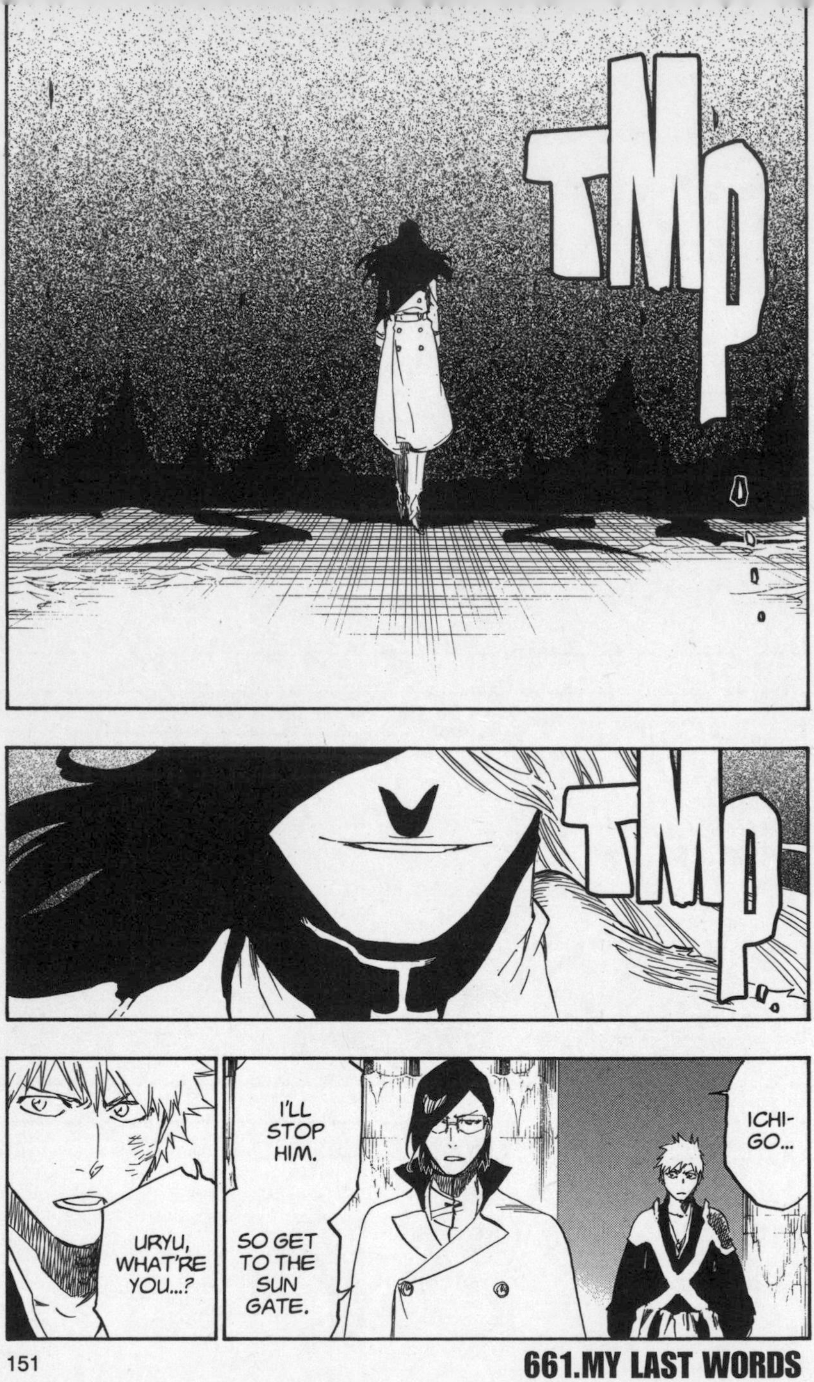
TMP
TMP
ICHI-GO...
I'LL STOP HIM.
SO GET TO THE SUN GATE.
URYU, WHAT'RE YOU...?

661.MY LAST WORDS

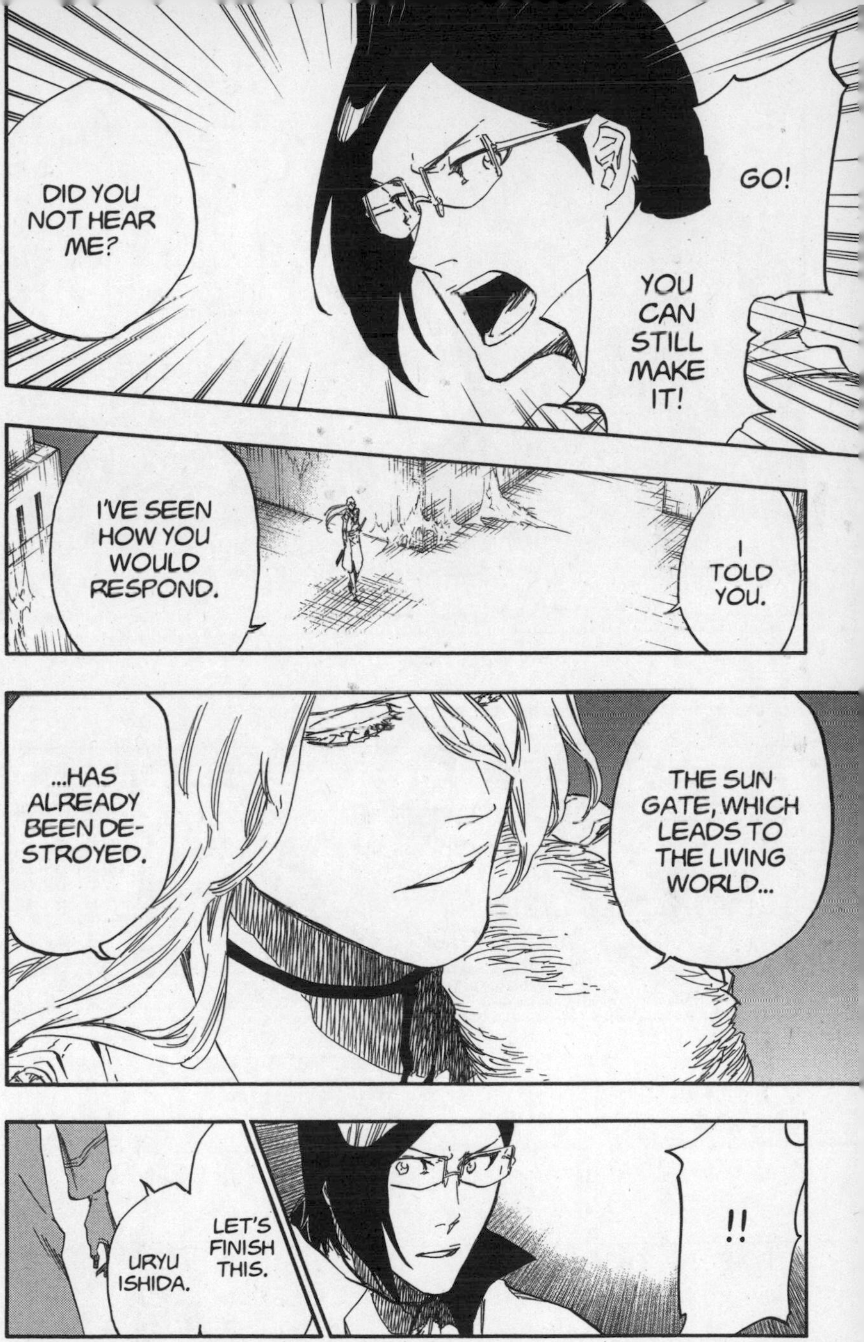
GO!
YOU CAN STILL MAKE IT!
DID YOU NOT HEAR ME?
I TOLD YOU.
I'VE SEEN HOW YOU WOULD RESPOND.
THE SUN GATE, WHICH LEADS TO THE LIVING WORLD...
...HAS ALREADY BEEN DE- STROYED.
!!
LET'S FINISH THIS.
URYU ISHIDA.

READ THIS WAY

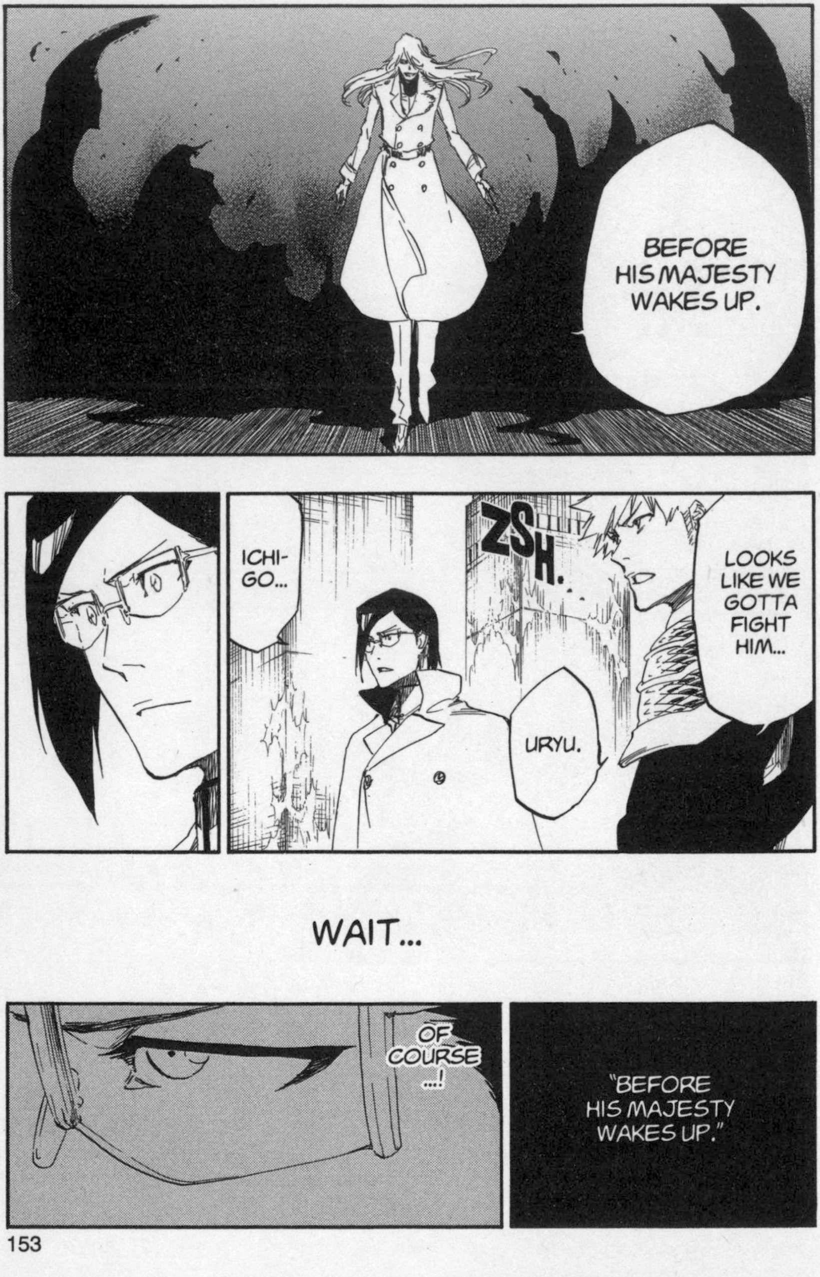

BEFORE HIS MAJESTY WAKES UP.
LOOKS LIKE WE GOTTA FIGHT HIM...
ZSH.
ICHI-GO...
URYU.
WAIT...
"BEFORE HIS MAJESTY WAKES UP."
OF COURSE ...!

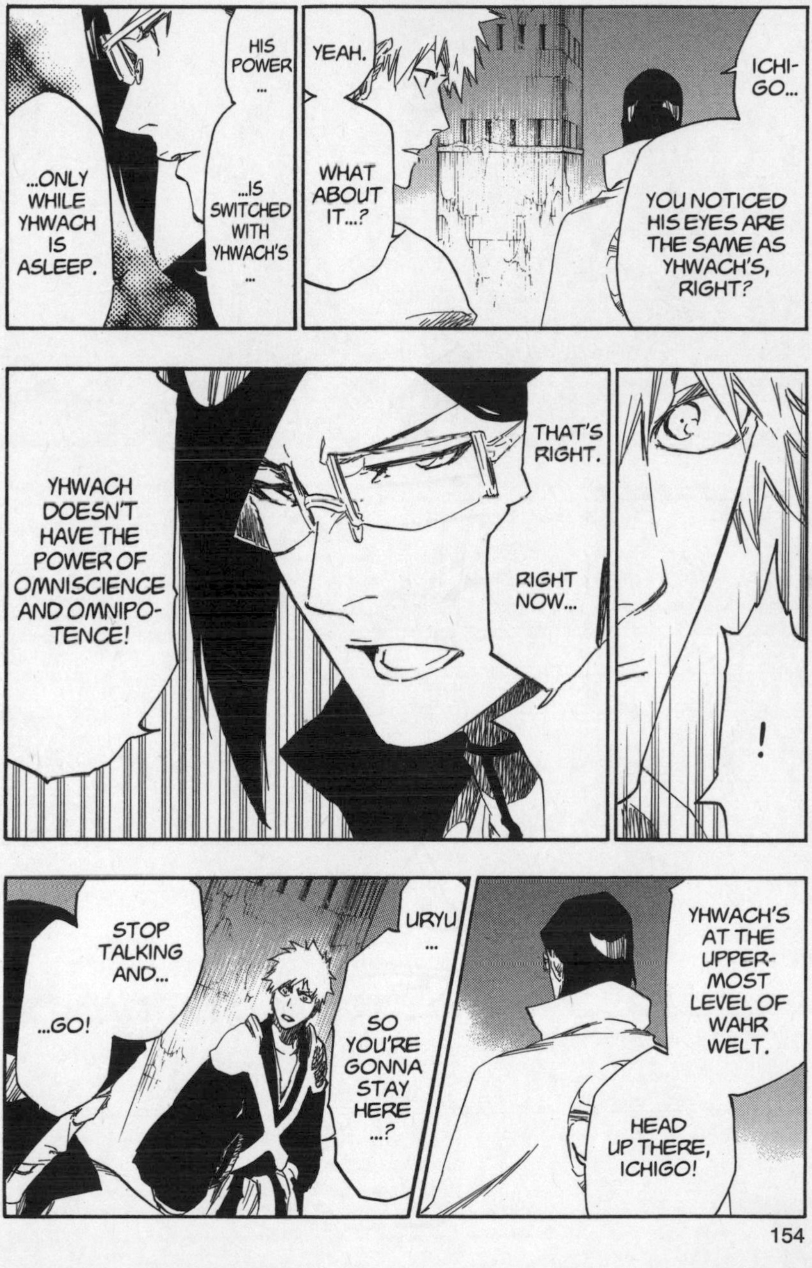
ICHIGO...
YOU NOTICED HIS EYES ARE THE SAME AS YHWACH'S, RIGHT?
YEAH.
WHAT ABOUT IT...?
HIS POWER ...
...IS SWITCHED WITH YHWACH'S ...
...ONLY WHILE YHWACH IS ASLEEP.
!
THAT'S RIGHT.
RIGHT NOW...
YHWACH DOESN'T HAVE THE POWER OF OMNISCIENCE AND OMNIPOTENCE!
YHWACH'S AT THE UPPERMOST LEVEL OF WAHR WELT.
HEAD UP THERE, ICHIGO!
URYU ...
SO YOU'RE GONNA STAY HERE ...?
STOP TALKING AND...
...GO!

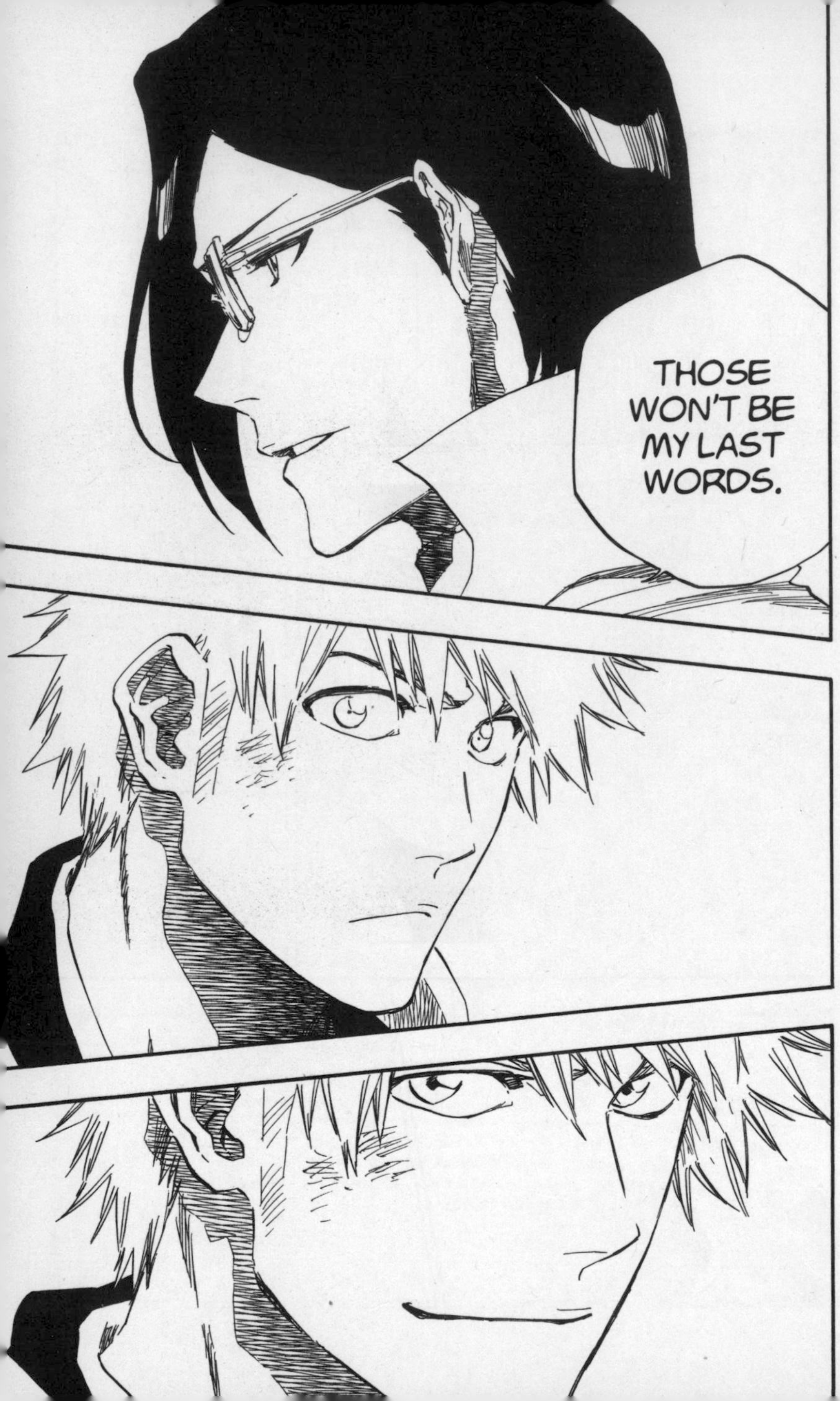
THOSE WON'T BE MY LAST WORDS.

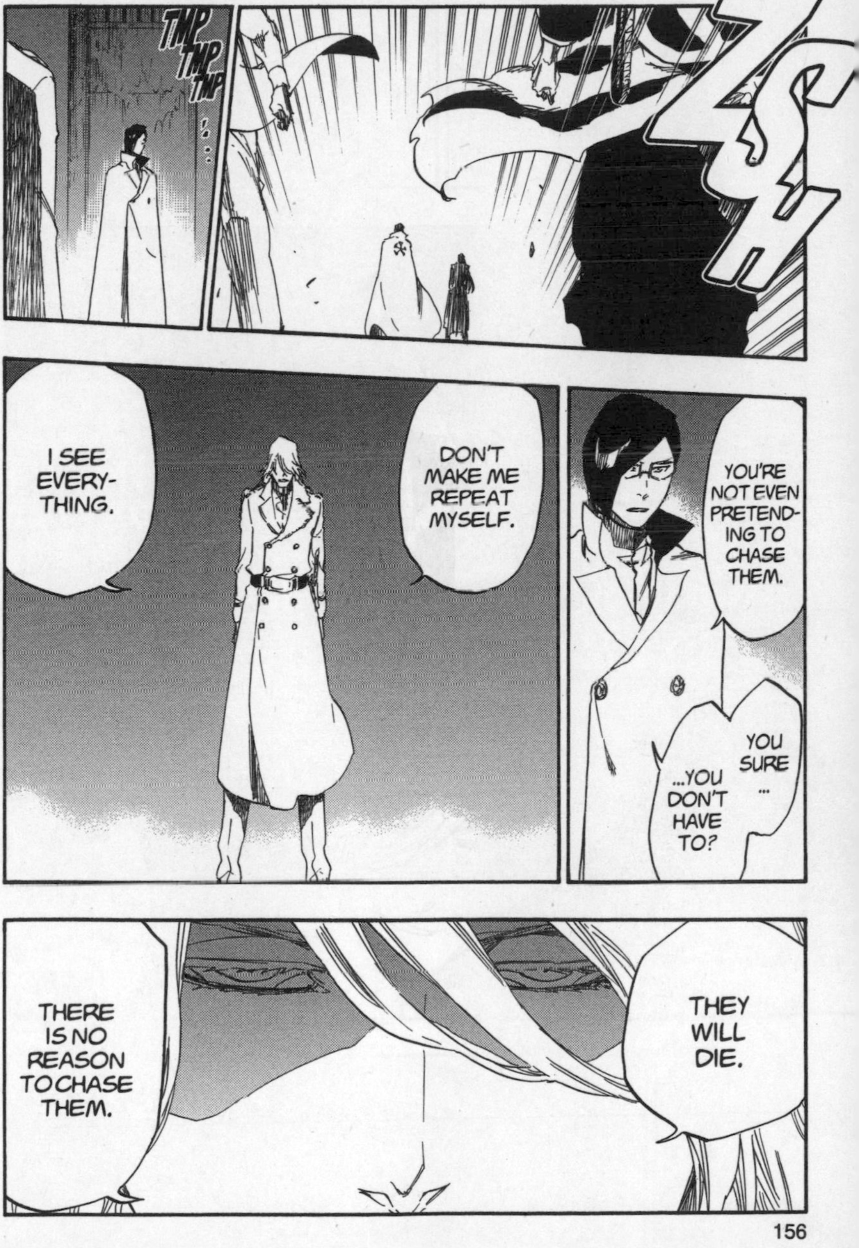
ZSH
TMP TMP TMP
...
YOU'RE NOT EVEN PRETENDING TO CHASE THEM.
YOU SURE...
...YOU DON'T HAVE TO?
DON'T MAKE ME REPEAT MYSELF.
I SEE EVERYTHING.
THEY WILL DIE.
THERE IS NO REASON TO CHASE THEM.

READ THIS WAY

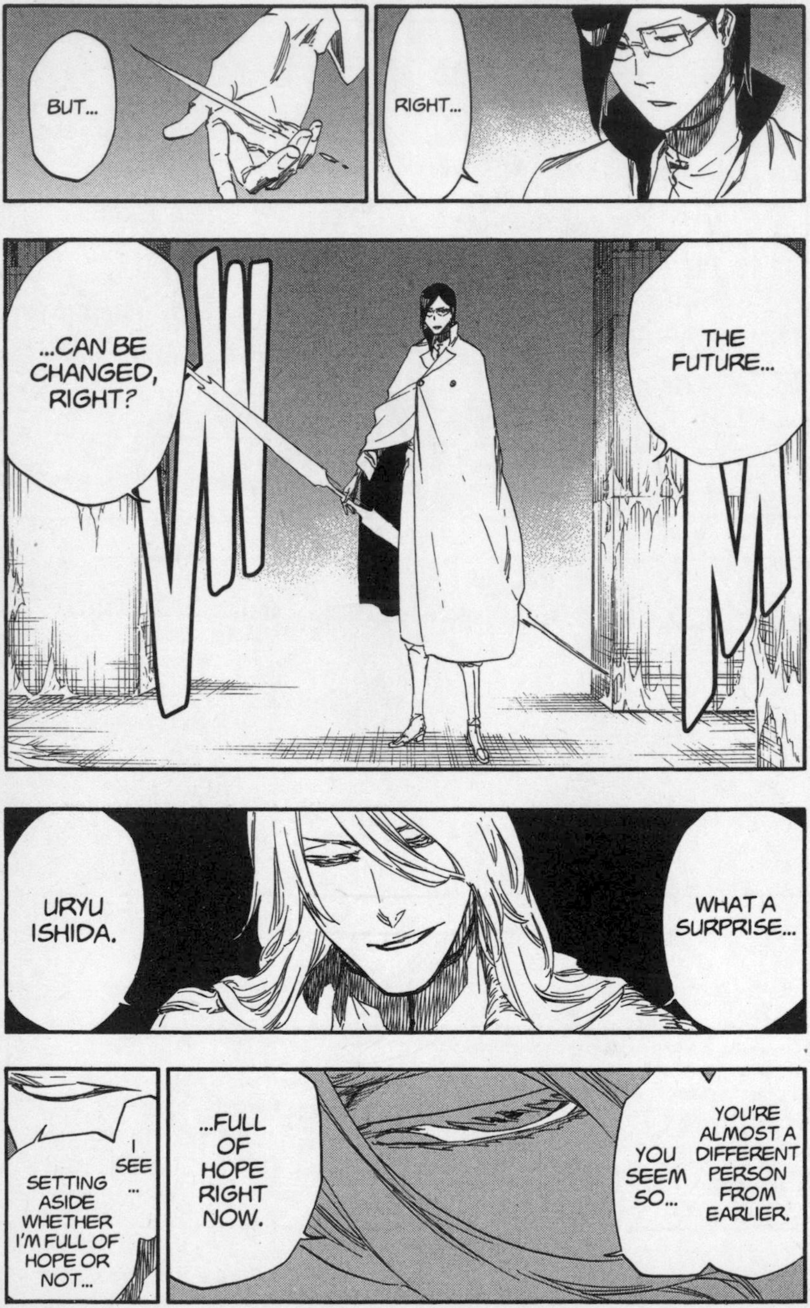
RIGHT...
BUT...
THE FUTURE...
...CAN BE CHANGED, RIGHT?
WHAT A SURPRISE...
URYU ISHIDA.
YOU'RE ALMOST A DIFFERENT PERSON FROM EARLIER.
YOU SEEM SO...
...FULL OF HOPE RIGHT NOW.
I SEE...
SETTING ASIDE WHETHER I'M FULL OF HOPE OR NOT...

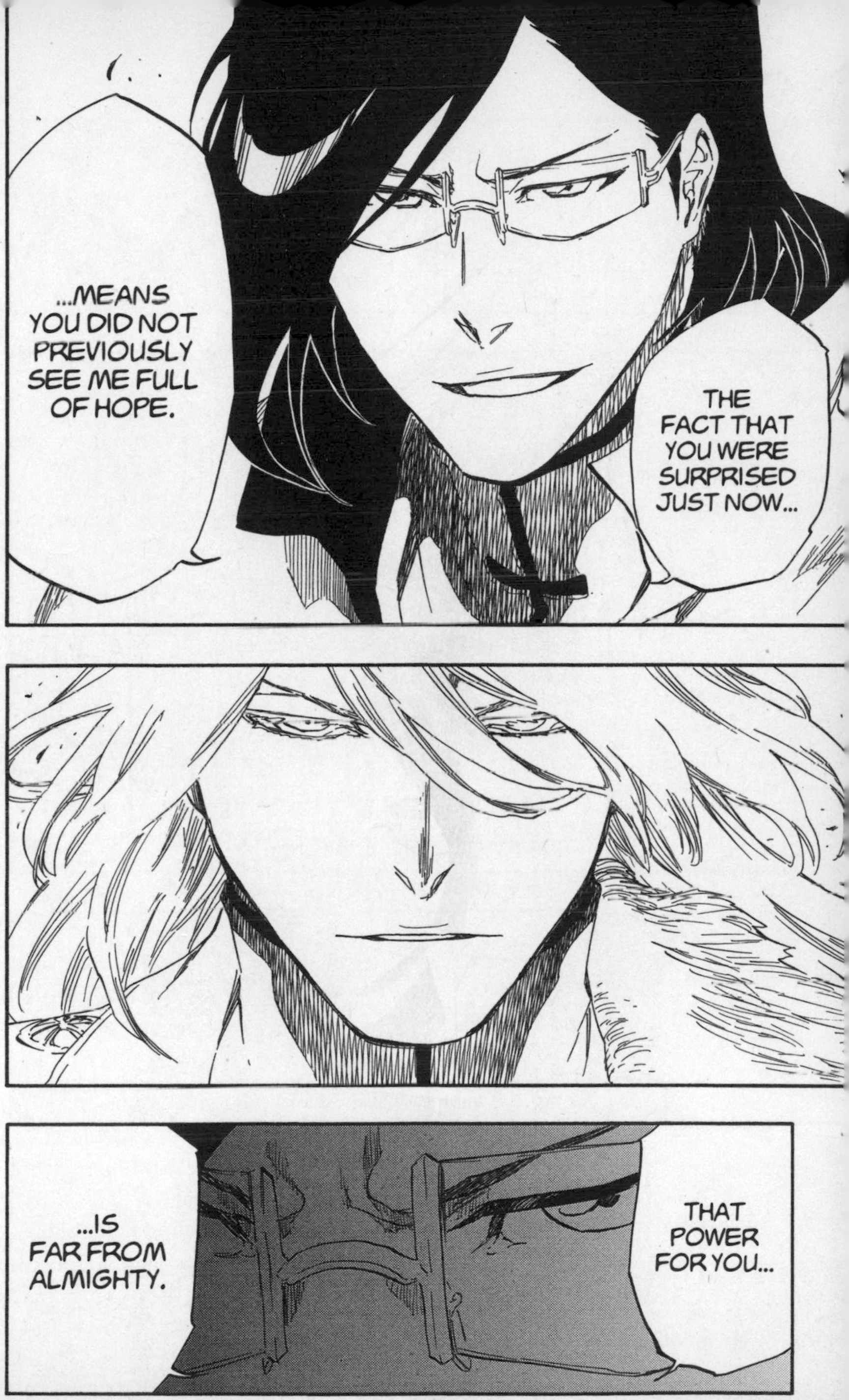
THE FACT THAT YOU WERE SURPRISED JUST NOW...
...MEANS YOU DID NOT PREVIOUSLY SEE ME FULL OF HOPE.
THAT POWER FOR YOU...
...IS FAR FROM ALMIGHTY.

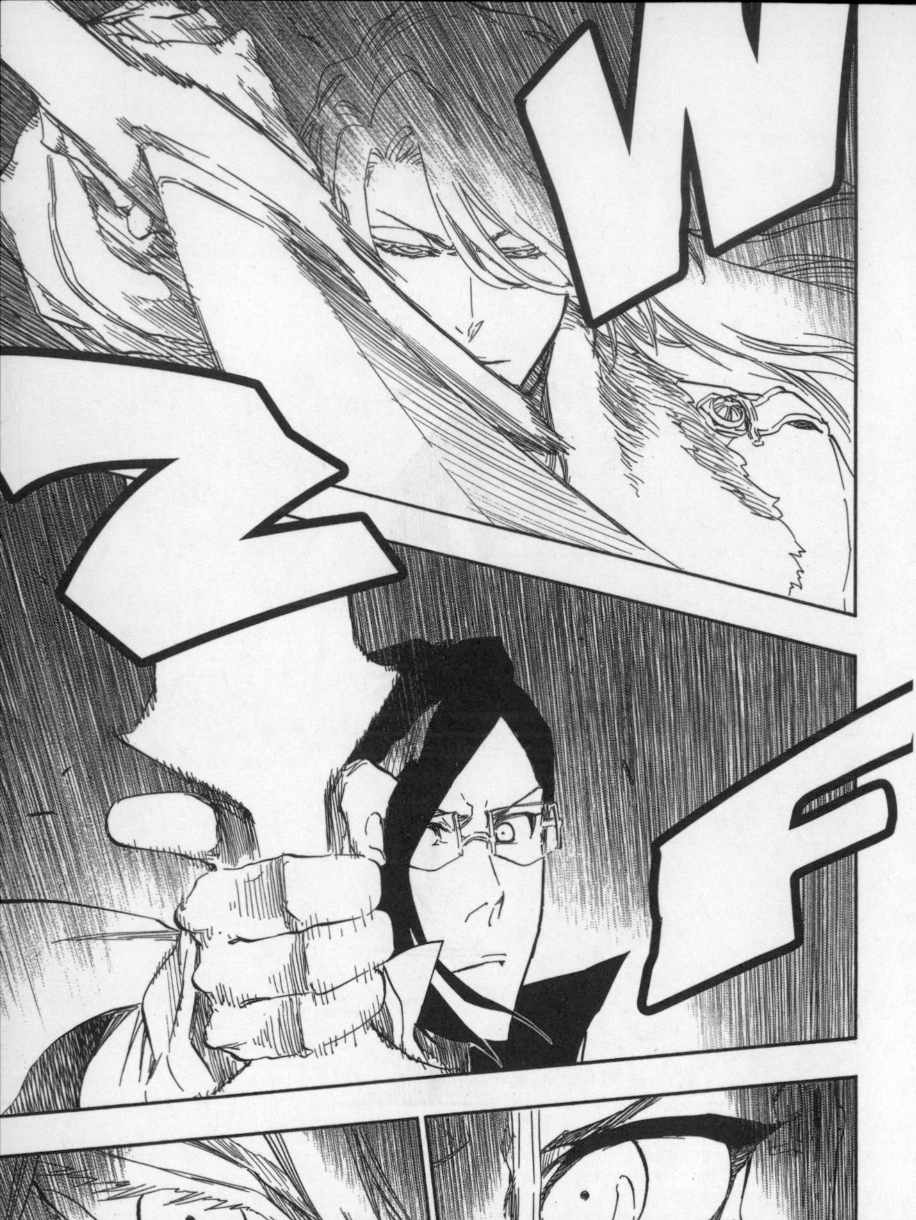

BLEACH 661.

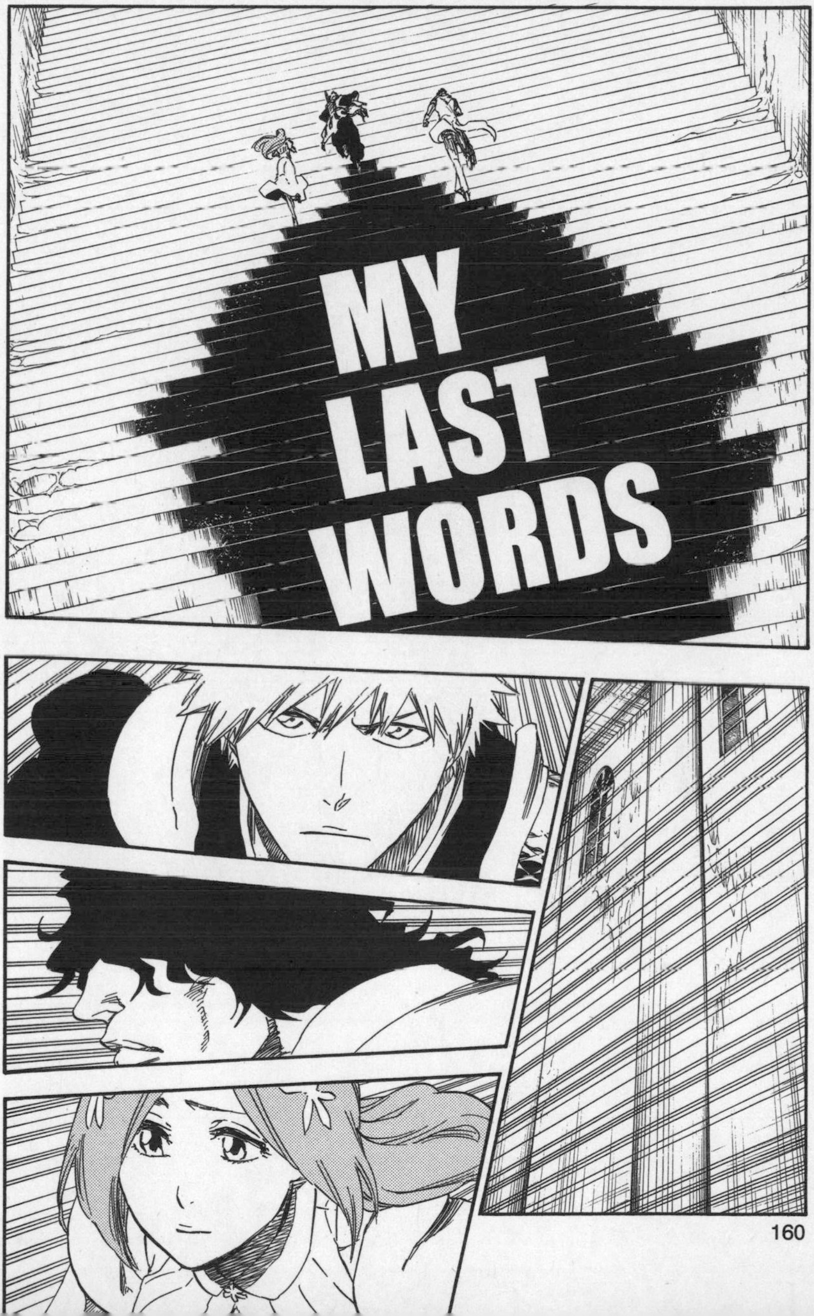
MY LAST WORDS

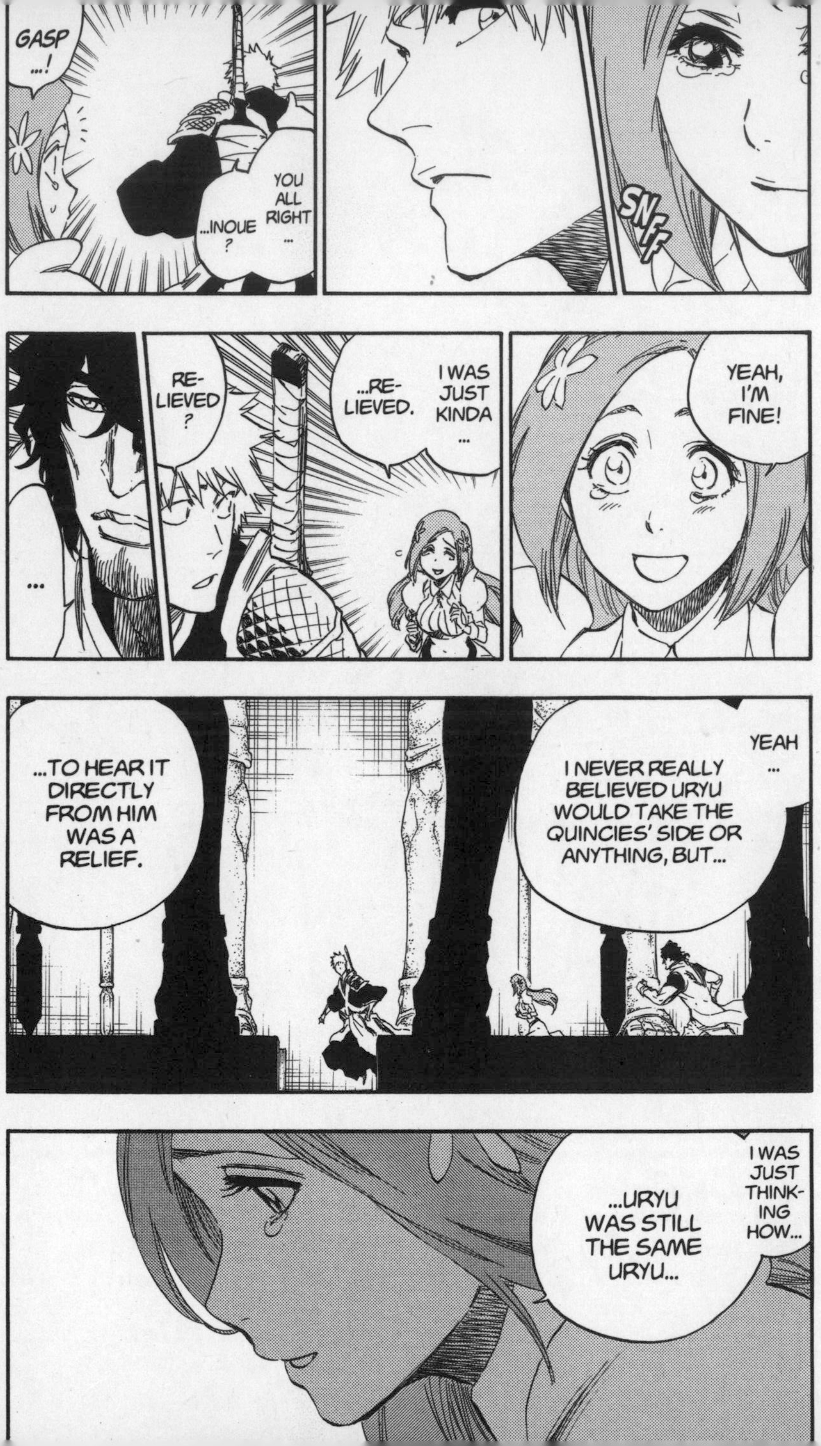
SNFF
...INOUE?
YOU ALL RIGHT...
GASP...!
YEAH, I'M FINE!
I WAS JUST KINDA...
...RE-LIEVED.
RE-LIEVED?
...
YEAH...
I NEVER REALLY BELIEVED URYU WOULD TAKE THE QUINCIES' SIDE OR ANYTHING, BUT...
...TO HEAR IT DIRECTLY FROM HIM WAS A RELIEF.
I WAS JUST THINKING HOW...
...URYU WAS STILL THE SAME URYU...

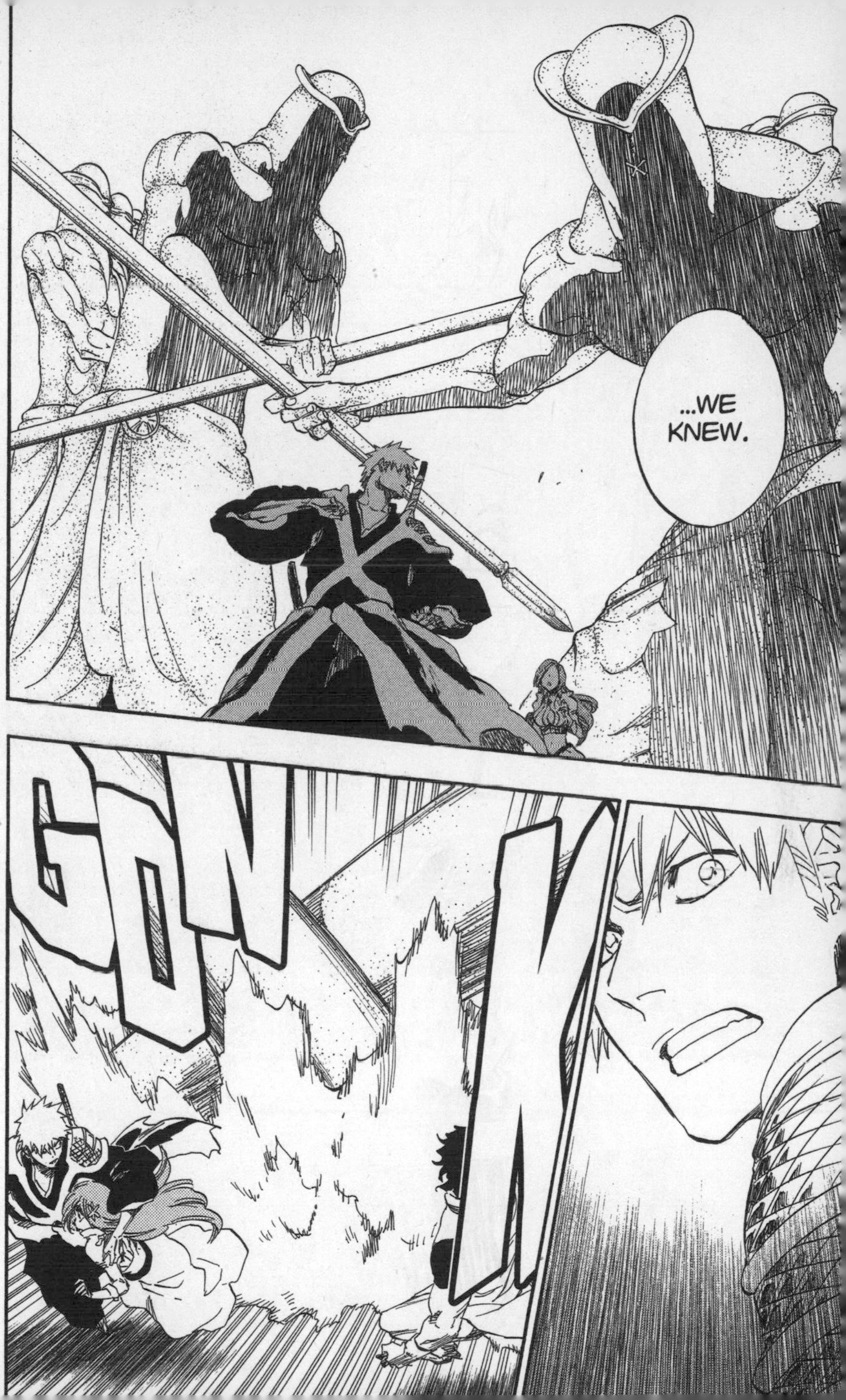
...WE KNEW.
GOON

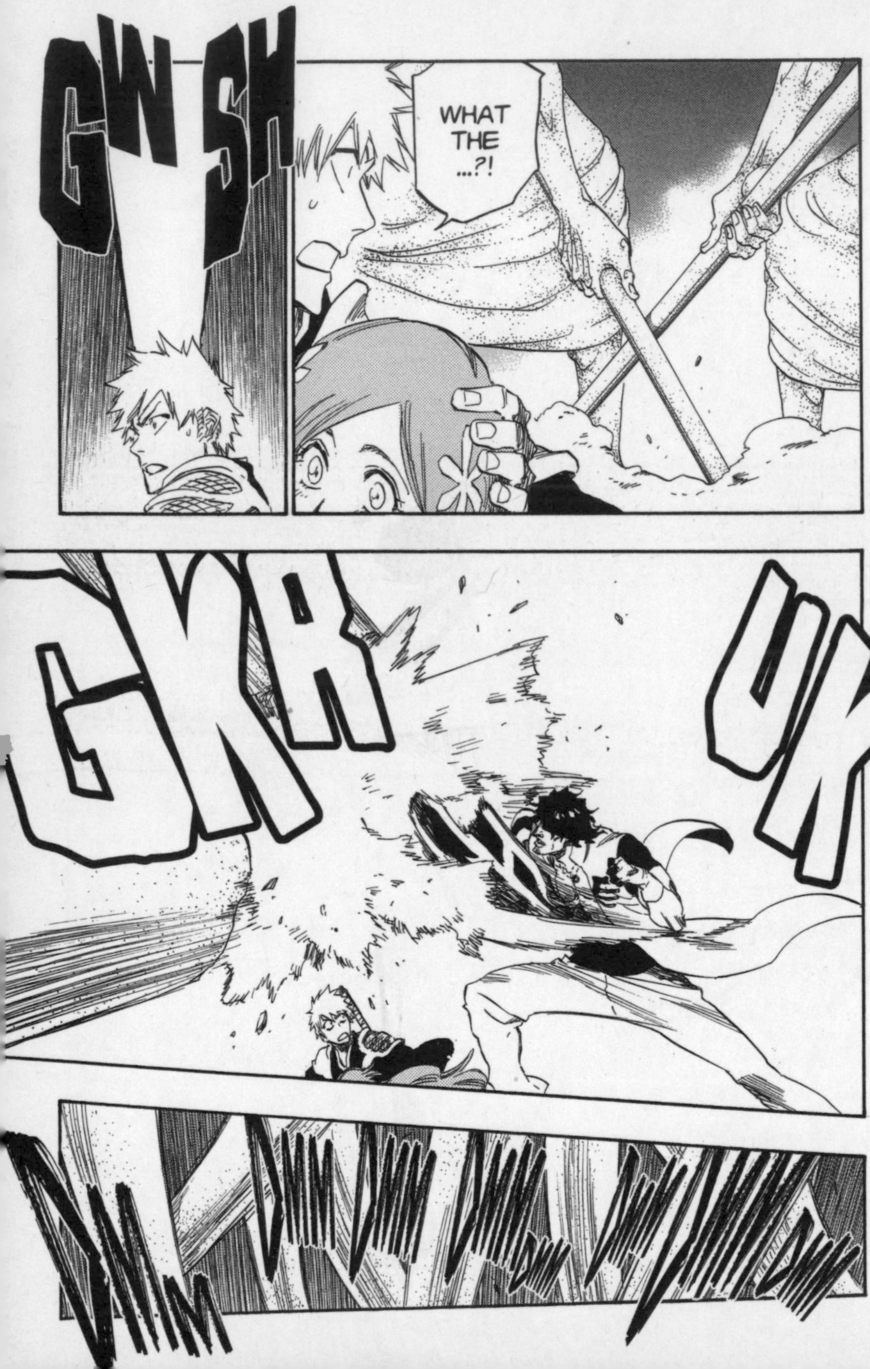
WHAT THE ...?!
GWSH
UK
GKRA

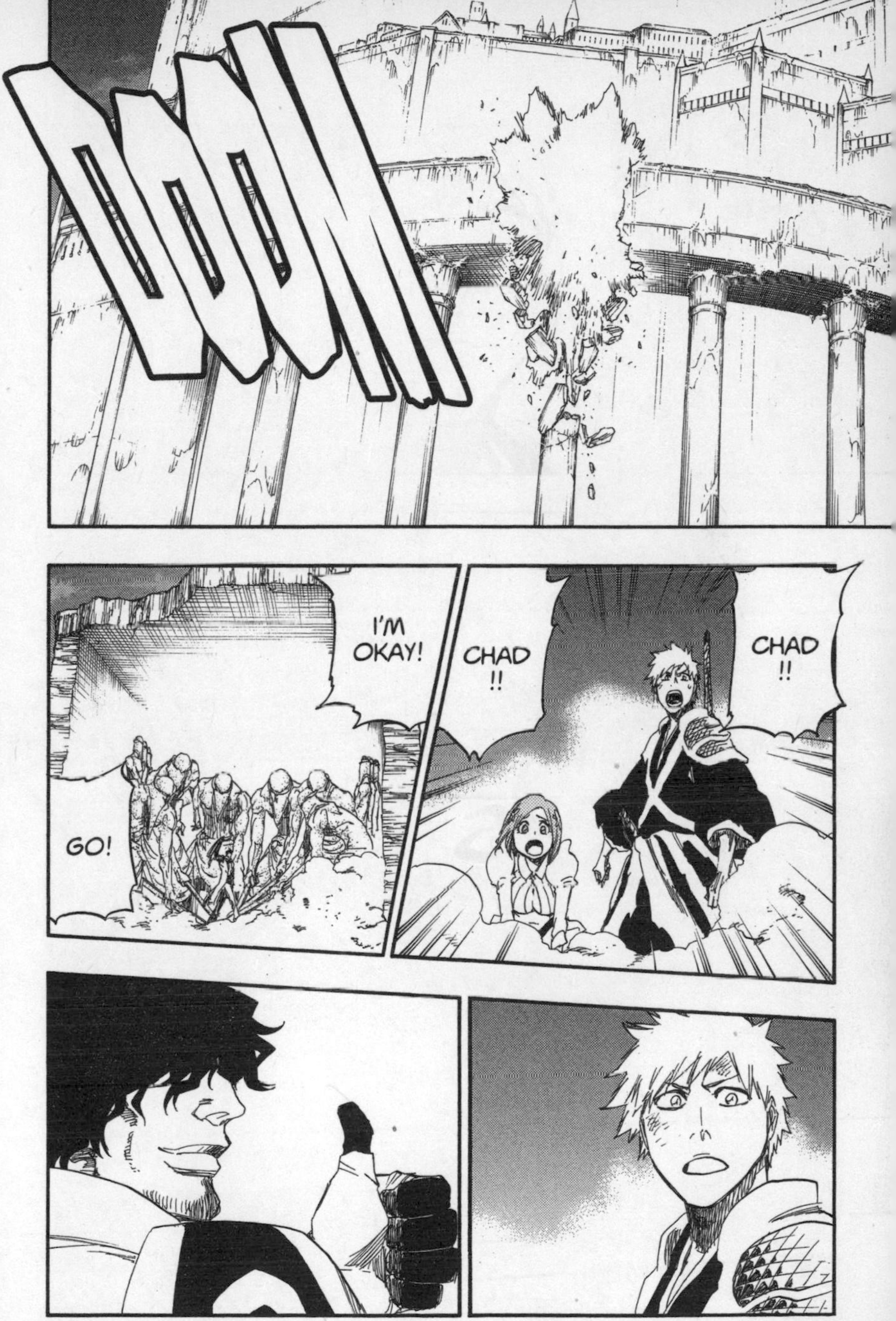
DOOM
CHAD !!
CHAD !!
I'M OKAY!
GO!

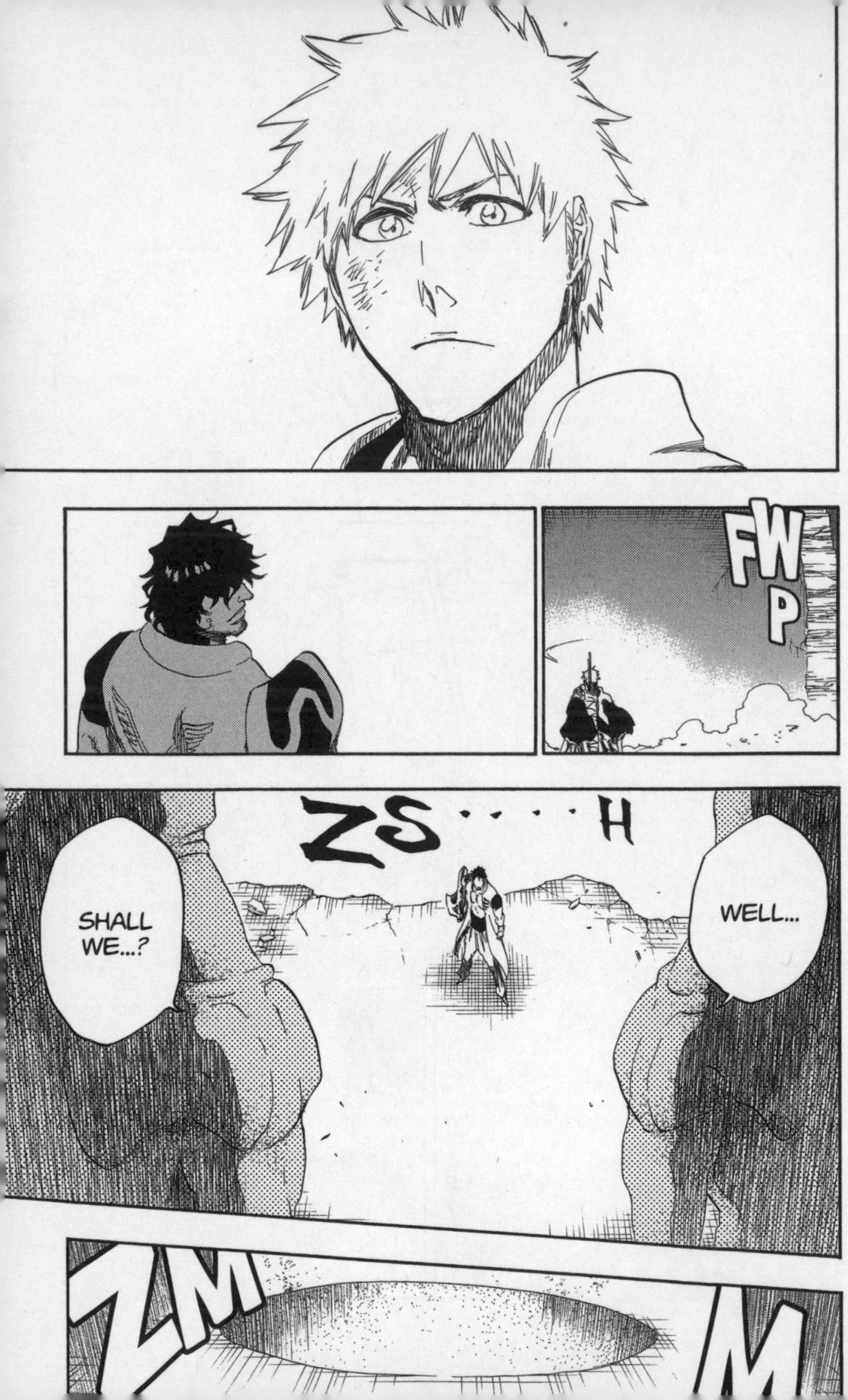
FWP
ZS...H
WELL...
SHALL WE...?
ZM M

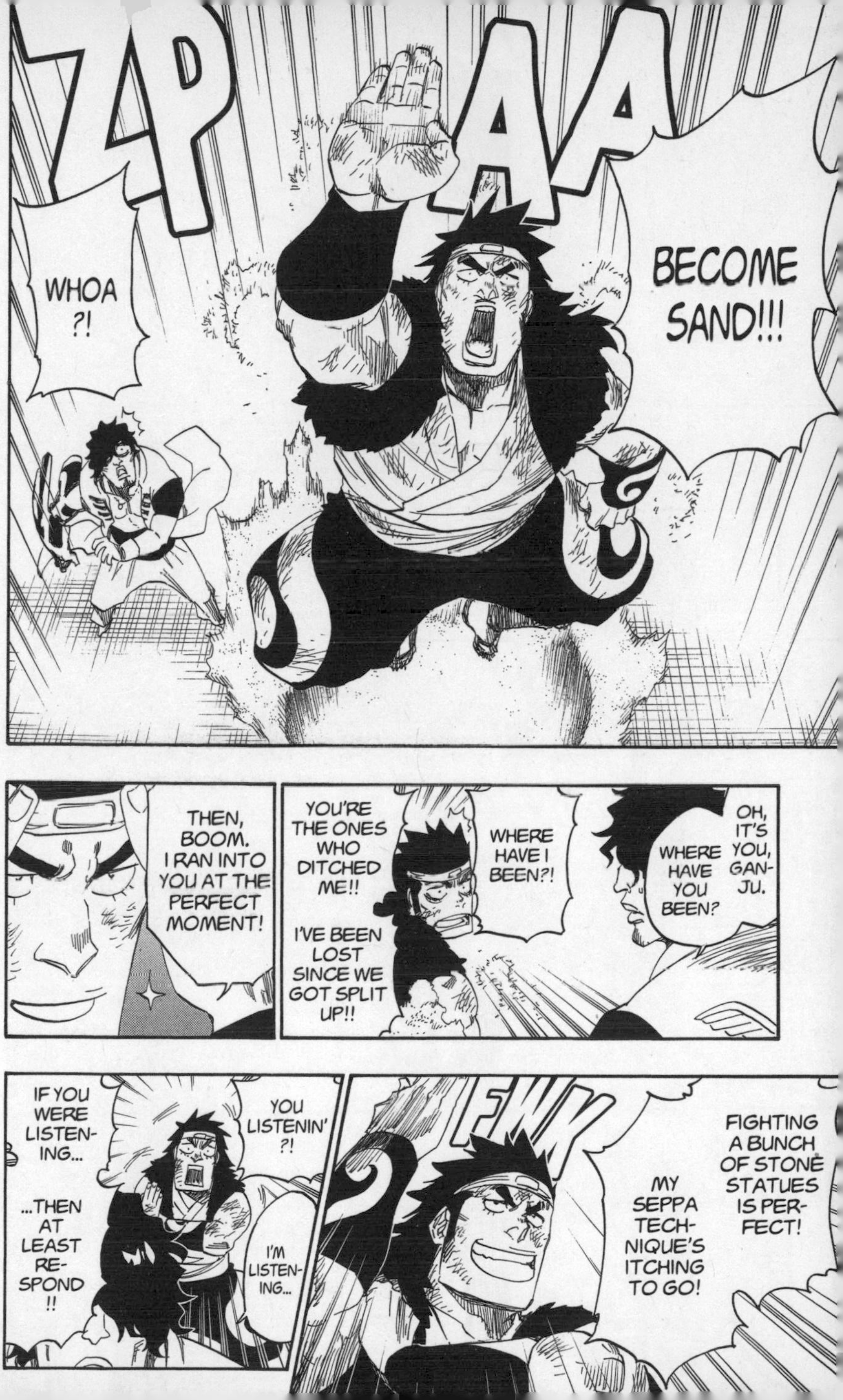
ZPAA
BECOME SAND!!!
WHOA ?!
OH, IT'S YOU, GAN-JU.
WHERE HAVE YOU BEEN?
WHERE HAVE I BEEN?!
YOU'RE THE ONES WHO DITCHED ME!!
I'VE BEEN LOST SINCE WE GOT SPLIT UP!!
THEN, BOOM. I RAN INTO YOU AT THE PERFECT MOMENT!
FIGHTING A BUNCH OF STONE STATUES IS PER-FECT!
MY SEPPA TECH-NIQUE'S ITCHING TO GO!
YOU LISTENIN' ?!
I'M LISTEN-ING...
IF YOU WERE LISTEN-ING...
...THEN AT LEAST RE-SPOND !!

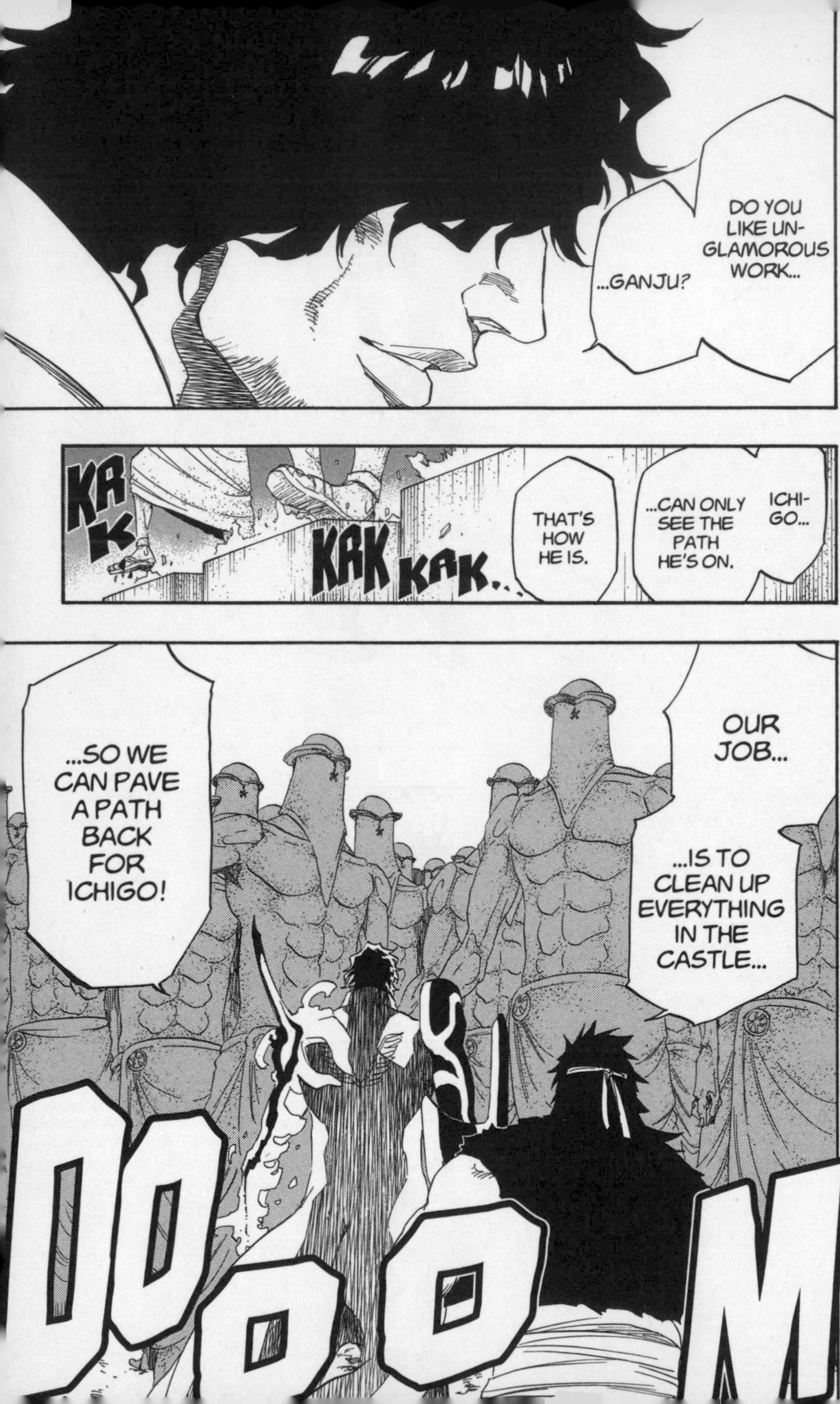
DO YOU LIKE UN-GLAMOROUS WORK...
...GANJU?
ICHI-GO...
...CAN ONLY SEE THE PATH HE'S ON.
THAT'S HOW HE IS.
KAK
KRK
KRK
OUR JOB...
...IS TO CLEAN UP EVERYTHING IN THE CASTLE...
...SO WE CAN PAVE A PATH BACK FOR ICHIGO!
DOOOM

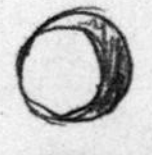

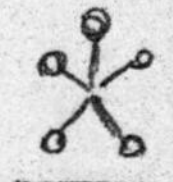

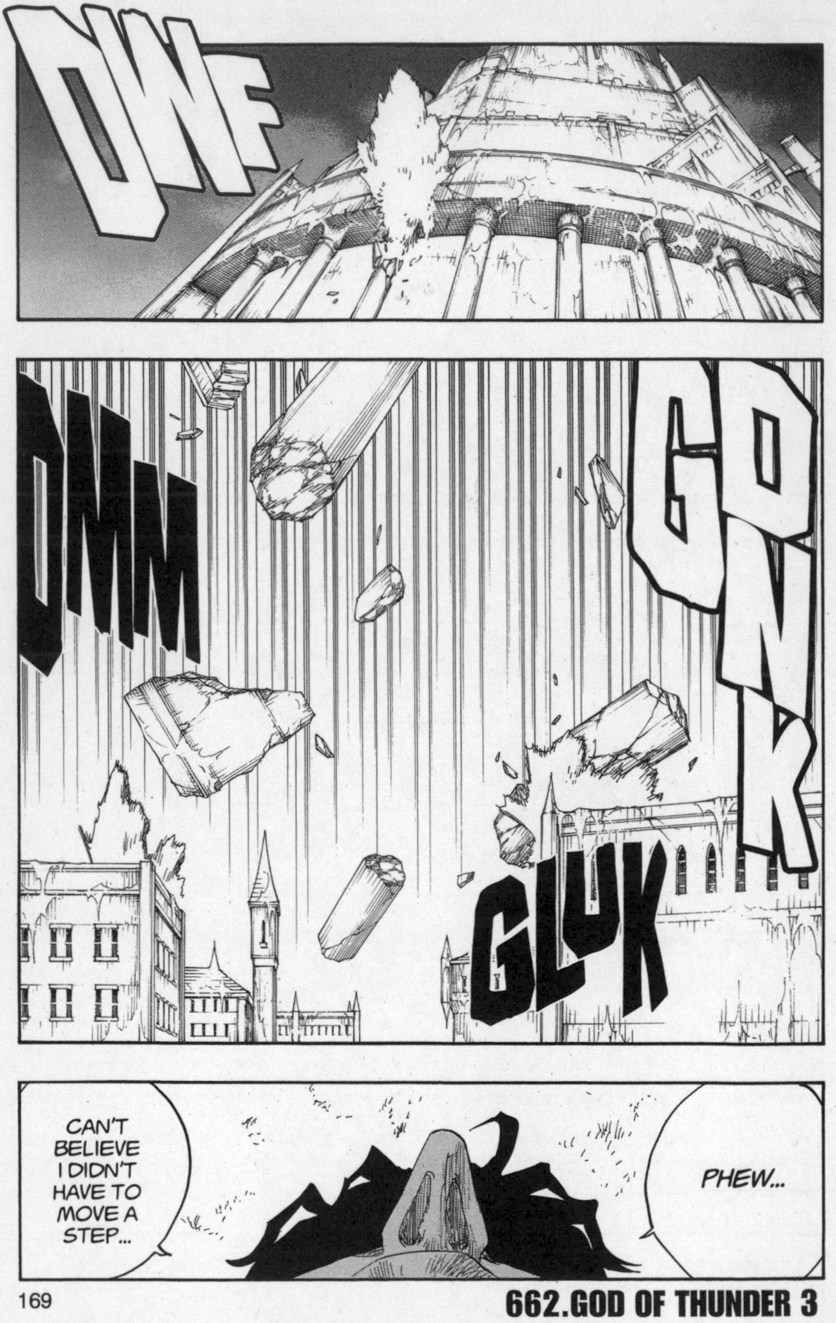
DWF
GONK
DMM
GLUK
PHEW...
CAN'T BELIEVE I DIDN'T HAVE TO MOVE A STEP...

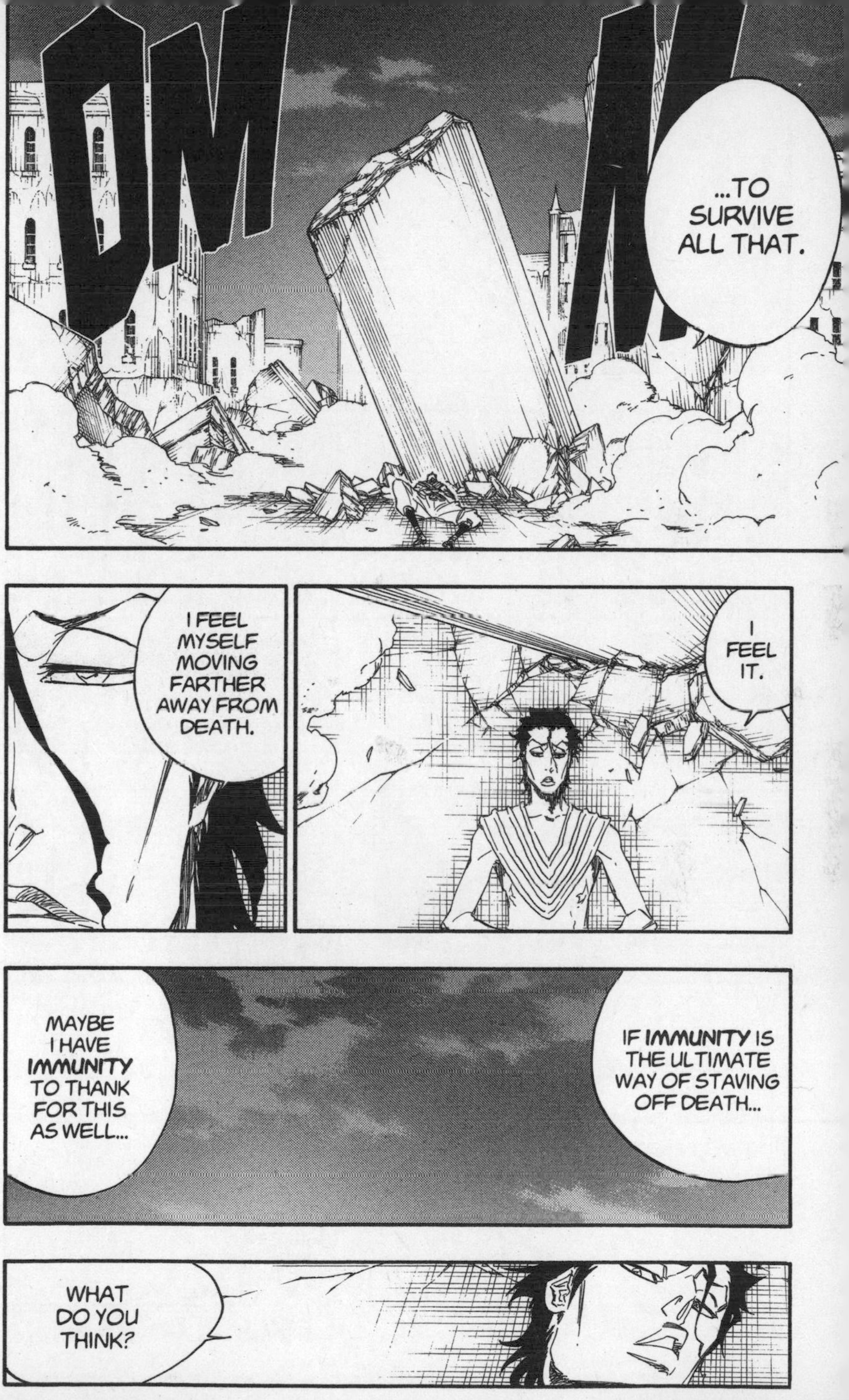
...TO SURVIVE ALL THAT.
I FEEL IT.
I FEEL MYSELF MOVING FARTHER AWAY FROM DEATH.
IF IMMUNITY IS THE ULTIMATE WAY OF STAVING OFF DEATH...
MAYBE I HAVE IMMUNITY TO THANK FOR THIS AS WELL...
WHAT DO YOU THINK?

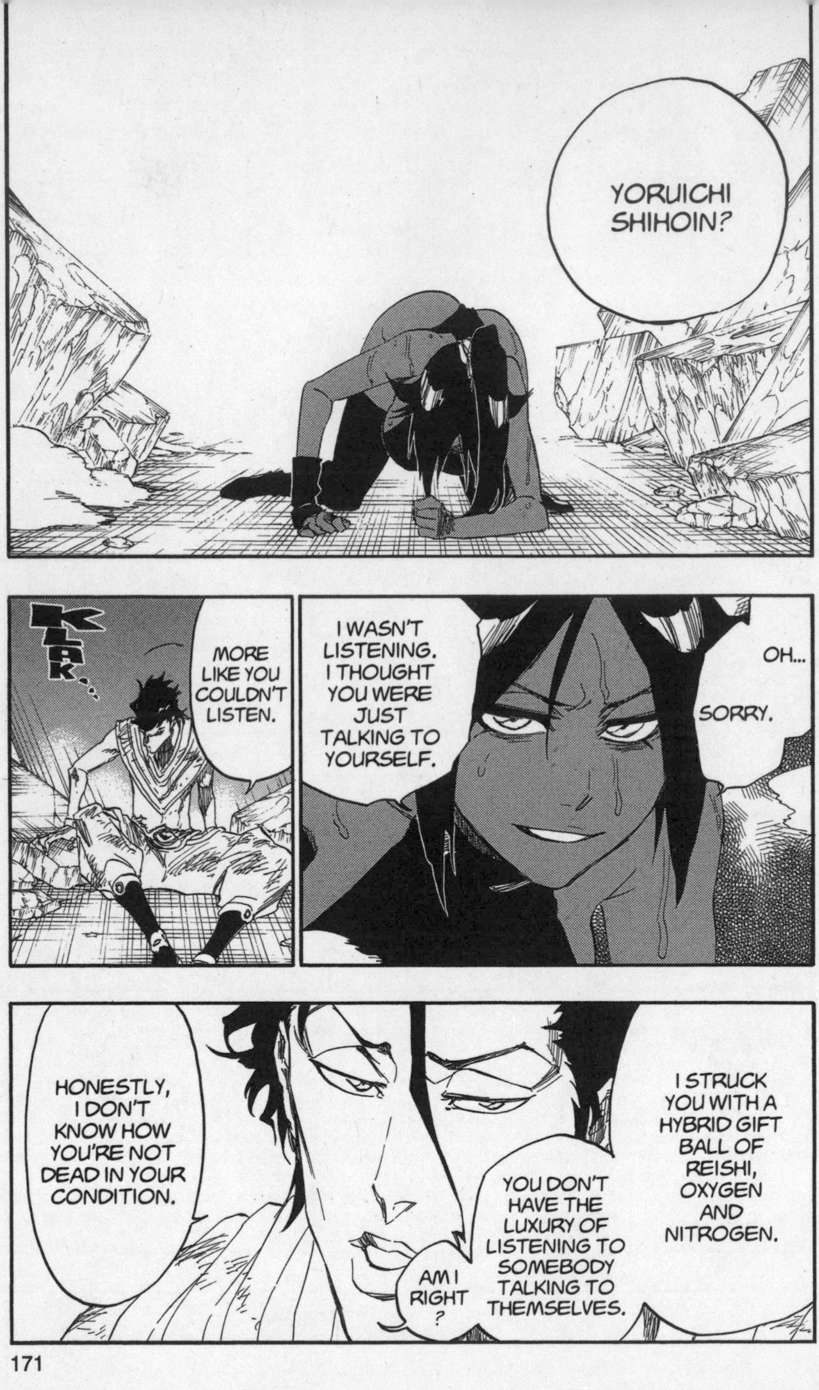
YORUICHI SHIHOIN?
OH... SORRY.
I WASN'T LISTENING. I THOUGHT YOU WERE JUST TALKING TO YOURSELF.
KLAK...
MORE LIKE YOU COULDN'T LISTEN.
I STRUCK YOU WITH A HYBRID GIFT BALL OF REISHI, OXYGEN AND NITROGEN.
YOU DON'T HAVE THE LUXURY OF LISTENING TO SOMEBODY TALKING TO THEMSELVES.
AM I RIGHT?
HONESTLY, I DON'T KNOW HOW YOU'RE NOT DEAD IN YOUR CONDITION.

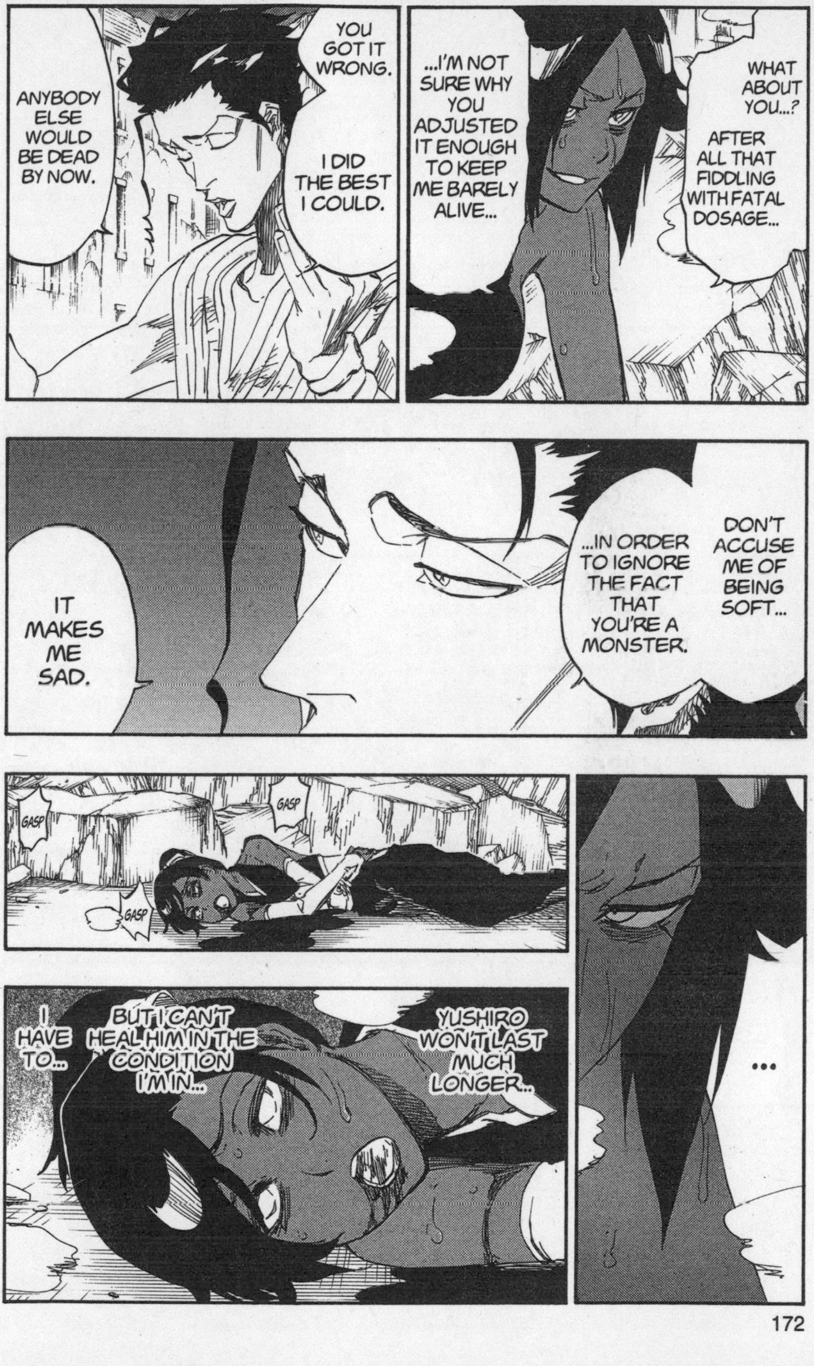
WHAT ABOUT YOU...?
AFTER ALL THAT FIDDLING WITH FATAL DOSAGE...
...I'M NOT SURE WHY YOU ADJUSTED IT ENOUGH TO KEEP ME BARELY ALIVE...
YOU GOT IT WRONG.
I DID THE BEST I COULD.
ANYBODY ELSE WOULD BE DEAD BY NOW.
DON'T ACCUSE ME OF BEING SOFT...
...IN ORDER TO IGNORE THE FACT THAT YOU'RE A MONSTER.
IT MAKES ME SAD.
...
GASP
GASP
GASP
YUSHIRO WON'T LAST MUCH LONGER...
BUT I CAN'T HEAL HIM IN THE CONDITION I'M IN...
I HAVE TO...

READ THIS WAY

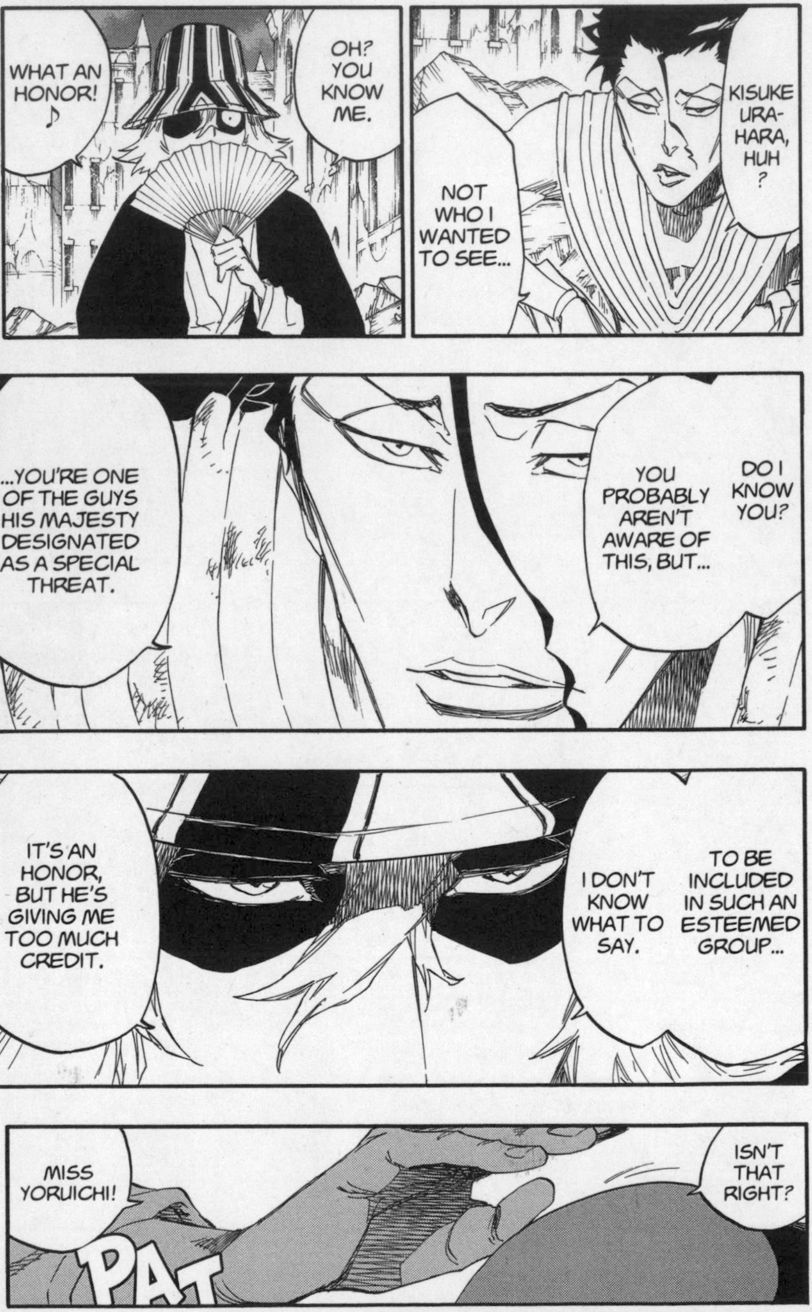

KISUKE URA-HARA, HUH?
NOT WHO I WANTED TO SEE...
OH? YOU KNOW ME.
WHAT AN HONOR! ♪
DO I KNOW YOU?
YOU PROBABLY AREN'T AWARE OF THIS, BUT...
...YOU'RE ONE OF THE GUYS HIS MAJESTY DESIGNATED AS A SPECIAL THREAT.
TO BE INCLUDED IN SUCH AN ESTEEMED GROUP...
I DON'T KNOW WHAT TO SAY.
IT'S AN HONOR, BUT HE'S GIVING ME TOO MUCH CREDIT.
ISN'T THAT RIGHT?
MISS YORUICHI!
PAT

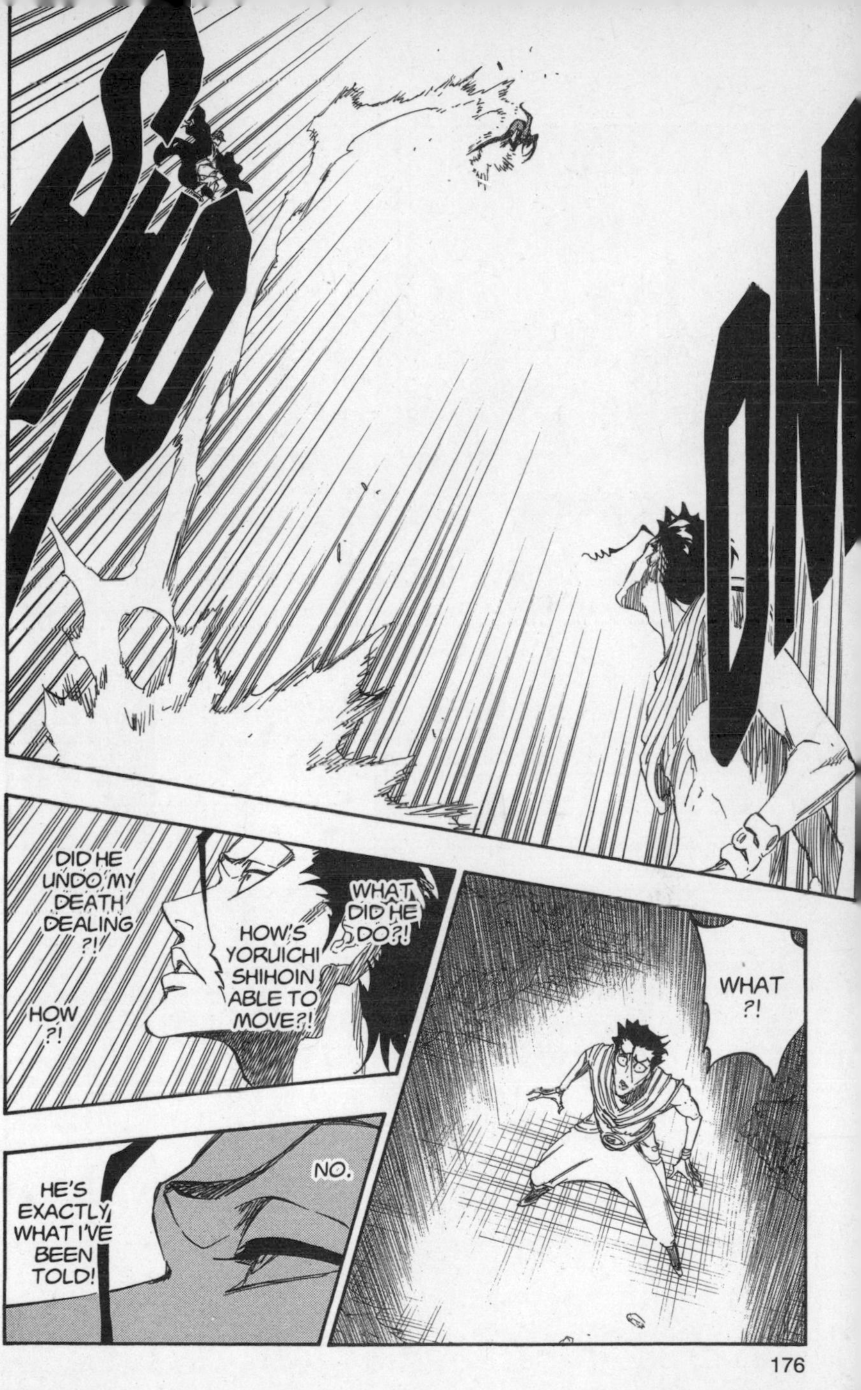
WHAT ?!
WHAT DID HE DO?!
HOW'S YORUICHI SHIHOIN ABLE TO MOVE?!
DID HE UNDO MY DEATH DEALING ?!
HOW ?!
NO.
HE'S EXACTLY WHAT I'VE BEEN TOLD!

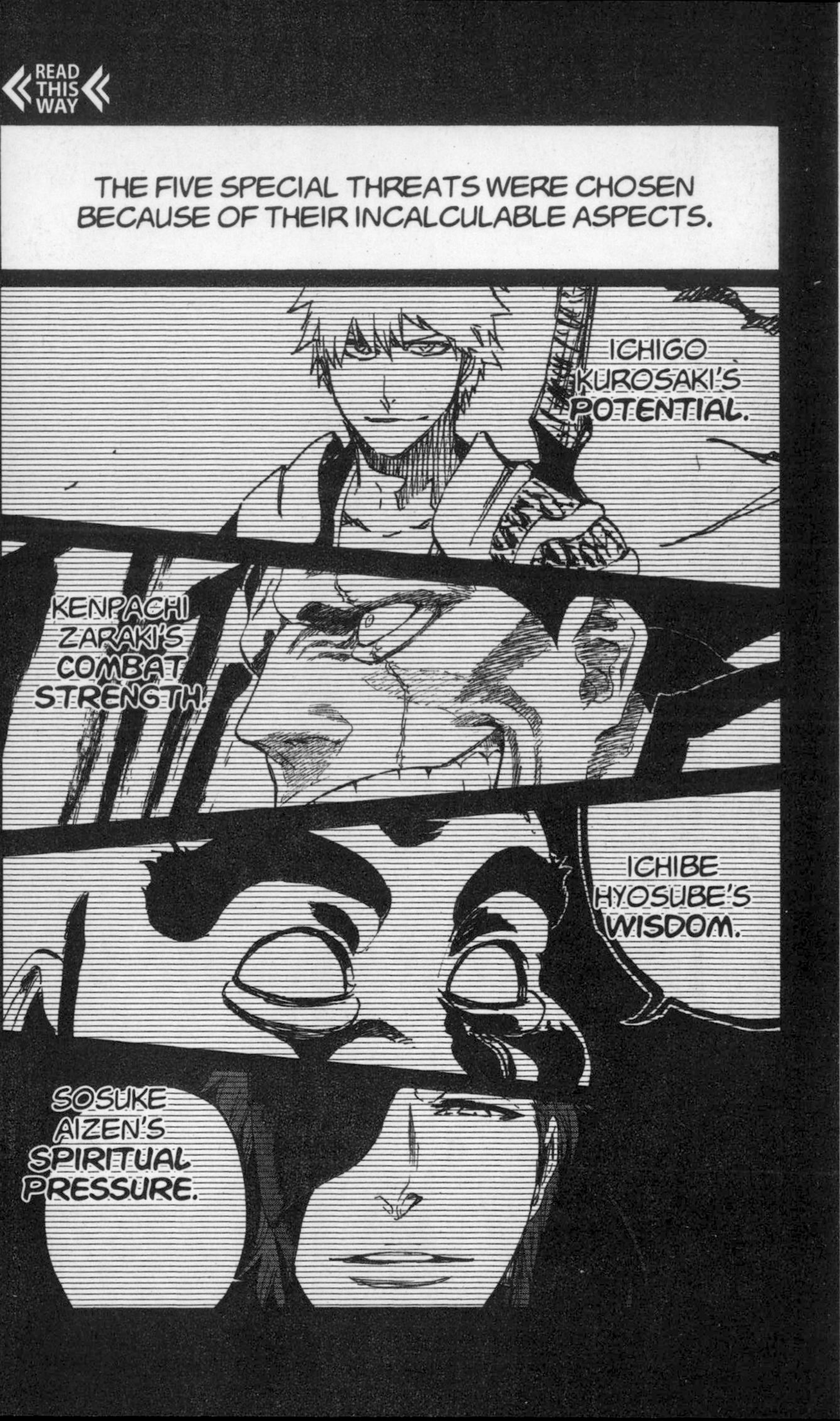
READ THIS WAY
THE FIVE SPECIAL THREATS WERE CHOSEN BECAUSE OF THEIR INCALCULABLE ASPECTS.
ICHIGO KUROSAKI'S POTENTIAL.
KENPACHI ZARAKI'S COMBAT STRENGTH.
ICHIBE HYOSUBE'S WISDOM.
SOSUKE AIZEN'S SPIRITUAL PRESSURE.

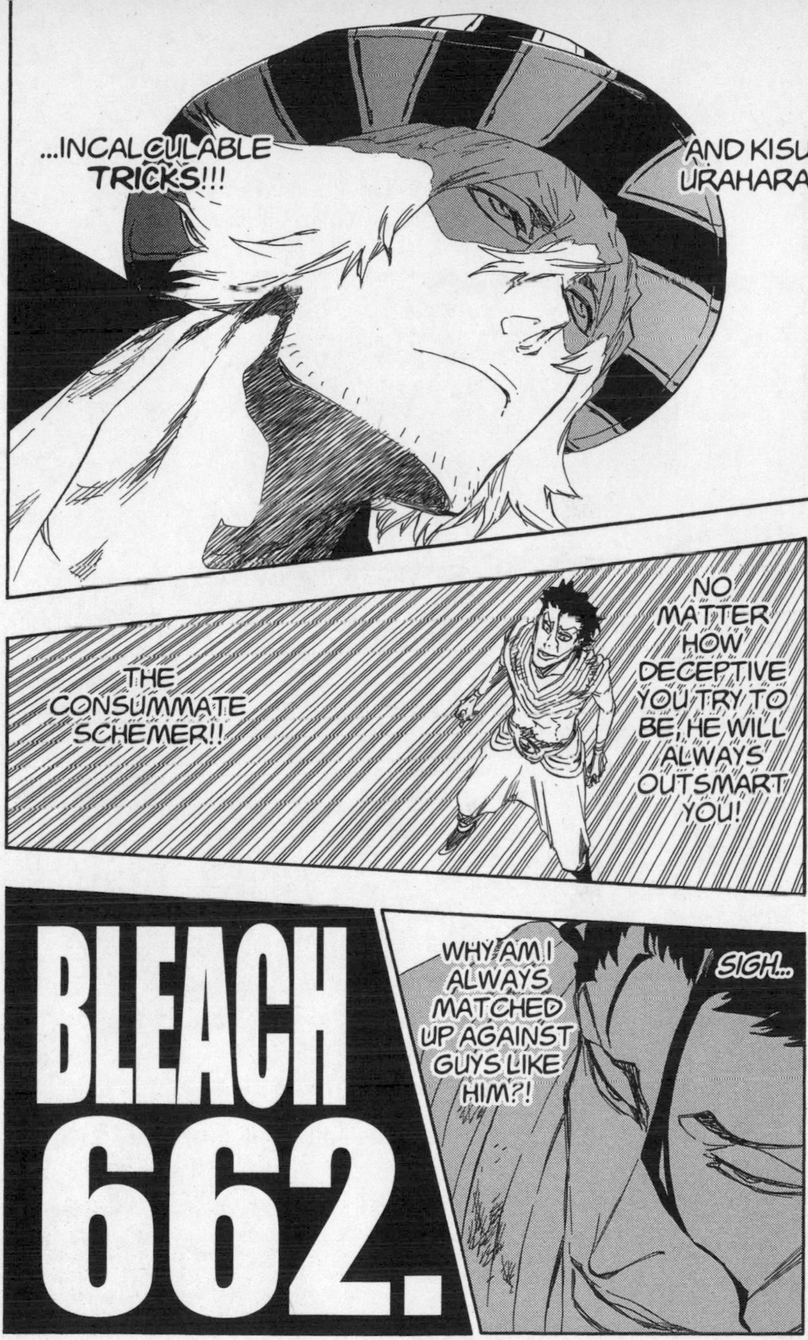
AND KISUKE URAHARA'S...
...INCALCULABLE TRICKS!!!
NO MATTER HOW DECEPTIVE YOU TRY TO BE, HE WILL ALWAYS OUTSMART YOU!
THE CONSUMMATE SCHEMER!!
SIGH...
WHY AM I ALWAYS MATCHED UP AGAINST GUYS LIKE HIM?!
BLEACH 662.

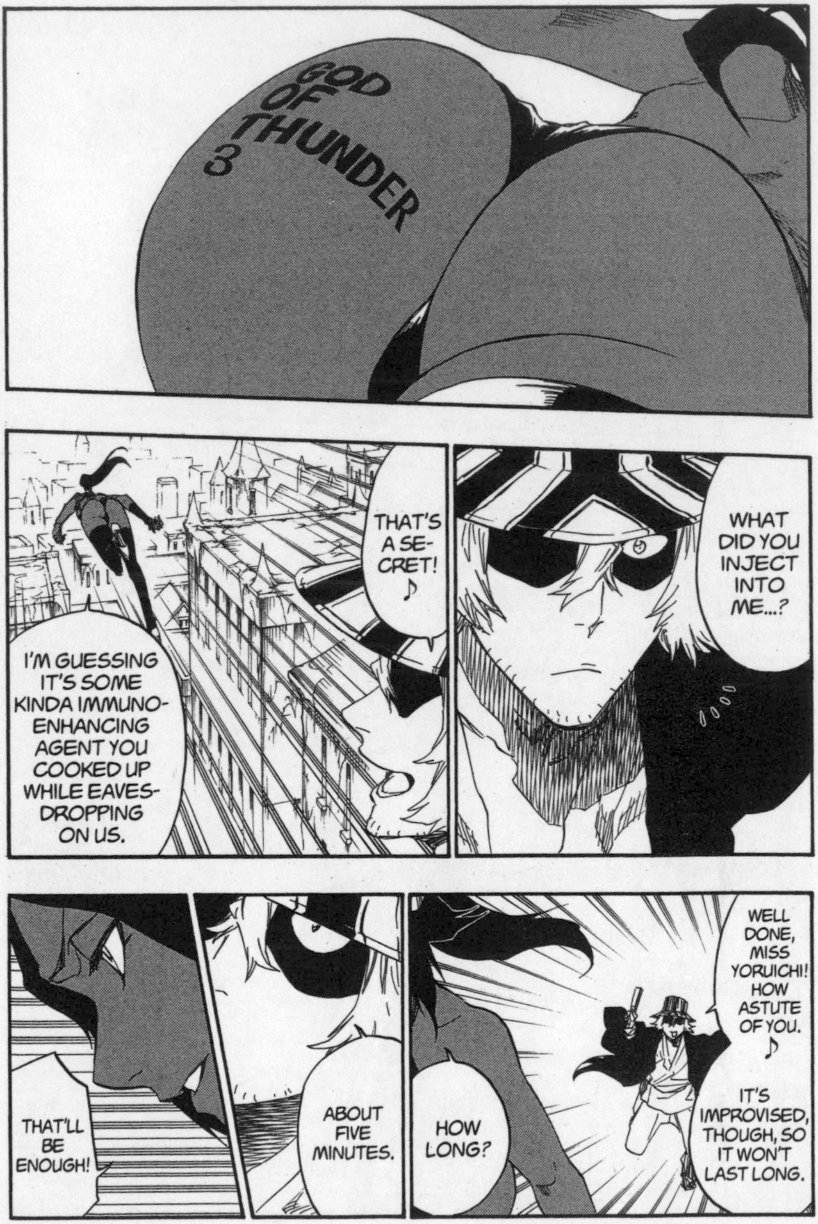
GOD OF THUNDER 3
WHAT DID YOU INJECT INTO ME...?
THAT'S A SE-CRET! ♪
I'M GUESSING IT'S SOME KINDA IMMUNO-ENHANCING AGENT YOU COOKED UP WHILE EAVES-DROPPING ON US.
WELL DONE, MISS YORUICHI! HOW ASTUTE OF YOU. ♪
IT'S IMPROVISED, THOUGH, SO IT WON'T LAST LONG.
HOW LONG?
ABOUT FIVE MINUTES.
THAT'LL BE ENOUGH!

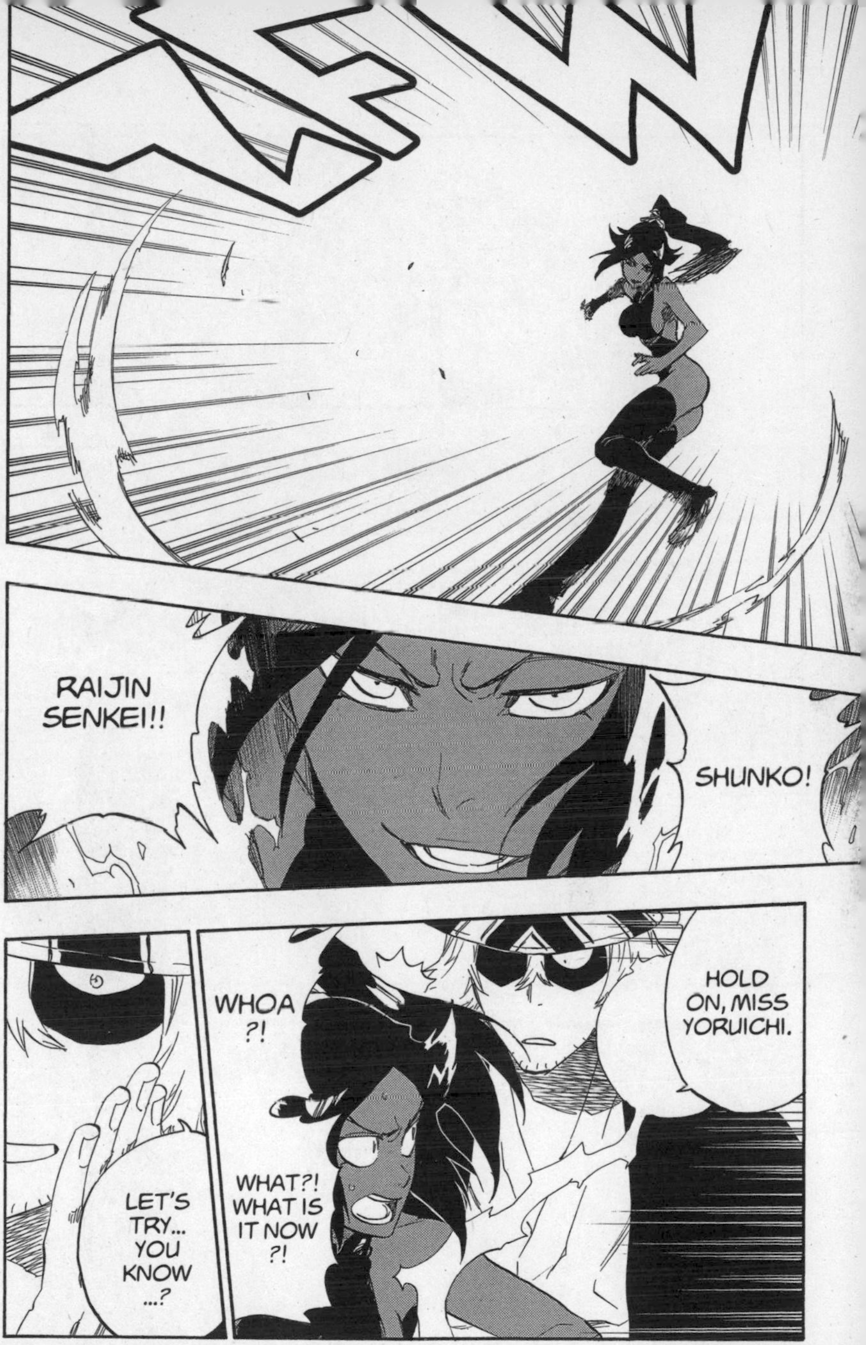
SHUNKO!
RAIJIN SENKEI!!
HOLD ON, MISS YORUICHI.
WHOA ?!
WHAT?! WHAT IS IT NOW ?!
LET'S TRY... YOU KNOW ...?

READ THIS WAY

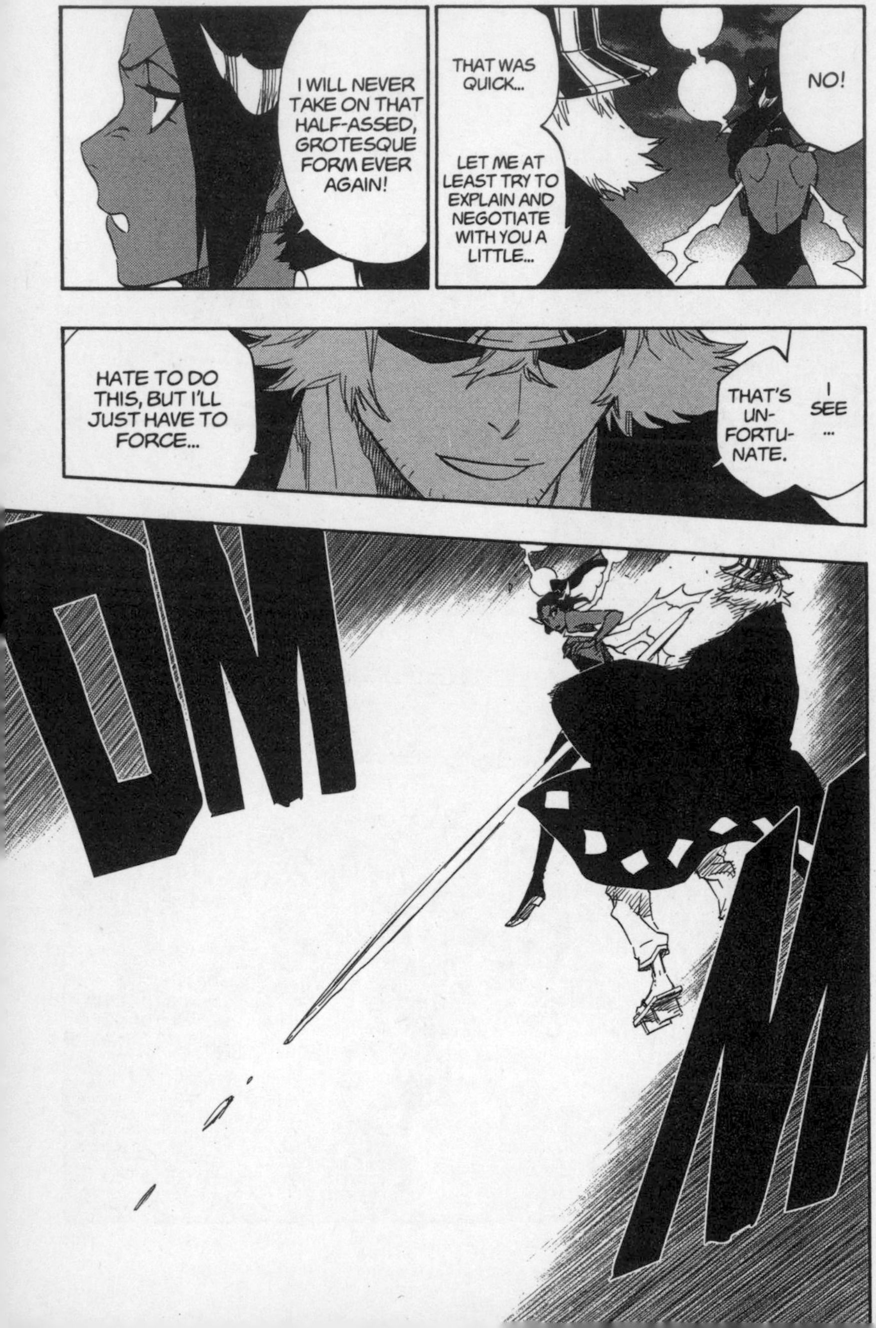
NO!
THAT WAS QUICK...
LET ME AT LEAST TRY TO EXPLAIN AND NEGOTIATE WITH YOU A LITTLE...
I WILL NEVER TAKE ON THAT HALF-ASSED, GROTESQUE FORM EVER AGAIN!
I SEE...
THAT'S UN-FORTU-NATE.
HATE TO DO THIS, BUT I'LL JUST HAVE TO FORCE...
DOMM

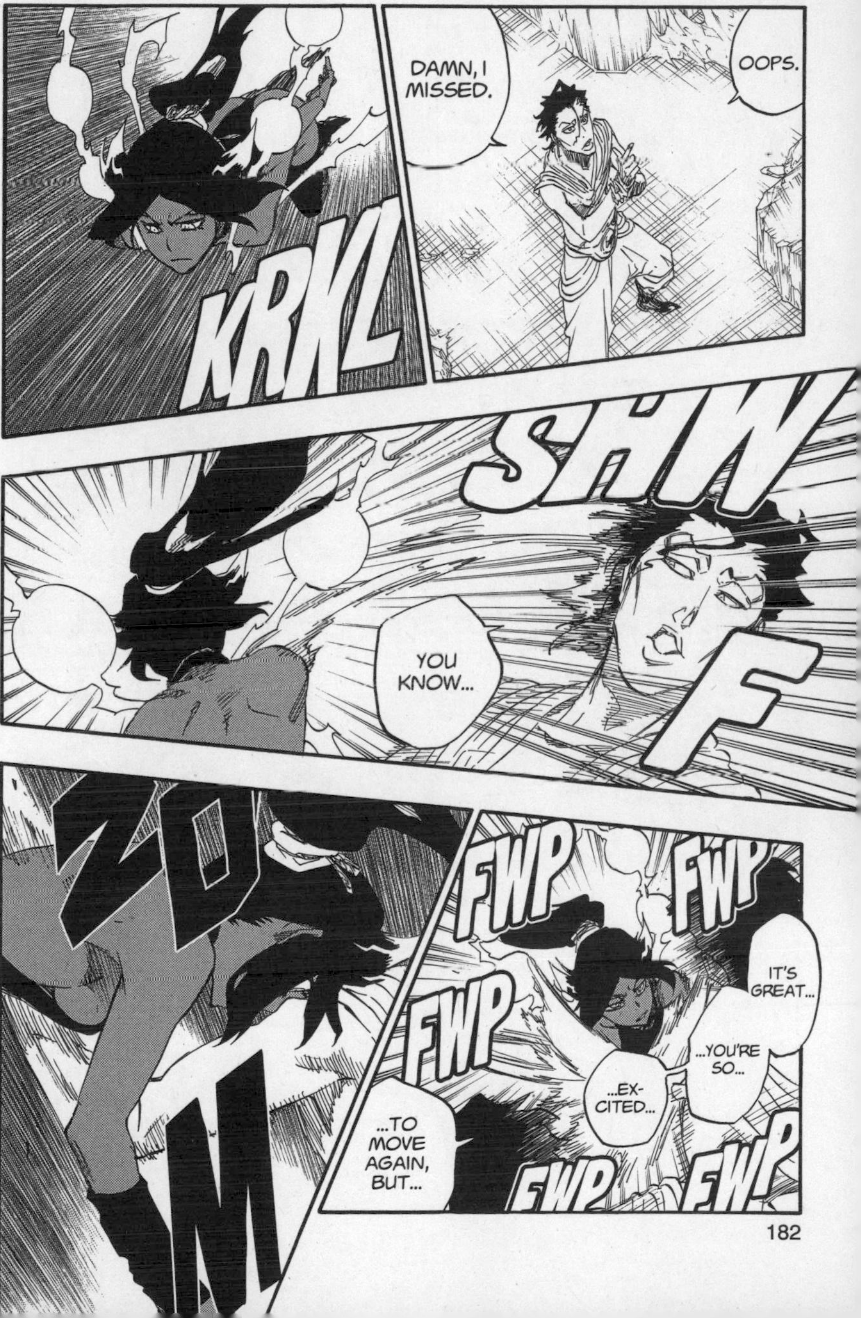
OOPS.
DAMN, I MISSED.
KRKL
SHIN
YOU KNOW...
F
FWP
FWP
IT'S GREAT...
...YOU'RE SO...
...EX-CITED...
...TO MOVE AGAIN, BUT...
FWP
FWP
FWP

READ THIS WAY

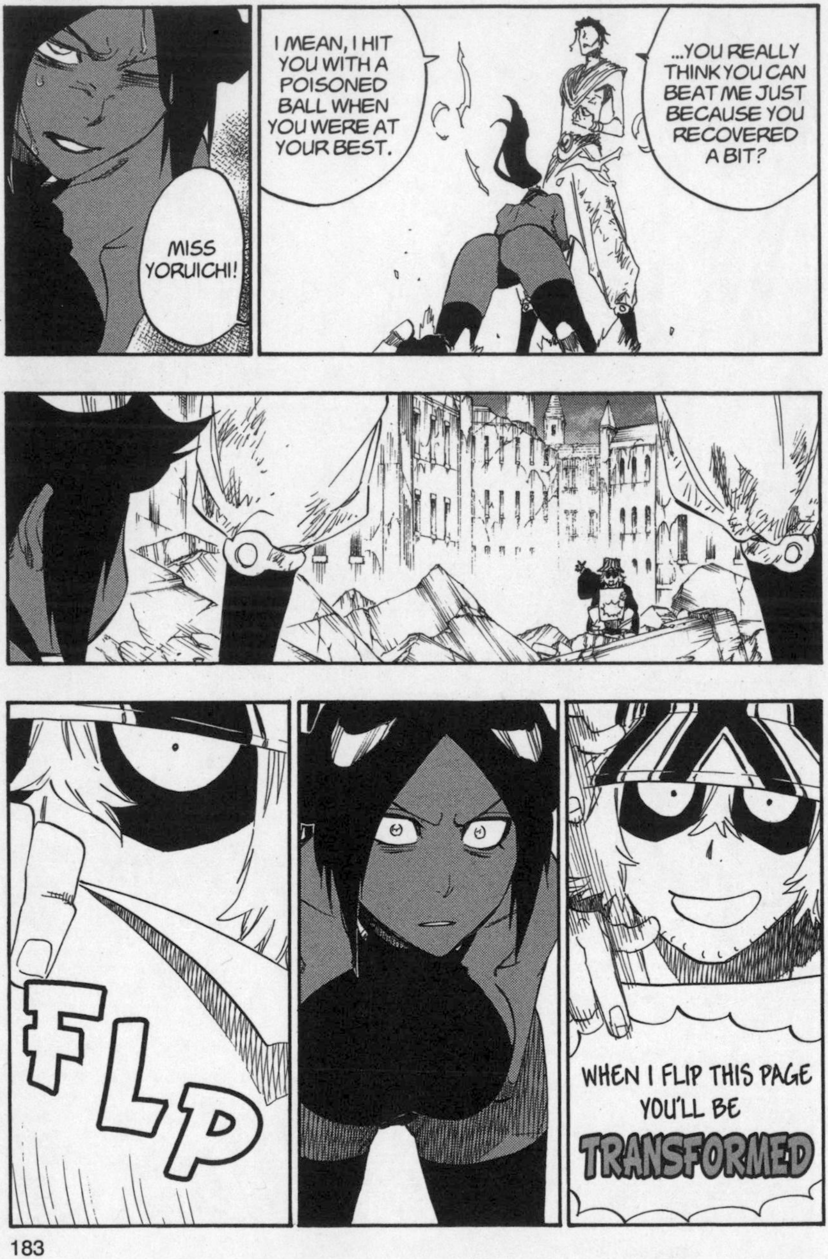

...YOU REALLY THINK YOU CAN BEAT ME JUST BECAUSE YOU RECOVERED A BIT?
I MEAN, I HIT YOU WITH A POISONED BALL WHEN YOU WERE AT YOUR BEST.
MISS YORUICHI!
WHEN I FLIP THIS PAGE YOU'LL BE TRANSFORMED
FLP

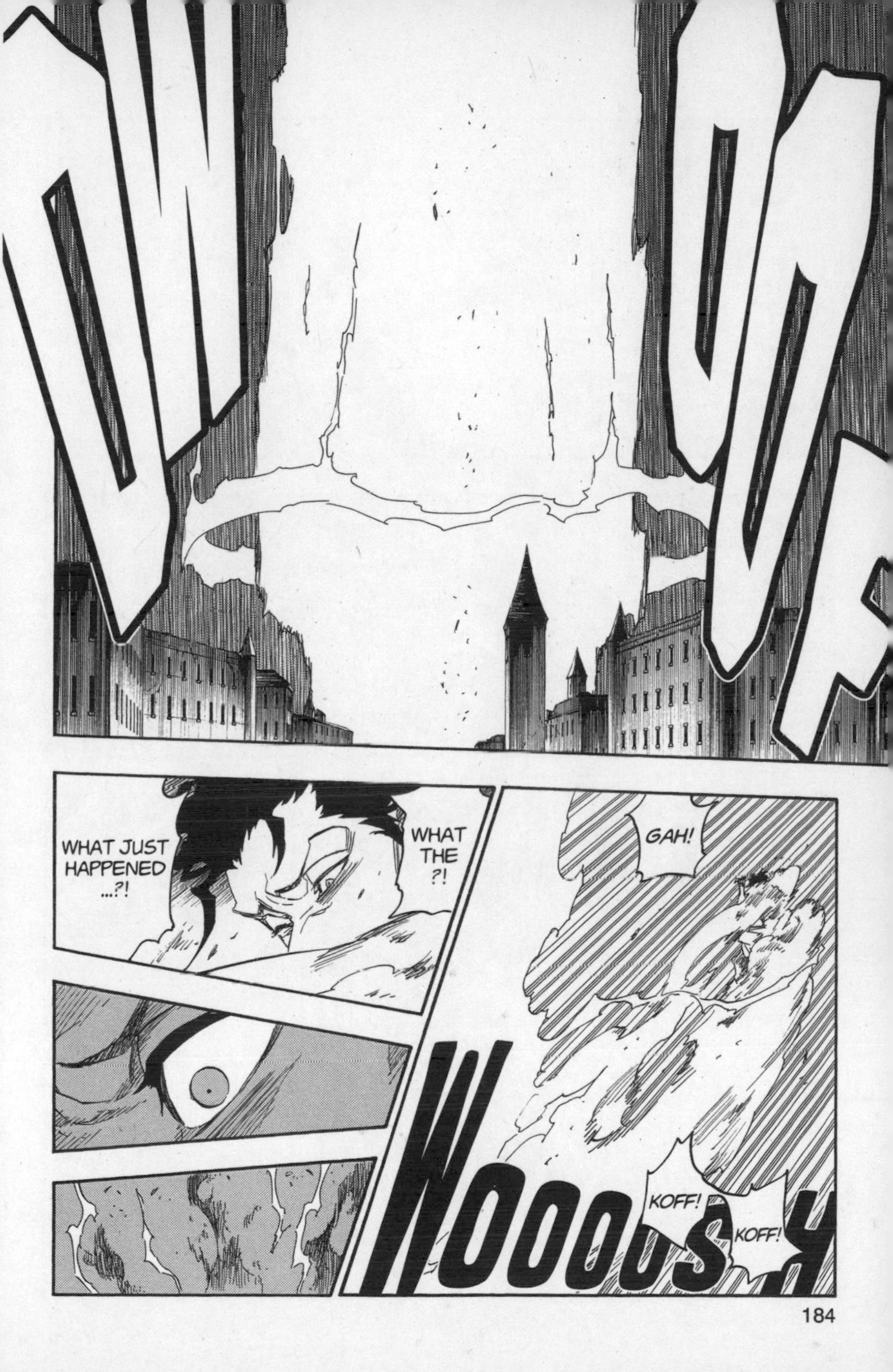
GAH!
KOFF!
KOFF!
WOOOOSH
WHAT THE ?!
WHAT JUST HAPPENED ...?!

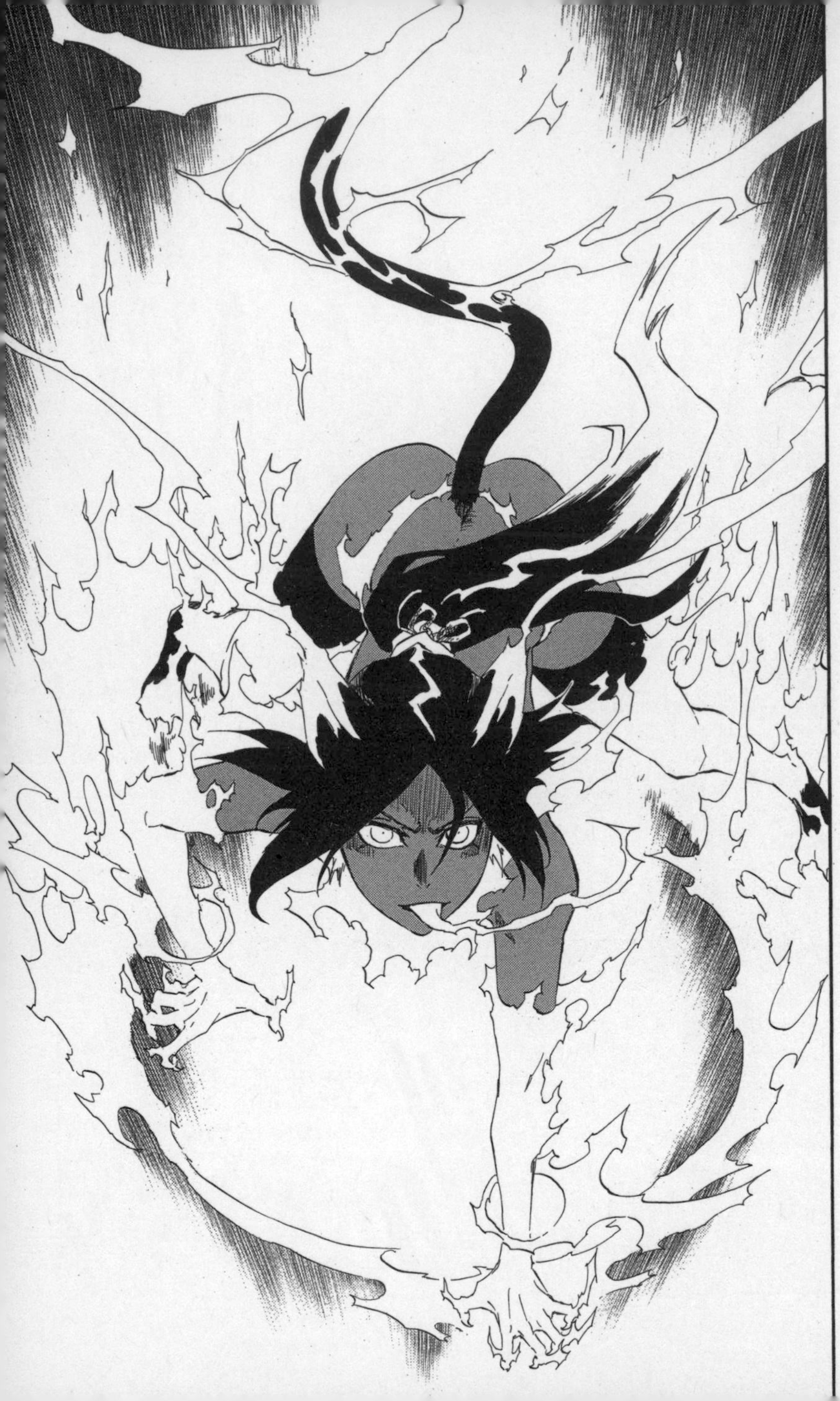

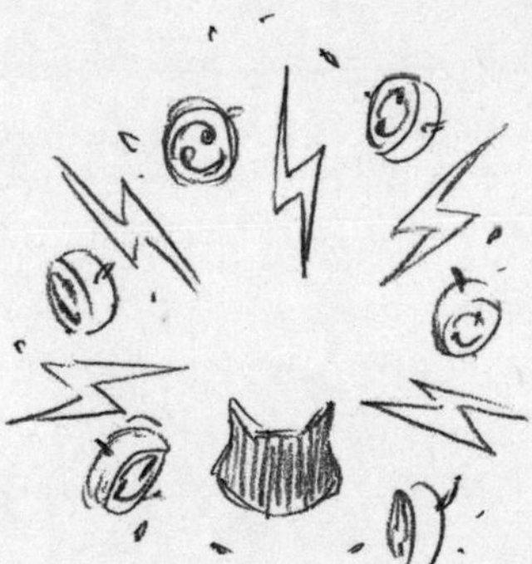

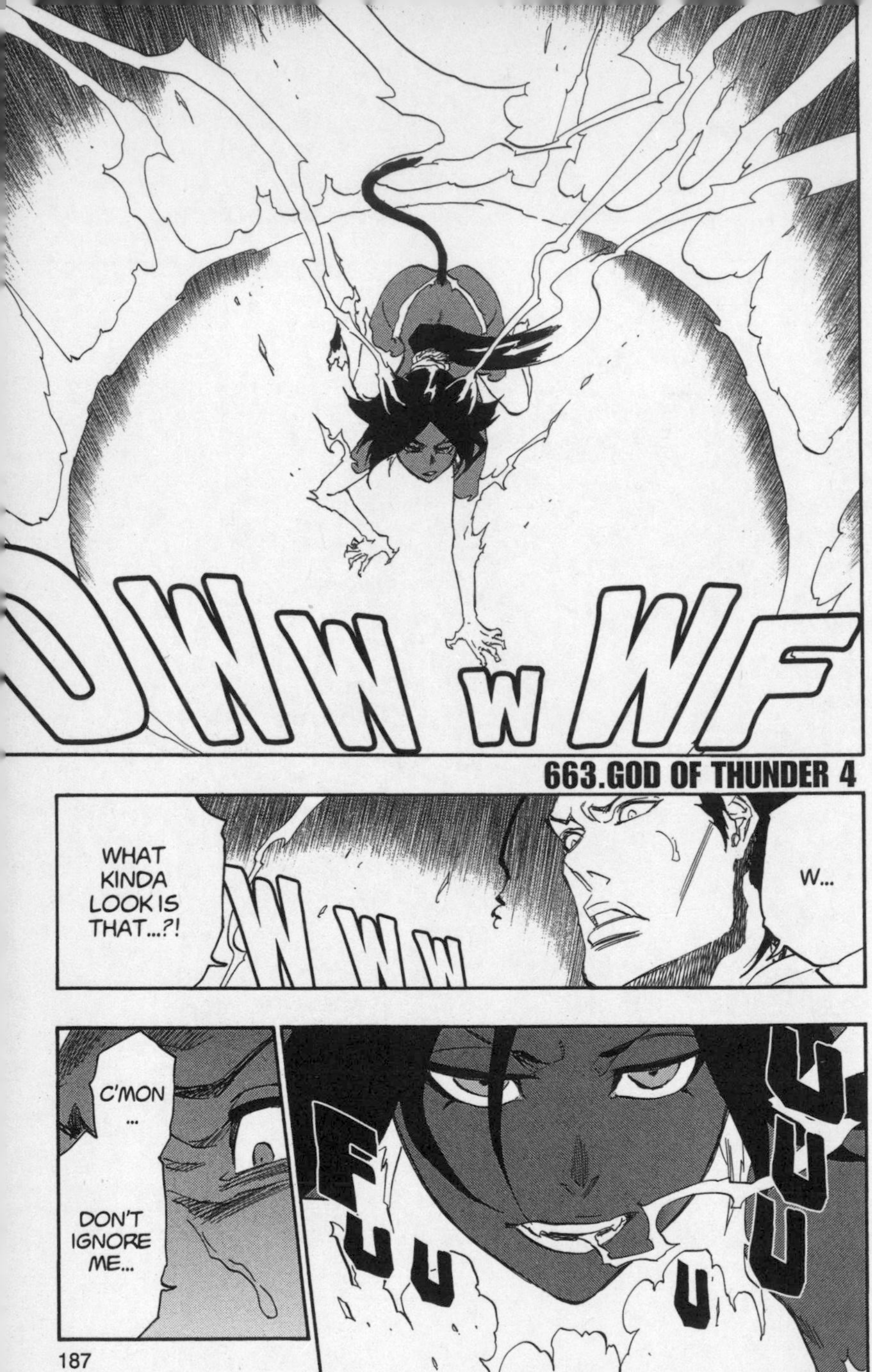
DWWWWF
663.GOD OF THUNDER 4
W...
WHAT KINDA LOOK IS THAT...?!
WWW
C'MON ... DON'T IGNORE ME...

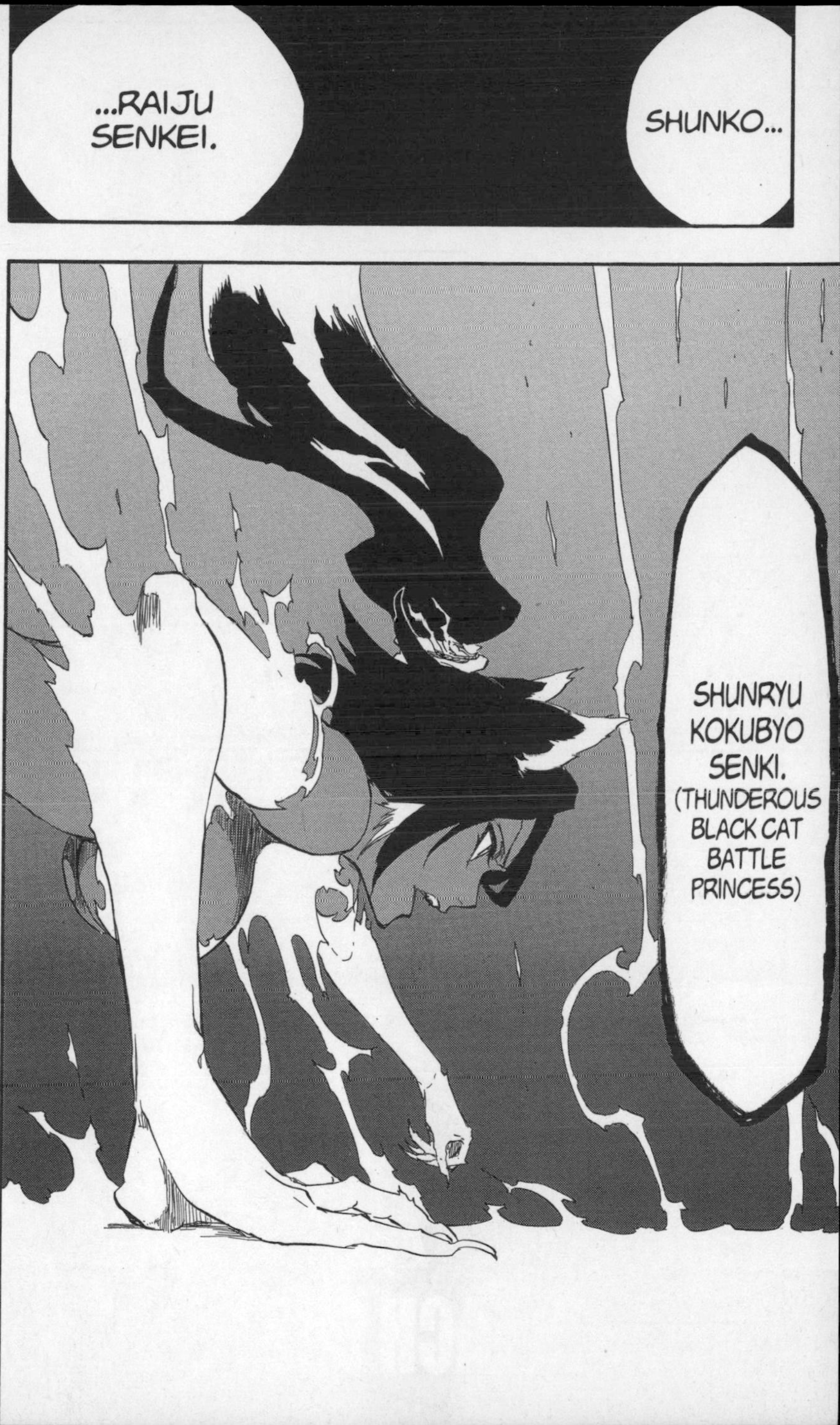
SHUNKO...
...RAIJU SENKEI.
SHUNRYU KOKUBYO SENKI. (THUNDEROUS BLACK CAT BATTLE PRINCESS)

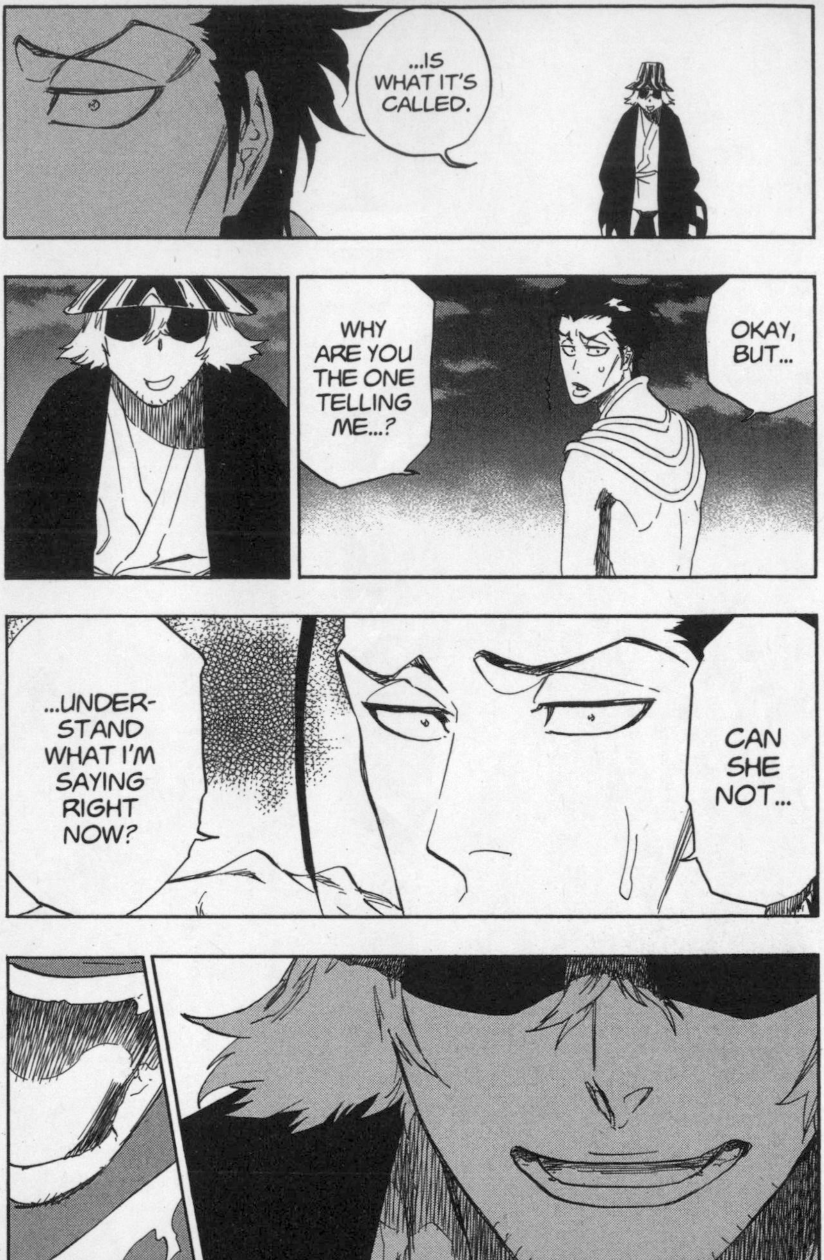
...IS WHAT IT'S CALLED.
OKAY, BUT...
WHY ARE YOU THE ONE TELLING ME...?
CAN SHE NOT...
...UNDER-STAND WHAT I'M SAYING RIGHT NOW?

BLEACH 663.

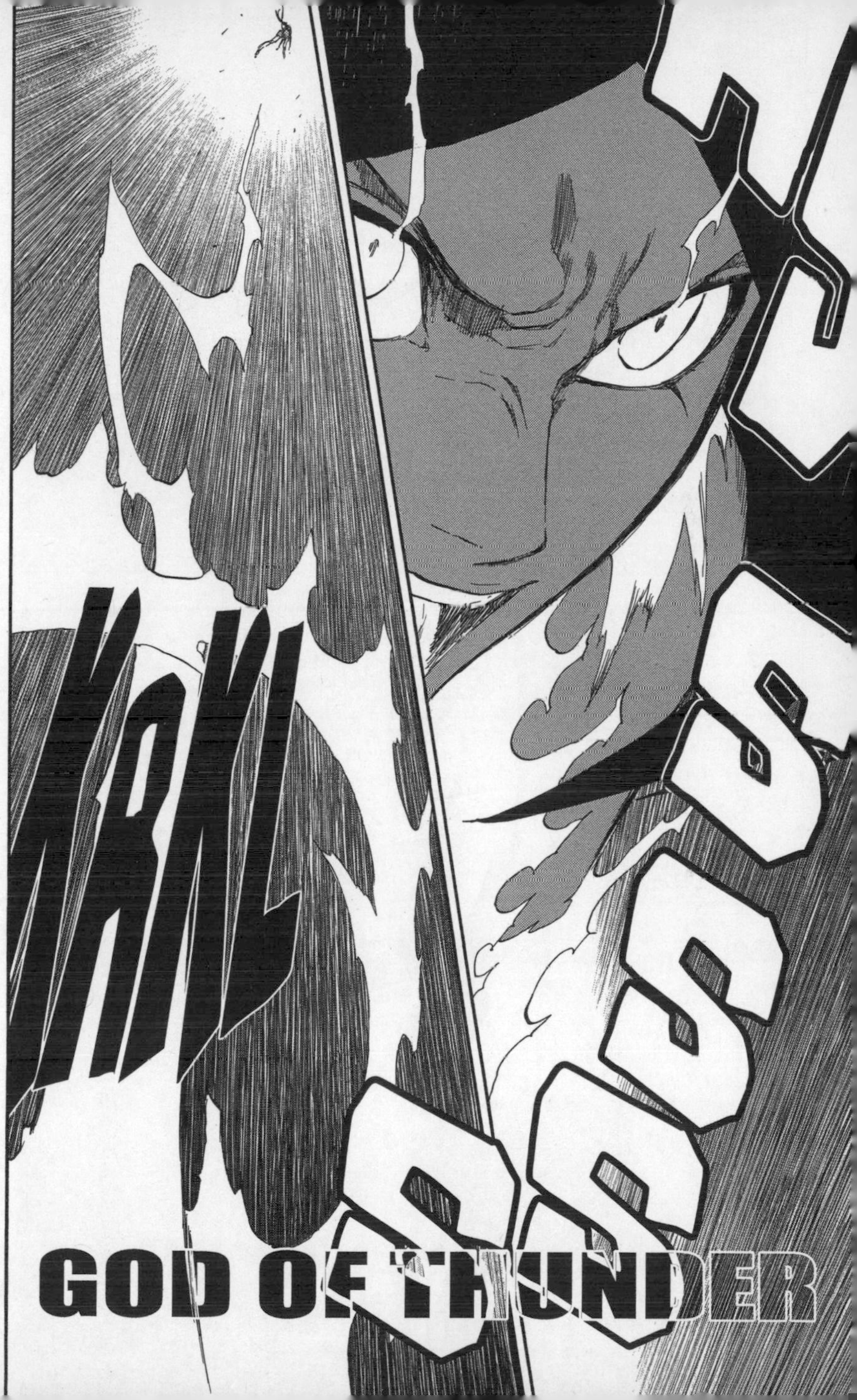
GOD OF THUNDER

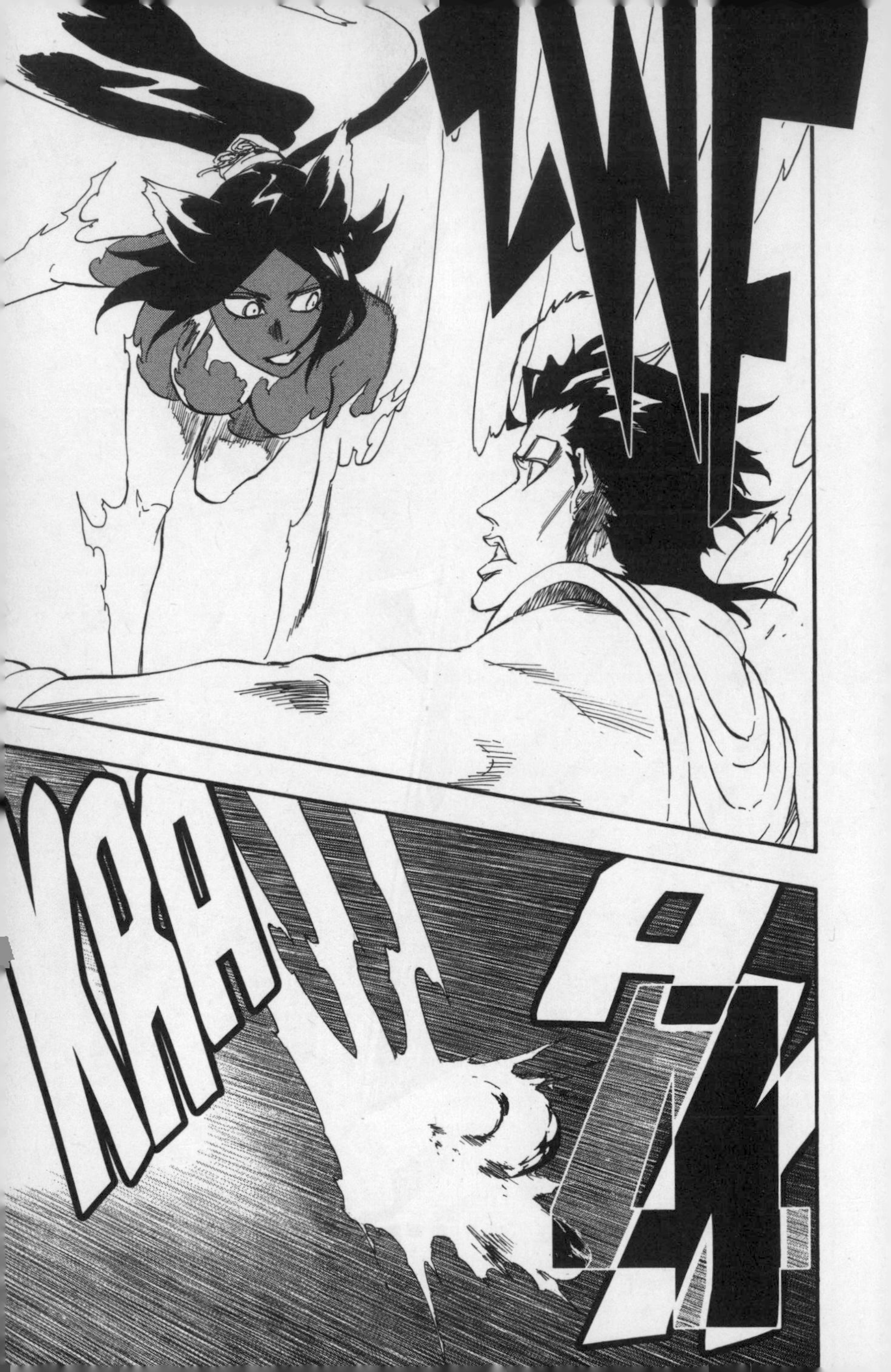

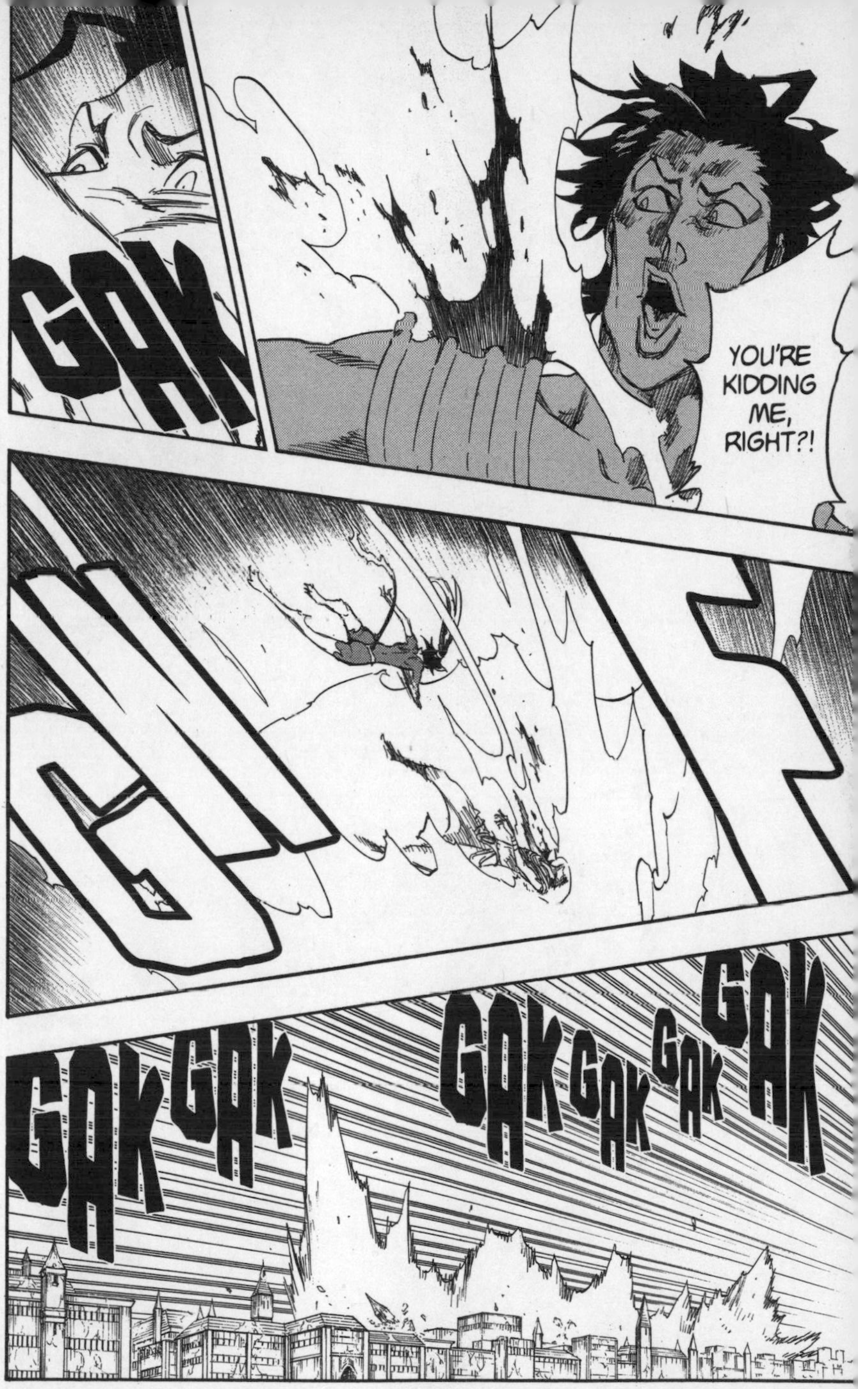
YOU'RE KIDDING ME, RIGHT?!
GAK
GAK GAK GAK GAK
GAK GAK

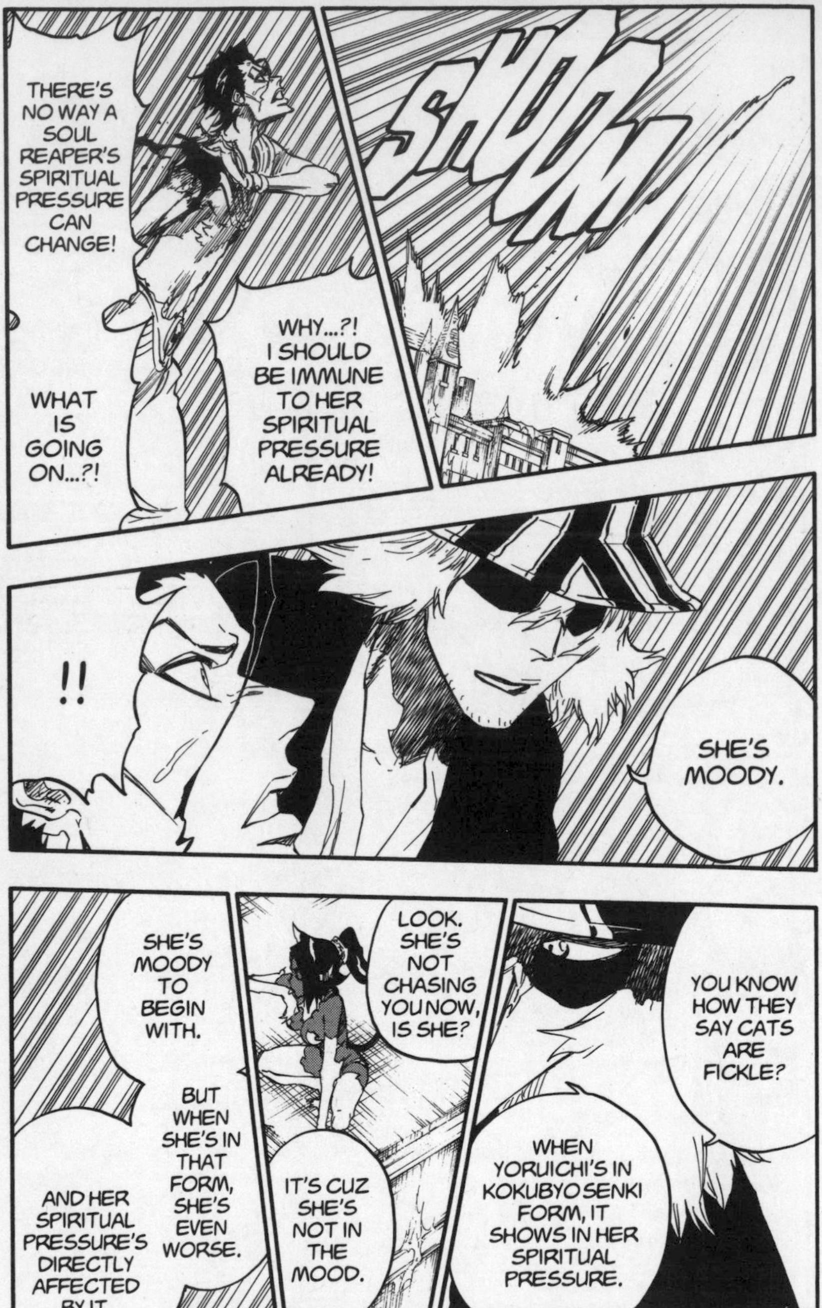
SHUM
THERE'S NO WAY A SOUL REAPER'S SPIRITUAL PRESSURE CAN CHANGE!
WHY...?! I SHOULD BE IMMUNE TO HER SPIRITUAL PRESSURE ALREADY!
WHAT IS GOING ON...?!
SHE'S MOODY.
!!
YOU KNOW HOW THEY SAY CATS ARE FICKLE?
WHEN YORUICHI'S IN KOKUBYO SENKI FORM, IT SHOWS IN HER SPIRITUAL PRESSURE.
LOOK. SHE'S NOT CHASING YOU NOW, IS SHE?
IT'S CUZ SHE'S NOT IN THE MOOD.
SHE'S MOODY TO BEGIN WITH.
BUT WHEN SHE'S IN THAT FORM, SHE'S EVEN WORSE.
AND HER SPIRITUAL PRESSURE'S DIRECTLY AFFECTED BY IT.

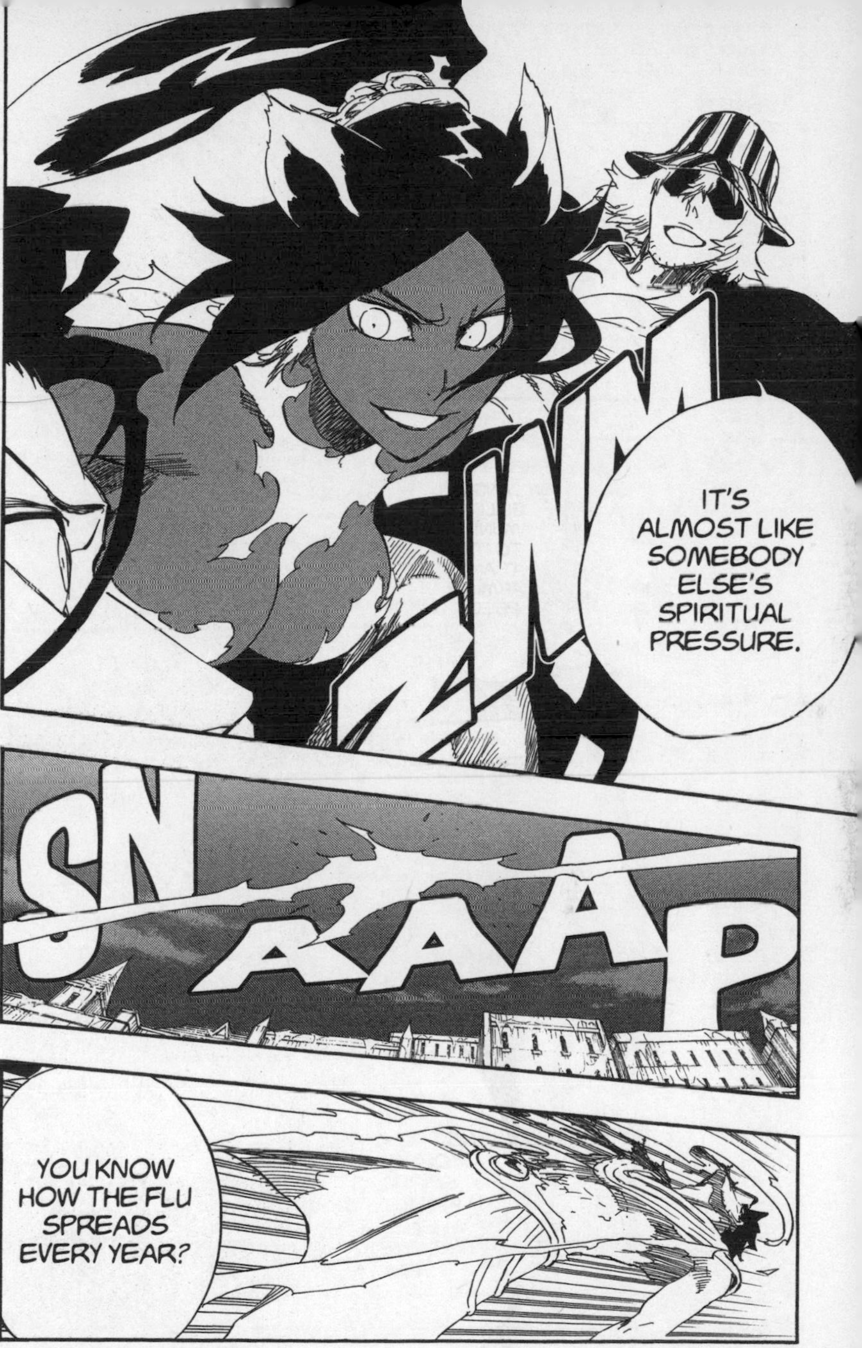
IT'S ALMOST LIKE SOMEBODY ELSE'S SPIRITUAL PRESSURE.
SNAAAP
YOU KNOW HOW THE FLU SPREADS EVERY YEAR?

READ THIS WAY

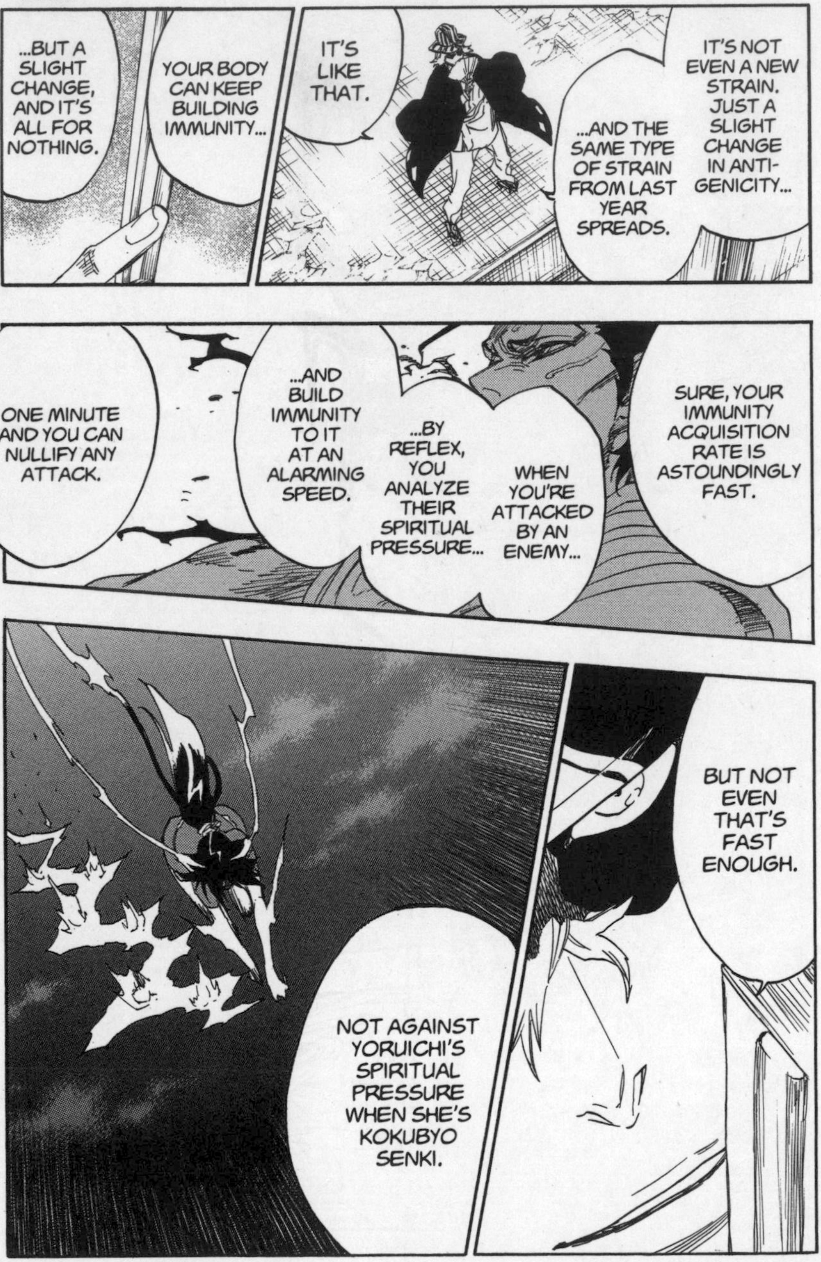

IT'S NOT EVEN A NEW STRAIN. JUST A SLIGHT CHANGE IN ANTI-GENICITY...
...AND THE SAME TYPE OF STRAIN FROM LAST YEAR SPREADS.
IT'S LIKE THAT.
YOUR BODY CAN KEEP BUILDING IMMUNITY...
...BUT A SLIGHT CHANGE, AND IT'S ALL FOR NOTHING.
SURE, YOUR IMMUNITY ACQUISITION RATE IS ASTOUNDINGLY FAST.
WHEN YOU'RE ATTACKED BY AN ENEMY...
...BY REFLEX, YOU ANALYZE THEIR SPIRITUAL PRESSURE...
...AND BUILD IMMUNITY TO IT AT AN ALARMING SPEED.
ONE MINUTE AND YOU CAN NULLIFY ANY ATTACK.
BUT NOT EVEN THAT'S FAST ENOUGH.
NOT AGAINST YORUICHI'S SPIRITUAL PRESSURE WHEN SHE'S KOKUBYO SENKI.

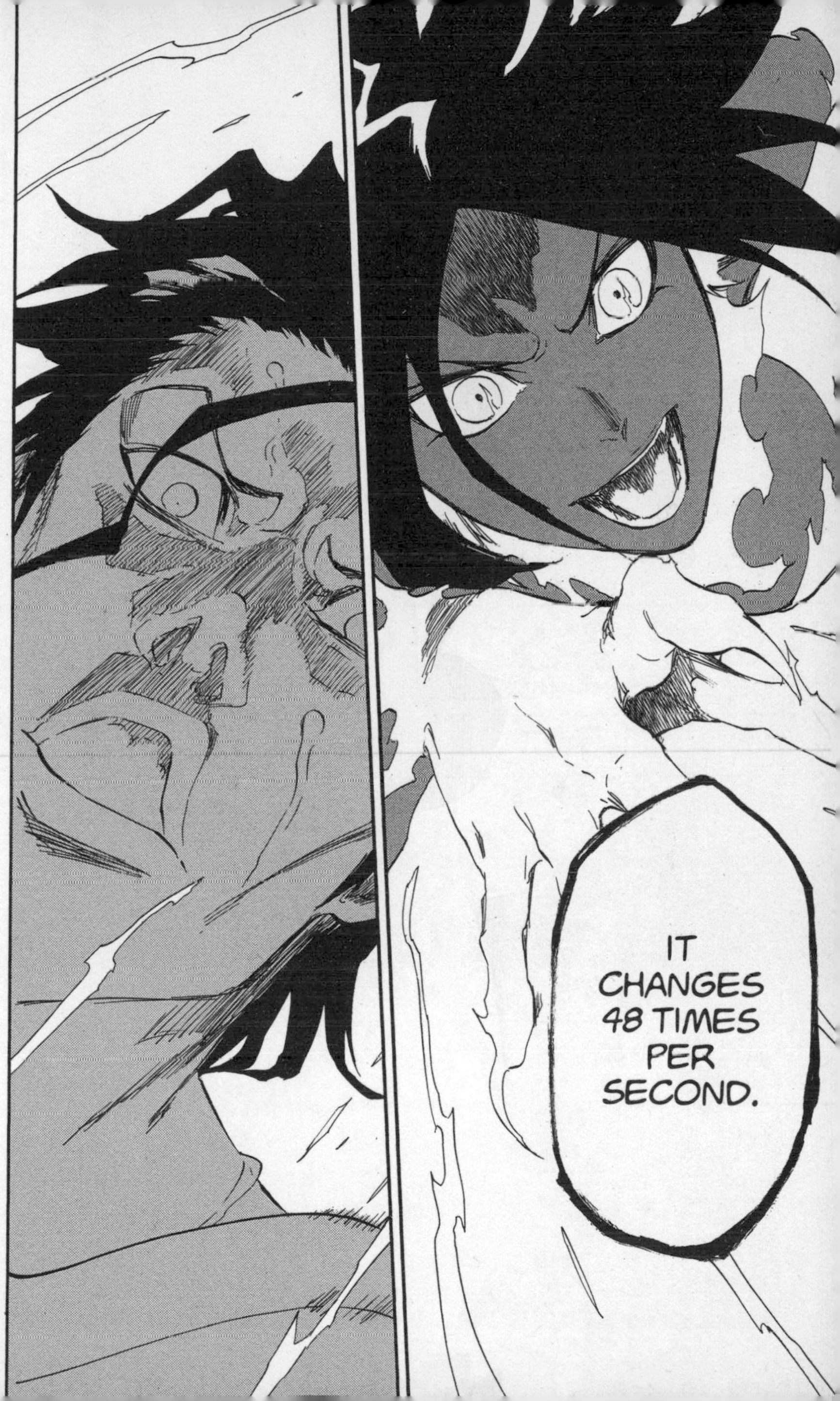
IT CHANGES 48 TIMES PER SECOND.

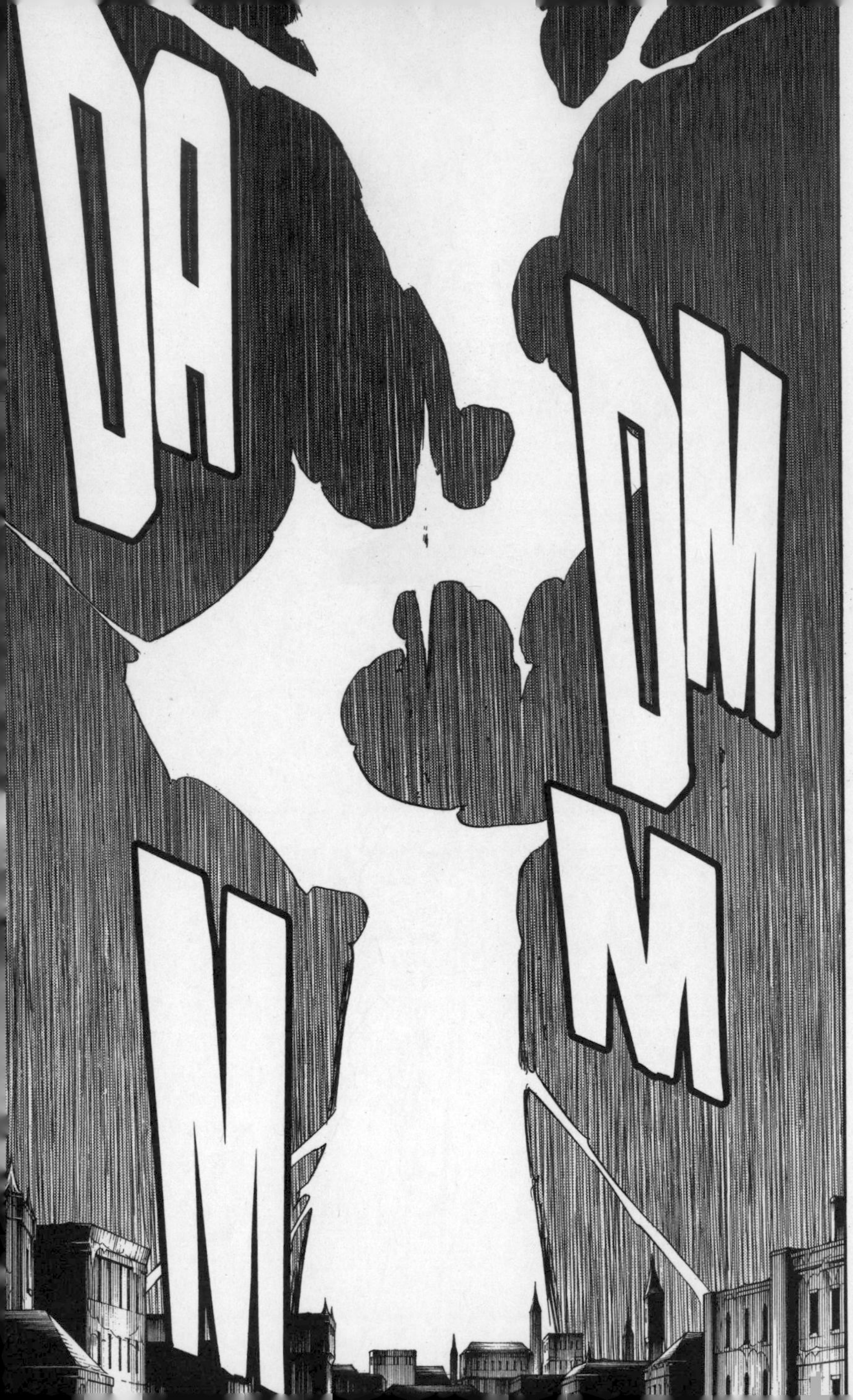
DMM
DAM

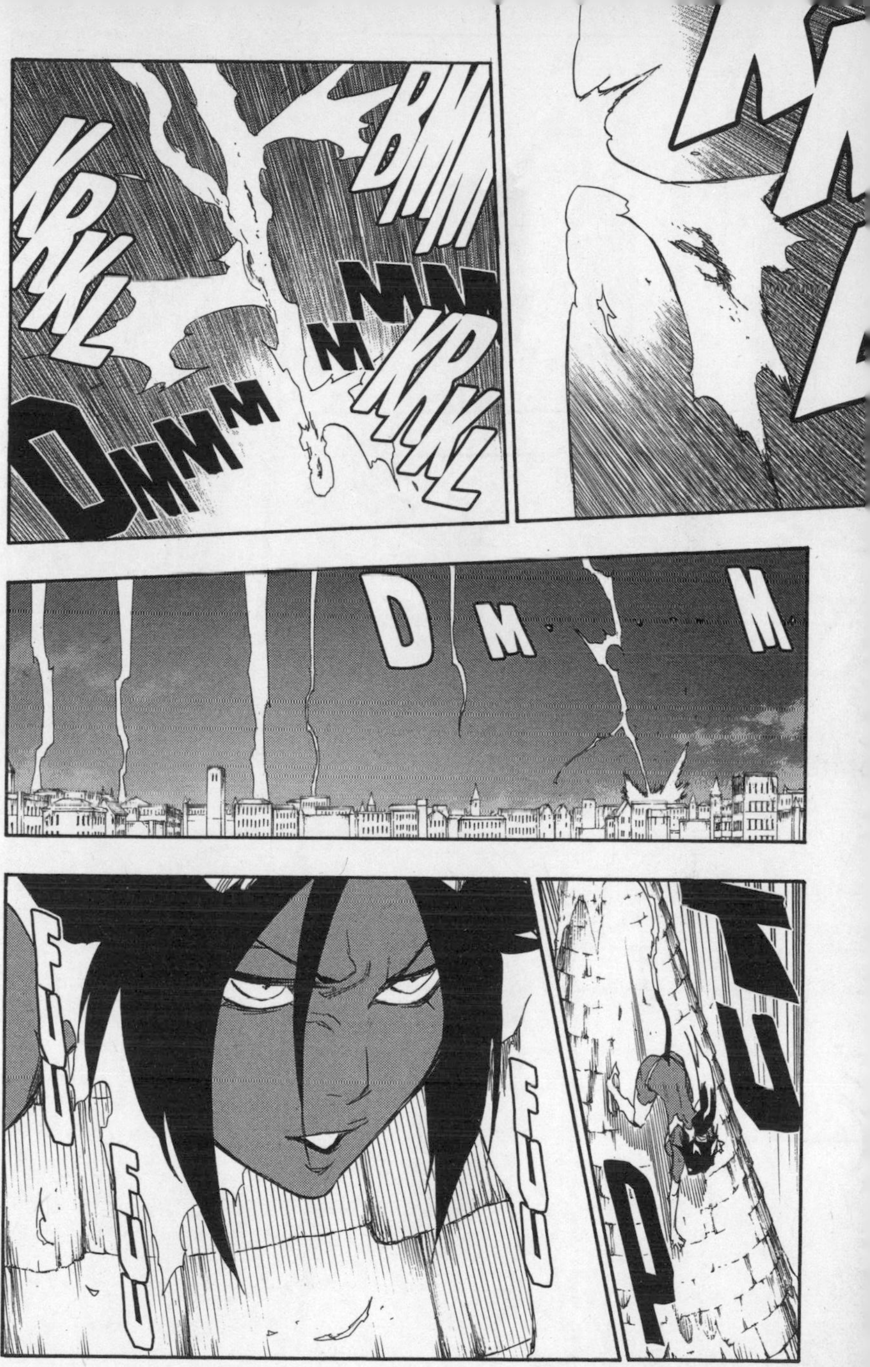
BMMMMM
KRKRKL
M
KRKL
DMMMM
DMM
TUP
FUUU
FUUU
FUUU

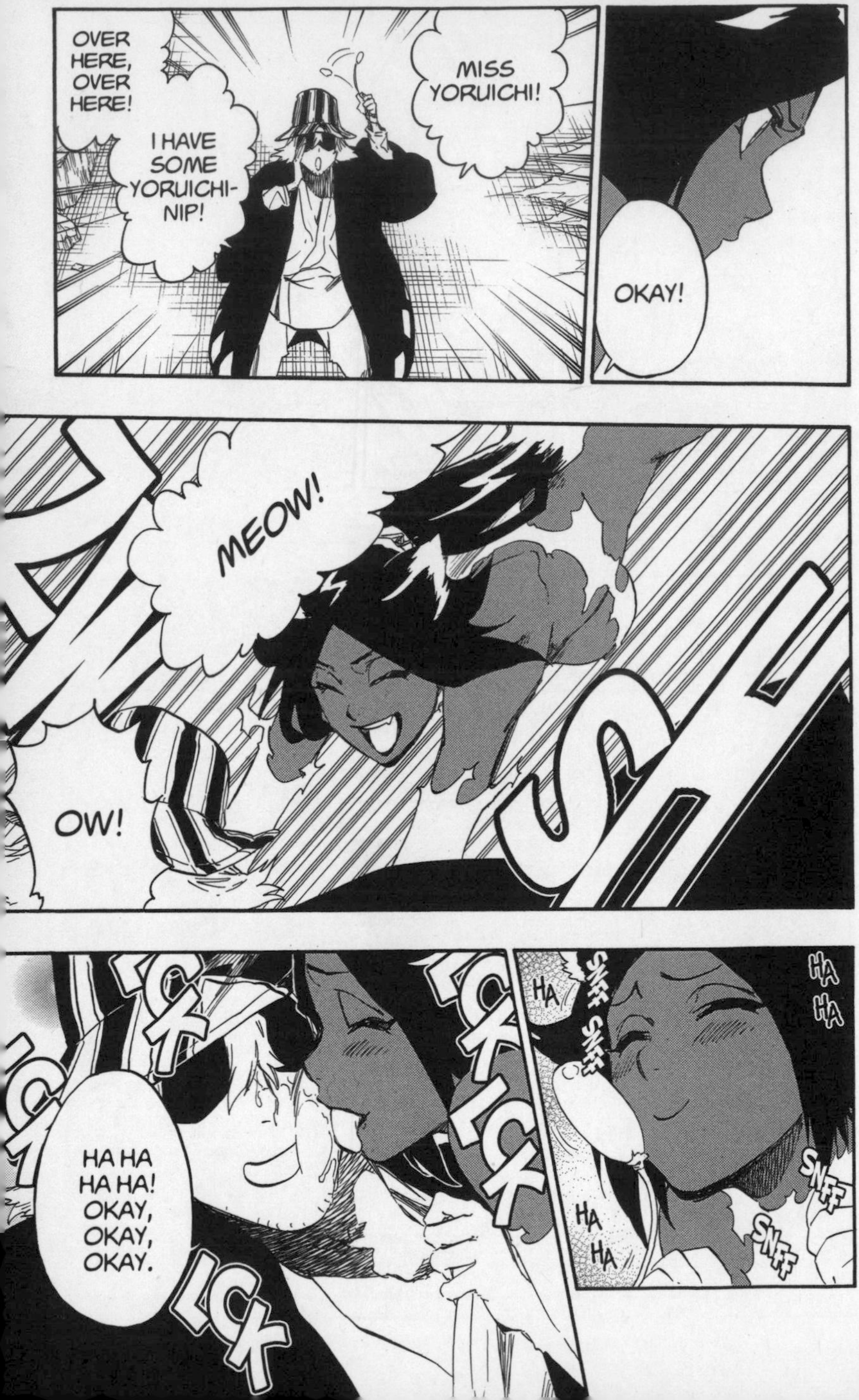
OKAY!
MISS YORUICHI!
OVER HERE, OVER HERE!
I HAVE SOME YORUICHI-NIP!
MEOW!
OW!
HA HA
SNFF SNFF
HA
SNFF SNFF
HA HA
LICK
LICK
HA HA HA HA! OKAY, OKAY, OKAY.
LICK

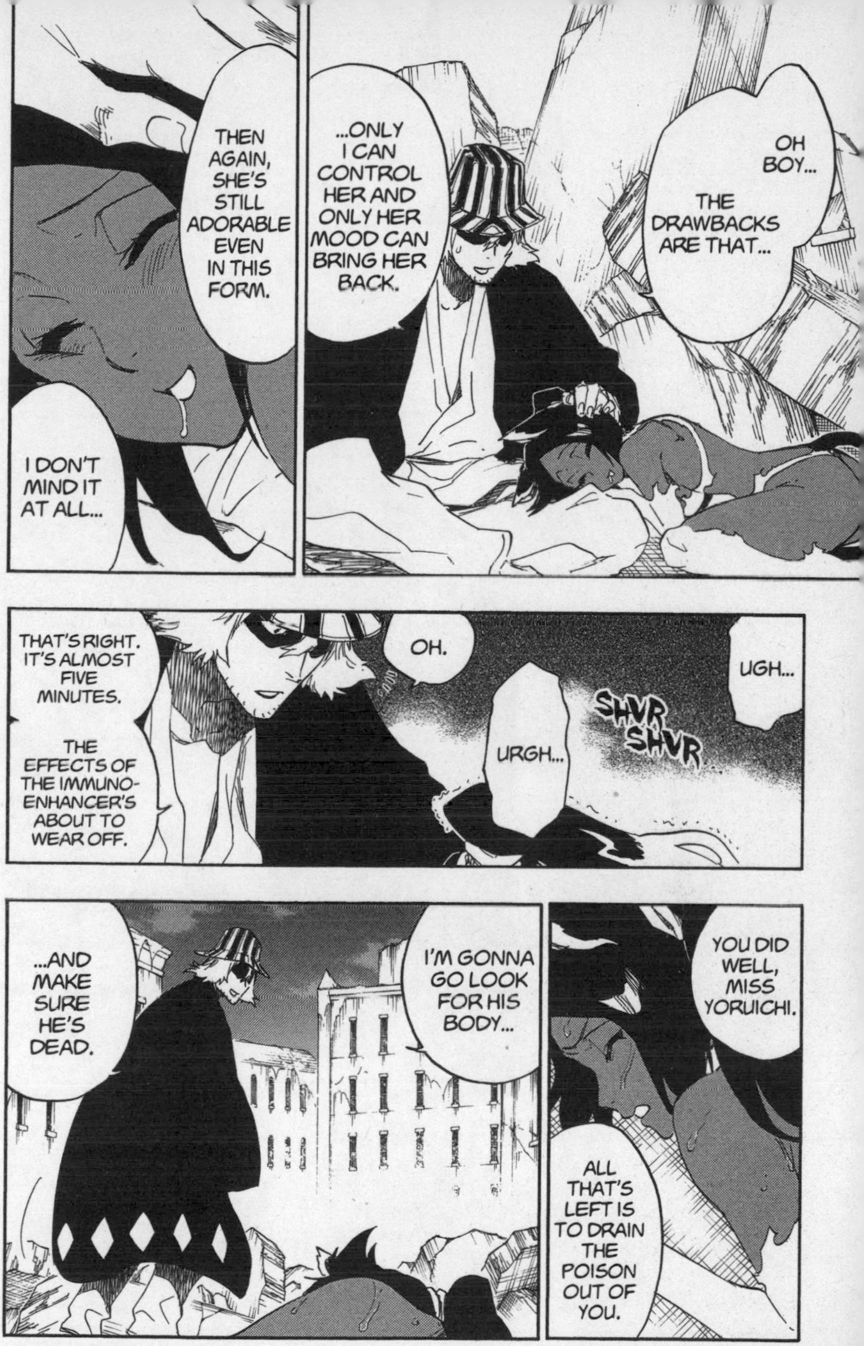
OH BOY...
THE DRAWBACKS ARE THAT...
...ONLY I CAN CONTROL HER AND ONLY HER MOOD CAN BRING HER BACK.
THEN AGAIN, SHE'S STILL ADORABLE EVEN IN THIS FORM.
I DON'T MIND IT AT ALL...
UGH...
SHVR SHVR
URGH...
OH.
THAT'S RIGHT. IT'S ALMOST FIVE MINUTES.
THE EFFECTS OF THE IMMUNO-ENHANCER'S ABOUT TO WEAR OFF.
YOU DID WELL, MISS YORUICHI.
ALL THAT'S LEFT IS TO DRAIN THE POISON OUT OF YOU.
I'M GONNA GO LOOK FOR HIS BODY...
...AND MAKE SURE HE'S DEAD.

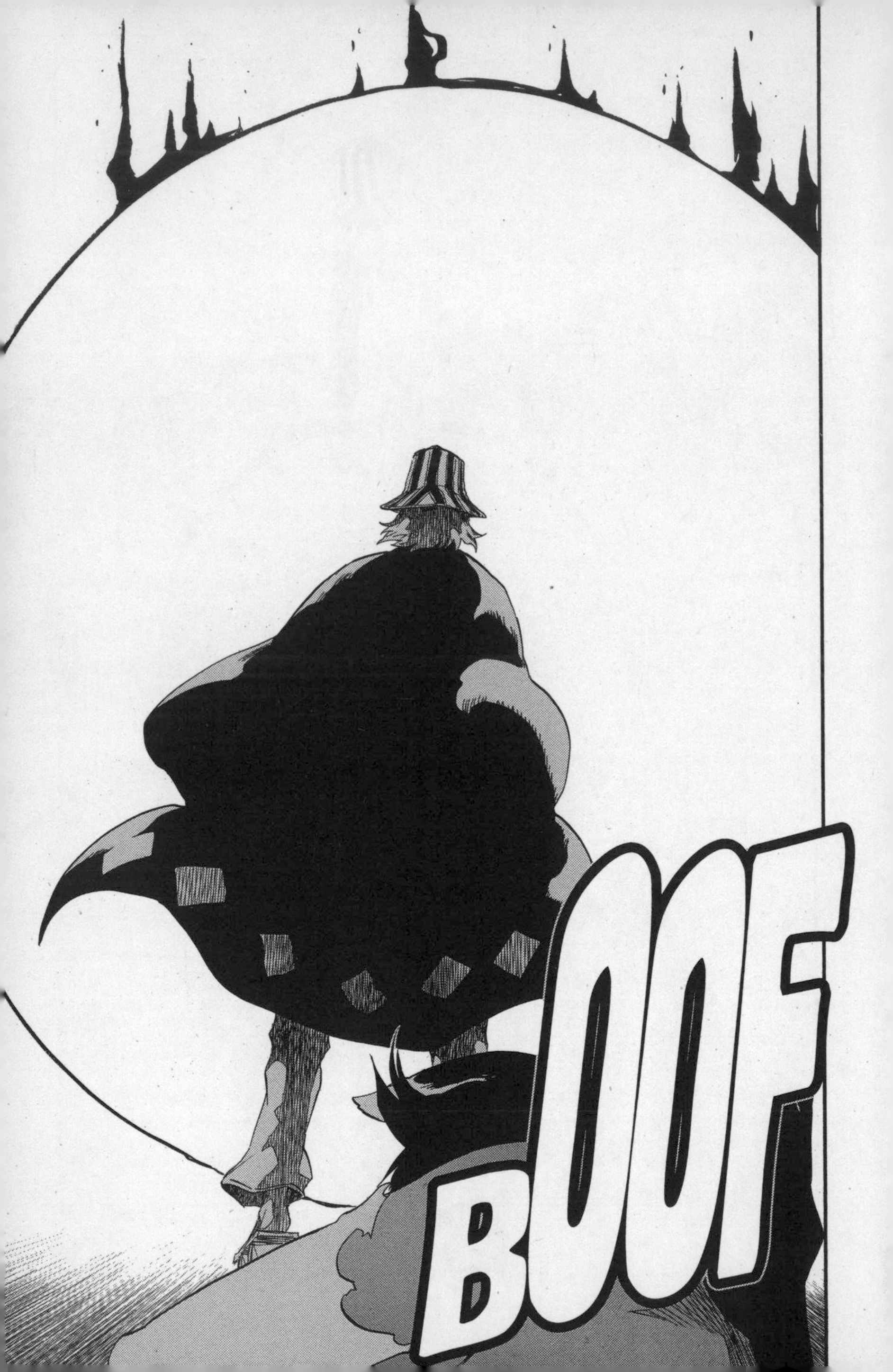
BOOF

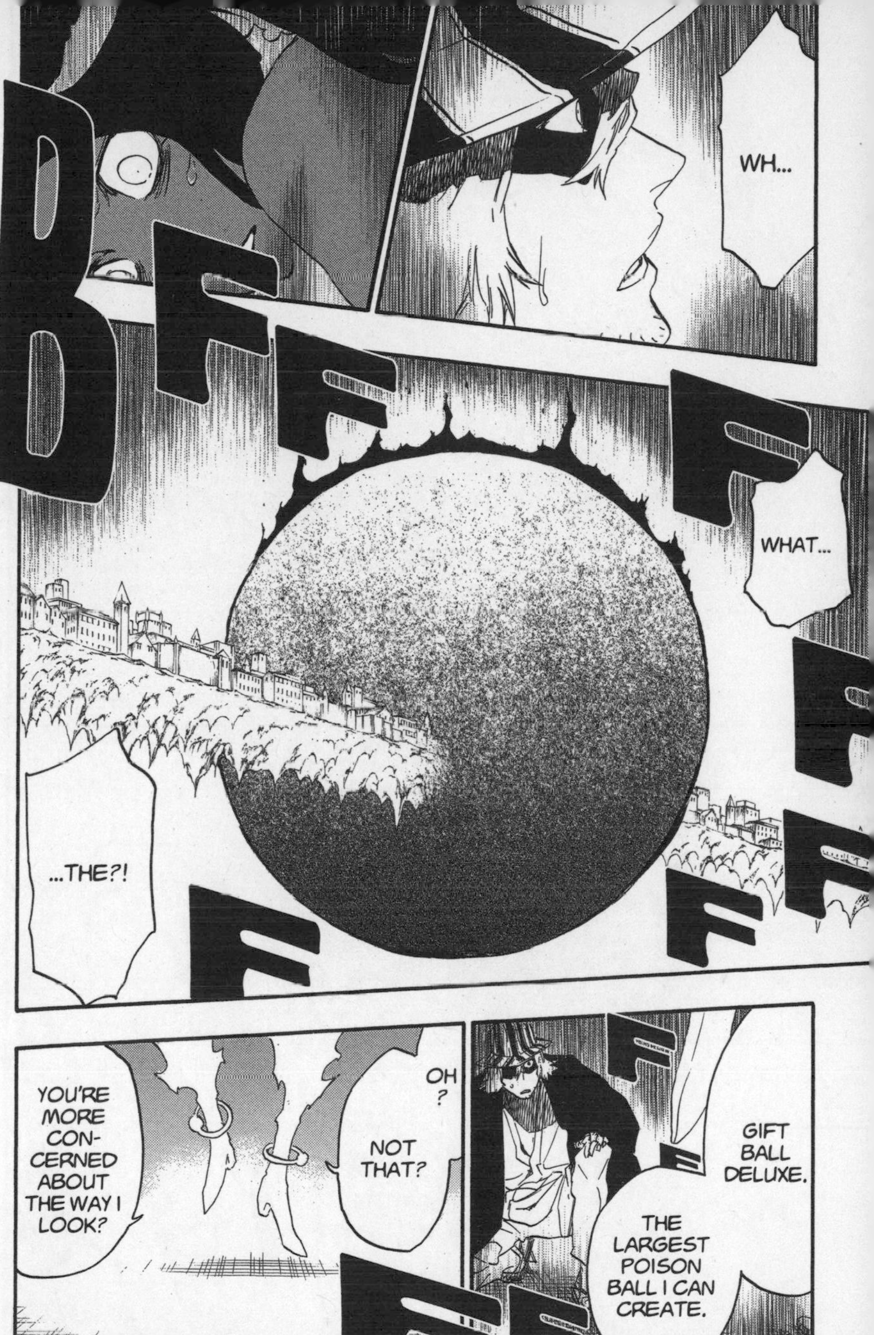
WH...
DFFFFFFFFF
WHAT...
...THE?!
GIFT BALL DELUXE.
THE LARGEST POISON BALL I CAN CREATE.
OH?
NOT THAT?
YOU'RE MORE CON-CERNED ABOUT THE WAY I LOOK?

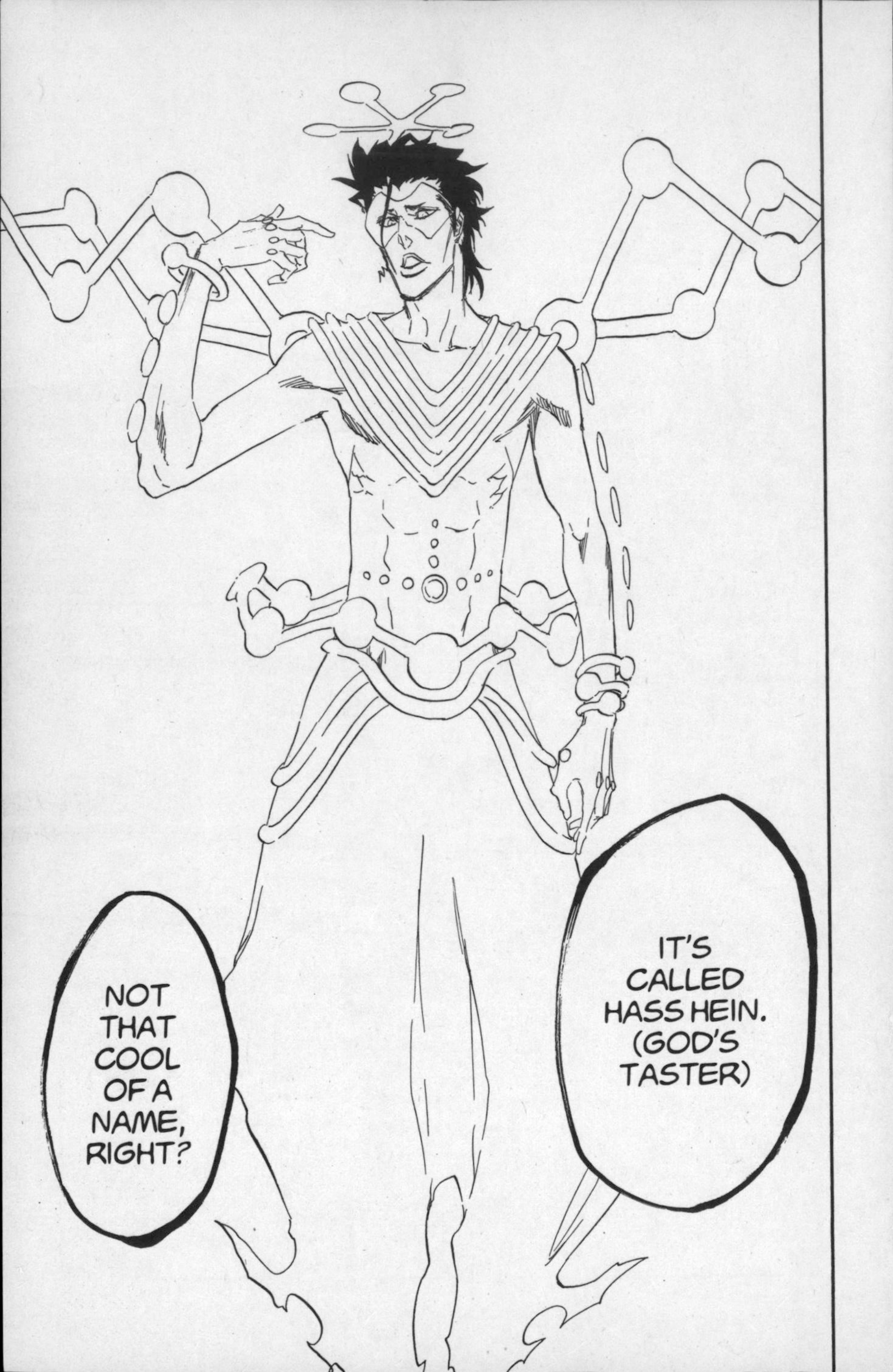
IT'S CALLED HASS HEIN. (GOD'S TASTER)
NOT THAT COOL OF A NAME, RIGHT?

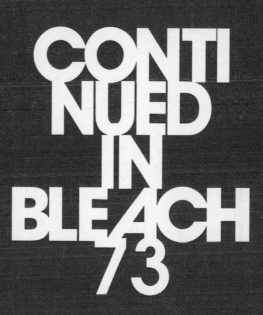

CONTI
NUED
IN
BLEACH
73

THE ACTION-PACKED SUPERHERO COMEDY ABOUT ONE MAN'S AMBITION TO BE A HERO FOR FUN!

ONE-PUNCH MAN

STORY BY
ONE | ART BY
YUSUKE MURATA

Nothing about Saitama passes the eyeball test when it comes to superheroes, from his lifeless expression to his bald head to his unimpressive physique. However, this average-looking guy has a not-so-average problem—he just can't seem to find an opponent strong enough to take on!

Can he finally find an opponent who can go toe-to-toe with him and give his life some meaning? Or is he doomed to a life of superpowered boredom?

ratings.viz.com

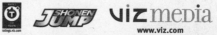
VIZ MEDIA
www.viz.com

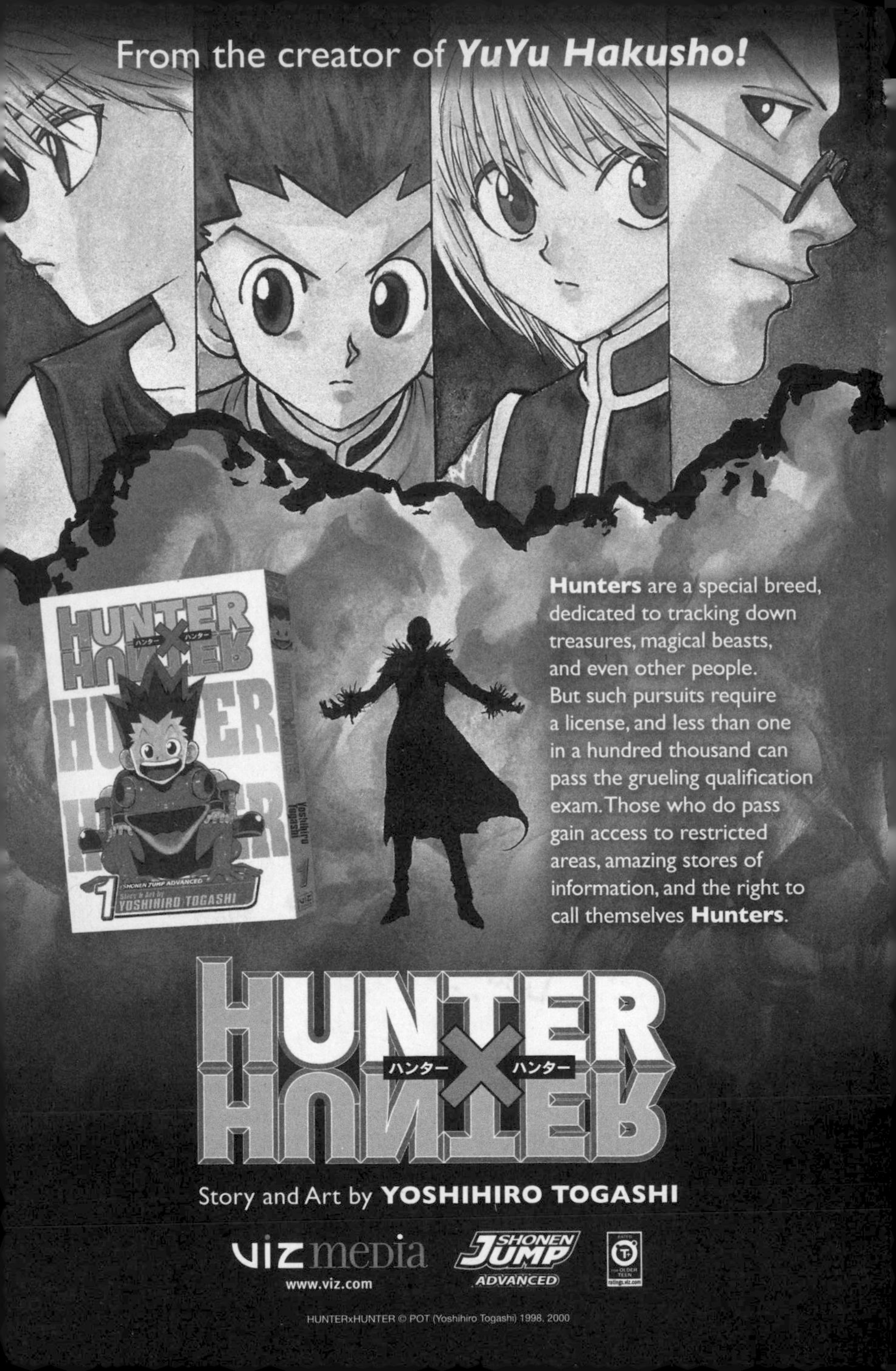
From the creator of YuYu Hakusho!
HUNTER × HUNTER
Hunters are a special breed, dedicated to tracking down treasures, magical beasts, and even other people. But such pursuits require a license, and less than one in a hundred thousand can pass the grueling qualification exam. Those who do pass gain access to restricted areas, amazing stores of information, and the right to call themselves Hunters.
HUNTER × HUNTER
ハンター ハンター
Story and Art by YOSHIHIRO TOGASHI
VIZ media
www.viz.com
SHONEN JUMP ADVANCED
HUNTERxHUNTER © POT (Yoshihiro Togashi) 1998, 2000

You're Reading in the Wrong Direction!!

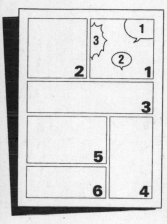

Whoops! Guess what? You're starting at the wrong end of the comic!

…It's true! In keeping with the original Japanese format, **Bleach** is meant to be read from right to left, starting in the upper-right corner.

Unlike English, which is read from left to right, Japanese is read from right to left, meaning that action, sound effects and word-balloon order are completely reversed… something which can make readers unfamiliar with Japanese feel pretty backwards themselves. For this reason, manga or Japanese comics published in the U.S. in English have sometimes been published "flopped"—that is, printed in exact reverse order, as though seen from the other side of a mirror.

By flopping pages, U.S. publishers can avoid confusing readers, but the compromise is not without its downside. For one thing, a character in a flopped manga series who once wore in the original Japanese version a T-shirt emblazoned with "M A Y" (as in "the merry month of") now wears one which reads "Y A M"! Additionally, many manga creators in Japan are themselves unhappy with the process, as some feel the mirror-imaging of their art skews their original intentions.

We are proud to bring you Tite Kubo's **Bleach** in the original unflopped format. For now, though, turn to the other side of the book and let the adventure begin…!

—Editor

◄ • • • • •